HOW THE BEATLES DESTROYED ROCK 'N' ROLL

OTHER BOOKS BY ELIJAH WALD

Josh White: Society Blues
River of Song: A Musical Journey Down the Mississippi (with John Junkerman)
Narcocorrido: A Journey into the Music of Drugs, Guns, and Guerrillas
Escaping the Delta: Robert Johnson and the Invention of the Blues
The Mayor of MacDougal Street: A Memoir (with Dave Van Ronk)
Riding with Strangers: A Hitchhiker's Journey
Global Minstrels: Voices of World Music

HOW THE BEATLES DESTROYED ROCK 'N' ROLL

AN ALTERNATIVE HISTORY OF AMERICAN POPULAR MUSIC

ELIJAH WALD

OXFORD
UNIVERSITY PRESS

2009

OXFORD
UNIVERSITY PRESS

Oxford University Press, Inc., publishes works that further
Oxford University's objective of excellence
in research, scholarship, and education.

OXFORD   NEW YORK

Auckland   Cape Town   Dar es Salaam   Hong Kong   Karachi
Kuala Lumpur   Madrid   Melbourne   Mexico City   Nairobi
New Delhi   Shanghai   Taipei   Toronto

WITH OFFICES IN

Argentina   Austria   Brazil   Chile   Czech Republic   France   Greece
Guatemala   Hungary   Italy   Japan   Poland   Portugal   Singapore
South Korea   Switzerland   Thailand   Turkey   Ukraine   Vietnam

Published by Oxford University Press, Inc.
198 Madison Avenue, New York, New York 10016

www.oup.com

Oxford is a registered trademark of Oxford University Press

Library of Congress Cataloging-in-Publication Data
Wald, Elijah.
How the Beatles destroyed rock 'n' roll : an alternative history
of American popular music / Elijah Wald.
    p.   cm.
Includes bibliographical references and index.
ISBN 978-0-19-534154-6
1. Popular music—United States—History and criticism.   I. Title.
ML3477.W35 2009
781.640973—dc22   2008042265

ROCK IT FOR ME
Words & Music by Kay Werner and Sue Werner
As sung by Ella Fitzgerald
© Copyright 1938 (Renewed) Words & Music, Inc., New York, NY
Used by Permission

"Rock the Joint" written by Harry Crafton,
Henry (Doc) Bagby, and Wendell (Don) Keene
Published by Andrea Music (SESAC)
Lyrics reprinted with permission of Andrea Music
and www.oldies.com (1-888-My-Oldies).

9 8 7 6 5 4 3 2 1

Printed in the United States of America
on acid-free paper

DEDICATED TO THE MEMORY OF JEFF McLAUGHLIN,
WHOSE SUPPORT AND CRITICISM HELPED ME SO OFTEN OVER THE YEARS,
AND WHOSE PRESENCE IN THIS BOOK AND IN MY LIFE IS SORELY MISSED.

DEDICATED TO THE MEMORY OF JEFF McLAUGHLIN,
WHOSE SUPPORT AND CRITICISM HELPED ME SO OFTEN OVER THE YEARS,
AND WHOSE PRESENCE IN THIS BOOK AND IN MY LIFE IS SORELY MISSED.

CONTENTS

ACKNOWLEDGMENTS

This is an exciting time to be writing about popular music. A flood of insightful, well-researched books and papers is transforming our view of the past, and the Internet has provided unprecedented access to recordings, documents, and scholars around the world. I cannot possibly acknowledge everyone whose work influenced and educated me over the course of this project, but I want to emphasize that I had a lot of help. I am pleased to have unearthed some interesting and unfamiliar tidbits and hope I convey some of the surprise I felt as my preconceptions were overturned, but I am following in the footsteps of a century of predecessors, many of whom were able to look at the evidence in greater depth and at closer hand, and I am very conscious of following the trails they blazed.

In the past two years I have talked and corresponded with dozens of historians, critics, and collectors, read hundreds of books and articles, and listened to thousands of recordings. It was a rich and fascinating process, and the names that follow are only a small sample of the people to whom I owe a debt for their efforts, aid, and advice.

I must give special thanks to the friends and colleagues who read parts of my manuscript, suggesting changes and catching my errors, and especially to Matthew Barton, whose breadth of knowledge never ceases to amaze me and who gave thorough notes on the whole damn thing. Also Lynn Abbott, Daphne Brooks, Ken Emerson, Robert Forbes, Reebee Garofalo, Bernard Gendron, Peter Guralnick, Keir Keightley, James Kraft, and Ned Sublette, as well as Susan McClary, whose encouraging words were much appreciated.

One of the great pleasures of this project was that it gave me an excuse to contact people whose names or work were familiar to me, as well as to look up some old friends. In general, I avoided doing interviews—largely because if I had started down that road I would never have finished the book—but in a few cases I couldn't resist, and I thank Charlie Gracie, Art Laboe, and Dale Hawkins for taking the time to talk with me. The list of other people I consulted could go on forever, and I hope I will not annoy anyone whose name is not here by mentioning Kate Bergh, Donald Clarke, Scott DeVeaux, Daniel Goldmark, Lawrence Gushee, Brad Kay, Michael Kieffer, Gene Lees, Jeffrey Magee, Dan Morgenstern, Dominic Priore, Ben Quinones, Bruce Boyd Raeburn, Rosetta Reitz, Christopher Robinson, Jody Rosen, Howard Rye, Marc Schechtman, Bruce Vermazen, Eric Weisbard, and Henrietta Yurchenko.

For their kind assistance in providing me with research materials, many thanks to the staffs of the Rutgers Institute of Jazz Studies; the Browne Popular Culture Library, Music Library, and Sound Recordings Archives of Bowling Green State University; the Hogan Jazz Archive at Tulane University; the Los Angeles Public Library; and, above all, to Bridget Risemberg and everyone at the University of California Los Angeles Music Library. Thanks also to Robert Walser and Raymond Knapp, who brought me to UCLA and made this task far easier than it would have been otherwise, as well as always being available for illuminating conversations.

I am indebted to Michael Fitzgerald for his Jazz Research Internet list, Scott Alexander for supplying me with Whiteman's recordings, Stephan Michelson for several boxes of books and magazines, Mike Daley for his dissertation on rock historiography, and the folks at Archeophone Records, redhotjazz.com, jazz-on-line.com, and numerous other Internet sites for making so much wonderful music available.

And last but far from least, thanks to all the people involved in the production of this book, including my agent, Sarah Lazin, who found it a good home; my editor, Suzanne Ryan, who believed in it from the first; Christine Dahlin and the production staff at Oxford; my copyeditor, Elaine Kehoe; and Sandrine Sheon and Martine Bruel, my wife and her mother, who along with moral support provided expertise in graphic design.

ACKNOWLEDGMENTS

This is an exciting time to be writing about popular music. A flood of insightful, well-researched books and papers is transforming our view of the past, and the Internet has provided unprecedented access to recordings, documents, and scholars around the world. I cannot possibly acknowledge everyone whose work influenced and educated me over the course of this project, but I want to emphasize that I had a lot of help. I am pleased to have unearthed some interesting and unfamiliar tidbits and hope I convey some of the surprise I felt as my preconceptions were overturned, but I am following in the footsteps of a century of predecessors, many of whom were able to look at the evidence in greater depth and at closer hand, and I am very conscious of following the trails they blazed.

In the past two years I have talked and corresponded with dozens of historians, critics, and collectors, read hundreds of books and articles, and listened to thousands of recordings. It was a rich and fascinating process, and the names that follow are only a small sample of the people to whom I owe a debt for their efforts, aid, and advice.

I must give special thanks to the friends and colleagues who read parts of my manuscript, suggesting changes and catching my errors, and especially to Matthew Barton, whose breadth of knowledge never ceases to amaze me and who gave thorough notes on the whole damn thing. Also Lynn Abbott, Daphne Brooks, Ken Emerson, Robert Forbes, Reebee Garofalo, Bernard Gendron, Peter Guralnick, Keir Keightley, James Kraft, and Ned Sublette, as well as Susan McClary, whose encouraging words were much appreciated.

One of the great pleasures of this project was that it gave me an excuse to contact people whose names or work were familiar to me, as well as to look up some old friends. In general, I avoided doing interviews—largely because if I had started down that road I would never have finished the book—but in a few cases I couldn't resist, and I thank Charlie Gracie, Art Laboe, and Dale Hawkins for taking the time to talk with me. The list of other people I consulted could go on forever, and I hope I will not annoy anyone whose name is not here by mentioning Kate Bergh, Donald Clarke, Scott DeVeaux, Daniel Goldmark, Lawrence Gushee, Brad Kay, Michael Kieffer, Gene Lees, Jeffrey Magee, Dan Morgenstern, Dominic Priore, Ben Quinones, Bruce Boyd Raeburn, Rosetta Reitz, Christopher Robinson, Jody Rosen, Howard Rye, Marc Schechtman, Bruce Vermazen, Eric Weisbard, and Henrietta Yurchenko.

For their kind assistance in providing me with research materials, many thanks to the staffs of the Rutgers Institute of Jazz Studies; the Browne Popular Culture Library, Music Library, and Sound Recordings Archives of Bowling Green State University; the Hogan Jazz Archive at Tulane University; the Los Angeles Public Library; and, above all, to Bridget Risemberg and everyone at the University of California Los Angeles Music Library. Thanks also to Robert Walser and Raymond Knapp, who brought me to UCLA and made this task far easier than it would have been otherwise, as well as always being available for illuminating conversations.

I am indebted to Michael Fitzgerald for his Jazz Research Internet list, Scott Alexander for supplying me with Whiteman's recordings, Stephan Michelson for several boxes of books and magazines, Mike Daley for his dissertation on rock historiography, and the folks at Archeophone Records, redhotjazz.com, jazz-on-line. com, and numerous other Internet sites for making so much wonderful music available.

And last but far from least, thanks to all the people involved in the production of this book, including my agent, Sarah Lazin, who found it a good home; my editor, Suzanne Ryan, who believed in it from the first; Christine Dahlin and the production staff at Oxford; my copyeditor, Elaine Kehoe; and Sandrine Sheon and Martine Bruel, my wife and her mother, who along with moral support provided expertise in graphic design.

HOW THE BEATLES DESTROYED ROCK 'N' ROLL

INTRODUCTION

You do not have to love a work of art or a style in order to criticize it, but you need to understand its attraction for someone who does.... Criticism has no significance and no importance if it is not accompanied by understanding—and that implies the comprehension of at least the possibility of love.

CHARLES ROSEN

The first record I ever owned was side two of *Meet the Beatles*. It was a birthday present from a Danish au pair, who had given side one to my younger sister. My sister's birthday is three days before mine, and in between the au pair neatly rewrapped the album, then gave me side two. It was 1965, and I was turning six.

I suppose I should have been aware of the Beatles before that, as my family had spent the previous year in England, but all I remember of that year was finding a bomb shelter and a hibernating hedgehog, and my enduring perplexity about a word I heard as "lava tree." And once, on a drive to London, noticing a person with long hair and a beard and being confused about whether it was a man or a woman.

In any case, I loved *Meet the Beatles*, and my sister and I would dance around the living room, singing along—I tended to skip over "This Boy" and "Till There Was You," which were sappy, but all the other songs were great. Within the next year or so, another au pair took us to see *Help!* and it instantly became my favorite movie. I saw *Help!* every year for the rest of my childhood. I also got the soundtrack album, along with *Beatles '65*, *Beatles VI*, and the first two Monkees albums.

Sometime in 1967, or maybe it was 1968, my much older half-brother gave my parents *Sgt. Pepper*. He didn't just hand them the album; he sat the whole family down and we listened to it from beginning to end. I could tell it was a masterpiece—my father, who was an amateur cellist, loved it—but it was not really my music. It was adult music, like Louis Armstrong or Pablo Casals. I played it occasionally, but nowhere near as often as the band's early records. It simply wasn't as much fun. Same with *Abbey Road* and *Magical Mystery Tour*, both of which I vaguely remember hearing when my parents bought them for us, but neither of which I can ever recall playing again. When *Yellow Submarine* came out, my mother took a group of my friends to it for my birthday party. I enjoyed the movie but had no interest in the soundtrack album.

The years passed, and between my sister and me, we gradually filled most of the holes in our Beatles collection. My tastes never changed, though. I can't remember playing *Revolver*, and although I definitely played *Rubber Soul*, it was mostly for the moments when it sounded like the earlier discs.

I heard all the songs, of course, on all the records, and was aware of how the Beatles' hairstyles were changing from year to year and listened for the clues that proved that Paul was dead and grew my own hair down over my ears. There was no way to avoid the Beatles' influence. Even if you hated them, you couldn't have missed being bombarded with the music, the pictures, and the news about their drugs and marriages and, eventually, their breakup. Twenty years later, a recently divorced friend defined his test for maturity as, "I'm not dating anyone who can't name all four Beatles." I was shocked to realize that there were young people who couldn't do that. I could understand not liking the Beatles—my own enthusiasm had dimmed a good deal as I discovered folk and blues—but not being able to *name* them?

Fast forward to 2004 or thereabouts. I had written a book about Robert Johnson and the history of blues, trying to place the early blues singers in the broader context of black popular music rather than treating them as folk artists. Over and over again, in interviews and conversations, I found myself saying that knowing about Johnson and Muddy Waters but not about Leroy Carr or Dinah Washington was like knowing about, say, the Sir Douglas Quintet but not knowing about the Beatles. My point was that in order to understand the music of any period, you have to be aware of the major artists of the time. If you are not aware of the Beatles, you cannot hope to understand any music of the 1960s, because they were ubiquitous and affected all the other music. Even if some musicians remained free of their influence, those musicians were still heard by an audience that was acutely conscious of the Beatles. They were the dominant, inescapable sound of the era.

It took a while, but eventually that thought began to nag me, because I was guilty of exactly the sort of mistake I was criticizing: I had been writing about the music of the 1920s for years but had never listened to a Paul Whiteman record. Admittedly, I had quite a bit of company. Virtually all the books I had read about the music of the '20s ignored Whiteman or mentioned him only in the negative—jazz historians remain angry that he was dubbed the "King of Jazz" and tend to mention him only in passing, as a barrier that the true jazz artists had to surmount. Nobody writing about blues or country music seems to feel any need to listen to him, nor do most jazz historians feel obliged to analyze his influence on the music they care about.

But, like the Beatles, Whiteman's orchestra was not only the most popular band of the 1920s, but was also enormously influential in every field of music. When that period is referred to as the "Jazz Age," conjuring up pictures of flappers, bearskin coats, and F. Scott Fitzgerald, the band that made that jazz was Whiteman's. In purely musical terms, his innovations were huge: He defined the arranging style that would be used by virtually every later bandleader. His band was the first to add a vocal group, the Rhythm Boys (which included Bing Crosby, the most popular singer in America for the next twenty years), and to hire a female vocalist, Mildred Bailey. If he didn't swing, he appreciated musicians who could and hired many of the most important white jazz artists of that era. And he was the first person to force a broad public to treat jazz as serious, important music rather than just a noisy fad. As the Beatles' *Sgt. Pepper* was for rock, Whiteman's *Rhapsody in Blue* was the breakthrough work in the struggle to have jazz recognized as art music, bringing it out of the saloons and dance halls and forcing "serious" music fans to take notice of it as the sound of their time. Duke Ellington always stressed his respect for Whiteman's innovations, and it would be hard to argue that the Beatles' music crossed racial lines as much as Whiteman's did.

There are other bases for comparison. In both the 1920s and the 1960s—the Jazz Age and the rock age—music served as a marker for deeper changes. "The older generation…pretty well ruined this world before passing it on to us," a young writer explained. "They gave us this thing, knocked to pieces, leaky, red-hot, threatening to blow up; and then they are surprised that we don't accept it with the same attitude of pretty, decorous enthusiasm with which they received it."[1] That was in 1920, but it could as easily have been written in the 1960s. And the fact that the eras' music symbolized the dreams and hopes of new generations gave the words "jazz" and "rock" a special weight. For many people, they were—and are—far more than musical styles. They were new languages, capable of expressing attitudes and emotions that other types of music could barely suggest. Because of that, they have inspired particular devotion and tend to be seen as not only separate from but also inimical to the pop music that preceded them and surrounded them in their youth.

I was a kid in the 1960s, and to me and my peers even the music of the 1950s seemed unimaginably old. I was taken by a grown-up friend to see a Chuck Berry concert around 1970, and I thought he was great, but it would have been incomprehensible for anyone my age to have played a record by Berry or Elvis Presley at a party. Those were already called "oldies"—a word that is still associated with the same records forty years later. The Beatles had changed everything—not by themselves, of course, but they were the standard-bearers—and although we could appreciate the rock 'n' roll pioneers as the roots of our music, we were living in a different era.

If early rock was already the sound of the past, then what interest could we possibly have in the popular styles that preceded it? The idea that we might have tossed a Glenn Miller record on the turntable was ridiculous: That music was already thirty years old! So it feels very odd to me when I ask my twelve-year-old nephew what he and his friends dance to at parties and the first band he names is the Beatles. He also listens to the Black-Eyed Peas and other present-day groups, of course. But kids, at parties, are putting on forty-year-old records! Much as I love a lot of older music, I find that incomprehensibly strange. After all, if kids in the 1960s had been dancing to the music of the most popular band of forty years earlier, they would have been dancing to...Paul Whiteman.

So I got interested, first in hearing Whiteman and his peers, and then in trying to make sense of how American popular music evolved over the course of the twentieth century. It was a way of forcing myself to listen to a lot of artists whom I knew by name but had never really heard, and of coming to terms with all the mainstream pop music that people like me have tended to disparage as "commercial." Instead of groaning over the fact that Whiteman was a bigger star than Louis Armstrong, that Dinah Shore outsold Dinah Washington, and that Guy Lombardo and his Royal Canadians were the most popular dance band of the century, I wanted to try to understand their music and the ways in which it affected the music I knew better.

One thing I concluded very early in this exploration was that the words "jazz" and "rock" were getting in my way. Both genres have inspired such devotion and spawned such vast critical and historical literatures that it is difficult to put them in perspective. In the creation of their canons, certain artists and styles have been examined in exhaustive detail while others have been ignored, often with little regard for which were more popular or more respected in their time. I understand the value of those canons—like all canons, they define an aesthetic and are both useful and illuminating—but because they account for such an immense proportion of the writing on American popular music, it has become hard to see beyond, around, under, and through them and to make sense of the broader picture into which they fit.

So I started trying to think of other ways to look at the evolution of popular music. One is to explore the effects of evolving technologies, as bandstands and parlor pianos gave way to Victrolas, transistor radios, and iPods and what was once a social lubricant became a way of creating a personal soundtrack. Another is to see the sweep of American music through the twentieth century as a story of African rhythm triumphing over European melody—an oversimplification, not least because Africa has produced plenty of melodies and Europe plenty of rhythms, but a cohesive way of tying together many of the century's key genres, from ragtime to jazz, swing, rock 'n' roll, funk, disco, and hip-hop.

The idea of a steady progression from ragtime to rap is tempting to a historian because it shows a clear line of development over an extended period of time. And if one accepts that continuum, then the Whiteman orchestra and the Beatles played very similar roles: not as innovators but as rearguard holding actions, attempting to maintain older, European standards as the streamlining force of rhythm rolled over them. Within the small world of music nuts, there have always been some who regard the Beatles in just this way. In their view, rock is rooted in African-American music, and its evolution was from blues and R&B through Little Richard, Ruth Brown, and Ray Charles toward James Brown and Aretha Franklin, and on to Parliament/Funkadelic and Grandmaster Flash. By the time the Beatles hit, still playing the rhythms of Chuck Berry and Carl Perkins, that style was already archaic and their contributions were to resegregate the pop charts by distracting white kids from the innovations of the soul masters, to diffuse rock's energy with effetely sentimental ballads like "Yesterday"—paving the way for Simon and Garfunkel, Crosby, Stills and Nash, Elton John, and Billy Joel—and then to drape it in a robe of arty mystification, opening the way for the Velvet Underground, Pink Floyd, Yes, and Emerson, Lake and Palmer. In other words, rather than being a high point of rock, the Beatles destroyed rock 'n' roll, turning it from a vibrant black (or integrated) dance music into a vehicle for white pap and pretension.

That is how a lot of jazz fans over the years have categorized the Whiteman band: as a temporary impediment to the music's evolution, substituting lilting strings and pretentious arrangements for swinging rhythms and group improvisation. It is incontrovertibly true that the Whiteman outfit lacked the rhythmic power and complexity of the King Oliver, Fletcher Henderson, or Count Basie bands, just as the Beatles lacked the rhythmic power and complexity of Motown, Stax, and James Brown. On the other hand, both the Whiteman orchestra and the Beatles pioneered a melodic and harmonic richness that was considered revolutionary for their genres, most dramatically in works arranged by Ferde Grofé, Whiteman's main arranger, and by the Beatles' producer, George Martin, who considered Grofé one of his musical heroes.

I don't want to overstate that analogy—the Beatles, unlike Whiteman, composed their own songs, were a loose, rowdy rock 'n' roll band before they got arty and, though they shared his commercial aspirations, would have mocked Whiteman's aspirations to respectability. But the differences in how they tend to be viewed by historians say more about the way jazz and rock history have been written than about the realities of their music and careers. Both were the dominant bands of their times, for better or worse—and, if we want to understand those times, for better *and* worse. That is, if one accepts that the Beatles and their peers transformed teenage dance music into a mature art form, then it isn't fair to deny Whiteman credit for doing much the same thing to jazz. And, conversely, if Whiteman is to be damned for attempting to turn jazz into white art music, why are the Beatles to be applauded for doing the same thing to rock?

Before I began writing about music, I was a working musician. Due to the limitations of my talent and the tastes of my audiences, I had few illusions about being an artist, but I was doing something I enjoyed and making a decent living at it. I was a reasonably skilled craftsman and took pride in the fact that I could play a wide enough range of styles to suit a lot of different kinds of people. And that is a key difference between the general run of musicians and most of the people who write music criticism and history. The writers are trying to define aesthetic positions, whereas the players, by and large, see aesthetic categories as limitations, cutting them off from jobs they are capable of filling. This attitude has inescapably shaped my understanding of music history: Any stylistic break, exciting as it may be, also seems to me to be a barrier. So as I survey the course of American music, I am always looking for connections, ways of linking styles and artists that usually are placed in separate boxes.

This does not mean that I favor continuity over change, but rather that I am fascinated by the continuities that show up even in the midst of the most dramatic changes. For example, there is no more perfect evocation of the thrill that came with early rock 'n' roll than the moment in Elvis Presley's 1954 recording of "Milkcow Blues" when, after singing a couple of slow, classic country blues lines, he stops the band, saying "Hold it, fellas. That don't *move* me. Let's get real, real gone," then breaks into a wild, whooping boogie. So I was charmed, listening to a record by Bennie Moten and his Kansas City Orchestra from 1928, to hear the trumpet player, Ed Lewis, interrupt Moten's perky piano introduction, saying "Hey, Bennie. Stop that ragtime. Let's get real lowdown," and go into a jazzy scat vocal.[2] The differences between Presley's music and Moten's are obvious, but so is their similar effort to signal a break with old rhythms—as well as, in both cases, to first signal their mastery of the older style.

So one of the main things I try to do in this book is to avoid the assumptions of genre histories, the divisions of eighty years of evolving popular styles into discrete categories like ragtime, jazz, swing, R&B, and rock. Not because those categories are necessarily inaccurate or objectionable, but because when I step outside them I hear the music differently and understand things about it that I previously missed.

This process inevitably has made me conscious of the ways in which my own experiences have affected my musical tastes. To stay with Presley for a minute, the fact that I was born in 1959 made it difficult for me to hear him as a musical revolutionary. I first recall seeing him in the 1973 television special *Aloha from Hawaii*, and his rhinestone jumpsuit, Vegas mannerisms, and orchestral bombast epitomized everything that was archaic, overblown, and ridiculous about mainstream show biz. I have since come to understand his importance and to appreciate the youthful excitement of his early Sun sides and his moody charisma in *King Creole*, but that was as much by reading about him as by listening to him or watching him—which is to say I like a lot of his work, but he has never been an important part of my life.

By contrast, Peter Guralnick, whose writings forced me to reconsider Presley's work, first saw him leaping off the television screen in 1956, when Guralnick was twelve. So, while he is always measured and incisive about Presley's abilities and does not shy away from the contradictions of both the life and the music, Guralnick is intensely aware of Elvis's initial impact: "The world was not prepared for Elvis Presley," he wrote in a groundbreaking essay for *The Rolling Stone Illustrated History of Rock 'n' Roll*. "Other rock 'n' rollers had a clearer focus to their music. An egocentric genius like Jerry Lee Lewis may even have had a greater talent. Certainly Chuck Berry or Carl Perkins had a keener wit. But Elvis had the moment. He hit like a Pan American flash, and the reverberations still linger from the shock of his arrival."[3]

That is the image of Elvis that dominates virtually all rock histories: the young revolutionary of "That's All Right" and "Hound Dog," signaling the arrival of a new era with his untamed vocals, swiveling hips, and rebellious sneer. And I have no argument with it, either aesthetically or historically. My favorite Elvis records are the rootsy, rocking sides, and when I read newspapers and magazines from the mid-1950s, he is universally hailed or damned for leading a blues-powered assault on the sedate and respectable bastions of Tin Pan Alley.

But if the stripped-down energy of the Sun recordings makes it easy to place Elvis in the company of rockers like Lewis, Berry, and Perkins, his success—the way he grasped his moment—very quickly put him in the company of Pat Boone and Perry Como, who rank just behind him as the top hitmakers of the 1950s. Guralnick tells me that Presley always expressed appreciation for Boone's ballad singing, and has written that it was Sun's owner, Sam Phillips, who pushed the young singer toward what we now call rockabilly. As Elvis told an interviewer in 1955, "I had never sung anything but slow music and ballads in my life at that time."[4] And when he left Sun for RCA, he quickly began to alternate the rock numbers with dreamy concoctions like "Love Me Tender" and "That's When Your Heartaches Begin"—an old Ink Spots hit he had recorded as a present for his mother during his first visit to Sun. The major label's choruses and studio musicians helped him sound like the movie stars he had idolized back in Memphis, and he would pick "It's Now or Never," based on Mario Lanza's version of "O Sole Mio," as his own favorite among his recordings.[5]

So with the advantage of hindsight one could think of Elvis as a 1950s equivalent of Bing Crosby, who established himself in Whiteman's band as the most jazz-oriented of white singers, then proved his mastery of older and more sedate styles, branching out into Tin Pan Alley ballads, Hawaiian exotica, cowboy songs, and Irish-American nostalgia. By 1956 Whiteman was a radio and television executive celebrating his fiftieth anniversary in show business, and his assessment of RCA's new star was "I think Presley's got the inner talent if it's handled well, but he'll have to develop his style in order to stay on top, like Crosby and Sinatra have."[6] And, with adjustments to fit the different eras, that is precisely what happened.

Or, more accurately, that is an alternate way of telling the story. Any history is a reflection of at least two periods—when the events happened and when one is writing—and also of the writer's personal experience. So when I write about

Elvis's arrival, I am writing about the 1950s, looking back from the thirtieth year of hip-hop, and hearing him with the ears of someone who grew up in the 1960s and 1970s. I can do my best to understand how he sounded when he burst out of car radios in 1955, but I inevitably remain aware of the power ballads that link him to Celine Dion, which I hear with tastes formed by the folk-blues revival. Some of my contemporaries deal with this by thinking of the Sun sessions as the real Elvis and the RCA ballad sides as irrelevant commercial confections, and that is a reasonable aesthetic judgment. But it doesn't explain why both "Hound Dog" and "Love Me Tender" spent over a month at number one in 1956. To say that something is timely—that it expresses its time—is a compliment, just as it is a compliment to say that something is timeless. But what made something timely is usually very different from what makes it timeless.

That is the essential divide between history and criticism. The critic's job is to assign value and importance on an artistic level, which necessarily is a judgment about how the work stands up in the present. The historian's is to sort out and explain what happened in the past, which means attempting to understand the tastes and environment of an earlier time. And the latter task also involves sorting out and understanding how earlier critics and historians were affected by their own times.

Anyone researching rock's beginnings is necessarily thrown back on the work of the early rock historians, who began writing in the late 1960s. Those writers were still living in the midst of the rock revolution, and they created a picture of the 1950s in which Elvis, Berry, Lewis, Big Joe Turner, Little Richard, Ruth Brown, Buddy Holly, the Drifters, and dozens of other artists pioneered a new style and forever transformed popular music. They drew strict boundaries between these artists and mainstream imitators like Boone and Georgia Gibbs, and completely ignored older, unrocking singers such as Como and the McGuire Sisters. One result is that today it is hard to come up with much in-depth, reliable information about the scene that produced Boone, Gibbs, Como, and the McGuires. Another is that the artists who have been celebrated and hailed as pioneers have been separated from their broader context. When Presley and Boone were the two most popular singers among American teens, were they really the idols of opposing camps? Or does that way of seeing them just reflect the fact that the few teenage music fanatics who went on to become rock critics had different tastes from the millions of teenagers who swooned over both? And did even the critics all draw that distinction when they were teenagers in the 1950s, or did some only learn to despise Boone as they matured through Motown, the Beatles, and Jimi Hendrix?

Ellen Willis, one of the few women writing about rock in the 1960s, was also the only prominent critic to answer that last question in the affirmative. In 1968, she wrote:

If we who grew up with rock and have always loved it feel smug these days, the smugness is tainted—at least for some of us. We all knew Elvis was great…but who among us has soul so pure that he never liked Pat Boone? My own taste was not only less discriminating than it could have been but often discriminating in the wrong way. I tended, for instance, to prefer the tamer, white versions of rhythm-and-blues records to the black originals. Partly this was because the imitators were pushed on the radio, but partly it was because Georgia Gibbs *sounded better* to me than LaVern Baker; I was one of the white teen-aged reasons the music was being watered down.[7]

Most of Willis's male peers claimed precisely the purity of soul that she admitted lacking, which is probably one reason she phrased her memory as an admission. And I do not think it is coincidental that a female critic was the lone admitted Boonian—or at least recovering Boonian—in the 1960s rock fold. Reading through the histories of both jazz and rock, I am struck again and again by the fact that although women and girls were the primary consumers of popular styles, the critics were consistently male—and, more specifically, that they tended to be the sort of men who collected and discussed music rather than dancing to it. Again, that is not necessarily a bad thing (some of my best friends…), but it is relevant when one is trying to understand why they loved the music they loved and hated the music they hated.

Obviously, as I survey the history of popular music, I am just as affected by my own time, gender, race, and class as the writers of the 1930s or the 1960s were by theirs, with my own prejudices and experiences. I am sure I would have written this book very differently before hip-hop, or if I were not a guitarist or the son of two middle-class, Jewish college professors with strong left-wing politics, one of them born in 1906 and the other an Austrian refugee, classical pianist and prominent feminist, or if I hadn't spent years playing bar gigs or writing for a newspaper, or so on and so forth…

So I am not claiming any clearer vision than previous writers; I am just trying to be conscious of who they were and how that affected their tastes and judgments. In the late 1930s and 1940s a lot of critics made rulings about what was and was not jazz, and in the late 1960s and 1970s other critics defined a canon of what was and was not rock, and we can respect those rulings without accepting them as definitive or even accepting those categories as useful ways for us to sort the music of those times. The critical choices have affected the way I hear the music, and continue to affect it, but, like the surviving magazines, playbills, interviews, and the music itself, those choices are now historical artifacts. There are no definitive histories because the past keeps looking different as the present changes.

This book is an attempt to go back and look at some familiar ground with fresh eyes and to strip away some layers of past opinion. Like any history, it omits far more than it includes, and if I have left out a lot of familiar stories and revered figures that is in general because they are covered at length and in depth in other books or because they do not happen to intersect the particular trails I am following.

One thing I want to stress is that I am trying to write history, not criticism—that is, to look at some of the most influential movements and stars of the twentieth century and explore what links and divides them without worrying about whether they were marvelous or pernicious, geniuses or frauds, or whether I personally enjoy their work. Even allowing for strong tastes, one can still attempt to separate artistic judgments from historical ones. I prefer Vincent van Gogh's paintings to Paul Cezanne's, but although that is my heartfelt aesthetic judgment, my historical judgment is that one could trace a solid, cohesive chronology of modern art without including Van Gogh—though it would lack some wonderful paintings and interesting connections—whereas without Cezanne one cannot understand how Picasso and Braque came to create cubism and thence explain all the other abstractions, geometric and otherwise, of twentieth-century academic art. Similarly, I prefer Picasso to the average painter of sunsets, and yet am aware that outside the academies and museums most people looking for pictures to hang on their walls still tend to prefer competent representations of pretty girls and landscapes to the innovative explorations of the twentieth century. So I can imagine a broad and accurate history of modern art that would treat museums and academies as serving an elite and largely irrelevant taste and recognize Van Gogh for having designed a fabulously popular and influential poster of sunflowers.

As it happens, that is how most histories of popular music are written: We tend to leave classical and symphonic styles out of the story, as if they existed in a separate world, just as historians of classical styles tend to give at best a glancing nod to pop trends. In a choice that seems odd to an outsider, the classical music historians also tend to regard most of the new, classically based orchestral compositions of the twentieth century—radio, film and television scores, easy listening and mood music, the orchestral sections of *Sgt. Pepper*—as falling outside their field. And, equally oddly, the jazz and rock canons tend to mimic the classical canon in this respect. Jazz historians, by and large, have no more interest in Paul Weston, Nelson Riddle, and Henry Mancini than classical historians have, and only minimally more interest in Glenn Miller. And while there are dozens of scholarly discussions of the Velvet Underground, there are virtually none of KC and the Sunshine Band.

To a great extent, that is because music criticism demands studious, analytic listening, and the people who listen that way tend to value music that rewards careful attention and analysis over styles that are just fun, relaxing, or danceable—which, again, is perfectly reasonable but automatically separates them from most of the people buying and dancing to popular music. And in the same way, historians tend to focus on unique, original musicians rather than typical, generic ones, even when they are supposedly studying trends and movements rather than exceptional achievements.

This is particularly true for historians of music from the past hundred years, because we can hear so much of it. Historians of earlier styles necessarily devote a lot of attention to generic performance practices because, unless the styles involved written notation, that is pretty much all we have to study, and even where notation exists, we need to understand how it was translated into sound. For the twentieth century, we have millions of recordings available, so we not only can read the sheet music for "Stardust" and study the composers and musicians who were active in its heyday, but can also listen to the ways different artists of that period played it. This is obviously an advantage, but it tempts us to think of those recordings as representative even when they are not and—because we have our own tastes and must listen to the records we are studying over and over—to pay more attention to records that excite us than to records that we find boring. For example, when we study the music of the 1920s we are tempted to focus on Louis Armstrong's Hot Five, even though we know that it never performed outside the recording studio, and to avoid Guy Lombardo, because he made hundreds of records. We can't write about them intelligently without listening to a representative sample of them, and they bore us.

Which brings me to my final point, at least for now: The most difficult thing about understanding the past is appreciating choices and tastes that seem strange or disagreeable and trying to confront them on their own terms. I began this introduction with a quotation from the classical pianist and historian Charles Rosen, and I want to end with another. Rosen notes that one of the things that makes it hard for us to appreciate new and unfamiliar styles is that they demand that we accept not only sounds that are strange to us but also the absence of qualities that we consider necessary. One reason that the music of Whiteman and the Beatles was so phenomenally popular was that it blended styles that older listeners found abrasive and unmusical with familiar elements, so those listeners could enjoy it without abandoning their previous standards and feel broadminded and modern without essentially changing their tastes. But as Rosen writes, "The appreciation of a new style is as much an effort of renunciation as of acceptance."[8] And the same holds true for any idea, old or new, that is drastically different from our own.

A wealth of new ideas, technologies, and musical styles were born over the course of the twentieth century, and the ones that achieved popularity required both acceptance and renunciations. Electricity, automation, ragtime, movies, jazz, radio, air travel, amplification, and rock 'n' roll were all wonderful in some ways and destructive in others. And to trace their evolutions we need to remain conscious of the losses as well as the gains, and to accept that some of the changes that most excite us were difficult for plenty of decent, intelligent, and talented people. For example, without recording we could not hear any of the music I write about in this book, and yet in some ways there has been no more musically destructive force than the phonograph. So I will begin this story with a look at what musical life was like before recording.

1

AMATEURS AND EXECUTANTS

Of all the ways in which music changed over the course of the twentieth century, the most fundamental was the shift from being something people played to something they consumed and from being part of a larger experience to being a thing that is often heard alone and out of any set context. Audio recording, simply by existing, separated sound from performance. Until recording, music did not exist without someone playing it, and as a result music listening was necessarily social. There was no way to hear a musical group without other people being present—to play even a duet, there had to be two people in the room. It is hard to think about how different that must have been, as everyone reading this book has listened to music alone. Indeed, with Walkmans and MP3 players, it has become common to use music to shut out the rest of the world.

Strange as it may seem, my own earliest musical memories reflect that era before recorded sound. My mother grew up in Vienna, the daughter of a concert-quality pianist and herself a child prodigy on the instrument. My father was an amateur cellist, and I recall them playing duets sometimes on the weekends. We would also gather around the piano and sing together, reading the lyrics from the *Fireside Book of Folk Songs* as my mother played the accompaniment. And my father would sing the popular hits of his youth, usually at the dinner table. I still know many of his favorite songs: "Sheik of Araby," "Lena Was the Queen of Palesteena," "Mammy," "Oh, by Jingo," and odd scraps like "Your Wife and Your Boarder, They're All Right." We owned a record player and my parents had dozens of classical albums, so I'm sure I heard those at times, and we even had some children's records which I must have listened to, since I still recognize songs from them. But I have no memories of listening to recorded music before that Beatles album on my sixth birthday.

Even in the early 1960s that was fairly unusual, and today it is extremely rare. But, with some variations, it is typical of how pretty much everyone first heard music, pretty much everywhere in the world, until well into the twentieth century. And that is something any modern reader needs to understand in order to follow the evolution of popular music from the ragtime era into the jazz years and beyond: For much of that time, records remained relatively unimportant. We tend to give them a lot of historical weight because we still have them, but for their first half century they were considered brief, fuzzy snapshots of popular music, not the thing itself. Live performances, most of them by players and singers who would never be recorded, remained the norm—indeed, the whole idea of "live music" did not arrive until well after the dawn of recording, as until then there had been no dead music.

When they first appeared, audio recordings were faint and scratchy novelties, and no one could have imagined a time when amateur performers would be complimented by being told that they sound "just like a record." Only the most pessimistic were more prescient, and the most famous of these was John Philip Sousa, who coined the term "canned music" and summed up his feelings in a 1906 diatribe, "The Menace of Mechanical Music."[1] By that time the phonograph had become a fairly common object in homes and entertainment arcades, with Sousa's popularity accounting for some of its greatest successes. The first Columbia Records catalog, published in 1890, included fifty cylinders by the U.S. Marine Band, then under his direction, and over the next decade his marches were among the most frequently recorded and best-selling tunes.

From the beginning, though, Sousa was ambivalent about the new technology. The Marine Band that recorded for Columbia was just an eight-man subgroup, as the acoustic recording process could not accommodate a full brass ensemble, and Sousa himself never set foot in the Columbia studio. After he broke off to form his own group in 1892, Sousa's Band would be credited with some 1,770 recordings, but only eight of those were made under his personal supervision.[2] He preferred to leave recording to his assistants while concentrating his own efforts on composing and, more important, bringing "good music" to a mass public.

Sousa considered himself first of all a classical musician, and his concerts, which routinely drew crowds numbering in the thousands, mixed his famous marches with a broad selection of European concert works. He would also include a small sample of light, hummable pop tunes, but to his way of thinking these were there as sweetener for the more serious material. A ragtime march like Kerry Mills's "At a Georgia Camp Meeting" or a sentimental parlor ballad like Charles K. Harris's "After the Ball" would act as a bridge to Wagner and Beethoven. That said, Sousa was acutely conscious and respectful of popular tastes. He noted with pride that the snootier classical orchestras could not match his concert receipts and ascribed this not only to the expertise of his musicians but also to the democratic spirit of his repertory.

From a modern perspective, it can be hard to understand the breadth of music Sousa popularized. Now that brass bands are heard only in parades and at sporting events, we tend to think of them as rousing, blaring calls to action. But brass band concerts included waltzes and ballads as well as marches. "After the Ball," for example, was a sentimental waltz:

After the ball is over, after the break of morn;
After the dancers' leaving, after the stars are gone;
Many a heart is aching, if you could read them all;
Many the hopes that have vanished after the ball.[3]

This song was the biggest sheet music seller of the 1890s, and it remained phenomenally popular well into the twentieth century. In a large part this was due to how easily it could be sung around the parlor piano or used as a tearjerker by professional balladeers, but when Harris looked back on the song's early life, he credited its overwhelming success to Sousa. The 1893 Chicago World's Fair was the first such event to draw visitors from all over the country, and Sousa was its musical superstar: "There were thousands of visitors to the World's Fair who heard Sousa's band play the song as only he could render it," Harris later wrote. "They would then invariably buy copies in Chicago's music stores to take back home with them, to show the home folks the reigning song success of the World's Fair. That was one of the reasons why the song spread throughout the world as no ballad of its kind had ever done before."[4]

The idea that people would hear his band play music and be inspired to go home and perform it themselves was integral to Sousa's mission. It is a bit of a stretch to compare him to Pete Seeger, but like Seeger a half century later he dreamed of a country full of amateurs making music for one another. It was part of the democratic American dream: The aristocratic arts of Europe would be made common property, rubbing shoulders with the rough songs of the pioneers and the latest dances of the vibrant new cities. Sousa differed from Seeger in that he not only wanted everyone to play, but also hoped they would play the works of the great European composers, but for both men, the most important thing was getting instruments into everyone's hands and encouraging them to make music. (And, although Seeger is best known for championing the songs of nonprofessional folk artists, he also recorded banjo transcriptions of Bach, Beethoven, and Stravinsky and wrote a book on sight-reading.[5])

Sousa's objections to "canned music" were not purely aesthetic. He was a businessman as well as an artist, and until 1913 recordings were not subject to copyright and paid no composer's royalties, so his marches were selling millions of cylinders and discs for which he received not a penny. But he also had more altruistic reasons to dislike the new technology, and although he granted that his polemic might be read as both alarmist and partisan, to a modern reader it seems prophetic—as well as being a reminder of a lost world of popular music making.

Sousa started by celebrating America's success in democratizing musical performance: "There are more pianos, violins, guitars, mandolins, and banjos among the working classes of America than in all the rest of the world," he wrote, "and the presence of these instruments in the homes has given employment to enormous numbers of teachers who have patiently taught the children and inculcated a love for music throughout the various communities."

> Right here is the menace in machine-made music! The first rift in the lute has appeared. The cheaper of these instruments of the home are no longer being purchased as formerly, and all because the automatic music devices are usurping their places.
>
> And what is the result? The child becomes indifferent to practice, for when music can be heard in the homes without the labor of study and close application, and without the slow process of acquiring a technic,...the tide of amateurism cannot but recede, until there will be left only the mechanical device and the professional executant....
>
> When a mother can turn on the phonograph with the same ease that she applies to the electric light, will she croon her baby to slumber with sweet lullabys, or will the infant be put to sleep by machinery?
>
> Children are naturally imitative, and if, in their infancy, they hear only phonographs, will they not sing, if they sing at all, in imitation and finally become simply human phonographs—without soul or expression? Congregational singing will suffer also, which, though crude at times, at least improves the respiration of many a weary sinner and softens the voices of those who live amid tumult and noise....
>
> The country band with its energetic renditions, its loyal support by local merchants, its benefit concerts, band wagon, gay uniforms, state tournaments, and the attendant pride and gayety, is apparently doomed to vanish in the general assault on personality in music....
>
> The country dance orchestra of violin, guitar and melodeon had to rest at times, and the resultant interruption afforded the opportunity for general sociability and rest among the entire company. Now a tireless mechanism can keep everlastingly at it, and much of what made the dance a wholesome recreation is eliminated....[6]

We have long lived in the world Sousa dreaded. Only a small minority of Americans still bother to master a musical instrument, and many readers will be puzzled by his reference to the country band with its bandwagon and gay uniforms, never having seen such an amateur group leading a local parade or giving a concert in a park. Virtually all dancing is now commonly done to recordings, played without pause, whether at clubs or at private parties. And although some mothers (and fathers) still hum lullabies and most religious congregations still sing together, it is becoming increasingly common for recorded music to be used even in these situations.

On the flip side, the fact that the "tide of amateurism" has been widely replaced by "the mechanical device and the professional executant" means that we can hear music performed not only by our family members and neighbors but also by the finest artists, alive or dead, who have ever been recorded anywhere in the world, and we can hear it whenever we want, wherever we go, in whatever order and at whatever volume we please. The musicians of the last hundred years have been able to study not only with local music teachers but also by listening to a range of performers and styles that were never previously available to anyone, no matter how rich or well traveled, and it has given them a breadth of experience and created a wealth of fusions that would have been unimaginable in Sousa's day.

So there have been plenty of gains to offset the losses. But some of the changes have been so fundamental that present-day music listeners do not even think about them, and it is worth taking a moment to consider how different music was before recording arrived and became a popular medium.

First of all, we need to remember that in the century or so before Sousa's diatribe, music had already undergone a huge change because of the wide dissemination of printed scores. The nineteenth century was the dawn of "popular music," as separate from "folk music," though few if any critics or historians were yet drawing that distinction. At root both terms are identical, and both originally referred to the music of the common people as opposed to styles composed for the pleasure and edification of a social or educational elite. But over the years they came to be understood quite differently, with folk music being what people made in their communities and popular music being the commercial styles they got from professionals.

As for the elite styles, commonly called "art," "serious," or "classical" music, they are usually discussed as if they formed a separate world, but as both Sousa's repertoire and the work of scholars such as Lawrence Levine have shown, in the nineteenth century highbrow and popular styles overlapped far more than they do today. To a great extent the reason was that both were mostly played at home. Composers and songwriters made their income not from the performance of their works but from sales of printed songs and instrumental arrangements, and most consumers bought and played everything from theater songs, "peasant melodies," and patriotic anthems to Strauss and Beethoven, often grouped in the same folios. Concert artists would likewise mix popular hits and operatic arias on the same program and in both cases tended to embrace the latest works. Today, we expect most classical concerts to be devoted to old music played in an old-fashioned manner, but until the latter half of the nineteenth century, concert programs were overwhelmingly devoted to contemporary compositions and settings. Even when one played the works of older composers, these were routinely adapted to suit current tastes—expanded orchestral settings of Haydn matched the opulent stage settings of nineteenth-century Shakespeare productions—and when both high and low culture were expected to keep up with the times, it was much easier for popular and art styles to overlap.

Concerts, in any case, made up only a small part of musical life, even in the classical field. The vast majority of compositions were written and marketed for people to play at home, which meant that the vast majority of musical performances were by people who, if they bothered to think of themselves seriously as players, thought of themselves as amateurs—literally, lovers of music—rather than as musicians. It was analogous to dancing, the only art that people still practice themselves more often than they pay to have it done by professionals. We dance at home, go out to social events built around dancing, and when we get into a new style like salsa or tango, we take some lessons, then practice with our friends or use our skills as a way to meet people. Far more of us dance than go to watch professional dancers, especially when we're young, and very few of us, even when we are taking lessons, give any thought to becoming professionals ourselves.

Playing music used to be like that. People sang as children and often learned to play an instrument, and many continued to play at least occasionally throughout their lives. What made a song popular was not that a concert artist was using it to wow sedentary crowds, but that hundreds of thousands of people were playing and singing it. Stephen Foster's "Old Folks at Home" was the runaway hit of 1851, and a columnist for the *Albany State Register* described its impact in a wry paragraph:

> Pianos and guitars groan with it, night and day; sentimental young ladies sing it; sentimental young men warble it in midnight serenades; volatile young "bucks" hum it in the midst of their business and their pleasures; boatmen roar it out stentorially at all times; all the bands play it; amateur flute players agonize over it at every spare moment; the street organs grind it out at every hour; the "singing stars" carol it on the theatrical boards, and at concerts. ...[7]

Note that the "singing stars" don't appear in that list until item nine, and no particular star is associated with the song. Today, we associate hits first of all with particular stars. It remains true that virtually none of us hear them for the first time at concerts, but a ubiquitous song tends to be heard in a recording by someone like Christina Aguilera, and though it still may permeate our lives, being heard at dance clubs and shopping malls and blaring from the windows of passing cars, it is always the same arrangement backing the same voice. At the turn of the twentieth century, hits were still heard and played in multifarious arrangements and sung by anyone who thought she could carry a tune.

That is one reason so many of the favorite art music composers of the nineteenth century have fallen from favor today. In competition with Beethoven, they now suffer from their comparative ordinariness and simplicity, but those were not drawbacks when amateurs had to play the music on their own instruments or with a few friends from the neighborhood. Beethoven was considered the highest of high art and scared a lot of amateurs, but even his work was by no means written exclusively for the concert hall. Although he was the most celebrated composer in Vienna, only two of his thirty-two piano sonatas were given public performances there during his lifetime. All of his string quartets were performed in concert, but the piano sonatas were considered "house music" for people to play at home or for professionals to play at small gatherings of amateurs.[8] Few composers could count on wealthy patrons or large commissions—the only sources of income aside from sheet music sales—so they carefully tailored their work to amateur performance. A reminder of this is all the pieces that were written for "piano, four hands." In concert, piano duets were played on two pianos, but few homes had more than one, so composers wrote duets to be played on the single keyboard. A piece that could be played only by concert artists might bring fame, but if you wrote a piece that people wanted to play at home, everyone needed to buy copies of the music.

Most of the famous composers and concert virtuosos were men, but it is worth noting that, in middle- and upper-class homes of the nineteenth century, the majority of musicians were female. Boys could sometimes escape the torture of music lessons, devoting themselves instead to sports or conjugating Latin verbs, but any properly brought up young lady was expected to be able to perform on the keyboard, guitar, violin, or some other common parlor instrument. A modern girl would keep up with the latest compositions, both serious and light, and a typical evening's playing might range from Beethoven to "The Old Folks at Home."

I keep emphasizing that overlap because it formed the foundation of popular music well into the twentieth century. Ragtime and jazz were both dependent on generations of performers and listeners whose musical world ranged from the latest popular songs to the most elevated concert works. Of course, part of what made people think of some works as elevated was that they were associated with a smaller, more educated audience, but that made them all the more attractive, especially when mixed with lighter fare. Today, orchestras that want to educate their audiences tend to perform a "difficult" piece by someone like Lutoslawski sandwiched between more accessible works by Beethoven or Schubert. In the nineteenth century, high and low arts were not so rigorously defined, so performers might "gild...the prodigious pill of Beethoven by the most irresistible polkas and Grand-Exhibition-of-all-Nations waltzes, mazurkas and redowas." That quotation is from an 1853 magazine review of the violinist Paul Julien, anticipating an American tour on which he promised a program of "Beethoven, Haydn and Mozart, with a colossal orchestra and no clap-trap performance but a genuine matter. He will interweave a lighter music so daintily, that our feet will insensibly glide from the solemn marches of the great masters to the airy pulsations of Strauss, and Lanner, and Julien himself."[9] Meanwhile Julien's singing star, the German soprano Anna Zerr, would perform not only selections from Mozart's *Magic Flute* but also

"The Old Folks at Home." With its lilting melody and nostalgic, rural flavor, Foster's song was a particular favorite of visiting concert artists: The Swedish prima donna Christine Nilsson, who was chosen to sing the opening performance at New York's Metropolitan Opera, made it a feature of all the concerts on her first American tour.

Julien's arrival was a newsworthy event in American music circles, and it may have been in response to it that Foster compiled what was then his most ambitious folio of parlor music, *The Social Orchestra*, a collection of vocal and dance arrangements of "the most popular operatic and other melodies," including a selection of his minstrel songs alongside pieces by Mozart, Beethoven, Donizetti, and Strauss, "arranged for flutes, violins and violoncello or piano forte."[10]

In an age when anyone who took music lessons was likely to be familiar with both Foster and Beethoven, it was common not only to find classical artists singing pop hits but also to hear classical music in minstrel shows and town band concerts, and later in vaudeville and on pop radio shows. Bing Crosby often had classical virtuosos as guests on his *Kraft Music Hall*, and when Bessie Smith made her Chicago debut in a black vaudeville program, the cast included an operatic "prima donna" (along with a blackface comedy duo, a trio of child dancers, and a juggler).[11] Many musicians who are best known for their pop work also played some classical pieces: When Louis Armstrong appeared in a theater orchestra in the late 1920s, his specialty number was an aria from Pietro Mascagni's 1890 opera, *Cavaleria Rusticana*. Even illiterate rural players such as Mississippi John Hurt typically played at least one formal parlor piece, "Spanish Fandango," which had been composed as a beginning guitar exercise by Henry Worrall in the early nineteenth century and became so common that its irregular tuning was called "Spanish" by everyone from Delta blues guitarists to writers in *Etude* magazine.

I could cite other examples, but it is important to remember that all the facts that researchers have assembled about our musical past are only glimpses of larger, undocumented worlds. For example, when we think of black musicians in the Mississippi Delta, we automatically imagine guitarists such as Hurt or Charlie Patton, just as, when we think of black musicians in New Orleans, we tend to think of jazz bands. But in both places, and in any town big enough to have even a few people who aspired to middle-class status, black or white, the most numerous and in many ways the most influential professional musicians were teachers. Some teachers performed as well, but the vast majority earned a living through pedagogy, not performance. And those teachers remained a potent conservative force through the ragtime and jazz eras and beyond, insisting that students from Clarksdale to California learn "good" music, perfect their reading skills, and become familiar with the classics.

Of course, there were also musicians who learned their instruments by ear, especially in the countryside, and because their music was unique or regional they were often the artists who attracted record company scouts and who continue to interest us today. But the fact that we are more interested in Patton or Gid Tanner's Skillet Lickers than in all the kids who took piano or violin lessons only testifies to how much more common the latter were. Likewise, when Armstrong recorded, the producers chose to preserve his unique performance of "Potato Head Blues" rather than one more version of *Cavaleria Rusticana*, and when Fats Waller and James P. Johnson recorded, they didn't play Chopin, although both prided themselves on their classical expertise. For many professionals, the classics remained "house music," something they enjoyed, practiced, and maybe played for friends or as accompaniment to silent movies or background music for dining, but there was no reason anyone would have bothered to record them playing a piece that had already been recorded by the Sousa Band or Artur Rubinstein.

Dance music was among the most common types of professional performance, and once again the word "performance" is somewhat misleading. After a century of recordings, it is natural that when we go out dancing to a live band we expect to dance in a way that fits the music. We associate certain bands with certain styles, and we don't go to hear a salsa band if we want to waltz or a rock band if we want to dance a tango. But in the days before recording, it was the bands' job to play whatever music suited the dancers, rather than vice versa. That is the reason that "St. Louis Blues" includes a tango section and rural fiddlers could play semiclassical waltzes like "Over the Waves." Muddy Waters is remembered solely as a blues musician, but when he was discovered by the folklorist Alan Lomax on a plantation outside Clarksdale, Mississippi, he said that his most popular numbers at local dances included "Chattanooga Choo-Choo" and "Darktown Strutters' Ball," and in a later interview he recalled, "We had pretty dances then. We was black bottoming, Charleston, two-step, waltz, and one-step."[12]

Before recordings made it possible to hear twenty different bands in an hour, dance musicians had to be versatile: Whatever step was in fashion, they had to be able to provide accompaniment for it. On the other hand, before recordings made the world's most popular bands available at any dance, there was no need for the locals to be particularly expert beyond that basic versatility. It was like the old joke about two guys being chased by a bear, in which one says to the other, "I don't have to be able to outrun that bear; I just have to be able to outrun *you*." A band in Clarksdale, Mississippi, or Montpelier, Vermont, didn't have to be able to play a tango as well as someone in Buenos Aires or ragtime as well as someone in St. Louis—it just had to play them better than anyone in the same price range in Clarksdale or Montpelier. In the more isolated rural areas, it was common for bands to be made up of locals who could scrape a little on a fiddle or guitar and who might play one or two songs for a whole night. As the Virginia guitarist and banjo player John Jackson recalled, "You started to play one thing, and if it didn't suit them to dance you'd stop it and start on another one and, if that suited them, that's what they wanted. You sat right there and played that one song all night, and when you got tired of playing it, two more people'd move in the corner and go to playing...."[13] I once attended a village dance in the Lacandon rain forest of Southern Mexico at which the band was so pedestrian that after sitting in on guitar I switched to *guitarón*, which I had never played before, and eventually to fiddle—an instrument that not even my closest family can stand to hear me play—without the dancers seeming to notice.

One reason that such inept or limited accompaniment was acceptable was that in many cases the dancers could barely hear the instruments. Sound carried much better in the days before cars, coolers, dishwashers, and other machinery created a steady hum of background noise, but in a room full of dancing feet the best one could hope for was often just to feel the rhythm.

The difficulty of being heard also affected music in other ways. Some instruments, notably the guitar, were simply too quiet to be played for large audiences. Any professional singer or instrumentalist had to be able to project, and subtlety and individuality were secondary considerations. At large events it is common to read of a half-dozen pianos played in unison and of choruses and orchestras numbering in the thousands. Naturally, these huge outfits were not made up entirely of professionals but drew from the well of amateurs who were constantly giving community concerts throughout the country.

There was also the world of religious music, which, like the classical world, is often treated as separate from the popular music scene, although it provided an important underpinning for popular styles. Of course, many people still sing in church without any help from recordings or amplification, so it is easier to cast ourselves back and imagine what this experience would have been like a hundred years ago. What is harder is to understand the degree to which religious singing defined many people's musical lives. The oft-repeated cliché about people dancing to the Devil's music on Saturday night, then singing God's tunes on Sunday morning, vastly understates how often church folk used to sing together—and how often people who might not have been otherwise religious got together to sing hymns or spirituals. There were school groups and church groups but also "singing schools," a movement encouraged in the late eighteenth century by publishers of hymn books who were eager to expand their markets. Singing-school teachers traveled all over rural America, holding week-long sessions at which community members would gather to learn note reading and part singing.

"Camp meetings" were another kind of popular gathering that served both religious devotion and the desire of people from isolated communities to get together with folks from neighboring areas. Because, unlike the singing schools, they were not primarily concerned with selling songbooks, they spawned a repertoire of orally transmitted devotional songs that overlapped and drew on the "Negro spiritual" tradition. Many camp meetings were interracial, and a Swedish tourist recalled attending one in the countryside near Charleston, South Carolina, in 1850 at which whites were seated on one side and blacks on the other, each with preachers of their own race, but all sang together in a "magnificent choir" and "most likely the sound proceeded from the black portion of the assembly, as their number was three times that of the whites, and their voices are naturally beautiful and pure."[14]

Many of the camp-meeting songs and spirituals were folk music in its purest sense—that is, their original creators were anonymous, and they were passed on entirely by oral transmission within communities, evolving through what would be dubbed the "folk process." That process is another thing that has become rare with the ubiquity of recording. Essentially, it is what happens when people make mistakes or alterations to a tune or lyric and pass them along without the change being noted. Spirituals, ballads, children's game songs, and dance tunes all changed in the process of oral transmission, and if no evidence remains of their original sources, all we have are the "folk" versions. Recording did not end this process: An apt later example is Elvis Presley's "Hound Dog," which he picked up from a live performance and, either because he remembered it wrong or because it had already evolved, has quite different words and music from the version Big Mama Thornton had recorded three years earlier. (Though not different enough to prevent the song's composers from collecting royalties.) Because Thornton's record survives, the difference is clear to anyone who cares to compare, but if it did not we would have no way of knowing what relationship Elvis's version of the song had to earlier sources. Likewise, plenty of folk songs undoubtedly started out as professional compositions, and the only reason we call "Old Folks at Home" or "The Baggage Coach Ahead" pop compositions, while calling "Barbara Allen" a folk song, is that we know the authors of the first two but not of the third.

One thing that distinguishes the folk process from other ways in which songs are created is that it places no value on originality. Elvis's version of "Hound Dog" made no claims to being a new arrangement of Thornton's; as far as anyone knows, it was just a poorly remembered version of the same song. Likewise, by the time anyone wrote down the words to "Barbara Allen," there were already hundreds of variants being sung, and although in some cases the song may have been greatly improved in its passage from singer to singer, the people who passed it along considered themselves to be singing an old song, and there is no evidence that any of them took particular pride in their improvements.

In the same way, the village orchestras, the country dance bands, the church and community singing groups, and the amateurs playing "house music" tended not to set a premium on individuality or innovation. Whether Muddy Waters's audiences demanded "How Long, How Long Blues" or "Chattanooga Choo-Choo," in neither case were they interested in hearing how he could transform the songs into his own style. They wanted to dance to the latest hits by Leroy Carr and Glenn Miller, and Waters's quartet was the only group playing that afternoon on Stovall's Plantation.

For almost all bands, almost all the time, that was the gig: You played old tunes for old folks, new tunes for young folks, fast tunes when people wanted to skip, and slow tunes when they wanted to sway. Twenty years after Lomax recorded Waters, the Beatles were working as the house band at the Star Club on Hamburg's Rieperban, and although both the situation and the music were very different, their job was still to play an assortment of current hits. On records, Waters and the Beatles made their names as innovators, because in that situation originality had some value—if your record wasn't special, why would anyone seek it out? But in live performance they were working bands, and they did their best to accurately provide the sounds their audiences demanded. Unfortunately, Lomax didn't have unlimited discs, so we will never know how Waters sounded singing Gene Autry, but we have George Harrison imitating Carl Perkins's twangy guitar and Paul McCartney mimicking Little Richard's falsetto whoop, and they sound like good journeyman bar musicians who have done their homework.

Today, that tradition of playing whatever the audience wants to hear, in the style they have heard it in elsewhere, is carried on only by a few "general business" wedding bands. But until the latter half of the twentieth century, it was the norm for virtually all professional musicians, as well as for amateurs in parlors, saloons, and barbershops across America. That is probably the most important thing that our familiarity with recordings has obscured: that all the brilliant individuals and startling innovations preserved on discs were just the tiny, shining tip of a huge iceberg of popular music. The geniuses and innovations are exciting, but if we want to understand how the music sounded in its time and how it changed over the years, we need always to keep in mind the submerged mass of journeyman dance bands, part-timers, amateurs, and dancers who kept the whole mass afloat.

2

THE RAGTIME LIFE

John H. Hand and his musicians play "Lohengrin" and "Siegfried" selections at Lincoln Park for the delectation of the crowd which assembles there one evening each week to listen, and Park Commissioner Dunton says that it is a mistake. He declares that the young girl on the diamond frame [bicycle], and the people on tandems, who have been spinning down the Sheridan Road, as well as those who visit Lincoln Park in their carriages, want "rag time" music.

"CHICAGO'S IDEA OF MUSIC," *NEW YORK TIMES*, AUGUST 28, 1898

In the mid-1700s, a French immigrant to rural New York State wrote back to the old country describing the music he now enjoyed: "If we have not the gorgeous balls, the harmonious concerts, the shrill horn of Europe, yet we dilate our hearts as well with the simple Negro fiddle."[1] It was the first of many similar effusions. European Americans have thrilled to the playing of African-American musicians for hundreds of years, and if the simple fiddle has evolved into the digital mixing board, much in the relationship of musicians and consumers has remained the same. "Black music for white people," to take a phrase from the cover of a Screamin' Jay Hawkins album, has not always dominated the pop charts, but it has accounted for each of the principal evolutions of the American pop mainstream in the modern era: ragtime, jazz, swing, rock, and hip-hop—and I could throw in R&B and disco as well, but let's stick to basics for a moment.

Ragtime was the first pop genre, in the sense that we have understood pop genres ever since. Before that, there were popular styles of presentation and popular dances, but not what we now would call genres. Minstrel music was noted for its banjos, bones, and tambourines and for some songs with syncopated rhythms, but also for sentimental melodies like "Old Folks at Home" and, in later years, for a range of styles that could even include opera singers like Sissieretta Jones, the "Black Patti" (a stage name that capitalized on the success of the Italian diva Adelina Patti). What distinguished minstrelsy was the blackface makeup and comic stage business more than any particular music, which is why the form was able to survive through a hundred years of shifting musical styles. The waltz, which in the early 1900s was often compared to ragtime as a once-scandalous dance craze, was only a dance, or more accurately a time signature: Anything in three-quarter time is a waltz, be it a classical composition or a cowboy ballad, and whether it is filed as ragtime, jazz, or rock.

Ragtime arrived shortly after commercial phonograph recording, and although the music was spread overwhelmingly by other means, its historical role is bound up with mechanization and mass marketing. Like jazz and rock 'n' roll, ragtime was perceived not simply as a type of music or dance but as the symbol of a new era:

> I've got a ragtime dog and a ragtime cat,
> A ragtime piano in my ragtime flat.
> I'm wearing ragtime clothes from my hat to my shoes,
> I even read a paper called the *Ragtime News*.
> I've got a ragtime accent, I talk that way,
> I sleep in ragtime and I rag all day.
> I've got ragtime troubles with my ragtime wife,
> I'm certainly living a ragtime life![2]

Like the jazz life or the rock 'n' roll life, the ragtime life was generally considered to be both young and urban, its sounds compared to the whir and crackle of electricity and the propulsive rhythms of locomotives and factory machinery. To conservatives, it conjured up pictures of youth gone astray: "A wave of vulgar, filthy and suggestive music has inundated the land," a writer in the *Musical Courier* lamented in 1899. "Nothing but ragtime prevails and the cakewalk with its obscene posturings, its lewd gestures. It is artistically and morally depressing, and should be suppressed by press and pulpit."[3] And, as always, the heralds of progress celebrated what the old folks bemoaned: "Ragtime is a perfect expression of an American city," a writer countered in 1917. "With its bustle and motion, its multitude of unrelated details, and its underlying rhythmic progress toward a vague somewhere. . . . It is today the one true American music."[4]

The stretch of almost two decades between those quotations saw a lot of musical change, and some purists insist that true ragtime held sway only for a few years near the start, denying that title to either the earlier cakewalk marches or the later Tin Pan Alley hits. But, like jazz and rock, ragtime remained the popular name for up-tempo dance music until a new name came along. On purely musical grounds I sympathize with the people who insist that Irving Berlin's "Alexander's Ragtime Band" and its ilk are "spurious rags";[5] certainly, these songs have neither the sophisticated structure nor the complex rhythms of Scott Joplin's work. And if some modern historians will leap to defend Berlin, even those broad-minded souls tend to flinch at the terminology of the pioneer jazz historian Henry Osgood, who in the 1920s called "Alexander" the "first milestone of jazz songs."[6] Nonetheless, like jazz after it, ragtime was a word that caught the public fancy, and sometimes precise definitions obscure as much as they clarify. In any case, before blundering further into the thicket of nomenclature, I'd like to spend a little time looking at the qualities that link ragtime, jazz, and rock. Some of these are arguably musical, but the most telling ones are mythic.

In 1934, writing about jazz, Roger Pryor Dodge neatly summed up the essential, conflicting myths of all three styles: "Criticisms on the subject seem confusedly to hover around on the one hand, the spirit of America, the brave tempo of modern life, absence of sentimentalism, the importance of syncopation and the good old Virginia cornfields; and on the other hand, the monotonous beat, the unmusical noises, the jaded Harlem Negro, alcoholism, and sexual debauch."[7] Later jazz and rock critics would shift the rural roots from Virginia cornfields to Louisiana bayous and Mississippi cotton fields, and Kansas City, Chicago, or Los Angeles have sometimes replaced Harlem, but those basic images, complete with their inherent contradictions, have held steady. And, like most myths, they all have elements of truth.

The pop music world that began with ragtime is fiercely democratic. Whatever its underlying commercial foundations, it claims to be the music of all America, rich and poor, country and city, black and white (and yellow, red, and brown, when it bothers to acknowledge such subtleties). The only gap it does not strive to bridge is that of age: Each shift of genre blazons the arrival of a new generation and threatens all doubters with the ignominy of hunching over their canes and mumbling impotent imprecations as youth dances by.

Meanwhile, as the names changed, there were always some older folks who argued that the music remained essentially the same. Sidney Bechet is recalled as one of the transcendent New Orleans jazz masters, but he insisted till the end of his life that he was playing ragtime. "Jazz, that's a name the white people have given to the music," he recalled in his 1950 memoir. "When I tell you ragtime, you can feel it, there's a spirit right in the word. It comes out of the Negro spirituals, out of [my grandfather] Omar's way of singing, out of his rhythm. But Jazz—Jazz could mean any 'damn thing: high times, screwing, ballroom. It used to be spelled *Jass*, which *was* screwing. But when you say ragtime, you're saying the music."[8]

Louis Armstrong, who outlived Bechet by a dozen years, would extend that thought into the rock era:

At one time they was calling it levee camp music, then in my day it was ragtime. When I got up North I commenced to hear about jazz, Chicago style, Dixieland, swing. All refinements of what we played in New Orleans. But every time they change the name, they got a bigger check. And all these different kinds of fantastic music you hear today—course it's all guitars now—used to hear that way back in the old sanctified churches where the sisters used to shout till their petticoats fell down. There ain't nothing new. Old soup used over.[9]

There's no right or wrong here. All music draws on earlier sources, all music evolves, and all genre divisions are arbitrary—not because the divisions are not based on real differences but because there is always both continuity and change. Music is like speech: The way people talk varies from neighborhood to neighborhood, year to year, and region to region, and decisions about how to divide all those ways of talking into languages tend to have more to do with politics and historical hindsight than with linguistics. The fact that Dutch and Flemish are typically classified as two different languages while the varieties of Arabic spoken in Egypt and Morocco are typically classified as dialects of a single language makes no sense in linguistic terms, but it reflects the historical reality that the Dutch and Flemish have preferred to accentuate their differences while the Moroccans and Egyptians have preferred to stress pan-Arabic unity. Similarly, there is no overriding musicological reason why Scott Joplin and Fats Waller should be placed in different categories—ragtime and jazz—while Waller and Chick Corea are both considered jazz musicians. The reason most historians agree that ragtime was supplanted by jazz in the late 'teens but that jazz continues to evolve in the twenty-first century is that in the first instance the balance of critics chose to signal a split while in the second they chose to emphasize continuity.[10]

Musicologists often distinguish ragtime from jazz on the basis of the shift from a two-beat rhythm to a four-beat rhythm, and that makes perfect sense. There was a marked and genuine shift in dance rhythms that began in the late 'teens and had solidified by the late 1930s, and it is a logical dividing line. But for Bechet, who was comfortable with both rhythms and kept playing through the shift and for many years afterward, it made more sense to say that both rhythms fell within a single style.

Bechet blamed white Northerners for the change in nomenclature, and there is plenty of evidence to back up his position. Most of the earliest bands to whom the word "jazz" (or "jass") was applied seem to have been white, and although one can easily argue that the jazz craze was just a white discovery of music that had already been played by black musicians and danced to by black dancers for at least a decade, that does not change the fact that the word was instituted as part of that white craze. In this sense jazz was like rock 'n' roll, a new name that signified white dancers catching up with black styles rather than a new music.

Race is a touchy subject, especially for white people, and nowhere more so than in the history of the American pop scene. It is easy to build a case that all the main evolutions in popular music since the 1890s have been spurred by black innovators, while the fame and wealth have overwhelmingly been reaped by white imitators and businessmen. I have made that case myself, often, and in some situations I will continue to make it vociferously and defend it against all comers. But as with all simplifications, it tells only part of the story, and the way the case has been formulated is itself largely a white construction. The vast majority of people who have defined American pop styles in books and newspaper articles, radio playlists, record stores, and discographies have been white and, whatever our race, they have inevitably influenced our ideas about popular music. That fact is an ugly relic of American racism, but it is a fact. And the reactions of white audiences and critics have also shaped the music itself. W. C. Handy, "The Father of the Blues," explaining in the 1920s how he settled on his trademark style, recalled, "The crude expressions, snatches of songs and idioms of my people always held a fascination for me, but when I heard an untutored band of three in a small Mississippi town play a weird melody with no definite end and witnessed white dancers paying for this, I saw commercial possibilities as well as esthetic value."[11] That is, Handy's business sense led him to imagine a popular style that, though based on black folklore, would overflow racial boundaries. When his blues hits swept the country, he did everything he could to get them performed and recorded by white artists as well as black, and one sign of his success was that many white dancers and listeners thought of blues as a new style rather than as a racial style.

It is standard practice to write rock history as a story of white musicians building on black foundations, but for seventy years it has been anathema to write ragtime or jazz history that way. So it is worth recalling that in earlier times it was not only possible but common to do exactly that. Not because it is a more accurate way of telling the story, but because by exploring the ways in which ragtime and jazz at their peaks of popularity could be regarded as largely white styles, we not only get a broader picture of the ragtime and jazz eras but also some perspective on rock.

There were at least two distinct periods when America went ragtime crazy. The first was at the turn of the twentieth century, when compositions like Kerry Mills's "At a Georgia Camp Meeting" and Scott Joplin's "Maple Leaf Rag" swept the country. This style is now often referred to as "classic ragtime," a term which was used at the time by Joplin's publisher, John Stark, and which was given added weight by Harriet Janis and Rudi Blesh in their 1950 book, *They All Played Ragtime*. Blesh and Janis helped spark a ragtime revival that culminated in the 1970s, when Joplin's rags provided the soundtrack to *The Sting*, and by separating the black, classically oriented Joplin (who gets 131 citations in their index) from the white, pop-oriented Mills (who gets two), they helped shape the modern perception of ragtime as a refined, though catchy and syncopated, piano style.

"Maple Leaf Rag" and "At a Georgia Camp Meeting" share the multimovement structure that is common to all classic ragtime compositions, setting them apart from the simpler ragtime songs popularized by minstrel and "coon" singers and later by the likes of Irving Berlin. This structure was explicitly modeled on European concert music and is one of the reasons that "classic" or even "classical" are appropriate labels for the style. Joplin, in particular, saw himself as a classical composer inspired by African rhythms, and one of the tragedies of his life was that the elite concert world was not prepared to accept him as such. As we shall see in later chapters, he was far from the last African-American musician to have that problem, and Blesh and Janis suggested that the "Maple Leaf Rag" would have been received very differently if it had been introduced by Antonín Dvořák and titled "Étude in Syncopation." Similar thoughts occurred to Joplin himself, and he subtitled "The Chrysanthemum," one of his later rags, "An Afro-American Intermezzo." This reflected not only his desire to be respected by the classical music establishment but also the fact that his compositions were sold as sheet music to amateur pianists who presumably would play them at home alongside other études and intermezzi.

Today, ragtime is generally thought of as piano music, but the ragtime era did not make that distinction. The piano was the most common home instrument, at least for people who read music, so sheet music sales in every genre were geared to pianists, but ragtime was also sung, danced, and played on whatever instruments came to hand. Kerry Mills, for example, was a violinist, and string ensembles were among the most common purveyors of classic rags. And when it came to large-scale concerts, there was no performer more influential in the spread of ragtime than—once again—John Philip Sousa. On records, Sousa's successes were matched by the banjo virtuoso Vess Ossman and a broad array of singers, but records did not reflect public performance, and through the 1890s brass music remained so popular that Joplin himself doubled as a cornet player.[12]

It was primarily Sousa who made "At a Georgia Camp Meeting" the first instrumental ragtime hit—his band recorded the piece at least eight times between 1898 and 1912[13]—and if the composer of "Stars and Stripes Forever" seems a strange herald for the ragtime era, it may make things clearer to read the song's sheet music cover, which describes it as "a characteristic march, which can be used effectively as a two-step, polka or cake walk."[14] Marching and dancing—especially dancing to African-derived rhythms—might seem like the most disparate poles of human movement, but the cakewalk brought them together. A satire of the "grand march" that opened most society balls, it was a contest dance with a cake as the prize and featured couples marching arm in arm in time to music, with the most elegant or flamboyant couple "taking the cake."

The cakewalk was often done by nonprofessionals, but it was a display dance, not a social dance like the polka or the waltz, and its association with early ragtime is a reminder that, though I have called ragtime the first modern pop music, the musical shift was a process of evolution rather than a clean break with the past. At least in part, this was an evolution from white people watching black people to white people trying to liberate or modernize themselves through the adoption of black styles—the shift from minstrel shows to jazz. Once again that is a simplification, but it captures a key difference between the cakewalk and, say, the fox-trot. And the shift from spectator to participant went along with another shift in American culture: Acting black became an ethnic leveler, a way for Jews, Irish, and Central and Southern Europeans to assimilate into the white mainstream.

Minstrelsy was by far the most popular form of ethnic mimicry in the United States, but European comedians had been exploiting racial stereotypes for centuries and the blackface performers of the ragtime era shared theatrical bills with all sorts of other "ethnic delineators." It is common to describe this dialect humor and makeup—the hook-nosed "Hebrews," the red-wigged "Paddys," the bushy-mustached "Wops"—as racist stereotypes maintaining a white nativist power structure, but white nativists were by no means the only people laughing. Looking through ads and reviews from the segregated black vaudeville circuit, one comes across performers like Louis Vasnier, who boasted of his "natural face expressions in five different dialects, no make up—Negro, Dutch, Dago, Irish and French.... The only colored comedian who can do it."[15]

An article in the *New York Times* of February 26, 1886, gives a hint of the ethnic complications that already surrounded cakewalk exhibitions a decade before ragtime. The headline is "Intruding at a Cake Walk: A White Man among Colored Champions Caused to Retire," and the story reads, in part:

> It was no novices' cake and cane walk that took place at Caledonia Hall, on Horatio-street, last night. The colored population of the Ninth Ward can boast of more prize walkers than even the precincts of Thompson-street.... [This was before black New Yorkers moved north to Harlem, and Greenwich Village was still a notably black neighborhood.] When the band—and there was great joy in the colored breast when it turned out to be a white band—droned into the funeral march, 16 couples appear[ed] for competition....
>
> They started on the parade as stiff as though it were Judgment Day. Every gentleman of color placed his left hand on his left hip and filled his lungs with air. Every lady held on to her partner's right elbow convulsively with one hand while the fingers of the other rigidly pointed downward. No smile flitted across their ebon features, and even the jeers and shouts of the white spectators produced no response....
>
> [But then] it began to be whispered that the third walker was no other than Maurice Jacobs, the poultry dealer of Barclay-street. Mr. Jacobs had taken advantage of his dusky complexion in his pride as a pedestrian to enter a colored cake walk.... It was great and good enough to have a white band; it was bad enough to have all the Irish of the Ninth Ward crowded in the galleries, but it was too much to have a white man try to win the cake....[16]

That ethnic stew—dusky Mediterraneans, brawling Irish, and an exhibition by "colored" dancers—was a commonplace of the urban scene, and the reference to "jeers" from the white spectators is indicative of how the solemn, well-dressed cakewalkers were regarded by the culture at large. It is common to read of cakewalks being accompanied by watermelon-eating contests and even of an event at which "two professional cakewalkers were brought in concealed in a huge watermelon."[17] A cakewalk at Coney Island that attracted almost a thousand spectators was preceded by the pavilion owner creating "a state of hilarious merriment by turning loose a score or more of newsboys and street arabs of all colors and descriptions ... and throwing handfuls of pennies into the air for them to scramble for."[18]

The idea of cakewalks as a parade of black dancers for the entertainment of whites reached back to slavery. The black entertainer Tom Fletcher wrote of older relatives who recalled evenings when white slave owners would sit on their verandas and watch what was then known as the "chalk line walk":

> There was no prancing, just a straight walk on a path made by turns and so forth, along which the dancers made their way with a pail of water on their heads. The couple that was the most erect and spilled the least water or no water at all was the winner. "Son," said my grandfather, "your grandmother and I, we won all of the prizes and were taken from plantation to plantation. . . . We'd have these dancing contests and a watermelon contest, and the singing would round out the evening.
>
> "The plantation is where shows like yours first started, son," he said.[19]

The shows that Fletcher's grandfather was referring to were minstrel shows, which typically ended with a grand "walk-around" in cakewalk style, as well as later productions such as 1898's one-act operetta, *Clorindy—Or the Origin of the Cake Walk*. *Clorindy* was not only performed by but was also written by African Americans—the poet Paul Laurence Dunbar and the composer Will Marion Cook—and its success helped to pave the way for a generation of writers and musicians who would reshape the racial balance of American popular music. Both Dunbar and Cook were educated in the European high-culture tradition, and their idea was to use the cakewalk theme as a way of tempting audiences accustomed to minstrel buffoonery to take a broader view of black folk styles. This was a tricky business, and it is hard to say how well they succeeded. Historians of African-American show business see *Clorindy* as a breakthrough, but many white spectators undoubtedly saw it as a new kind of minstrel show and many black leaders continued to decry any and all cakewalks as retrograde.[20]

Like the dances and music that would follow, the cakewalk was an ambiguous mix of white and black traditions. Some later historians have sought to trace it back to the religious "ring shouts," which clearly descend from African dance worship, but the only link is that both are often danced in a circle, which is true of dances all around the world—and, as Fletcher indicates, the early walks were not necessarily circular. A more obvious derivation is from white ballroom styles, which black dancers mocked by exaggerating the elegant formality of both dress and bearing. The plantation tradition was maintained by servants dancing for the delectation of their bosses, and newspaper reports from the late nineteenth and early twentieth centuries often mention middle- or upper-class white women providing fancy clothes and accompanying their black cooks or maids to cakewalk competitions. Fletcher recalls that resort hotels from Coney Island to Palm Beach expected the "colored help" to end the season with a special display and "would give men and women Cake Walkers easy work during the season in order to have them on hand for the Cake Walk contest."[21]

Before the ragtime era, cakewalks were not associated with any particular kind of music: A typical contest might start out with something as sedate as the funeral march mentioned earlier or a chorus of "John Brown's Body," then move on to a minstrel hit like "Goodbye, Liza Jane" and an Irish comic march like "The Mulligan Guards."[22] By the end of the century, though, the two styles were firmly associated, as can be seen in dozens of ragtime song lyrics. Joplin assiduously tried to avoid minstrel or "coon song" connections, giving his compositions such elegant titles as "Solace," "Weeping Willow," "The Cascades," and "Elite Syncopations," but many of his competitors were less discriminating. Although there is a story that Mills conceived "At a Georgia Camp Meeting" as an attempt to rescue African-American folk traditions from minstrel stereotypes, the song's lyrics were anything but respectful: "I thought them foolish coons their necks would break / When they quit their laughing and talking and went in to walking / For a great big chocolate cake!"[23] Even Joplin was not immune: The original 1899 sheet music for "Maple Leaf Rag" showed a clumsy sketch of two black couples doing what appears to be a sort of cakewalk, and when lyrics were added five years later, the new cover showed a bowing, grinning blackface figure wearing a straight razor on a necklace, and the language was typical minstrel dialect.

Such lyrics highlight one of the main differences between ragtime and later pop styles. Though African-American rhythms were sweeping the country and being hailed and damned as a reflection of modern urban life, the white people who were dancing to them showed little inclination to adopt black styles or slang, and the black people pictured in the songs remained usually rural and exclusively comic. There was a movement afoot in black show business to counteract this image, with the singer-songwriter Ernest Hogan wryly billing himself as "The Unbleached American" and the musical comedians Bert Williams and George Walker producing shows set in urban locations and even at a black college. As *Variety* wrote of Williams and Walker's *Bandanna Land* in 1908, "Since they must be comedians at least they can be funny in some other way than by stealing chickens, 'shooting dice' and using razors, the three conventions which have somehow or other come to be the inevitable earmarks of the comic negro."[24] But the show's title is evidence of the enduring stereotypes, albeit less offensively so than that of the first major all-black musical comedy, 1897's *A Trip to Coontown*.

There are reasons that the word "nigger" has survived in American speech, while "coon" and "darky" now sound archaic, and one is that, nasty as the former word is, it fits with the idea of African Americans—black men in particular—as tough and threatening, which remains a potent image in popular culture. By contrast, although the black characters in minstrel shows and coon songs were sometimes portrayed as wielding razors in alley crap games, even the biggest and angriest were buffoons, counterparts of the Irish country bumpkins who were a staple of English theater. Until at least the 'teens, pretty much the only white performers who got famous by trying to look or act like African Americans were blackface entertainers, and blackface makeup was clown makeup.

By the turn of the century, this image was already an anachronism. Most American cities had large African-American neighborhoods, and black, urban artists were having a profound effect on popular entertainment, but the stereotypes were still stuck on the plantation. Sentimental darkies of the Uncle Tom variety and grinning coons clutching watermelons remained the dominant images, and although Euro-American dancers were picking up steps that had been developed by African Americans, there was not yet any sense of adopting black fashions in clothing or slang. Indeed, the most striking example of ragtime slang was a sort of pig latin featured by Ben Harney, an influential white coon-song composer, who would "rag" the lyric of his "Cake-Walk in the Sky," turning the title phrase into "thege cagake wagauke gin thege skigi."[25] When the Original Creole Band—a black group from New Orleans that featured the music and instrumentation that would soon be dubbed jazz—made its groundbreaking vaudeville tour in 1914, its stage set was a rural cabin and the musicians interspersed their instrumental numbers with choruses of "Old Black Joe" and "Old Kentucky Home."[26]

Those stereotypes would hang on for many years—one of the most successful African-American dance bands of the late 1920s was called McKinney's Cotton Pickers, and we still have Uncle Ben's rice and Aunt Jemima syrup—but by the 'teens they were already considered old-fashioned even by people who did not care that they were racist. For one thing, the reality of black city life had become too obvious to ignore. As James Weldon Johnson, who had graduated from writing coon songs to editing the first major anthology of African-American poetry, wrote in 1921, "I do not deny that a Negro in a log cabin is more picturesque than a Negro in a Harlem flat, but the Negro in the Harlem flat is here, and he is but part of a group growing everywhere in the country, a group whose ideals are becoming increasingly more vital than those of the traditionally artistic group, even if its members are less picturesque."[27]

Meanwhile, Johnson noted, "for a dozen years or so there has been a steady tendency to divorce Ragtime from the Negro; in fact to take from him the credit of having originated it. Probably the younger people of the present generation do not know that Ragtime is of Negro origin."[28] Even in 1900, the hero of "I'm Certainly Living a Ragtime Life" was not walking for a cake at a Georgia frolic, nor does anything about the lyric suggest that he was anything but a bright, white go-getter. A dozen years later, Irving Berlin was leading the second wave of the ragtime craze, and the characters in his songs ranged as far from the plantation as could be imagined: The sheet music for "That Society Bear" showed a private ballroom filled with wealthy white New Yorkers in evening dress, and the lyric described

John D. Rockefeller, Jay Gould, and J. P. Morgan succumbing to the latest dance craze, while the steel baron Charles Schwab was heard "in a high-toned manner, playing the pianner," and "someone cried, 'Cuddle up to your Vanderbilt.'"[29]

Although Berlin's song was a fantasy, the first white amateurs to attract notice by adopting black dance styles were indeed members of New York's richest families. In 1898, newspapers exulted in the spectacle of William K. Vanderbilt, yachtsman, motor racer, and scion of the New Amsterdam aristocracy, triumphing at a society cakewalk. Fletcher described how he tutored the Vanderbilts (William was married to the silver-mining heiress Virginia Fair) and acted as parade leader for their prize-winning walk at Mrs. Stuyvesant Fish's annual Newport Gala. The spectacle of high society disporting itself in this manner inspired widespread hilarity, and various black cakewalk champions, including Williams and Walker, immediately challenged the Vanderbilts to meet them in public competition—a challenge that was quietly ignored.[30]

To put this upper-crust cakewalking in perspective, Mrs. Fish was also famous for hosting an annual ball at which her guests would dress up as their own servants. Secure in their social positions, the young Vanderbilts and Fishes could cheerfully masquerade as butlers and maids or cavort like colored minstrels. Old fogies might grump about "historical and aristocratic names joining in this sex dance...a milder edition of African orgies,"[31] but a cakewalking Vanderbilt remained a Vanderbilt. Cakewalking Cohens, Corellis, or Clancys would have been on far shakier ground, since their claims to whiteness were still considered rather tenuous by America's more conservative arbiters of ethnicity. So, at least for the time being, the cakewalk remained largely a black—or blackface—spectacle, and a brief society fad.

The prancing Vanderbilts did open a door, though, and by 1910 a new generation of white and off-white dancers would be two-stepping through it.

3

EVERYBODY'S DOIN' IT

In the second decade of the twentieth century, the only music that seemed to matter was dance music. "Dance-Mad Denizens of the Metropolis Keep on the Whirl from Luncheon to Breakfast Time" cried a headline in the *New York Times*.[1] Ragtime syncopation vied with the rhythms of Brazil, Cuba, and Argentina; songwriters rushed out tunes to fit the latest steps; and restaurateurs cleared away tables to make room for hectic fox-trotters and lithe aficionados of the tango. This trend owed as much to shifting demographics as it did to innovations in music or dance, and the zeitgeist can be glimpsed in the contrasting stories of the era's key figures in each art: Irving Berlin and the dance team of Vernon and Irene Castle. Berlin and the Castles conquered Broadway together in 1914 with a musical revue called *Watch Your Step*, but they got there by very different routes, and their stories exemplify two of the dominant myths of what would soon be known as the Jazz Age.

Berlin, originally named Israel Baline, was born in Russia in 1888 and arrived in New York with his parents at age five. His father, a Jewish cantor, died when "Izzy" was thirteen, and soon the boy was living on his own on the Lower East Side, singing for tips in saloons. He learned the fine points of this trade by acting as lead boy for a singer named Blind Sol, just as many rural blues singers got their start by leading blind black buskers. Like them, Berlin never learned to read music and picked up his skills through the oral tradition, lending credibility to the many early writers who referred to his compositions as folk songs. But rather than wandering the dusty roads of the rural South, he was in the middle of America's most active commercial music scene, where songs were a product to be knocked together on an assembly line and rushed out in bulk. Berlin got his first taste of that process as a song plugger for Harry Von Tilzer, the man who, according to one story, gave Tin Pan Alley its name with his jangly office piano. Though almost certainly apocryphal, the legend testifies to Von Tilzer's prominence. His songs were models of commercial savvy, from the sentimentality of "She's Only a Bird in a Gilded Cage" and "I Want a Girl Just Like the Girl Who Married Dear Old Dad" to the winking "I Love My Wife but Oh You Kid!" and such ethnic numbers as "Rastus Thompson's Rag-Time Cake Walk" and "Under the Anheuser-Busch." (Meanwhile, his brother Albert wrote "Take Me Out to the Ballgame.") Von Tilzer also ran his own publishing company, and he hired Berlin to sing one of his numbers in an act at Tony Pastor's vaudeville music hall. (Coincidentally, the act featured the Three Keatons—the third Keaton being a rambunctious youngster named Buster.)

Berlin had a famously weak and reedy voice, and his career as a song plugger was brief. By 1904, he had settled into a regular gig as a singing waiter at a joint on the Bowery, the Pelham Café—better known as "Nigger Mike's" after its dark-skinned Jewish owner, Mike Salter. He remained at the Pelham until 1907, the year he wrote his first song lyric. Two employees of a rival Bowery saloon had produced a minor Italian dialect hit, "My Mariucci Take a Steamboat," and on Salter's urging Berlin teamed up with the Pelham's pianist to produce the competitive "Marie from Sunny Italy."

Later that year Berlin was fired over some confusion about missing funds and took to songwriting in earnest. Over the next three years he published more than a hundred compositions, and gradually learned to shape tunes as well as lyrics. Nonetheless, till the end of his life he remained musically illiterate and had to dictate his melodies to a transcriber. His early efforts were a typical hodgepodge of Alley clichés, from the exotic dance parody "Sadie Salome, Go Home" to the mildly naughty "My Wife's Gone to the Country—Hurrah!" and a symphonic pastiche, "That Mesmerizing Mendelssohn Tune," as well as various ethnic dialect numbers.

In 1911, Berlin broke out of the pack with "Alexander's Ragtime Band," which became the most popular song in the country. The fact that it had only one syncopated phrase has led later chroniclers to dub it "fake" ragtime, but that did not prevent it from sparking a second ragtime craze nor Berlin from being hailed as king of the genre—and the views of those historians should be balanced by Scott Joplin's claim that Berlin's melody was stolen from his then-unpublished opera, *Treemonisha*.[2] Indeed, Berlin was dogged throughout this period by rumors that he was stealing tunes from black artists, from vague stories about "a little colored boy" he employed as a regular ghost writer to the specific charge that "Alexander" had been composed by Lukie Johnson, a black pianist who sometimes played at the Pelham. (Johnson denied this.)

Whatever he may have learned from black composers, Berlin helped to separate ragtime from its "coon song" associations, most obviously by dragging in other ethnicities—"Sweet Marie, Make Rag-a-Time-Dance with Me" and "Yiddle on Your Fiddle Play Some Ragtime"—but more generally by writing perky lyrics that portrayed it as the up-to-date rhythm that was setting feet tapping all across America and beyond. His "International Rag" boasted that "the world goes 'round to the sound of the International Rag," and the cover of its sheet music showed Uncle Sam conducting a choir with a Dutch girl, a German hussar, a gaucho, a Turk, and a Chinese coolie—but not a single black face.[3]

Nor would black dancers tend to be prominently mentioned in connection with the new ragtime steps. The cakewalk had always been associated with black Southerners, but the turkey trot, despite being similarly derived from African-American styles, was associated with wild and nutty youth. The original version apparently arrived in New York around 1910, as an import from the saloons of San Francisco's Barbary Coast, and was basically a two-step with flapping elbow movements, but it became so popular that after a while the name was used generically for any rowdy ragtime dancing. By 1911, it had been adopted by the Broadway and society crowd, and Berlin's popular dance hit "Everybody's Doin' It" acquired a new tagline: "Doin' what? Turkey trot!"

Over the next few years, every week seemed to bring new steps, twists, and bends, each with a distinctive name, from sexy Latin imports to goofy "animal dances." Most were marked by close partner holds, syncopated rhythms, and the horror they provoked in respectable observers. The Texas evangelist Mordecai Ham—best remembered as the man who "saved" Billy Graham—provided a particularly exhaustive catalog of the craze, reaching back to the first close-couple dance, the waltz, then tracing the "progress of sin" through its myriad sequelae:

> [The] two-step, one-step, and all their family known by such names as turkey trot, grizzly bear, bunny hug, honey bug, gaby glide, pollywog wiggle, hippo hop, ostrich stretch, kangaroo canter, dizzy drag, hoochie cooche, Salome dance, necktie waltz, Bacchanalian waltz, hesitation waltz, love dance, shadow dance, wiggle-de-wiggle, pickaninny dandle, fuzzy-wuzzy, terrapin toddle, Texas Tommy, Boston dip, kitchen sink, cartel waltz, boll weevil wiggle, Arizona anguish, Argentine ardor, lame duck, chicken flip, grizzly glide, maxixe, shiver shake, cabbage clutch, puppy snuggle, fado foxtrot, syncopated canter, lemon squeeze, hug-me-tight, tango, etc., etc.

Impressive as this list was, Ham assured his readers that its apparent variety was a distraction: "No matter by what name they go all are just plain hugging set to music.... There are only two places where indiscriminate hugging is tolerated: the brothel and the ball room."[4]

To be fair, most people in urban America already viewed the waltz and two-step as harmless and even rather old-fashioned—waltzing remained very popular, but by the 'teens both two-steps and the Sousa marches that had inspired them were regularly ridiculed as quaint and stodgy. Still, some country folk and recent immigrants had not yet accommodated to the idea of closed-position dancing. Many rural communities continued to favor the old ballroom squares, complete with French calls—*allemand, dos-à-dos* ("do-si-do"), *chassé* ("sashay")—and immigrant families in New York and Chicago still joined hands in village circle dances. Polkas and waltzes had been ballroom stalwarts for half a century, but respectable young people did them only at private functions, and there were plenty of parents who shuddered at the idea of their daughters twirling in the arms of a stranger. As the reformed dance instructor Thomas Faulkner wrote in his frequently reprinted *From the Ballroom to Hell*, "Any woman with a nature so cold as not to be aroused by the perfect execution of the waltz, is entirely unfit to make any man happy as his wife, and if she be willing to indulge in such pleasures with every ballroom libertine, she is not the woman any man wants for a wife."[5]

Whatever its potential perils, the waltz had at least arrived from Europe and, more respectably yet, from Germany. The new dances came straight from the fleshpots of the Barbary Coast, and it was hardly surprising that parents worried. The surprise was that so many of the parents were soon themselves spinning and hopping to ragtime melodies, even on weekday afternoons and at Manhattan's poshest hotels. The credit for that transformation goes largely to a couple who billed themselves sedately as Mr. and Mrs. Vernon Castle. Vernon Castle (born Vernon Blythe) was a dancer and actor with a slim form and an impeccable English accent. His wife, Irene, was a doctor's daughter from New Rochelle, equally slim, and famous for her bobbed hair and innovative fashions. The Castles were lovely dancers, but what was perhaps more important was that they were proper, married Anglo-Saxons, quite unlike the Jews, Irish, and Mediterraneans who dominated so much of show business. Vernon had danced and done comedy on Broadway, but he carried no whiff of East Side tenements or Bowery saloons, and when the pair made their debut at Times Square's Café de l'Opéra in 1913, they were fresh from a success at the Café de Paris in Paris, France. Their performances were uniquely understated and refined: They would sit quietly at a private table near the Café's dance floor until the stroke of midnight, then rise and float gracefully around the room like a couple of charming customers who just happened to move more beautifully than anyone else.

Like many other famous innovators, the Castles actually arrived a little late on the scene. A New York-born Frenchman named Maurice Mouvet had set the trend they carried forward, preceding them at both the Café de Paris and the Café de l'Opéra. Mouvet had started as a ragtime dancer while living in Europe, inspired by a troupe of African-American cakewalkers at Paris's Nouveau Cirque, and toured the continent under the Americanized name of Morris before returning stateside as Monsieur Maurice. By 1911, he was teaching well-heeled New Yorkers to tango, waltz, and tone down the jerkier aspects of the turkey trot, omitting "the grotesque movements of the shoulders which made it so unpopular among people of refinement and good taste."[6] However, compared with the Castles, Monsieur Maurice was a somewhat dubious character. His most famous specialty was the violent apache dance, a pantomime of a street tough abusing a prostitute, which he claimed to have invented after a visit to the criminal dives of Les Halles. Even when doing more sedate steps, he was the prototypical Latin lover, and though he and his partner, Frances Walton, were one of America's favorite ballroom teams, he was hardly the sort of man to be trusted with one's wife or daughter.

The Castles, by contrast, were as chaste as a married couple could be. Gilbert Seldes, one of the period's most influential cultural critics, described the smoothness of Vernon's movements as being accented by his "rigid body," while Irene was admirably "unimpassioned" and "cool," and their teamwork was "the least sensual dancing in the world; the whole appeal was visual.... It was all that one ever dreamed of flight, with wings poised, and swooping gently down to rest." Irene, who treasured that description, would add only that Seldes had missed their "bubbling joy," remarking that "if Vernon had ever looked into my eyes with smoldering passion during the tango, we would have both burst out laughing."[7]

Anyone who has marveled at the airy ease of Fred Astaire and Ginger Rogers has had a taste of the Castle style. Irene, in particular, had an influence that still resonates today, her boyish, athletic figure forever banishing the generous curves of the nineteenth-century Gibson girls. Barely a year after arriving in New York, they were presiding over a small empire: Castle House, a dance studio across 46th Street from the Ritz-Carlton, welcomed "the highest echelon of New York society" to "a pretty little marble foyer with a fountain at one end of it and a double stairway leading up either side to two long rooms ... [which] hold a colored band for jazz enthusiasts and a string orchestra for the tango and maxixe."[8] (The maxixe was a Brazilian dance the Castles marketed as the "tango brésilienne.") Sans Souci, a basement club on Fifth Avenue, drew customers who might drink whatever they chose but were in any case obliged to buy champagne as payment for their tables. When the Castles opened on Broadway in *Watch Your Step*, they followed their nightly appearance by hosting a pair of clubs in the 44th Street Theatre: Castles-in-the-Air, where they led rooftop dancing from 11 p.m. until 2 a.m., and the private Castle Club in the basement, where members could trip on till dawn and beyond. Then, to beat the summer heat, they adjourned to a Long Island resort dubbed Castles-by-the-Sea.

Like Monsieur Maurice, the Castles taught variations of the animal dances but dismissed the exaggerated movements of the original versions as "ugly, ungraceful, and out of fashion." Asked by a reporter how he had come to take up the modern styles, Vernon explained, "I was broke, and in Paris. They asked me to show them how to dance the turkey trot. I had never seen the turkey trot danced, but my wife and I got up and showed them how I thought it ought to be danced. The result was the dance that is known by our name." That was the Castle walk, a superbly simple step that could be learned in a few minutes by almost anybody and was fun without being even mildly suggestive. "Do not wriggle the shoulders," the "Castle

House Suggestions for Correct Dancing" advised. "Do not shake the hips. Do not twist the body. Do not pump the arms. Do not hop—glide instead. Avoid low, fantastic, and acrobatic dips.... Remember you are at a social gathering and not in a gymnasium."[9]

In effect, the Castles were transforming flamboyant black dance styles into simple and civilized steps that could be enjoyed by the most respectable matrons and businessmen. A *New York Times* reporter, casting a wry eye on Broadway's luncheon, tea, supper, and late-night dance emporia, described the result: He watched one couple "plod a painstaking course about the room. She is of generous figure, defiant of waistline. He is of medium height, thickset, and wears glasses, a long mustache, and an expression of solemnity...a middle-aged man whose head looks tonsured executes fantastic steps.... One man who must be fully seventy glides about with a tall, slender lady, in perfect rhythm and apparent absolute enjoyment."[10]

Yet, even as they were toning down the African-American aspects of ragtime dancing, the Castles were doing the opposite with their choice of music. Vernon was an amateur drummer who understood and cared about syncopated rhythms, and when it came to hiring a band for Castle House and his clubs, he turned to James Reese Europe, New York's most prominent black bandleader. Europe was a classically trained musician who had helped form the Clef Club, a prestigious association of black instrumentalists, and in 1912 and 1913 he staged concerts at Carnegie Hall featuring the music of African-American composers. Most of his career, though, was devoted to dance music, and he was already well known in New York's high-society circles before he began working with the Castles. His drummer, Buddy Gilmore, was the first extrovert drumming star, setting the pattern for Chick Webb, Gene Krupa, and Buddy Rich, and he gave Europe's ensemble a propulsive power that made it an influential forerunner of the big swing bands.

In its broader instrumentation, Europe's Society Orchestra was quite unlike later black dance orchestras. His biographer, Reid Badger, writes that Europe considered strings more appropriate than brass instruments for "communicating the soul of African-American music,"[11] and although the recordings he made under Vernon Castle's sponsorship in 1913 and 1914 included a clarinet and cornet and concert programs sometimes listed a trombone as well, the core group consisted of violins, bass, cello, and various sizes of banjos and banjorines (a small four-string banjo, tuned like a mandolin). Except for the banjos, this was the instrumentation that had always been typical for society dances, Broadway pit orchestras, and restaurant mood musicians—in many venues, black string groups replaced Gypsy bands, and reviewers sometimes compared the banjos to balalaikas. And, like most such ensembles, Europe's group played whatever music the clients wanted to hear and dance to. His recordings include not only hot ragtime tunes but also a tango, a maxixe, and an original waltz, "The Castle Lame Duck." Europe was also among the earliest artists to popularize W. C. Handy's "Memphis Blues," the first national blues hit, and it was his version of this tune that inspired the Castles to create the fox-trot that is their most enduring contribution to American dance.[12] (Meanwhile, in Memphis, Handy acknowledged the new ballroom trends with the tango bridge of his follow-up hit, "The St. Louis Blues.")

Castle insisted on using Europe's group, or occasionally other black bands, to the point of defying the musicians' union and bringing them into Times Square's vaudeville theaters. (The union banned black musicians from the theater pits, so Europe's orchestra sat at the back of the stage.) And if he was more insistent than other white sponsors, he was by no means alone. In 1913 Florenz Ziegfeld hired Will Vodery, a black composer and bandleader who would go on to orchestrate one of George Gershwin's first major works and act as a mentor to Duke Ellington, as arranger for his rooftop Frolics. Tom Fletcher recalled that in this period, "All the popular dance places, large and small, in and around New York and in lots of other large cities, had colored bands," including Europe at Castles-in-the-Air, Tim Brymn at the New York Theater Roof Garden, William "Bill" Tyers at the Strand Roof, and Fort Dabney at the Amsterdam Roof.[13] (In those days before air condition-ing, rooftop venues replaced indoor nightclubs for the duration of the Manhattan summer.)

Soon James Weldon Johnson was quoting a European-American performer's plaint that "the poor white musician will be obliged to blacken his face to make a livelihood or starve," and backing this claim with a telling anecdote:

> A society lady called up on the telephone a man who makes a business of supply-ing musicians, and asked the price for a band of ten men. The man she called up is a colored man and supplies colored musicians [it could have been Europe, who along with leading his own orchestra also booked ensembles of varying sizes and instru-mentation], but as his office is on Broadway, such a thought seems not to have been anywhere near the lady's mind. He told her what ten men would cost for an evening. She was amazed and said to him, 'Why I can get colored musicians for that price.'"[14]

It was a moment that would never be repeated, when wealthy white dancers demanded not just African-inflected rhythms but genuine black musicians to play them, and were willing to pay extra for the privilege.

If that sounds progressive, it is important to remember that the bands were hired help. As with the fashion for black butlers and maids, who lent a romantic touch of Southern aristocracy to Newport mansions, the demand for black dance bands did not mean that any black guests were welcomed or that the musicians were treated with much respect. The pianist Eubie Blake remembered a private party in a wealthy home at which the butler served Europe's band dishwater instead of soup. What particularly struck Blake about the incident was not the insult but Europe's reaction: The bandleader calmly ate the slop, and Blake noted, "Jim Europe didn't get where he is with the white folks by complainin'."[15]

Europe was committed to elevating the stature of black composers and instrumentalists, but he was also a pragmatist in the Booker T. Washington mold. Even in his most elevated concert performances, he gave tacit support to a separate-but-equal ideology, stressing the Negro's "natural" rhythm and "indigenous" affinity for ragtime syncopation, and Blake recalled that Europe's musicians were forbidden to use written music:

> The *white* bands all had their music stands, see, but the people wanted to believe that Negroes couldn't learn to read music but had a natural talent for it.... I'd get all the latest Broadway music from the publisher, and we'd learn the tunes and rehearse 'em until we had 'em all down pat.... All the high-tone, big-time folks would say, "Isn't it wonderful how these untrained, primitive musicians can pick up all the latest songs instantly without being able to read music?"... Now this is the truth. Europe's orchestra was filled with readin' *sharks*. That cornet player, Russell Smith! If a fly landed on the music, he'd *play* it, see, like *that*. But we weren't supposed to read music![16]

The emphasis on natural gifts over conservatory training was not just a matter of race, although that was the most obvious factor. As we shall shortly see, some of the first white jazz stars were similarly cagey about their literacy, and stories about Irving Berlin regularly stressed his inability to read music or to play piano in more than one key. In that context, we also need to remember that by the standards of early-twentieth-century New York, race was not just a matter of black and white. Like many of his Tin Pan Alley contemporaries, Berlin was a Russian Jew, and several early critics compared the soulful inflections of blues and jazz to Jewish cantorial singing, while Europe argued that "the music of our race springs from the soil, and this is true today with no other race, except possibly the Russians."[17] In New York, as in many American cities, there were clubs and neighborhood associations that discouraged or explicitly barred Jews, and my father recalled that when he was at New York University in the 1920s, the Jews, Italians, and Latin Americans who made up most of the student body distinguished their Christian and less obviously ethnic classmates as "white men."

Black performers did face unique barriers. No amount of literacy would have made it possible for a black violinist to join a mainstream symphony or theater orchestra, whereas literate Jewish, Italian, and Irish players had plenty of opportunities that their illiterate kin lacked. Still, the stereotype of poor people playing and dancing in ways that are natural and thrilling reaches back at least to the Elizabethan pastorals and the *Beggar's Opera*, and long before white sophisticates began making trips to Harlem, tourists were "slumming" in the dives of the Bowery and the Barbary Coast. In the 1840s, Charles Dickens was taken to a rough Irish saloon in New York's notorious Five Points neighborhood (he incidentally saw the black dancer Juba there, but the point was to visit an Irish dive), and the first mention

Berlin received in the press was when, as a singing waiter at the Pelham, he received a ten-cent tip from the visiting Prince Louis of Battenberg.[18] Guides specialized in leading tourists through opium dens and sleazy dance halls, and Herbert Asbury would even write that in some joints on the Barbary Coast, "for the benefit of the sightseers, who looked on from the slummers' balconies, fake fights were staged on the dance-floors, with occasionally the flash of a knife-blade or the dull gleam of a pistol-barrel; and each night several couples were ceremoniously ejected for indecent dancing."[19]

One of the earliest mentions of the turkey trot came from just such a tour, when the Russian ballerina Anna Pavlova visited "the Coast" with a group of symphony and society people and made headlines by joining the locals in the new step. "The life and intensity of it appeal to me very strongly," she told reporters. "I like it. I will use it. I am going to dance it and introduce it in Russia and throughout all Europe.... It is the only American dance I have seen that is original, in which there is no evidence of borrowing from something else."[20]

The moves that thrilled Pavlova were to a great extent developed by black dancers, and San Francisco's reputation as a source for them was probably due in a large part to the city's relatively relaxed racial climate. There was segregation on the Barbary Coast, but it was much looser than back east, and the city also benefited from all the ships arriving via New Orleans, Texas, the Caribbean, and points south. Sid LeProtti, a black pianist who led a band there from 1906 to 1920, recalled that some of his finest players came from New Orleans and Martinique and that the dance-hall girls came from all over the Americas and beyond.[21] It was an atmosphere in which a Cuban step could fuse with a pseudo-Middle Eastern "Salome dance" and race mixing added spice to the rowdier late-night joints. As a result, innovations in the east regularly turned out to have antecedents in the Bay Area. The bunny hug, for example, hit New York around 1910, but in 1901 the hero of a slang sonnet cycle by the San Francisco versifier Wallace Irwin was already lamenting, anent his lady love, "Last night when at the Rainbow Social Club / She did the bunny hug with every scrub."[22] Al Jolson told a group of New York social workers that as a lad he had sold newspapers outside Barbary Coast saloons and seen half-drunk sailors doing all the moves Manhattan considered shocking ten years later: "The orchestra would hit it up, and they would rag it a bit, and then strike out on the minors that are more seductive, I guess—and get closer and closer, and snap their fingers, and—and I guess I've said enough."[23]

Such stories are a valuable reminder that the roots of ragtime dancing were in working-class dance halls, not stages or hotel salons. It is easy to get caught up in the glittering world of the Castles, Maurice and Walton, society orchestras, Broadway ballrooms, and wealthy matrons fox-trotting at *thés dansants*. Those were what made the news, along with the latest ragtime revues, musical shows, Follies, Frolics, and vaudeville turns, and, like the short stories of F. Scott Fitzgerald and

Rudolph Valentino's cinematic tango, they were entertaining to rich and poor alike. Ballroom dance classes and instruction manuals promised clerks and shop assistants that they could whirl as lightheartedly as the Castles—in Hollywood dreams, a shopgirl could even capture the heart of a handsome young millionaire with her unique combination of fleet feet and simple virtue—and the upper-class styles certainly exerted an effect on working-class tastes.

But the turkey trot, grizzly bear, and bunny hug, and the hot rhythms that propelled them, were not originally conceived as raw material for professional performers and instructors. The whole point of the dance craze was that, to an ever-increasing degree, the professionals and aristocracy were on the sidelines. Square dances, waltzes, and polkas had arrived as fashionable European ballroom importations, then trickled down to the common folk, but in the ragtime era that process was reversed. Vaudeville stars and wealthy amateurs got the ragtime dances late and usually in adulterated versions. This period set the pattern that would be repeated throughout the century, in which anyone who wanted to see the latest styles at their wildest and best had to seek them out among young, working-class couples dancing for their own pleasure. Ten years after the Castles' heyday, a reporter for *Variety* wrote of the white "sheiks" and "shebas" who went dancing at Chicago's Arcadia Ballroom: "The boys and girls would probably regard a team of professional dancers with disdain. And at that, very few professionals could imitate some of the dancing pulled by the Arcadia amateurs."[24] So if we want to understand this fundamental shift in America's musical culture, we need to try to dig beneath the stars and celebrities.

A first step is to understand that before the ragtime era the idea of "going dancing" as we now know it did not exist. People went to dances, which was a quite different thing. Whether it was a debutante ball or a country hoedown, each dance was a unique event, scheduled and eagerly awaited, and drew not only dancers but also a lot of people who had no intention of getting out on the floor. Older relatives would go to see one another and incidentally to watch the young folk twirl, and even some of the young folk might watch as much as they took part. The more complex figures—the cotillion, the minuet—were never intended to be danced by everyone present. Though he was an enthusiastic waltzer, the German writer Johann Wolfgang von Goethe would remark: "Nobody ventures unconcernedly to dance unless he has been taught the art; the minuet in particular is regarded as a work of art and is performed, indeed, only by a few couples. Such a couple is surrounded by the rest of the company in a circle, admired, and applauded at the end."[25] And the idea that dancers might be a skilled minority was not just an upper-class affectation. Plenty of working-class styles, from the kazatsky to break dancing, have been intended more for display than participation.

Another important point is that most public life, and nightlife in particular, was directed exclusively at a male clientele. Some saloons had "family rooms" in which women could drink, but the main barroom was an exclusively male preserve. In vice districts such as the Bowery and the Barbary Coast, there were plenty of bars with women in them, but those women were working. They were not necessarily prostitutes, but that was the standard assumption, and in any case they were part of the entertainment, sitting with men and being treated to frequent glasses of "whiskey" that was often just tea or colored water. Dance halls attached to these saloons were the only places where a nonprofessional could go dancing every night of the week, and the clients were men who came to buy some time with the hostesses and entertainers, not couples looking for a fun night out. Numerically, even such halls were a relative rarity. A study of Chicago saloons published in 1900 listed 163 establishments, but only six of them included dance halls, and the suggestion was that these tended to be involved in prostitution, the author referring to places with "a dance hall in the rear and a house of ill-fame above, all under one management."[26] There are occasional mentions of early-morning joints where prostitutes, pimps, and entertainers might dance for their own enjoyment after the clydes had gone home to bed, and these undoubtedly gave birth to some popular steps, but the general rule was that women did not go dancing on their own and that single men paid for dances, at least by buying drinks.

By the early 1900s, though, America's urban population was growing at an unprecedented pace, and social mores were changing to suit new demands. In the cities, young women as well as young men were required for office, shop, and factory work, and for the first time thousands of them were arriving on their own, both from the country and from other countries. The historian Kathy Peiss writes that in turn-of-the-century New York there were 343,000 wage-earning women, almost one-third of them between sixteen and twenty years old, and four-fifths of them single.[27] Most lived with relatives or in private lodgings with some sort of older female supervision, but they still had a degree of economic independence—and, perhaps more important, a sense of personal independence—that was quite new. In general, they lacked the social options they would have had back home: They couldn't limit their socializing to friends of their families, because those friends were back in Poughkeepsie or Poland. So if they wanted to go out, they had to take some chances that their mothers would not have taken, and it was inevitable that new kinds of dancing establishments would emerge to suit their needs.

Like all societal shifts, this one took time, and it is not easy to trace precise developments. Newspapers did not bother to cover dances in working-class neighborhoods unless someone got shot or stabbed, so most of the surviving reports are from reform organizations, and these saw public dancing as a danger and described only the aspects that were relevant to their agenda. They rarely mention what music was played or specific dance styles, except when noting unseemly behavior: "Men and women held each other in a tight grasp, the women putting their arms right around the men.... He [held] the woman right to him with both hands on her backside ... [there were] frequent hugs, 'feels' of breast and posterior extremities."[28]

Nonetheless, such reports give some sense of how public dancing evolved. For example, when Chicago's Juvenile Protective Association began studying dance halls in the early 'teens, there were already more than three hundred registered in the city, though the dances remained irregular events, given either by the management or by some private club or society. "Dances are advertised by 'pluggers,' bright colored cards with the dance announcement on one side and a popular song, often indecent, on the other," one report explained. "They are distributed in the halls ... and announcements of future dances are also made at the halls through a megaphone." The report went on to mention some typical hosting organizations: the Put Away Trouble Club, the Merry Widows, the Fleet Foot Dance Club, the White Rose Benevolent Association, and the Dill Pickle Club.[29] Other groups, especially immigrant organizations and young people's clubs such as the YMCA and YMHA, had their own buildings, or, if they were sufficiently respectable, they might use a large room in a school or town hall. In general, those dances would have been more sedate, with chaperones to prevent any turkey trotting, but reformers noted that such rules were by no means universally enforced.

The simple reality was that dances were one of the few places at which young people could meet and socialize with members of the opposite sex. The precise styles of dancing were almost beside the point; one could argue about whether the turkey trot was sexier than the waltz, but in either case decent young women were going to dances without family supervision. Before, parents had made sure that girls danced with a variety of partners at every ball, just as in the 1950s they would try to prevent their daughters from "going steady." Now, women went out dancing with their boyfriends, or might even meet and dance with strangers. Both the advertised club dances and the full-time halls that began opening in the early 'teens often let women in at reduced rates or even for free, on the assumption that their presence would draw men. It became common for groups of young women to go to dances together, keeping an eye on one another and giving each other courage. In New York, at least, they could signify that they were interested in meeting partners by starting a dance together, at which point a pair of men were expected to step in and "break" them.[30]

Scare stories described these women as in imminent danger of falling *From Dance Hall to White Slavery*, in the title of one popular text,[31] but most reformers admitted that there were plenty of decent young people to be found even in the sleazier halls. Jane Addams, Chicago's most famous anti-dance-hall crusader, observed "the number of young men, obviously honest young fellows from the country, who stand about vainly hoping to make the acquaintance of some 'nice girl.' They look eagerly up and down the rows of girls, many of whom are drawn to the hall by the same keen desire for pleasure and social intercourse which the lonely young men themselves feel." And, despite the dangers, "occasionally the right sort of man and girl meet each other in these dance halls and the romance with such a tawdry beginning ends happily and respectably."[32]

Addams was writing in 1909, when this was still a rather radical idea. The changes of the 'teens, especially regarding women's social freedoms, brought about a seismic shift in American music and culture. Public dancing went along with women's suffrage and birth control, all scandalous novelties that we now take for granted. And, like birth control, the change in dancing patterns affected not only young, single women but also married couples. Today some writers accuse the baby boomers of being a generation that refuses to grow up, as if that were something new, but the same charge was already being leveled at the middle-aged fox-trotters of the 'teens and would continue to be made as, with Arthur Murray's help, their successors cavorted alongside new crops of youngsters to the Charleston, Lindy hop, rumba, jitterbug, mambo, and twist.

ALEXANDER'S GOT A JAZZ BAND NOW

I wouldn't say I know what jazz is, because I don't look at it from that angle. I look at it from music—we never did worry about what it was in New Orleans, we just always tried to play good.

LOUIS ARMSTRONG

In January 1917, a quintet of white New Orleans musicians called the Original Dixieland Jass Band started a residency at the 400 Club, a small restaurant in the Reisenweber Building on Columbus Circle in midtown Manhattan. The following month they recorded two numbers for the Victor Talking Machine Company: "Livery Stable Blues," a fast fox-trot punctuated with animal imitations, and the "Dixieland Jass Band One-Step." The importance of these events has been debated by fans and historians for much of the intervening ninety years, but one thing is certain: The month before the ODJB opened in New York, there were maybe a half-dozen groups in the United States that called themselves jazz (or jass, or jaz, or jasz) bands, and within a few months of their record release, there were dozens.

In a way, it was the turkey trot all over again. A wild style that had been circulating for years in black and working-class saloons and dance halls had arrived on Broadway, and suddenly the whole Western world was taking notice. Like the turkey trot, jazz was traced back to San Francisco and New Orleans—with a stop-off in Chicago—and at first was hailed even by its fans largely for its nutty energy, its resemblance to "a chorus of hunting hounds on the scent, with an occasional explosion in the subway thrown in for good measure."[1] And, like the turkey trot, it was considered part of the ragtime craze.

To the extent that jazz had a separate meaning, it signaled a new emphasis on improvisation, or as it was then known, "faking." J. Russell Robinson, who would shortly take over as the ODJB's piano player, claimed that the band's music was nothing but ragtime played by ear, and his partners emphasized their rough illiteracy with smart-ass remarks like "I don't know how many pianists we tried before we found one who couldn't read music."[2] Faking was not necessarily improvisation in the modern sense of making up a new melody or harmony every time you played. It was just playing something you had worked out yourself, without written music, and the ODJB is a perfect example of a band that faked everything but rarely seems to have improvised—each musician presumably worked out his own part, but once he had something he liked, he would play it pretty much the same way from then on.

Because jazz fans have made a fetish of improvisation, equating it with musical freedom, and because later jazz artists took the approach to levels that no other music has attempted, it is worth emphasizing that in its basic meaning—creating a spontaneous melody or harmony—the practice has been common in many kinds of music, all around the world. No other culture has developed an equally complex, multiperson improvisational language, and very few individuals can create music at the level of a first-rate jazz soloist or an Indian or Persian classical musician, but almost all of us start out improvising before we learn any proper songs, singing random scraps of "la-la-la" melodies. What is unusual in the great scheme of things is playing a precise part from written notation. That was an anomaly of the European classical tradition, and allowed its composers to create huge orchestral works that had not previously been possible. Nonetheless, even in that tradition, musicians continued to work out their own harmonies and cadenzas through much of the nineteenth century—like the ODJB, they might end up playing the same cadenza at every concert, but it was theirs, not a previous composer's. And in the broader culture, there were always plenty of musicians who did not rely on notation, from Swiss yodelers to minstrel banjo players, Gypsy restaurant ensembles, rural hoedown fiddlers, spiritual singers, and the bands that played at various kinds of ethnic dances.

For many musical jobs, faking was not just a virtue but a necessity: Lounge pianists still come to work with "fake books" that give basic chords and melody for thousands of standard songs to help them fill requests. In the days when variety entertainment was common in working-class saloons and cabarets, even professional singers rarely had their own written charts, so the musicians were expected to be able to create a suitable arrangement by ear. Recalling Wesley Fields, the house pianist at a famous black cabaret on the Barbary Coast around 1907, a younger musician would say, "The gals used to come in Purcell's and sing a song over to him once, and that's all he'd need; he'd play it back as an accompaniment for them."[3] Lesser musicians might need to hear a tune a few times before performing it, but Willie "the Lion" Smith, who held a similar job in Atlantic City, noted that you still had to be able to rework your arrangement on the spur of the moment: "A singer might change into any key on the piano at any time. They themselves didn't know half the time what key they worked in. . . . Some of the gals would start work at nine o'clock, singing in E-flat, but when a little draft was blowing, or they had taken on a few belts, they would be singing in G major by eleven, swearing they were still in E-flat."[4]

Pianists occupied a unique position because they often worked alone, providing the full accompaniment for a night's entertainment. A group of instrumentalists would generally need some rehearsal to work out their parts; they did not need to read music, necessarily, but would at least want to sort out a loose "head" arrangement. So pianists seem to have been the first ragtime players to put special emphasis on their improvisational abilities. You could get a job by besting ("cutting" in jazz parlance) a club's current ivory tickler, and a particularly effective way to do that was by running down a series of flashy, impromptu variations on a piece the other player had just finished. Pianists also "ragged" nonragtime melodies, including classical compositions—it was a perfect way to show off both your range of musical knowledge and your personal touch. And in later years, when the custom of giving individual players solo spots had become common, horn and reed players would engage in similarly ferocious cutting contests.

Along with faking and head arrangements, another important ingredient of what would become known as jazz was the blues. It is impossible to sort out exactly when or where people began using the word "blues" to describe a musical style, but it may have been as early as the first ragtime compositions. The term came to national attention in the early 'teens with the success of Handy's "Memphis Blues" and "St. Louis Blues," but in some musicians' reminiscences it appears to have surfaced earlier and to have been used generically. There are a few specific song titles that are recalled as blues, pieces such as "Alabama Bound" and "East St. Louis," but it seems likely that most people thought of blues as loose arrangements that a band might not even bother to name. As Dave Van Ronk would say many years later, "blues is like a kielbasa [a long, concentrically wound Polish sausage]: you don't play a whole blues, you just slice off a section." It seems to have been primarily an unwritten style, with simple melodies and few chord changes, played in the tougher clubs late at night, as dancers slowly did the grind and belly-rub.

As with the two-step, one-step, and animal dances, blues dancing did not require an instructor; you could pick it up in a few minutes as long as you were willing to grind against a partner in public. This change in dancing, from prescribed, varied sets to generic styles that were simple and repetitive, took a couple of decades and is integral to the story of the music and musicians who came along in the 'teens and '20s. Traditional ballroom accompanists like Europe's Society Orchestra played plenty of ragtime dance music, including the "Memphis Blues," but interspersed it with waltzes, tangos, and Brazilian maxixes. Though the Latin styles were new, they fitted the old idea that a night's dancing should involve multiple rhythms, with specific steps to go with each, and most dance bands kept playing varied sets from written charts for many years after the arrival of jazz.

That was not just true of bands playing for white society balls. Willie Smith recalled the dancing at Harlem's fanciest restaurant, the Libya, which seems to have hosted a largely African-American clientele: "The music was furnished by a string orchestra made up of members of the Clef Club. They were hidden in a grove of potted palms and were not allowed to rag it or beautify the melody using their own ideas—they had to read those fly spots closely and truly."[5]

In the terminology of the times, musicians who read scores and could play the full range of dance, theater, and light classical styles were known as "legitimate" or "legit." One of the standard jazz myths, at the outset, was that jazzers were the opposite of legit musicians—hence the ODJB's insistence on not being able to read—and it would be supplanted in later years by a myth in which the music was formed when New Orleans's legit Creole musicians began working with non-Creole black faking bands. There is some truth to the latter legend; take George Baquet, a clarinet player who would become a member of the groundbreaking Original Creole Band. Around 1904, Baquet was working with one of the most respected outfits in New Orleans, John Robichaux's Orchestra, playing formal ballroom dance sets: a schottische, a mazurka, a rag, a waltz, a quadrille, and the same sequence over again. Then late one night, after the regular clubs had closed, he happened into the Odd Fellows Hall and heard Buddy Bolden's group:

> I remember thinking it was a funny place, nobody took their hats off. It was plenty tough. You paid 15 cents and walked in. When we came in, we saw the band, six of them, on a low stand. They had their hats on, too, and were resting, pretty sleepy.... All of a sudden, Buddy stomps, knocks on the floor with his trumpet to give the beat, and they all sit up straight, wide awake. Buddy held up his cornet, paused to be sure of his embouchure, then they played "Make Me a Pallet on the Floor."... I'd never heard anything like that before. I'd played "legitimate" stuff. But this—it was somethin' that pulled me! They got me up on the stand that night, and I was playin' with 'em. After that I didn't play legitimate so much.[6]

That is the classic jazz conversion story, the legit player captured by the improvisational magic of the blues, but for many musicians such transformations were less a matter of personal taste than of changing times. Take Sid LeProtti, a black pianist born in Oakland, California, in 1886. He first learned classical music and written ragtime, but after an older minstrel singer told him his playing sounded too mechanical, he also learned to fake and work up his own variations. Around 1906, as the Barbary Coast was recovering from the great earthquake and fire, he got his first professional job at Sam King's saloon, where the orchestra leader was an old-school violinist, Jack Ross, and the repertoire consisted of "marches, mazurkas, two-steps, and waltzes of the day, and once in a while some character would come in and ask you to play a polka or schottische."

By that time, though, a lot of dancers were tired of the old society sets:

> The customers there would ask Jack to play a slow drag, or the blues as they called them. He was very stubborn and hard-headed about playin' tunes, and he'd just

ignore them. So when he'd step out to the restroom ... I'd play the blues and the floor would be full'a people dancin'. Well, Sam King, ... he noticed it. He put old Jack on the spot. He told him he'd have to play more blues and ragtime tunes. Old Jack said, "I'm runnin' the orchestra, and if you don't like the way I'm runnin' it, that's just too bad." They give him the customary two weeks' notice and let him go. There wasn't no union in them days, and that was it. They made me leader of the band.[7]

As with all musical changes, it was not just a matter of musicians breaking free and playing what they loved. Some players did better because of the new styles, but others did worse, and in either case they had to suit their playing to the tastes of the customers, the management, and the particulars of each job. Tastes evolved at different speeds in different regions, and from club to club and hour to hour, depending on the age, social status, background, and mood of the clientele. To a modern reader, the most surprising thing about LeProtti's reminiscence may be that in an African-American saloon on the Barbary Coast there were still dancers who wanted to do the schottische, but styles do not shift overnight. In New York, Willie Smith recalled playing at one of the toughest black clubs, formally denominated Drake's Dancing Class but better known as the Jungle Casino, where longshoremen from Savannah and Charleston were still dancing cakewalks and cotillions in the 'teens:

[They] would start out early in the evening dancing two-steps, waltzes, schottisches; but as the night wore on and the liquor began to work, they would start improvising their own steps and that was when they wanted us to get-in-the-alley, real lowdown. It was from the improvised dance steps that the Charleston dance originated ... all it really amounted to was a variation of a cotillion step.[8]

It is impossible to trace the evolution of unrecorded musical styles with precision, especially when those styles were not respected by anyone who bothered to write about music or dancing. Printed arrangements are helpful up to a point for the compositions that were issued in that form, but because they use standard European notation, they give only relatively formal versions of each piece, and they tended to be prepared by journeyman arrangers who often had quite different skills and tastes from those of the original songwriters or the most popular interpreters. Even recordings, once they appeared, are often misleading. The groups that recorded were not necessarily typical bands, nor were their recordings necessarily typical of their performance style or repertory. Until the mid-1920s, the acoustic recording process could not handle bass or drums, so the all-important rhythm sections of earlier dance bands were not preserved. The ragtime and jazz historian Rudi Blesh insisted that the ODJB also played much faster on its records than in live performance, because that was the only way they could fit their full arrangements on a three-minute 78-rpm side.[9] What was recorded could be influenced by what songs a publisher wanted to promote, by which arrangements seemed likely to work best on record, or, conversely, by which specialties a band might want to keep unrecorded to limit imitators.

There was also a strong prejudice in favor of white, urban tastes. Quite a bit of blues was recorded in the 'teens, but it was not the slow, grinding blues that black musicians recall playing at dances. And it may be that our idea of ragtime is similarly off-kilter. The written and recorded versions of "Pork and Beans," a popular composition by the black New York pianist Charles Luckeyth "Luckey" Roberts, make it seem like a fairly intricate multisection rag, but that is not how the publisher Edward B. Marks recalled the piece: "The new dancing was rhythm, almost bare of melody, and Lucky Roberts, one of the hardest-pounding colored piano players of any weight, gave us 'Pork and Beans,' a perfect example of the genre. An Englishman once asked the Castle House orchestra for 'that song without any tune,' and they immediately responded with Lucky's composition."[10]

Without going out on a limb, it seems safe to say that by 1910 there were a lot of "songs without any tune" being played at black and mixed dances—and by some black bands and a few white ones at white dances—and that faking ragtime and blues arrangements was fairly common in the less formal venues. Similar memories have been gathered on both coasts, as well as in Kansas City, Chicago, and other places with large African-American populations, and undoubtedly many more could have been gathered if anyone had bothered to try. There were regional variations, but a lot of musicians were traveling, both on their own and with vaudeville, minstrel, and circus bands, so styles seem to have spread fairly quickly.

New Orleans deserves a special place in this story, and local boosters were already insisting on its uniqueness a half-dozen years before the jazz craze hit. "Now that a siege of erotic dances has started in New York, it may be as well to place New Orleans on record as the home of 'the Grizzly Bear,' 'Turkey Trot,' 'Texas Tommy,' and 'Todolo' dances," *Variety*'s Crescent City correspondent wrote in 1911. "Fifteen years ago, at Customhouse and Franklin streets, in the heart of New Orleans' 'Tenderloin,' these dances were first given, at an old negro dance hall. The accompanying music was played by a colored band, which has never been duplicated. The band often repeated the same selection, but never played it the same way twice."[11]

There are hundreds of books on New Orleans jazz, so there is no need to explore that particular heritage here, but I need to emphasize both that New Orleans musicians were uniquely influential in the formation of the style that hit in 1917 and that plenty of non–New Orleans musicians and historians have disputed their primacy. One of the first serious jazz scholars, Winthrop Sargeant, argued that bands featuring saxophones and jazz-style rhythm sections were around as early as 1905, mentioning Will Marion Cook's Memphis Students and writing that "it may have been indifferent jazz, some of it encumbered with vaudeville clowning, some of it mawkishly sentimental. But it all spoke a new syncopated musical language."[12]

(Contemporary reviews mention no saxophones, describing the Students as a vocal group accompanied with mandolins and guitars, but do highlight their "broken measures."[13]) In his landmark study of the Creole Band, Lawrence Gushee catalogs theories ranging from a pure New Orleans root to a universalist position that treats "jazz" as nothing more than a new name for ragtime dance music, before throwing up his hands and concluding, "One thing for sure, New Orleans jazz began in New Orleans."[14]

If we grant for a minute that the New Orleans style was what defined jazz as separate from the broader field of ragtime, then the Creole Band can be considered the first jazz outfit to have reached a widespread audience. Led by a bass player named Bill Johnson and featuring the cornet virtuoso Freddie Keppard, the group—at first billed as the Original New Orleans Orchestra and Ragtime Band—toured in vaudeville from 1914 to 1918 (after which Robinson settled in Chicago and hooked up with King Oliver, who assumed the Creole Band name). In some ways, it was a pretty old-fashioned act: The musicians dressed as ragged plantation characters, performed vocal renditions of "Old Folks at Home" and "Old Black Joe," and traveled with a stage set that included a log cabin, a jug of moonshine, a trained chicken, and a backdrop of cotton fields. But aside from a violin, the instrumental lineup was what would come to be considered the standard jazz or "Dixieland" combination: cornet, trombone, clarinet, guitar, bass, and drums.

The Creole Band also had a different rhythmic approach from most ragtime groups. LeProtti recalled hearing them when they came through San Francisco and realizing that he would have to rethink his own style: "I listened, and I says to the fellas, 'You know that old heavy two beats we play—you know we've got to get that four beats like them boys.'" He had to fire his drummer and hire a younger man who could make the switch, and he also told his bass player to stop bowing and instead pluck the strings, "because that was the Louisiana-type."[15]

A newspaper review from 1914 of what seems to be the Creole Band—the group is not named, but the dates and instrumentation match—presaged the florid jazz critiques of a few years later. The venue was the Golden West Café in the Central Avenue neighborhood near downtown Los Angeles, and a reporter evocatively named Johnny Danger described it as "a resort . . . where women and men of all colors go to blow off steam." An accompanying illustration showed a blonde woman drinking with a broadly caricatured black man, and as for the band:

[A] strange orchestra was producing melody which would have caused an Apache redskin to emit a blood-curdling yell and go on the warpath. The music had a weird minor strain and a rhythm so enticing that the temptation to dance was almost overwhelming. . . . The fiddler rolled his eyes ceilingward and jigged madly without leaving his seat. The cornetist bent to the floor and then leaned backward until it seemed as if he would go over, chair and all, while he blew uncanny sounds from his horn, interspersing through the music imitations of yelping dogs, crowing roosters, locomotive whistles and terrible groans. In a corner the bass-fiddler shuffled about, hitching his shoulders and guffawing in joy. From time to time he spun his instrument around like a top.[16]

Coincidentally, the first confirmed appearance of the word "jazz" was likewise in Los Angeles. The *Los Angeles Times* of April 12, 1912, quoted a pitcher for the Portland Beavers as calling his special curve "the Jazz ball" because "it wobbles and you simply can't do anything with it."[17] The next sighting was similarly in a baseball context, in a column about the San Francisco Seals, who returned from their Boyes Springs training camp in 1913 "full of the old 'jazz'." This time the reporter appended a definition: "What is the 'jazz'? Why, it's a little of that 'old life,' the 'gin-i-ker,' the 'pep,' otherwise known as the enthusiasalum. A grain of 'jazz' and you feel like going out and eating your way through Twin Peaks." He also hinted at a musical connection, writing that the Seals had "trained on ragtime and 'jazz'," and as it happened a local drummer named Art Hickman—who will shortly reappear—had led a band that year at the training camp. But in retrospect Hickman explained that, rather than referring to his playing, the word came from the effervescent "jazz water" of the springs, whence it traveled to the ball ground, where "when action was wanted, the boys would call out, 'come on, let's jazz it up.' "And, he concluded, "that is how an orchestra with life came to be known as a 'Jazz orchestra.' "[18]

Slang terms are notoriously elusive, and although Hickman's etymology fits the first appearances of "jazz" in print, it has plenty of competition: John Philip Sousa told Paul Whiteman that the word came from vaudeville, "where at the end of a performance, all the acts came back on the stage to give a rousing, boisterous finale called a 'jazzbo.' "[19] Ferde Grofé—another figure who will shortly reappear—reported that it was used in San Francisco cafés when singers joined in an ensemble chorus, but "there was no extra 'pepping up' . . . in these choruses and the word appears to have had no special significance as regards the music."[20] Sidney Bechet, as previously mentioned, said that before it had a musical meaning the word was just slang for "screwing," which seems to be the most widely accepted derivation. And possible linguistic roots have been found in Arabic, French, Old English, Spanish, Gaelic and several African languages.[21]

In any case, by 1915 the word had reached Chicago and meant a kind of music. The New Orleans trombonist Tom Brown, who brought a quintet of hometown boys north in May of that year, claimed that the Chicagoans tried to insult them by calling them jazz players—meaning that they played lowlife junk—and they adopted the term as a badge of honor. Bert Kelly, a banjoist who had played with Hickman in San Francisco, claimed that he had brought the word east with him a year earlier and was the first to use it in a band name. (The earliest surviving report calls Kelly's outfit the Frisco Ragtime Four, but group names in this period were perversely fluid.) One way or another, on July 11, 1915, the *Chicago Tribune* ran an article titled "Blues Is Jazz and Jazz Is Blues." It was a pretty silly effort, devoting most of its space to the discovery that blues/jazz could transform the most bumbling, tired commuter into an ardent fox-trotter, but near the end it made a stab at musicology:

> A blue note is a sour note. . . . It's a discord—a harmonic discord. The blues are never written into music, but are interpolated by the piano player or other players. They aren't new. They are just reborn into popularity. They started in the south half a century ago and are the interpolations of darkies originally. The trade name for them is "jazz."[22]

Both of the musicians quoted in the article were white, as were Brown and Kelly, and one of the two cartoons accompanying the piece showed a white couple preparing to rise and dance, but the other was of a caricatured black man teasing a flurry of "wooo" and "ooo" sounds from a saxophone. So the fact that no black jazz bands had yet been mentioned in print undoubtedly says as much about the patterns of press coverage as it does about the evolution of music.

Etymology aside, cornetist Ray Lopez, who came up from New Orleans in Brown's group (which he referred to as five "ragtime lugs"), recalled that a lot of people didn't know what to make of their style. An eccentric dancer named Joe Frisco had heard them in New Orleans and set them up with a job at Lamb's Café on the north side of Chicago's downtown Loop, but Smiley Corbett, the club's manager, was worried when they showed up without any sheet music: "He wanted to hear a sample," Lopez said. "We played 'Memphis Blues.' We kicked off, and twisted that number every way but loose. We worked it up to a pitch that used to kill the folks back home. . . . Corbett was white as a ghost. He roared: 'What kind of noise is that! You guys crazy—or drunk?' Well, we played our novelty tune, 'Livery Stable Blues.' The cashier made faces and held her ears."[23]

Despite this reaction, enough Chicagoans came around to make the band a hit, and the Lamb's gig was followed by a four-month foray into New York before the boys headed back to New Orleans early in 1916. By that time some other New Orleans players had followed them north, including the group that would mutate into the ODJB and set off the national jazz craze with its own version of "Livery Stable Blues."

How crazy was the craze? Even Thomas Edison, who joked that jazz records sounded better if you played them backward, got into the act.[24] In March of 1917, less than a month after the first ODJB recording, Edison Records had Arthur Fields in the studio singing "Everybody Loves a 'Jass' Band," and the sleeve notes for the 78-rpm record asked "Do you love a 'Jass' band? Doubtless you would if you knew what one was. You'll know all about it when you have heard this song. 'Jass' bands are all the rage this year in the 'Lobster Palaces' along Broadway."[25] ("Lobster

Palaces" were the expensive restaurants where New Yorkers went after the theater, and they were known for featuring the trendiest cabaret entertainers.)

Fields (born Abraham Finkelstein) had been touring in minstrel shows and vaudeville since near the turn of the century, and he was by no means the sort of singer we now associate with jazz. But his song was typical of a flock of similarly themed novelty numbers. Even before the ODJB hit New York, the blackface team of Collins and Harlan had recorded "That Funny Jas Band from Dixieland," and 1917 saw a flood of jazz-fad titles, including "Jazzing Around," "At The Jass Band Ball," "New Orleans Jazz," "Some Jazz Blues," "Johnson's 'Jass' Blues," "Keep Jazzin' It, Ras," "Everybody's Jazzing It," along with such oddities as "Lily of the Valley Jazz One-Step," "Oriental Jazz," and the unforgettable pairing, "Cleopatra Had a Jazz Band" and "Alexander's Got a Jazz Band Now." What Irving Berlin thought of that last title is not reported, and in later years he often expressed a distaste for jazz, but for the moment he chimed in with a composition called "Mr. Jazz Himself." Meanwhile, W. C. Handy got a chance to make his recording debut and, rather than performing "Memphis Blues" or "St. Louis Blues," cut "That 'Jazz' Dance (The Jazz Dance Everybody Is Crazy 'Bout)," backed with a cover of "Livery Stable Blues." By that summer, the grand finale of Ziegfeld's Midnight Frolic featured Marion Harris, the white "Queen of the Blues," singing "When I Hear That Jazz Band Play."[26]

This wave of publicity brought a ferocious demand for jazz bands. But what exactly was a jazz band? The short answer was, damn near any group that could play fast and frantically. Some existing bands just pulled a speedy name change: Borbee's Tango Orchestra had recorded a couple of sides the same week as the ODJB's debut, and when the record was released, the label read Borbee's Jass Band. Others made more substantial alterations: The saxophone virtuoso Rudy Wiedoeft assembled a group he called the Frisco Jass Band and cut a string of discs that, if hardly jazz by modern standards, still sounded a good deal looser than his previous work. Earl Fuller, whose Rector Novelty Orchestra was a society dance band featuring strings and xylophone, set a precedent that would be followed by many later orchestra leaders by organizing a smaller recording quintet called Earl Fuller's Famous Jazz Band, whose members included the soon-to-be superstar Ted Lewis. A Victor advertisement for the group's first disc explained that "the sounds as of a dog in his dying anguish are from Ted Lewis' clarinet"—an all-too-accurate description, but not one likely to have been considered good advertising after the first flush of the jazz craze. The same ad tried to educate consumers by pointing out that they should "notice the two little chords at the end of each number. This is how you know for certain that a Jazz Band is playing."[27] With that sort of support, it is easy to understand why a lot of musicians and critics disdained the jazz label. A reporter hailing the vaudeville singer Blossom Seeley's band—which featured Ray Lopez leading what would now be considered a pretty serious group of white jazzmen—went out of his way to separate them from the craze, describing them as "not a jaz band, but a Group of Talented Artists."[28]

Since they were already credited with playing the wildest and most rhythmically infectious dance music around, virtually all black dance bands were now saddled with the jazz label. The most notable in that first year was Wilbur C. Sweatman and His Jass Band, the second "jass" group to get a record into stores. Sweatman was a redoubtable instrumentalist, famed for his ability to play three clarinets simultaneously, and some historians cite these records as the first surviving examples of true jazz improvisation. Be that as it may—there is no way to know if he was improvising or not, and whether his music was jazz or ragtime is a matter of opinion—Sweatman was a major figure in the black entertainment world. He had toured with Handy as early as 1902, was a friend of Scott Joplin's (reputedly making the first recording of "Maple Leaf Rag," though no copy has turned up), and composed the popular "Down Home Rag," which James Reese Europe recorded for the Castles. The jazz craze gained him new notoriety, and over the next few years he would update his group with such soon-to-be-famous youngsters as Coleman Hawkins and a Washington, D.C., pianist named Duke Ellington.

With the ODJB setting the style, white musicians made up much of the first rush of jazz recording artists, but some people had apparently concluded that a real jazz band ought to consist of African Americans. When the manager of the Royal Hotel in Hamilton, Ontario, decided he had to have a jazz outfit for his grand reopening gala, he turned not to the nearby Chicago scene but to the established black orchestra purveyors of New York's Clef Club, and when they came through with a group, he crowed that "they are sending Jass bands to Europe and all parts of the continent, and I consider myself lucky in being able to secure one." The group he had hired was advertised as the Dixieland Jass Band, and although its leader was a cellist and there is no reason to think it played anything but society-style ragtime, what mattered was less the music than the sense that one was keeping up with current trends. Inspired by this example, a group of black Ontarians hastily formed their own quintet of violin, banjoline, piano, cymbals, and drums and named themselves the Whang Doodle Jazz Band.[29]

For the time being, few people seem to have cared whether the music was called jazz or ragtime as long as it was fun to dance to. In 1918, Chicago's most popular black dance hall, the Dreamland Café (soon to play host to King Oliver and Louis Armstrong), was still advertising its New Orleans Jazz Band as "the best ragtime band in Chicago,"[30] and some writers continued to use the two words interchangeably well into the 1920s. A piece in the 1919 *New York Times*, though, could aptly serve as the older form's obituary: "Ragtime! Respectable, conservative ragtime, about which learned men are writing solemn essays to prove that it is America's great contribution to the world's rhythms. The frantic jazzer of today has forgotten it or, if he remembers, he calls it 'old stuff.' "[31]

5

CAKE EATERS AND HOOCH DRINKERS

If the ragtime era already seemed old-fashioned in 1919, the 1920s have remained a lively source of pop culture into the twenty-first century. Flappers, speakeasies, and gangsters; Charlie Chaplin, Greta Garbo, and Rudolph Valentino; Louis Armstrong, Jelly Roll Morton, and Bessie Smith are still familiar touchstones. But the more we think we know about a time, the harder it can be to see it clearly. As someone once said, history may repeat itself, but historians repeat other historians. Certain stories and images get recycled ad infinitum, and alternative stories and images are ignored or disappear entirely as witnesses die and papers are thrown away.

The musical history of the Jazz Age has been complicated by the fact that "jazz" came to mean something very different in later years. The musicians who have been the focus of most jazz scholarship, with their records widely reissued and celebrated as pioneering masterpieces, were not the most popular or typical artists of that era but the ones who captured the imagination of later fans. Race had a lot to do with that. As jazz became defined by many historians as an essentially African-American art form, the Jazz Age was recalled as a blossoming of black culture. The Harlem Renaissance writers and artists, the pioneering dancers, and the amazing generation of hot black soloists and blues singers have deservedly been hailed for transforming American culture. In the process, white stars like Ted Lewis, Ben Bernie, Vincent Lopez, and Paul Whiteman have faded from the picture or been held up as examples of the era's racism and wrongheadedness.

My own tastes were formed a half century after the 1920s and tend to match those of the mainstream jazz historians. So I was surprised when I started listening to Whiteman's records—not because I found them more exciting than Armstrong's or Duke Ellington's but because I had to confront the fact that I didn't know a damn thing about the decade's most popular bandleader or any of his main competitors. Ellington frequently acknowledged his debt to Whiteman, and Armstrong consistently named Guy Lombardo's Royal Canadians as his favorite orchestra, but the discussions I had read of white artists in early jazz typically focused on how people like the ODJB and Bix Beiderbecke related to their black counterparts, not about the effect of Whiteman's *Rhapsody in Blue* and Lombardo's swooning saxophones on white and black alike.

As it happened, I had an alternate history close at hand. My father was born in 1906 and started going to dances sponsored by the Brooklyn YMHA (the Jewish equivalent of the YMCA) around 1921, while he was in high school. He recalled that the dancers at that time were divided into two groups, the cake eaters and the finale hoppers. His older brother was a cake eater:

> They wore very tight collars, so tight that when my brother buttoned his shirt collar he would then pull his neck out so that it would sort of roll over the top of the collar. They wore very narrow neckties and bell-bottomed pants and tight-waisted jackets. When he was dressed the way he thought was real sharp, his face was a bright red, because he was essentially choking. That was considered the right thing for a cake eater.

My father, meanwhile, was a finale hopper.

> We patterned our lives on what we believed and hoped were college fashions. The boys wore loose clothes—no bell-bottoms, but loose, just the opposite of the cake-eaters, and made of grey flannel, or tweeds if you could possibly lay hands on them. The girls invariably wore galoshes, which were left completely open. They had a special way of walking: They sort of slid along, and meanwhile the open buckles of the galoshes were waving in the breeze and making a clatter. When we danced, it was in entirely different styles. You danced like a finale hopper or you danced like a cake eater, and never the twain would meet.[1]

Cake eaters and finale hoppers don't tend to turn up in books, but if one looks through newspapers of the early 1920s, the former at least are pretty common. They were more or less the same as "sheiks"—both terms suggest a gigolo or pimp—and the tight jackets and bell bottoms were typical across the United States. The *Los Angeles Times* described a young dude who wore "not ordinary trousers, but honest-to-goodness Follies of 1922-Valentino-cake-eater trousers. They were corduroy, high-waisted, tight along the thigh and knee and belled at the bottom. In lieu of a cuff they were laced in true Spanish matador style."[2] The Spanish touch, reminiscent of Valentino's tango dancer in *The Four Horsemen of the Apocalypse*, seems to have been a Los Angeles variant, but the bell bottoms were universal. In Kansas City, a contest for the "best dressed 'caker' (boy) and flapper (girl)," judged the boy by the width of his bells, which in that region apparently reached a yard in circumference, with rows of yellow or blue buttons in lieu of matador lacing.[3]

Finale hoppers are more elusive. A couple of sources use the term purely for females: A film script from 1923 has a scene on New York's Lower East Side with a cake eater and his finale-hopper dance partner, and a newspaper article from 1922 locates the term in the environs of Columbia University, as "a new designation for ultra-modern girls...the young women who are a year ahead of the present, or think they are doing now what the rest of their sex will be doing at some time in the future."[4] One article that matches my father's usage is a *New York Times* feature from 1928 that looks back on "that sprightly coterie of youthful clerks and sales-men formerly known in the city's vernacular as 'finale hoppers' but now rejoicing in the more dignified designation of 'collegiates.'"[5] These youths were credited with spreading a wave of hatlessness that had started around Columbia and the uptown campus of New York University (not to be confused with the larger, less prestigious outpost in Greenwich Village that was my father's alma mater). And if the name was unique to New York, the look once again was national: In Mississippi, William Faulkner wrote of hatless university men who "looked down upon the town boys who wore hats cupped rigidly upon pomaded heads, and coats a little too tight,"[6] and a *Los Angeles Times* article on the various sorts of "he-flappers" includes the type with a "'college cut-up' air [who] disdains to wear a hat [and whose] trousers hang loosely. It is doubtful whether they touch the wearer's legs."[7] The article adds that cake eaters and collegiate types frequented the same dance halls, "although the high-waisted 'jazz suit' is evidently a favorite over the loose-fitting English mode." What it does not note is what kinds of orchestras accompanied the dancing or what music they played. Nor did my father.

That is one of the tricky things about trying to survey the music of the Jazz Age. Most later fans and writers have naturally focused on the music that remained interesting in later periods—hot jazz—rather than on the era's mainstream dance accompanists. And although the literature of the '20s includes thousands of arti-cles, novels, and short stories about "flaming youth," these almost never say any-thing specific about bands or music. F. Scott Fitzgerald's characters flit in and out of myriad drunken parties, but the closest he comes to specifying the entertain-ment is a reference to "a special orchestra, special even in a day of special orches-tras,...headed by a famous flute-player, distinguished throughout New York for his feat of standing on his head and shimmying with his shoulders while he played the latest jazz on his flute. During his performance the lights were extinguished except for the spotlight on the flute-player and another roving beam that threw flicker-ing shadows and changing kaleidoscopic colors over the massed dancers."[8] (Disco lighting was already fairly common: A recollection of a dance featuring King Oliver at Chicago's Lincoln Gardens includes "a big crystal ball that was made of small pieces of reflecting glass and hung over the center of the dance floor. A couple of spotlights shone on the big ball as it turned and threw reflected spots of light all over the room...."[9])

Surveying the era's most popular records, one can form some idea of the ideal band—Whiteman led the pack, and his competitors included Vincent Lopez, Ben Bernie, the California Ramblers, and Isham Jones—but that leaves out such figures as Fitzgerald's flutist, whose distinguishing skill would not have translated to disc, and in any case no group that was either that famous or that big would have been likely to play for my father's dances in Brooklyn or at most other events across the country. Even if, on special occasions, a local social club hired a Whiteman band, it would have been one of the many satellite versions, which did not include Whiteman himself or the musicians who appeared on his records. At that time, the idea of a "name" dance band was still quite new and was as much a matter of creating a reliable brand as of designating a specific group of musicians—in 1925, Lopez boasted that he had twenty-two orchestras and that his dream was to have one "in every city of any size in the U.S."[10] Along with such established stars as Whiteman and Lopez, youngsters like Duke Ellington often functioned secondarily as band brokers, fielding impromptu ensembles for parties, and Meyer Davis, the enduring dean of East Coast society bandleaders, kept no musicians on his staff, simply hiring players according to how many were contracted for each job and sometimes sending out two dozen or more groups on a single evening.

Virtually all mainstream dance bands relied largely on "stock" arrangements—instrumental charts bought from the publisher rather than arranged by or for a particular orchestra—and hiring a group from a big-name front man such as Davis or Whiteman was considered a guarantee of quality rather than implying that it would play in any distinctive, personal style. Nor did dancers feel shortchanged because they were not getting something original or unique. After all, they didn't go to dances to listen to the band; they went to dance. That is one of the great, universal truths, often forgotten or underemphasized by music critics and historians. Any musician who has played dance gigs knows that dancers can be a very critical audience, but they show their appreciation by dancing and their disapproval by sitting down or leaving, and they are not typically the sort of people who write reviews or who necessarily buy a lot of records.

For dancing, the most important thing is not innovative arrangements or brilliant soloists but a rhythm that makes you want to move around the floor. It can be a hot rhythm or a sensuous one, and although jazz record collectors have concentrated on heat, young couples on dates also cared about the slow dances. So the top bands were adept at both, and because it was the dancers' tastes rather than the musicians' that determined the repertoire, white and black bands that were working the same kinds of jobs played roughly the same range of music. Through the 1920s there was a certain cachet to having a black jazz band, so some of the more expensive white venues hired black players just as they had in the Castle era. But as a general thing, dancers were accompanied by players who looked more or less like them, with black bands in the black and mixed clubs and white (or at least Italian or Jewish) bands in the white ones.

My father's area of Brooklyn had plenty of ethnic strife, but it was between Jews, Irish, and Italians. He didn't know any black people, and until he moved to Manhattan to go to college in 1923 it is unlikely that he would have heard any black bands. Indeed, one of the striking things about the cake eaters and finale hoppers as compared with later white hipsters is that neither seem to have been much affected by black styles. The music they danced to was certainly influenced by African rhythms, and some of their body movements were undoubtedly influenced by African-American dancers, but, as in the ragtime era, their slang and fashions were still coming from other sources. It was not in emulation of black women that the female finale hoppers slid around the floor in galoshes; according to a *New York Times* fashion writer, women on rural Ivy League campuses came up with the unbuckled footwear as a winter compromise that was equally suited to trudging through snow-filled college yards and sitting in hot classrooms, and she fancifully suggested that it came to the city when

> some damsel coming down from Vassar or up from Bryn Mawr inadvertently wore her collegiate footgear, and perhaps it snowed that fateful week-end and every one was jealous of the college girl's comfortable protection against swirling snow and slushy street corners. At any rate, galoshes appeared on Fifth Avenue and Broadway and on numerous cross streets, and they continued to appear every day, rain or shine, snow or sun... and when the headliners of the vaudeville shows and the choruses of the "Follies" were costumed in flippery flapping galoshes the success of the style was assured.[11]

The fashion became so popular that it is sometimes cited as the source of the term "flapper." In fact, that word was being used in England well before it hit New York, and by now most of us think of flappers as kicking up in perky Charleston steps, not sliding their feet along the floor so their rubber boots won't fall off. But like the hatless lads in loose tweeds, the galoshes are a reminder that for a lot of young people the Jazz Age was about college styles. In many cases this was more a matter of emulation than situation—in 1928, only 12 percent of eighteen- to twenty-one-year-olds were continuing their formal education beyond high school—but college enrollment had doubled over the course of the decade, and collegians were considered models of up-and-coming youth.[12] One of the era's most popular singers was Rudy Vallée, a Yale boy who had his biggest hit with the University of Maine's "Stein Song," and many dance bands were insistently collegiate. The *New Yorker* reported that to be a member of Fred Waring's orchestra, "you must be young, a collegian, and not bald," and a fellow musician recalled the Waring boys' "long overcoats... trousers much too long, and huge galoshes open and flapping."[13] In memoirs like Hoagy Carmichael's *Stardust Road*, one gets the sense that hot music was a campus specialty, and in 1925 Whiteman wrote an article for a music trade journal bemoaning the effect of "college boy" bands that played for next to nothing "as a lark" and were replacing professional orchestras during the summer season, naming two of the era's most successful bandleaders, Ted Weems and Jan Garber, as outgrowths of such outfits.[14]

These enthusiastic amateurs, like the cake eaters and finale hoppers, do not normally figure in pop music histories, but their involvement helps explain why "trad" or "Dixieland" jazz—later terms for the small-band style of the late 'teens and '20s—would by the 1950s be overwhelmingly associated with a white, middle-class audience. As in the rock era, the white college students who chose to become part of a wild subculture had a safer, more mainstream appeal than black or working-class musicians. Furthermore, college kids could afford to dedicate themselves single-mindedly to the music that excited them, while musicians who needed to make a living and support their families had to be willing to play waltzes and tangos.

The problem of making a living in music got more serious in the 1920s with the arrival of Prohibition. The Eighteenth Amendment to the U.S. Constitution made the sale and public consumption of alcohol illegal throughout the country as of January 16, 1920, and it was not repealed until the end of 1933. Obviously, this had a profound effect on nightlife of all kinds, and the American Federation of Musicians reported that it "resulted in some 56,000 men or two-fifths of the Federation's membership losing their jobs . . . in hotels, restaurants, resorts and beer gardens."[15] Given this fact, it is startling how little attention has been paid to the effects of Prohibition on popular music. In histories of the period, jazz is routinely mentioned alongside speakeasies and bathtub gin, and it is easy to get the sense that everybody was partying like crazy, drinking more than ever and dancing up a storm. The reality was far more complicated, which is why repeal was greeted with widespread relief even by a lot of people who did not drink.

One reason that this subject has been ignored may be that we tend to see the 1920s as a period of musical revolution, so it is normal for us to concentrate on styles and players that flourished in the unusual conditions. We look at the bands that exemplified the "Roaring Twenties" rather than at all the musicians who were thrown out of work when old-fashioned venues were forced out of business. To take an example often cited by writers of that time, the elegant Broadway restaurants and cabarets that had produced Maurice and the Castles disappeared forever. In Herbert Asbury's typically florid description:

Within half a dozen years after the Eighteenth Amendment went into effect, virtually everything that had made Broadway famous was gone, and the amusement area had been transformed into a raucous jungle of chop-suey restaurants, hot-dog and hamburger shops, garish night clubs, radio and phonograph stores equipped with blaring loud-speakers, cheap haberdasheries, fruit-juice stands, dime museums, candy and drug stores, speakeasies, gaudy movie houses, flea circuses, penny arcades, and lunch counters which advertised EATS![16]

In a similar vein, a reporter in Kansas City wrote that as he drove around what had been the city's main entertainment district:

> The only music to be heard floated out as the final stanzas of a burlesque show. There are a number of places that furnish music for their diners, but the orchestra makes an early exit to fill an engagement at a picture show. There are no more places of the old-fashioned cabaret variety.... At the hotels one hears merely the efforts of a jazz orchestra. There is no pretence at anything more varied. You may dance if you choose. The crowds there consist in the main of the town's debutantes and their escorts.[17]

It is easy to forget that there were people who regarded the replacement of traditional cabarets and all-purpose dance bands with a "mere" jazz orchestra as a loss. Furthermore, because of Kansas City's reputation as a hard-swinging jazz center, some modern readers may imagine the debutantes and their escorts jumping to an earlier equivalent of the Count Basie band. In fact, the likeliest nominee for that evening's hotel orchestra would have been the Coon-Sanders Nighthawks or a similar white ensemble. These "sweet" bands—some of which could also play with a fair bit of heat when needed—dominated the ballrooms of the 1920s and remained a major component of the Big Band scene into the 1950s and beyond. Even for them, though, the Prohibition era was not a golden age. Guy Lombardo's Royal Canadians became one of the most popular dance orchestras in the United States in the later 1920s, but he recalled it as a tough time for musicians, because without liquor revenues all but the most successful hotels found it difficult to pay top talent.[18] As for smaller rooms, they could rarely afford an orchestra of any kind. As Joe Darensbourg, a New Orleans clarinet player who led a quartet in a roadhouse in southern Illinois, recalled, "They never had any big groups in these road-houses.... They was set up with booths and they had a little piano that you could wheel round and play at the booths. Each booth had a curtain, so that a guy could go in there with his girl and be drinking."[19] Some roadhouses near the biggest cities had full bands, but they were few and far between, and those little pianos that could be rolled from table to table were popular from New York to California.

For urban speakeasies noise was a problem, and many dispensed with music entirely. Illicit alcohol was enough entertainment by itself, and even if the cops were on the take, there was no point in attracting undue attention or disturbing the neighbors. New York in particular seems to have hosted more drinking establishments during Prohibition than during the 'teens,[20] but most were in basements or rooms set back from the street, often on residential blocks, with minimal furnishings and little or nothing extra in the way of amenities. The last thing they needed was a band that could be heard from the sidewalk.

Of course, the situation varied from town to town and year to year, with some administrations cracking down and others turning a blind eye. Kansas City's importance as a jazz center was in a large part due to its particularly lax enforcement of liquor laws, which allowed black clubs to operate around the clock and feature loud, swinging horn bands. Other cities insisted that the more visible venues make at least a show of sticking to nonalcoholic beverages: In New York and Chicago, nightclubs and dance halls served ginger ale at champagne prices and charged for ice as if it were whiskey, assuming that customers would have a hip flask along. Such subterfuges became more common with practice, and as it became obvious that Prohibition was accomplishing little beyond making previously law-abiding citizens contemptuous of the police, public opinion swung behind repeal. By the latter half of the 1920s, city and state legislatures from New York to Montana were voting to abandon local enforcement and leave the job to the overextended federal authorities.

Nonetheless, the failures of Prohibition did not keep it from affecting America's musical life. Especially during the first couple of years, when the law tended to be most strictly enforced, tens of thousands of venues went out of business. The old-fashioned saloon with a piano all but disappeared, and with it much of the tradition of amateur male singing. Where there was work for musicians, the situation was often quite different than in the old days. Some of the chop suey parlors that replaced Broadway's great restaurants continued to feature bands—when the Palais d'Or went Chinese, it not only retained its name but in 1930 was still mounting a thirty-person revue, and *Vanity Fair*'s New York nightlife guide listed eleven places with chop suey and dancing—but the clientele was no longer in dinner dress, and the production values and pay scales were undoubtedly a lot lower than they had been in the street's glory days.[21]

In 1925, a study of dance venues conducted by the City of New York's Advisory Dance Hall Committee listed sixty-five restaurants but noted that at many of these the dancing was incidental to the food, which most likely meant that the music was provided by a single piano player, a small string group (perhaps with a Gypsy violinist or a Hawaiian guitarist), or simply a phonograph. Overall, the researchers found that the number of dance halls had actually increased by 60 percent since 1920, but because they could no longer defray the upkeep by selling beer and wine, the old community groups had been replaced by commercial management. The commercial halls were also growing bigger, as profits had to be made on the dancing itself. "Dance palaces" such as the Roseland and a bit later Harlem's Savoy Ballroom held anything from five hundred to six thousand patrons, had two orchestras so the music could continue uninterrupted through the evening, and charged an entrance fee that often included only the first few dances, with an additional charge for each subsequent turn on the floor. (There were also "closed halls," where female customers were not admitted and men paid to dance with hostesses, but these provided a pretty wretched musical experience: The bands were notoriously third rate, and a typical dance lasted under a minute.)[22]

Jazz of some sort was common in almost all of these venues, but in a lot of restaurants and cabarets the basic instrumentation had not changed much since the reign of the Castles. Even in Harlem, the band at Connie's Inn in 1926 was still featuring violin and cello.[23] Other uptown nightspots had hotter, horn-driven bands, and though they accounted for only a tiny fraction of New York's nightlife, the relatively lax law enforcement in what was already considered a marginal area gave them a special cachet in the Prohibition years. In 1924, Fletcher Henderson had proved his commercial primacy among black bandleaders by getting a downtown residency at Broadway's Roseland Ballroom, but by 1930 the white customers were heading north and his orchestra was the house band at Connie's. The *Vanity Fair* guide called Harlem "the town's current hot-spot," and listed Connie's as featuring the district's "fastest show," adding that "its clientele is wholly white and, for the most part, dressy."[24] Indeed, much of the Harlem Renaissance was fueled by white customers coming uptown to drink, and many of the clubs instituted white-only customer policies or at least strongly discouraged black patronage, even though they maintained all-black entertainment and service staffs. Another popular nightlife guide was titled *New York Is Everybody's Town*, but its description of the Cotton Club specified that "You see no negroes here except among the performers."[25]

Considering the exorbitant drink and food prices, most local residents could not have afforded to patronize upscale rooms like Connie's and the Cotton Club in any case. For the average African-American urbanite who wanted a night out, Prohibition was the era of "rent parties" and "buffet flats." Private apartments were turned into makeshift saloons, and their musical entertainment—if they had any besides a phonograph—was typically a pianist or, especially in the South and Midwest, a guitarist or guitar-and-piano duo. Georgia Tom Dorsey recalled that the smoother, more urbane blues style that made him, Tampa Red, and Leroy Carr into popular recording artists in the late 1920s was developed because the louder blues singers who filled theaters and attracted attention on street corners would have drawn complaints in apartment buildings.[26] Meanwhile, stride pianists like Willie the Lion, James P. Johnson, and Fats Waller were regulars on the Harlem rent party circuit, and those gigs provided them with a freedom to improvise and stretch out that was rare in more conventional venues.

Downtown, an equally distinctive style of Prohibition-era nightclub appeared, where the food was notoriously lousy and raids by Federal agents seem at times to have been regarded as part of the entertainment. Hosted by such celebrated characters as Texas Guinan, Helen Morgan, Harry Richman, and Jimmy Durante, these clubs are recalled as glittering examples of Jazz Age New York nightlife, but they were small and expensive and very few New Yorkers ever set foot in them— indeed, they existed largely for the benefit of well-heeled out-of-towners like the

Midwestern beef and dairy magnates Guinan dubbed "big butter-and-egg men." They had music, but mostly to accompany singers and scantily clad chorus girls who roamed from table to table, and although the larger ones had orchestras, others got by with just a pianist, trio, or quartet.

Of course, there were plenty of entertainment venues that had never served alcoholic beverages, and these were relatively unaffected by the new laws. Vaudeville weathered Prohibition just fine—though it was soon to be destroyed by sound movies and the Depression—and some musicians who played dance gigs before and after the 1920s spent at least part of that decade touring with vaudeville stars like Blossom Seeley and Sophie Tucker or developed their own stage acts. As we shall see in the next chapter, Paul Whiteman turned more and more to concerts, commissioning pieces like *Rhapsody in Blue* and hiring singers and specialty performers to alternate with his orchestral selections, and although he might have made some of those choices in any case, it seems likely that economic pressures played a role.

Prohibition lasted for thirteen years and overlapped the arrival of both radio and sound movies, so any attempt to sort out which musical developments were stimulated by it and which were impeded is to a great extent speculation. That said, the liquor laws very likely account for one of the era's most striking musical anomalies: that many of its most exciting jazz groups never performed in public. To cite the most famous examples, Louis Armstrong, Jelly Roll Morton, and Bix Beiderbecke all made their greatest recordings during these years with small bands—Armstrong's Hot Fives and Sevens, Morton's Red Hot Peppers, and the Beiderbecke-Trumbauer groups—that existed only for those record sessions. In public, Morton was leading a larger dance orchestra, Beiderbecke and Trumbauer were with Whiteman, and Armstrong was doubling with Carroll Dickerson's Savoyagers and Erskine Tate's Vendome Theater Orchestra.

Large orchestras went along with large dance halls, and without liquor revenues there was no way for a smaller club or restaurant to generate the money to pay a name act. Had alcohol remained legal and the popular saloons and cabarets been able to evolve naturally, the revolutionary small bands could have taken over from predecessors like the ODJB and worked seven nights a week rather than being relegated to occasional record dates and late-night jam sessions. And if the greatest hot soloists had stayed in smaller groups and ballrooms had not ballooned in size, the swing-era big bands might never have evolved or might have evolved very differently.

Instead, most of the hot players had to make their livings in mainstream dance orchestras, and that undoubtedly affected both their individual styles and the sound of the large outfits. The musicians improved their reading skills and got used to playing organized arrangements, and the orchestras found ways to capture some of the energy of the small groups and to showcase hot soloists. Both of those developments might have happened without Prohibition, but in any case large orchestras were the dominant sound of the 1920s. That fact needs to be emphasized, because most of the histories of this period's music have been written by jazz fans who are understandably drawn to the smaller, hotter bands, so it is easy to get the impression that the big swing bands of the 1930s evolved from small groups like the Hot Seven and Red Hot Peppers. In reality, large dance orchestras dominated both periods—though the most successful kept growing in size right through World War II—and their main stylistic shifts were driven less by brilliant soloists than by innovations in arranging and section work. Which is to say that much as we may love the small-band recordings of people like Armstrong and Beiderbecke, and much as they inspired and influenced later jazz soloists and arrangers, the overall Big Band style owed far more to the example of Paul Whiteman.

6

THE KING OF JAZZ

[Paul Whiteman] is directly responsible for the artistic recognition of jazz and for many of its instrumental methods...however...it is characteristic that he always acknowledges his esthetic debts. "Somebody had to do it," he says.

THE NEW YORKER, 1926

In 1936, at the height of the big band era, a slim volume called *Secrets of Dance Band Success* appeared, with advice for young musicians from a dozen of America's most popular orchestra leaders. It began with a few encouraging words from Paul Whiteman:

> So you want to become a musician. Well, if you really like music better than anything else, that is sufficient justification to make it a career. The most fun in life comes from doing what you want to do and getting paid for it. You will find plenty to discourage you, no doubt your parents who will want you to go into something like law or medicine. Many of our successful musicians today were discouraged by their parents. I happen to be an exception. My dad put a violin in my hands when I was a youngster and taught me to play it.[1]

Whiteman was born in 1890, in Denver, Colorado, where his father was the supervisor of music for the city schools and conducted student productions involving thousands of singers and musicians. (The Denver schools were racially integrated, and the black bandleaders Andy Kirk and Jimmie Lunceford both remembered studying with the elder Whiteman.) At age three Whiteman was being trotted out to perform on a tiny violin for family guests, and by age seventeen he was playing first viola for the Denver Symphony and picking up theater and dance dates on the side. He recalled that he and a friend used to amuse the older symphony musicians by "ragging" the "Poet and Peasant Overture" and other familiar classics.

In 1914, Whiteman moved to San Francisco, which was gearing up for a World's Fair–style event, the Panama-Pacific Exposition. He wangled a job with the Exposition orchestra, then moved on to a more prestigious position with the San Francisco

Symphony and also a chair in the Minetti String Quartet, one of the most respected chamber groups on the West Coast. Classical music did not pay particularly well, though, so in between he got gigs with some of the larger hotel orchestras.

It was during this period that he first heard a jazz band, at a sleazy joint on the Barbary Coast: "Men and women were whirling and twirling feverishly there," he remembered. "Sometimes they snapped their fingers and yelled loud enough to drown the music—if music it was. . . . Raucous? Yes. Crude—undoubtedly. Unmusical—sure as you live. But rhythmic, catching as the small-pox and spirit-lifting. That was jazz then."[2]

Whiteman was thrilled by the new sounds and joined a local jazz group, but found that he could neither understand nor play the style properly: "It was as if something held me too tight inside. I wanted to give myself up to the rhythm like the other players. . . . But it was no good."[3] No one who has heard Whiteman's playing will doubt this part of the story, but many are dubious about the sequel: He wrote that he labored long and hard for the next few months to create a score that would replicate the feel of jazz "faking," and in the end, eureka! He had composed the first jazz orchestration.[4]

Whiteman's detractors tend to deny that any of his early music deserves to be called jazz, orchestrated or not. But even granting that he would shortly be the leader of America's most popular jazz orchestra, it is highly doubtful that he developed its arranging style by himself in a San Francisco apartment. For one thing, the arrangements that would make his band famous were mostly done by its pianist, Ferde Grofé. For another, the foundation of that style was laid by another San Francisco band before Whiteman left Denver. As the 1929 edition of the *Encyclopaedia Britannica* eloquently put it, "The inevitable movement to modify the hideous noisiness of early jazz was led by Art Hickman, a California orchestra leader, and later taken over by Paul Whiteman."[5]

Hickman, a nonreading musician whose main instrument was drums, is best remembered today as the composer of "Rose Room," a dance-band standard named for the ballroom in the Hotel St. Francis where his orchestra played from 1913 until the end of the decade. His style was not precisely like that of the later Whiteman band, but it set the pattern Whiteman followed: taking some ideas from the looser, rowdier jazz bands and using them to spice carefully arranged dance orchestrations featuring a saxophone section. Saxophones were still considered novelty instruments, and the idea of using a group of them as a counterpart to the traditional brass or strings was an innovation.[6]

The most important thing about the new style was its variety. Previous dance bands, at least if they were playing arrangements rather than faking, had tended simply to play the same arrangement over and over for as long as the dancers or the management wanted it to last. Even if they were faking, they would fake chorus after chorus as an ensemble—the essence of the early New Orleans style—rather than emphasizing different soloists or approaches in each chorus. Hickman and Whiteman would instead give each chorus to a different selection of instruments, so that even when the basic melody remained the same, the tonal and harmonic colors kept shifting. This had not been considered necessary for dance orchestras as long as they kept up a nice steady rhythm, but by the end of the 'teens records were taking on a new importance, and for home listening the varied arrangements made a huge difference. They also made the bands sound better at dances, and Hickman's orchestra would often play a single song for as long as fifteen minutes.

As records became more popular, they created an increased demand for orchestras that sounded not only good but unique. As long as live performances were all that mattered, it was not a problem that groups in New York, Chicago, and San Francisco were playing the same stock arrangements; if dancers liked an arrangement, the fact that they could hear it anywhere in the country was an advantage. For a recording career, by contrast, individuality was a selling point, because otherwise no one would care which band they were buying. Hickman and Whiteman were among the first bandleaders to realize this and to create records that were not just expert performances of a standard score—what classical orchestras had always tried to provide and continue to provide today—but unique arrangements that no other orchestra was performing.

By the late 'teens, the ODJB's recording of "Livery Stable Blues" had proved that a record could make a band into a national sensation, and this would be a key factor in Whiteman's success. That success was dependent not only on distinctive arrangements and expert musicianship but also on a superlative sense of publicity. And here it is interesting to compare Hickman's and Whiteman's public statements about jazz, because these had a great deal to do with Whiteman's unique fame in the 1920s, as well as his later erasure from jazz histories.

Hickman said that he first heard jazz as a messenger for Western Union: "I used to greet with joy the chance to deliver a message to some hop joint, or honky-tonky in the Barbary Coast," he told the *San Francisco Examiner* in 1928. "There was music. Negroes playing it. Eye shades, sleeves up, cigars in mouth. Gin and liquor and smoke and filth. But music! There is where all jazz originated."[7]

That sounds a lot like Whiteman's story about visiting a similar joint, but in 1920, when Hickman was a major recording star appearing at Ziegfeld's roof garden in New York, he went out of his way to stress his distance from those roots. "Jazz," he explained to a reporter, "is merely noise, a product of the honky tonks, and has no place in a refined atmosphere. I have tried to develop an orchestra that charges every pulse with energy without stooping to the skillet beating, sleigh bell ringing contraptions and physical gyrations of a padded cell...." At that time, jazz in New York was still in its novelty faze, led by Ted Lewis with his "gas-pipe" clarinet, battered top hat, and good-time clowning. Hickman wanted to make it clear that he was leading an innovative, professional dance orchestra, not latching onto a passing fad:

People...expected me to stand before them with a shrieking clarionet and perhaps a plug hat askew on my head shaking like a negro with the ague. New York has been surfeited with jazz. Jazz died on the Pacific Coast six months ago. People began to realize that they were not dancing, that the true grace of Terpsichore was buried in the muck of sensuality. If I can make New Yorkers appreciate the true spirit of the dance I will be happy.[8]

Many bandleaders of the 1920s, both black and white, were doing their best to differentiate their music from the sort of noisy hokum Hickman despised, and they objected to their groups being called jazz bands. Whiteman's stroke of genius was to claim the best of both worlds: In terms of his musical tastes and approach, he was in the Hickman camp, but he realized very early that "jazz," as a word, had the potential to outlive its early associations. So, while Hickman was distancing himself from jazz, Whiteman was appearing as "the world's first exponent of 'jazz classique.'"[9] He knew this would strike a lot of people as a bizarre juxtaposition, and a half-dozen years later, when he cowrote a book titled *Jazz*—not incidentally, the first extended work on the subject—he admitted that "'Livery Stable Blues' and 'A Rhapsody in Blue'...are so many millions of miles apart that to speak of them both as jazz needlessly confuses the person who is trying to understand modern American music." Nonetheless, he understood that he could win more fans by broadening the meaning of the word than by arguing about it, so he added, "I have become convinced that people as a whole like the word 'jazz.' At least they will have none of the numerous substitutes that smart wordologists are continually offering. So I say, let's call the new music 'jazz.'"[10]

To modern readers, "jazz classique" may seem like a quaint phrase, but the idea behind it has become more or less standard. We often find jazz referred to as "black classical music" or "American classical music"[11] and played in the most prestigious concert halls. As early as the 1930s, some critics were insisting that Duke Ellington was America's greatest composer, regardless of genre, and that his work should be seen in that light rather than being lumped together with other pop music. Ellington himself disliked the word "jazz," preferring to call what he played "American Negro music," and as soon as he got the chance he began composing extended concert pieces. He was also clear about his admiration for Whiteman: In the 1930s, both white and black publications quoted him calling Whiteman his favorite musician and the Whiteman Orchestra his favorite band, and as late as 1959, writing in a jazz magazine edited by critics who considered Whiteman the antithesis of everything they loved, Ellington still hailed him as "one of the truly great musicians of the jazz era."[12] Ellington expanded on Whiteman's approach with an imagination and brilliance its originator could not have imagined, but it was his model: The first ad for his Washingtonians appeared less than two weeks after Whiteman's groundbreaking concert at New York's Aeolian Hall, and it boasted of his group's

"Combination of Symphonic Jazz Plus Versatility"—precisely the Whiteman recipe.[13]

Back in 1920, the Aeolian Hall concert was still almost four years in the future, and "jazz classique" was a startling designation for a dance band, especially one that at the time had recorded only two 78-rpm records, the more popular of which featured a brass arrangement that still had traces of Sousa, a solo on slide whistle, and some mildly hot trumpet in the final chorus. That was "Whispering," which, with its backing track, a piece of pseudo-Oriental exotica called "The Japanese Sandman," sold over a million copies in its first few months. Neither arrangement was particularly jazzy or strikingly classique. Whiteman's next release might have rectified at least the latter matter, as it combined a medley based on the "Dance of the Hours" from the opera *La Gioconda* with a version of "Avalon," a pop song so openly copped from Puccini's *Tosca* that the opera's publishers successfully sued for all royalties. However, both were quite ordinary dance pieces, the former a tritely perky arrangement by Whiteman himself and the latter once again featuring slide whistle. In any case, the record did not sell particularly well.

It was only with the band's third release, a month after that first pair, that Whiteman produced something a modern listener might at least tangentially consider jazz. "Wang Wang Blues" was written by a trio of band members including the New Orleans clarinetist Gus Mueller, who led off with a catchy solo; and over the course of the 1920s the song would be covered by everyone from Ellington and King Oliver to blues queens, vaudevillians, and a Kentucky hillbilly trio.[14]

Mueller had an excellent pedigree for a white jazz player, having been one of the New Orleans gang that traveled north with Tom Brown's band in the mid-teens. However, far from being the linchpin of Whiteman's early success, he represented the sort of musician that jazz classique sought to supplant. "Men taken from symphonies are the easiest to train," Whiteman explained. "They have had good discipline and they usually leave the symphony because they are interested in jazz and want to experiment.... The real blues player is more hidebound in his way than the symphony man." Whiteman wrote that Mueller was a "wonderful" reed player but refused to learn how to read a written score, insisting on being taught every arrangement by ear:

I couldn't understand why he was so lazy or stubborn or both. He said he was neither.

"It's like this," he confided one day. "I knew a boy once down in N'Awleens that was a hot player, but he learned to read music and then he couldn't play jazz any more. I don't want to be like that."

A little later, Gus came to say he was quitting. I was sorry and asked what was the matter. He stalled around a while and then burst out:

"Nuh, Suh, I jes' can't play that 'pretty music' that you all play. And you fellers can't never play blues worth a damn!"[15]

Whiteman told this story without a hint of self-deprecation. He took pride in the fact that many of his musicians could have had symphonic careers, and he was not competing for any blues crown. Especially in later years, he would hire blues and "hot" soloists, including Bix Beiderbecke, Jack Teagarden, and the Dorsey brothers, but he expected them to be able to read and play section parts as well—and he paid them enough to make the extra study worth their while. Whiteman liked jazz, but he primarily wanted an orchestra that could execute complex orchestrations smoothly and perfectly, with a catchy dance beat and immaculate intonation.

Listening with modern ears, it is virtually impossible to hear how fresh and exciting the Whiteman band must have sounded in the early 1920s. We have had eighty years of film music, big bands, and vocal accompaniments based on his blend of classical skills and pop sensibility, and most of his records inevitably sound conservative and boring compared with, say, King Oliver's Creole Jazz Band. But what he was doing changed the face of both jazz and popular music. It was not simply a matter of making jazz into a sedate, European-American style, as some of his detractors would charge; rather, he applied scoring techniques that had previously been reserved for classical compositions to dance-band arrangements, capturing listeners' attention not with novelty noises—the slide whistle was a brief aberration—but with tonal and harmonic colors. If only a small proportion of his records have stood the test of time, we nonetheless can appreciate their liberating effect on all the hotter bandleaders who followed— not only white swing stars but also people like Ellington, Don Redman, Fletcher Henderson, and Jelly Roll Morton. The pioneering jazz critic Hughes Panassié criticized Henderson for bowing to commercialism in an attempt to become "the Paul Whiteman of the Race,"[16] but Henderson would not have taken that as an insult, any more than the Detroit bandleader Jean Goldkette—who led one of the decade's hottest white bands—objected to being advertised as "the Paul Whiteman of the West."

It is easy to forget the extent to which most Americans in the 1920s, and especially musicians, respected and listened to classical music. Up to the 1950s jazz musicians were still adapting ideas from composers like Ravel and Stravinsky; singers as disparate as Al Jolson, Frank Sinatra, and Elvis Presley were taking inspiration from opera stars; and popular variety programs from Bing Crosby's *Kraft Music Hall* to the *Ed Sullivan Show* regularly featured classical virtuosi. But in the 1920s, it was not just a matter of inspiration and guest appearances. Anyone who had taken music lessons had learned classical techniques and compositions, hit songs were being adapted from classical themes, and classical performers were household names. When *Talking Machine Journal* announced in 1923 that Whiteman had become the best-selling artist on Victor—the most popular record label in the world—he was taking over that honor from Enrico Caruso.[17]

The same article reported that a New York department store had "over a thousand standing orders to deliver any and all Whiteman records as they are released." That is, at this single store there were over a thousand customers who automatically bought every Whiteman record, a fair commitment considering that he had twenty-three discs issued in 1922 and nineteen in 1923. And when it came to the overall market, no other artist has come close to dominating a decade's music the way Whiteman dominated the 1920s. He was not only the biggest single seller, but set the style for the overwhelming majority of his competitors in the dance-band field, as well as theater orchestras and, by the end of the decade, vocal accompaniments.

Whiteman's effect on dance music was twofold: He forced old-fashioned orchestras to modernize and jazz musicians to play organized arrangements. As early as 1922, an article in *Variety* noted that "The Whiteman system of 'crooning' and orchestration has become so general among the musicians that it is now an isolated case where the boys simply step on it and make plenty of noise."[18] Of course, those changes were not simply due to Whiteman's influence and might have happened without him—pop bands have always adapted to changing times, and organized, jazz-influenced arrangements were a logical step—but he bestrode the era, and both fans and detractors considered him its defining bandleader.

In 1924, Whiteman became something more than that. On February 12 he gave the concert at Aeolian Hall whose repercussions are still being felt today. Titled "An Experiment in Modern Music," it was an attempt to present his version of jazz as a serious symphonic style—indeed, as the future of American art music. As he explained in a preconcert press release:

> Scoring for small orchestras is a fine art in America today. Instead of viewing our dance orchestras with alarm, I feel we should study them and use them as a power for good rather than evil. Furthermore, since I first started to orchestrate for the dance orchestra, thousands of other orchestras are making their own arrangements. This means that there are thousands of young men writing music today who are not influenced by any school, but are composing in the spirit of the times. Among those young people there must be several who will develop something for which we may all be proud. It is to encourage this development that I am anxious to present my case to you.[19]

James Reese Europe had made a similar attempt to introduce syncopated dance music to the classical concert audience, and composers from Scott Joplin to Claude Debussy had blended formal orchestrations with ragtime rhythms, but Whiteman's concert had an unprecedented effect on both the popular and classical music worlds. This was in part because the time was right for his blend of high- and lowbrow culture, which fitted well with the shifting aesthetics of the modern art world and the leveling effects of cinema and radio, but the overwhelming response to his "Experiment" was also due to two distinctive factors: He was the biggest star in American popular music, and the concert included the premiere of *Rhapsody in Blue*.

Because this piece is usually referred to as "George Gershwin's *Rhapsody in Blue*," I need to stress the extent to which Whiteman was responsible for its composition. As usual, his contribution was as a sort of ringmaster rather than as a musician or composer, but it is no less significant for that. He had worked with Gershwin before on *George White's Scandals of 1922*, which featured the Whiteman band and a bouquet of new Gershwin compositions that included not only the usual songs and dance tunes but also a one-act blackface opera, *Blue Monday Blues*, with lyrics by the songwriter B. G. De Sylva and orchestration by the African-American arranger Will Vodery. Though it is remembered today as an important precursor to 1935's *Porgy and Bess*, White deemed *Blue Monday* too depressing and canceled it after the show's first night.[20] Nonetheless, it alerted Whiteman to Gershwin's ambition to move beyond the standard Tin Pan Alley song format, and when he conceived the Aeolian Hall concert, he announced that the program would include a "jazz concerto" by the young songwriter. This was news to Gershwin, who had chatted with Whiteman about such a project but never committed to it, and who now found himself with only five weeks in which to have the piece written and rehearsed. It is an oft-told story, but the short version is that Whiteman assigned Grofé to score the piece as Gershwin wrote out the themes for piano, and they got it done just in time to perform it at a public rehearsal for critics and musicians on February 5—though its famous opening was not added until the following week, when clarinetist Russ Gorman suggested to Gershwin that what the pianist had written as an ascending scale would be more effective as a swooping glissando.[21]

Gorman's contribution is a reminder that, just as Duke Ellington would become famous for composing not for abstract instruments but for specific members of his band, Grofé scored the *Rhapsody* specifically for the Whiteman orchestra. As Maurice Peress would note when he recreated the Aeolian Hall concert in the 1980s, Grofé "did not write 'trumpet 1' or 'reed 3' to indicate *what* was to be played on a given staff, but 'Busse' and 'Ross,' to indicate *who* was playing" (in this case, trumpeter Henry Busse and Gorman).[22] Whiteman's original recording of the *Rhapsody*, with Gershwin on piano, reflects this individuality, sounding quirkier and less classically orchestral than other performances of the piece, including those by later Whiteman bands.

Rhapsody in Blue was the *Sgt. Pepper* of the 1920s, the work that forced a drastic rethinking of what popular music could be. It was so successful that Whiteman shortly repeated the entire "Experiment" at Carnegie Hall, then made an extended concert tour that featured the *Rhapsody* and included only a single dance appearance. It also called forth similar attempts by Whiteman's rivals—one, Vincent

Lopez, had apparently been planning his own experiment when Whiteman booked Aeolian Hall, which was why Whiteman's program was prepared in such haste—but none came close to matching his impact.[23]

Classical musicians and critics attended, listened, and fiercely debated the merits of symphonic jazz. Arnold Schoenberg announced that he had acquired a complete collection of Whiteman records and was playing them over and over to figure out the instrumental effects, while Sergei Rachmaninoff declared that Whiteman had "the finest orchestra of its size I have ever heard."[24] Others found such encomiums idiotic and annoying, insisting that Whiteman was producing middlebrow tripe. In either case, few could ignore him or continue simply to dismiss jazz as primitive noise. Like the Beatles, Whiteman brought the generations together, creating music that young people could dance to and their parents could appreciate as at least an attempt at serious art. The phrase of the moment was that he had "made a lady out of jazz."

The reaction among jazz fans was equally mixed. Some lovers of the rowdy, good-time style, the looser improvising groups, or, in later years, the equally complex but far more swinging works of Ellington, Benny Goodman, and their many heirs have argued that what Whiteman was playing was not even jazz. But a lot of solid jazz masters, black and white, were inspired by his accomplishments. Within the next few years, Ellington, James P. Johnson, and Fats Waller would write their own rhapsodies and concertos, and although they might well have wanted to do this in any case, it was Whiteman's success that provided the impetus and the public interest that got their compositions presented. Roger Pryor Dodge, a white dancer who loved hot jazz and despised Whiteman and Gershwin as middlebrow poseurs, recalled that the first time he heard the Henderson band, he was impressed with the inventive improvisations of the soloists, but the featured arrangement was a version of *Rhapsody in Blue*. Dodge spoke to Henderson about this, and the bandleader told him he considered Gershwin's music "outstanding." So, Dodge wrote, "I learned two things at once: that all the good music was improvised and that the scorn I felt for Gershwin and the enthusiasm I felt for the stuff Henderson and his men were playing, wasn't even completely shared by Henderson."[25] It was a lesson a lot of fans are still reluctant to learn.

At the time, Dodge was in the minority. Most people who wrote about jazz in the next few years treated Whiteman as the music's foremost figure. Along with Whiteman's own book, 1926 brought Henry J. Osgood's *So This Is Jazz*, and the only artists given full-chapter treatment were Whiteman, Grofé, Gershwin, and Irving Berlin, with a separate chapter on the Aeolian Hall concert. Critics were ready for a style that bridged the gap between high and low culture: In 1924 Gilbert Seldes had published an influential book called *The Seven Lively Arts*, in which he made the case for what would now be called "pop culture"—movies, comic strips, vaudeville, and popular music—as a valuable counterpart to the more academic arts. Unlike Osgood and

Whiteman, Seldes singled out a number of African-American musicians for positive comment, but he joined them when it came to awarding the jazz crown: "Nowhere is the failure of the negro to exploit his gifts more obvious than in the use he has made of the jazz orchestra," he wrote, "for although nearly every negro jazz band is better than nearly every white band, no negro band has yet come up to the level of the best white ones, and the leader of the best of all, by a little joke, is called Whiteman."[26]

If that comment seems hopelessly racist and shortsighted to modern readers, we might consider how similar it is to the treatment rock was accorded in the 1960s and 1970s and, to a great extent, continues to be accorded today. It is common to read that the Beatles, Rolling Stones, and other rockers who arrived in the mid-1960s built on the work of black precursors but took the music in new directions, and to find studies of their genre that give at best a cursory nod to their black contemporaries, who are usually filed separately in the "soul" category. This is a fundamental difference between the way jazz and rock history have been written: Most people continue to accept the idea that the later white rock style was its own genre, whereas later jazz critics have generally compared Whiteman to the black artists of his time and found him wanting. But in both cases there was a great deal of overlap and interchange between white and black styles, as well as some clear differences in the way they were marketed and accepted. So there is no good reason that we should consider the people who judged *Rhapsody in Blue* a greater work of art than "Dipper Mouth Blues" in the 1920s any more racist and shortsighted than those who considered *Sgt. Pepper* a greater work than "Papa's Got a Brand New Bag" in the 1960s.

That said, the Beatles regularly acknowledged their debt to African-American artists—a *16 Magazine* feature hailed James Brown as their favorite singer[27]—and Whiteman rarely made a similar effort. Hickman described black musicians as inspiring his love of jazz, but Whiteman's similar story included no mention of race, and, kind words from Ellington and Henderson notwithstanding, he was quite willing to elide the contributions of black artists from the jazz canon. He began his book with the stirring acknowledgment that "Jazz came to America three hundred years ago in chains," and commissioned concert works and arrangements from several African-American composers—for a year he even had William Grant Still as a staff arranger—but he preferred to frame the music's history as a shared American heritage, born of our inventive, pioneering spirit. The African-American critic Gerald Early has placed this in the kindest possible light:

> Inasmuch as Whiteman wanted to convince himself and his audience that it was an American music, he was bound to convince both himself and others that it was, officially, a white music. Otherwise, history taught him that the only way he could perform black music would be in blackface or as a kind of minstrel. Whiteman, whatever his faults, did not want jazz to become another minstrel music and it is, in part, through his popularizing efforts that the music did not become that.[28]

Unfortunately, it was not simply a matter of avoiding minstrel stereotypes. The one black performer Whiteman featured onstage in the 1920s was a "pickaninny" dancer and banjo player, ten-year-old Edwin "Snowball" Harris. And then there is Universal Pictures' 1930 extravaganza, *King of Jazz*, the all-color, all-singing, all-dancing apotheosis of all things Whiteman. In many ways an entertaining revue, with some terrific playing and spectacular dancing, it begins with a cartoon Paul discovering jazz in "darkest Africa," where the music is made by a lion, an elephant, a monkey, a dancing coconut palm, and a handful of broadly drawn natives. With that questionable exception, all the performers are white, which could be excused as a symptom of the times if the whole film did not lead up to a grand production number on the theme "America is a melting pot of music wherein the melodies of all nations are fused into one great new rhythm—jazz!" The nations parade across the screen: English huntsmen, Italian accordionists, Scottish bagpipers, Viennese waltzers, Irish harpers, Spanish guitarists, Russian balalaikists, and French military drummers. Whiteman stirs them up in a cauldron and out comes a bevy of jazz-dancing white chorines in cowgirl outfits . . . *et finis*, over a rousing chorus from *Rhapsody in Blue*.

Whiteman did not write the script of his namesake movie, but he had turned down several previous scripts and approved the final version. And though he occasionally appeared with black musicians in later years and made a record with Billie Holiday, he maintained an all-white band even after a lot of other bandleaders had integrated. But if his record on race issues is unimpressive, that does not alter the broader point, which is that he did more than anyone else to transform the mainstream perception of jazz: What had been considered the sound of low dives and wild youth was now a modern art music and the defining sound of its time. (Nor is "mainstream" in this case simply code for white. Educated, middle-class black people had also tended to disdain the style before Whiteman made it suitably symphonic.) By the mid-1920s, the equation of jazz with everything from Picasso to skyscrapers had become a ubiquitous cliché, with a writer on the *New Yorker* joking, "let one of the boys on the *Dial* [a well-known literary magazine] evolve an idea such as that, after all, New York City is just a great, glorified, baffling jazz composition, and, for at least five years it is good for a lead to every article written in the more enlightened journals, and for no fewer than eight hundred very bad paintings."[29]

After Aeolian Hall, Whiteman's fame continued to grow, and his music evolved in rather surprising directions. *Rhapsody in Blue* remained his signature piece, and over the years he commissioned and recorded orchestral works by everyone from Grofé and Ellington to the classical avant-gardist Eastwood Lane, but his most important changes in the later 1920s were to add vocalists and to hire some of the country's hottest white soloists. His band's stars from the first half of the decade have been forgotten by all but hardcore fans, but many of the new names are still recognizable today. The first batch were all alumni of the Jean Goldkette Orchestra, a Detroit band run by a French classical pianist who, like Whiteman, functioned as a leader rather than a performer. They included the Dorsey brothers, Beiderbecke, Frankie Trumbauer, Joe Venuti, Eddie Lang, and, perhaps most important, the group's principal arranger, Bill Challis.

By this time, Don Redman and Fletcher Henderson had created a more exciting variation of the old Whiteman model—in part inspired by the innovations of Louis Armstrong—and Whiteman's hotter style may have been a response to this. He covered "Whiteman Stomp," a virtuosic tribute-cum-satire composed for the Henderson crew by Fats Waller and arranged by Redman, then commissioned Redman to write some charts for his orchestra—a compliment Henderson returned by commissioning some arrangements from Challis and later by making a note-for-note cover of the Challis-Trumbauer-Beiderbecke hit "Singing the Blues."

When present-day jazz fans want to say something nice about the Whiteman band, they inevitably single out "San," a recording from this period arranged by Challis for a stripped-down group of ten musicians including several of the Goldkette crew. This goes along with the swing-era cliché that the hot players felt trapped in the huge Whiteman orchestra—Fred Astaire's character in the 1940 film *Second Chorus*, a minor-league jazz trumpeter, dismisses the idea of joining Whiteman with the comment, "Too big a band for me. If I'd've stayed with him, I'd've lost my individuality. Same thing happened to Bix." Some later historians have noted that Beiderbecke and Trumbauer were eager to work with Grofé because of his expertise in modern classical harmonies and arranging techniques, but Whiteman's own contributions are still frequently dismissed.[30] So it is worth highlighting Challis's memory of a gig with the Goldkette band at which Whiteman accepted an invitation from him and Beiderbecke to conduct a couple of numbers: Instead of dancing or talking, as they had been doing up to that point, the customers crowded around the bandstand, and Challis realized that "this is what our band needed all the time...with Whiteman there's so much presence there, that 'these are my boys'—that sort of thing. You didn't get that with the other guys...the applause we got, it was tremendous. The band never got applause like that."[31]

As Otis Ferguson wrote in the late 1930s, "[Whiteman] was a showman twenty-four hours a day and forty-eight on Sundays."[32] Even with the admixture of Goldkette players and later soloists including Jack Teagarden and Bunny Berigan, his orchestra was never principally a hot band. Like the other orchestras that led the dance field into the 1930s—Lombardo's, Leo Reisman's, Fred Waring's—it continued to be a crowd-pleasing, full-service musical aggregation, with Whiteman as its genial master of ceremonies. But it would pioneer one other major innovation—or two, depending on how one chooses to look at it. At the end of 1926, Whiteman hired a vocal duo called the Rhythm Boys, which he shortly turned into a trio—the first vocal group to be full-time members of a dance orchestra—and in 1929 he hired Mildred Bailey, the sister of one of the trio's members, as a vocal soloist.

Bailey was the first full-time woman singer with a big band, and hence the inspiration for virtually every female singing star of the next quarter century. In terms of overall influence on popular music, that could have made her the most important performer Whiteman introduced, were it not for the fact that one of the Rhythm Boys was Bing Crosby.

Again, one could argue that once there were microphones it was inevitable that big bands would feature vocalists and that Whiteman just happened to get lucky and sign up the most popular singer of the twentieth century. But Whiteman did not add singers because of new technology; he added them because the success of *Rhapsody in Blue* had led to his group becoming a concert orchestra—the first touring concert orchestra since Sousa and Pryor—and the vocal interludes helped flesh out his theater programs. Prohibition probably played a part in this evolution, but the "Experiments in Modern Music," which became annual affairs, also created a national audience that was interested in hearing what Whiteman was doing and felt that his music deserved their silent, seated attention.

Crosby was a new kind of singer, and it took some time before audiences accepted him and his partners, but Whiteman advised them, figured out ways to showcase their performances, and stuck with them until the audiences came around. When one listens to 1928's "From Monday On," recorded a month after "San" and to my mind a more striking performance, his singing has a combination of relaxed virtuosity and jazz inflection that is perfectly set off by the clever arrangement and a hot Beiderbecke solo. As with Gershwin, Whiteman not only chose to associate himself with a rising young star but also provided the perfect setting for Crosby's talent, and, as with Gershwin, there is no reason to think that talent would have taken the same path without Whiteman's support.

So in one decade Whiteman had not only become America's best-known musician and sold more records than anyone alive, but he had also transformed dance music, transformed the world's attitude toward jazz, and transformed popular singing. Whether he had transformed them for the better remains a matter of opinion, but it is hard to argue that any artist before or since has had a greater impact.

7

THE RECORD, THE SONG, AND THE RADIO

When we want to get a sense of Paul Whiteman or the other musicians of his time, it is logical for us to start out by listening to their records. After all, the best way to learn about any music is to hear it, and the only way to hear the music of the past is through recordings. Those recordings can still excite and amuse us, and give us the feeling that for a moment we have traveled back in time. We need to be careful about that feeling, though, because old records bear the same relationship to vanished bands that fossils and skeletons bear to extinct animals. Some allow for quite accurate reconstructions, but others leave us in the position of someone looking at the skeleton of a peacock: We can see the essential bone structure and imagine a squat little bird, but we don't see the spreading tail and iridescent feathers that are all we would care about if we were confronted by a live peacock. That may seem obvious, but a lot of popular music history is written as if the skeletons were peacocks. And it has become easier and easier to make that mistake as recordings have taken on a larger role in our musical environment.

Today, much of the music we hear exists only on recordings and bears little resemblance to anything that could be performed without recorded assistance. Writers such as Evan Eisenberg and Mark Katz have explored the ways in which both music and our relationship to music have been changed by evolving recording technologies, which have made it possible for us to own performances and listen to them at will.[1] Even when we go to a concert, we generally expect to hear material that is familiar from the artists' records—and that has been true for our entire lives, and in most cases for our parents' and even our grandparents' lives. As a result, although we may be aware of the technical limitations of old recordings and know that they give us only a fuzzy picture of the bands they preserve, we still tend to think of those bands in terms of their records—and, by extension, to imagine their fans thinking in those terms as well. So it is important to remember that in the early decades of the twentieth century records still played a relatively minor role in popular music, and people thought about them very differently than we do today.

For example, in the spring of 1923, *Talking Machine Journal*—the trade organ for phonograph salespeople—ran a story in its "Music Mart" section with the headline "2,000,000 Records of 'Whispering' Sold." Since Whiteman's recording of "Whispering" was one of the biggest hits of the decade and established him as a national figure, it would be natural for a modern reader to assume that this record was the focus of the article, but that was not exactly the case. In the early 1920s, the music industry was not yet focusing on particular bands or recordings, and although the article noted that Victor Records' version of "Whispering" (parenthetically referred to as "Whiteman-made") accounted for over half the total sales, several other companies had taken bites of the pie.[2]

At that time, it was standard for any hit song to be available on all the major labels. One of the regular features of the "Music Mart" was a list of the most-recorded songs of the previous three months, and it did not include the names of any bands or record companies, just the publisher of each entry. The music industry was still treating records as a kind of sheet music, and the *Journal* estimated that although sales of the biggest hits had fallen from a high of over a million to less than 500,000 copies each in printed music, they were making up for that by averaging over 860,000 on records. Victor's versions tended to lead the pack with about half a million copies, "the superior edge being accounted for by Whiteman"; Brunswick averaged about a third of that thanks to Isham Jones; OKeh was doing "astonishing things" thanks to Vincent Lopez; and Columbia was a strong contender with Frank Westphal, Paul Specht, Ted Lewis, and the Columbians.[3] Some bands and artists had devoted fans, but most customers were apparently still shopping for songs rather than specific performances: They would hear "Whispering" or "When Francis Dances with Me," go to a music store, and ask for a record of it. Whiteman's name was regarded as a guarantee of quality, but if the Victors were out of stock most people were happy to go home with an alternate version on Brunswick, OKeh, or Columbia.

Change is always more striking than continuity, but even the most dramatic technological developments at first affect us only in quite limited ways, because we tend to fit them into our old methods of dealing with the world. As a result, exciting as they may be, their deepest and most enduring effects often are not noticed for years or even centuries. For example, let's think about an earlier recording technology: Writing had been around for millennia and printing for centuries before people got used to thinking of written words as anything more than a preserved form of speech. Literature was dominated by plays and poetry, both of which had been developed for public performance rather than individual contemplation, and

Chaucer's *Canterbury Tales* were framed as stories told by travelers at roadside inns. Even after reading became more common, the first English novels were disguised as more familiar forms—*Pamela* as a collection of letters and *Robinson Crusoe* as the memoir of a shipwreck.[4]

As long as writing was considered simply a form of recording and dissemination, its limitations were more obvious than its advantages. It provided only the words, not the tone, timing, and gestures, and anyone who could see Chaucer or Shakespeare perform their work would have preferred that to just reading the part of their performances that could be frozen in ink. Eventually, though, as people got into the habit of reading silently to themselves and writers became used to the idea that their work would be absorbed in that manner, they began to realize that there were ways in which written works could be more intricate, subtle, and extensive than speech or performance, and to imagine purely written forms of literature: for example, the novel.

Phonograph records went through a similar process. Thomas Edison originally promoted the phonograph as a mechanical means of taking office dictation, and even after sound recordings became marketable commodities, they were still understood to be simply records of existing sounds—most commonly music, but also jokes, poems, and stories—and to offer nothing new except a means of preserving those sounds and making them portable. For a while the "talking machines" themselves were a novelty, and people paid to listen to them in nickelodeon parlors, but once they became common household furniture—and once the copyright and royalty issues had been sorted out—it was natural for the music business to treat records as a high-tech equivalent of sheet music. As Henry Osgood wrote in 1926, "The receipts from sheet music are nothing compared to what they were even ten years ago. People let the radio, the phonograph, the player piano, sing and play for them to-day, instead of taking the trouble to do it badly themselves."[5] This shift was spurred by the popularity of ragtime, jazz, and Latin rhythms, which were trickier for the average amateur to play and sing than such old favorites as "After the Ball" and "Sweet Adeline," but the parlor phonograph was generally seen as a variation on the parlor piano.

Like that piano, the early records rarely provided performances by famous concert artists. Instead, they preserved generic versions of classical compositions, current songs, marches, and whistling or laughing novelties. In part this was because recording was a slow and grueling process. As with the hand-copied manuscripts that preceded printing, every early phonograph cylinder was unique: Musicians played or sang into a bank of acoustic horns, each of which was connected to a needle that cut an impression of the sound waves in the groove of a wax cylinder. The number of cylinders that could be made at one time was limited by the number of machines that could be crowded closely enough together to capture the music clearly, and because some horns were necessarily closer to the musicians on one side of the room and some closer to the musicians on the other, each cylinder was slightly different. A recording session consisted of playing the same piece over and over, with the recording engineer putting new cylinders on the machines as each was finished. To make a thousand records of a song, assuming that you could fit ten horns into the room and that every cylinder recorded properly—which was rarely the case—you would have to perform a song a hundred times.

As a result, only a small proportion of early cylinders were made by major stars. Someone who could earn a good living by singing a few songs in a musical show had no interest in spending hours in a stuffy, soundproofed room, endlessly repeating a single song, nor could most voices survive those working conditions. The most prolific recording artists were therefore relative unknowns with endurance. An extreme example was Silas Leachman, whom an 1895 article in the *Chicago Daily Tribune* described as having made almost 250,000 records in his living room over the previous four years, three at a time for four hours a day: "As soon as he has finished one song he slips off the wax cylinders, puts on three fresh ones without leaving his seat, and goes right on singing until a passing train compels him to stop for a short time.... He has been doing this work until his throat has become calloused so that he no longer becomes exhausted."[6] Rather than being sold on the reputation of the performer, such discs were marketed as generic performances: a popular song, a banjo player, an operatic aria—or, in Leachman's case, "ballads, negro melodies, and Irish, Chinese, and Dutch dialect songs," as well as "a negro sermon and an imitation of an Irish wake."

This sort of generic marketing remained common even after records became flat objects that could be recorded once and stamped out by the thousands.[7] When George M. Cohan's "Give My Regards to Broadway" became one of the biggest hits of 1905, people who wanted to listen at home had to satisfy themselves with versions of the song by record singers such as Billy Murray or S. H. Dudley rather than by Cohan himself. But that would not have seemed odd to them, since they would in any case have been listening to the song performed by people other than Cohan at concerts, in vaudeville shows, on street corners, at restaurants, in saloons, or at home around the piano. My father never associated a song with a particular performer, and that was typical for the 'teens and '20s. A new hit might be introduced by a star like Sophie Tucker, but it was sung and played by everybody.

In the days when printed music was the lifeblood of the music business, this was vitally important, because if a song became so closely associated with a single performer that no one else wanted to sing it, that would hurt the sheet music sales. In most cases, rather than getting a single big boost from a major star or a Broadway show, a song would be circulated by people hired by the publisher as song pluggers, and the idea was to get it sung and played by as many different artists and in as many different venues as possible. Until 1913 publishers received no royalties from recordings of the songs they controlled, so they considered phonographs a threat, and even after a royalty system was established they still saw no advantage in a song being connected to a particular artist, because the more people who recorded it, the better. (Nor did that change in later years. "Yesterday" was not the Beatles' best-selling record, but it was by far the most profitable of Lennon and McCartney's copyrights because so many other people did it.)

Through the early 1950s it remained standard for all the major record labels to get out their own versions of any big hit and for at least two or three versions to turn up on the charts—in 1951, "If" and "My Heart Cries for You" made *Billboard* magazine's pop top thirty in eight and nine versions respectively. *Your Hit Parade*, which started on radio in 1935 and survived on television into 1959, was a popular Saturday-night program that broadcast each week's top songs, and although some of the cast members who sang those songs were famous—Frank Sinatra was a regular for several years—most were just versatile vocalists accompanied by the house orchestra, performing the hottest hits of the moment. It was only with the coming of rock 'n' roll that it became standard for songs to be linked to particular artists, and right through the 1960s there were examples of two singers going head to head with similar versions of the same number.

Of course, once vaudeville and concert stars began to make recordings, there were also buyers who wanted those specific discs. By the 'teens, Tucker, Caruso, John McCormick, Al Jolson, and Bert Williams were all known as major record sellers, and an issue of *Talking Machine Journal* from 1920 features a shop window display made up entirely of Marion Harris records, pictures, and other advertising material that the Columbia label was sending to dealers. The record companies had contracts with performers rather than with songwriters, so they stood to gain if buyers could be trained to seek out a particular artist. As an example of how this changed the business, in 1921 a typical advertisement in the *Chicago Defender*'s entertainment pages was from a publisher pushing "Arkansas Blues," and it advised customers that versions of the song were available on four different record labels and from three piano roll manufacturers. A year later, all the ads in the same section were from record companies, each claiming that their artist was the world's greatest blues singer—Trixie Smith had even received "the prize cup...presented by Mrs. Vernon Castle"[8]—and that her latest record was unique. When a hot song came along, though, all the companies still tended to jump on board: Bessie Smith got her first hit with "Down Hearted Blues" in 1923, but her version on Columbia was matched by competing versions on eight other labels.

Songs remained the essential currency of the pop music world, but the growing popularity of blues, jazz, and country music meant that more people were beginning to want records of unique performances. The laughing specialists and virtuoso whistlers of the 1890s had already represented styles that could not be sold in printed form, and by the 1920s it was becoming clear that the record business was in some ways quite different from the sheet music or live music businesses. Ethnic recordings, for example, found ready consumers in immigrant neighborhoods, and thanks to mail order they could reach homesick clients in towns that did not have large enough communities to support an Italian or Yiddish variety show. In 1920 the runaway success of Mamie Smith's "Crazy Blues," the first blues record by a black singer, alerted dealers to the similar market for African-American, or "Race," recordings,[9] and by the mid-1920s they had also found that a tidy profit could be made on records by white "hillbilly" players and idiosyncratic black street musicians. Fiddlin' John Carson and Blind Lemon Jefferson would have been laughed off most vaudeville stages, but their records racked up impressive sales not only in the rural South but also in cities like Chicago and Detroit, where Southerners had gone in search of industrial jobs.

Like the immigrant recordings, these "Race" and "Old Time Tunes" discs were segregated in specially numbered series so that dealers—often employees of furniture stores that sold records as a sideline to selling phonographs—would have an idea of which releases to show to which customers. Such ethnic and regional divisions were the ancestors of the separate charts in magazines like *Billboard* and the separate sections in record stores, and thus of most of our modern musical genres, which at root are simply marketing categories—that is, we call something jazz or rock less because of any inherent musical characteristics than because we think it will be of interest to people who consider themselves jazz or rock fans.

Before the rise of recording there had been little sense in dividing music by style. "After the Ball" was performed by amateur parlor players, string quartets, brass bands, Appalachian fiddlers, African-American guitarists, blackface minstrels, and vaudeville sopranos, and no sane publisher or songwriter would have wanted it any other way. Stores filed sheet music alphabetically by title, with a further division by instrument, and for the first few decades they tended to file records the same way. Even when they used more precise categories, these bore no resemblance to such modern divisions as rock, folk, hip-hop, and jazz. An 1894 catalog of recorded "plates" (a foretaste of the later slang term "platters") available from the Berliner company was divided mostly by instrumentation—band music, instrumental quartet, cornet, baritone—plus two plates of children's songs, two of American Indian songs, and one of a recitation.[10]

More than a quarter century later, most stores were still filing records by catalog number, with a salesperson handy to help the customers find what they needed. In 1920, an article in *Talking Machine Journal* argued that this was a mistake, because "In the idea of filing according to the *character* of the record there is big sales possibility that ought to appeal to every dealer. The first important point about this system is that it hitches on to the idea of making a record purchaser, also a record collector." Nonetheless, the example that followed was still a traditional sheet music category: A customer who liked the violin might be persuaded to become a collector of violin records. The writer went on to suggest that "this policy can be

developed in any department—operatic, vocal, orchestral, dance, humorous, juvenile, educational, etc., etc.," but the idea of a jazz or ragtime collector seems to have
been beyond him.[11]

Though they may seem odd to us, these old categories were at least as logical as
today's genre divisions. Violin records, as a group, have as much in common as the
varied congeries of styles grouped in the jazz or rock sections, and it was no accident that when the Beatles released "Yesterday," it attracted a lot of people who
had always preferred string quartets to electric guitars. If we are trying to understand the way people used to think about music, it is worth paying attention to the
labels they used. We cannot go back to the 1920s, but it can give us a better sense of
that time if we try to think of Louis Armstrong's "Ain't Misbehavin'" not as a jazz
classic but as what it is called on its label: a "fox-trot...with vocal refrain."

Did many people actually fox-trot to Armstrong's record? During the late 1920s
and early 1930s he was still making much of his living at dance jobs, but he performed that particular song in a Broadway show, and even his instrumental records
with the Hot Five were bought by a lot of people who listened to them the way
fans listen today: as if they were a kind of hot chamber music. So although people
might have been thinking about music in different terms, they were already treating some jazz records in a quite special way. Indeed, jazz—in our modern sense of
the term—had a special relationship to recording. The ODJB became national stars
not because of great songs or a major tour but because they made exciting records,
and the music they played was transmitted largely through that medium. By some
standards, they were the first nationally famous band since the heydays of Sousa
and Pryor, but whereas young musicians who wanted to play Sousa arrangements
bought the sheet music, incipient jazzers spent months hunched over a turntable.
Bix Beiderbecke learned Nick LaRocca's cornet parts from the discs, and other
players were soon learning Beiderbecke's solos and Armstrong's in the same way.
The vast majority of dance orchestras continued to work from printed charts, and
by 1927 you could buy *Louis Armstrong's 50 Hot Choruses for Cornet*, but woodshed-
ding with records became a standard way of picking up new techniques and even of
learning entire arrangements.

Unlike printed music, records made it possible to mass-produce a unique performance, and in that way they were not just different from sheet music but its exact
opposite. The whole point of written music is to help a wide variety of performers
to play the same thing, but records preserve what is different in the way a particular
performer sounds. So, to the extent that we think of jazz as a music of improvisation and personal touch, it can survive only through recordings. Without recording we could still get a sense of Duke Ellington's, Ferde Grofé's, and Don Redman's
orchestrations from the 1920s, but Armstrong's genius would exist only in legend. It might be a potent legend, and specialists might be aware that Armstrong's
solos inspired some of Redman's greatest arrangements, which in turn helped to

change the course of dance-band orchestration. But it would be Redman, not Armstrong, whose work would live on—just as most of us know of Mozart but only a few scholars can name the Viennese virtuosos who commissioned or inspired his compositions.

This makes the early jazz recordings immeasurably precious, but also tempts us to extract them from their time and ignore what they meant to their original listeners. For us, they are letters from the past, and it is easy to forget that, like letters, they are just brief précis, jotted down quickly in atypical moments and directed at particular audiences. To stay for a moment with Armstrong, I have mentioned his stint with the Erskine Tate and Carroll Dickerson orchestras, which ran from the fall of 1925 until the spring of 1929. That means that for three and a half years he was working virtually every day, for many hours, in orchestras that performed a range of music that ran from stock dance arrangements to operatic overtures. But if we want to hear what he sounded like on those gigs, there are precisely two 78-rpm discs, one by each orchestra, adding up to about ten minutes of music; and as both are recordings of obscure specialty numbers, it is safe to assume that they are not typical of what those bands played over the course of even one evening. Meanwhile, on twenty-seven days spread out over the course of those years, Armstrong got some young players together and made the Hot Five and Hot Seven records that are now widely considered to be his greatest work.

Why, if the Dickerson and Tate bands were more saleable on the Chicago entertainment scene than Armstrong's small groups, did they not record more? And why, if the Hot Fives and Hot Sevens were worth recording every few months over several years and are still considered among the greatest bands in history, was their leader working his lips off in a couple of orchestras that today are all but forgotten?

I have already touched on the effect of Prohibition on small-band venues, but a more general answer to both questions is that records were still a specialty market. There was no particular reason to record the Dickerson and Tate groups, because dance and theater orchestras all over the country were playing essentially the same arrangements and, if they played a number you liked, you could buy a record of it by Whiteman, Henderson, or Isham Jones. The Armstrong small groups, meanwhile, were selling to the same specialty jazz audience that was buying the small-band records that Beiderbecke and Trumbauer were making as a sideline from their jobs with Whiteman. Hundreds of musicians were fascinated and inspired by these records, and they were joined by a lot of college kids—spiritual ancestors of the young men who in later years would worship rock guitar heroes. But the broader audience, both black and white, tended to favor records by larger dance orchestras and singers and had no interest in specific solos or who happened to be playing them. When Armstrong started singing he acquired a lot of fans who had not known his name when he was just a trumpet player, and it helps put his records in context to note that OKeh's ads in the *Chicago Defender* paired them with discs by guitar-accompanied Southern blues singers like Bo Carter and the Mississippi Sheiks—for example, Armstrong's recording of "Stardust" was advertised alongside Carter's "My Pencil Won't Write No More," a double-entendre song about sexual impotence.[12]

Carter and the Sheiks were working at picnics in the Mississippi Delta rather than in urban ballrooms and theaters, but like Armstrong they made a lot of their day-to-day living playing popular hits learned from sheet music. And, like Armstrong in his instrumental period, they recorded hardly any of this material. The mainstream was covered by the major orchestras, so groups like the Sheiks and the Hot Five were recorded specifically to reach an ethnic or specialty audience—which is one of the main reasons that their records still sound fresh and interesting today, while the mainstream dance bands tend to sound dated. But that, once again, reflects our modern tastes, not what the average person was hearing in the 1920s.

As it happens, by the time Armstrong and Carter were being advertised together, there were relatively few record buyers of any kind. The Depression that began in 1929 had a devastating effect on the record business, which had already been badly hit by the incursions of radio. The first commercial radio station in the United States, Pittsburgh's KDKA, went on the air in 1920, and within two years there were over two hundred stations providing regular broadcasts to radio sets in some three million homes. By 1925, some estimates placed the radio audience at fifty million people, and by 1928 NBC had linked sixty-nine affiliate stations in the first coast-to-coast broadcasting network, so that 80 percent of that audience could tune in simultaneously to a single show.[13] By contrast, even successful records had rarely sold more than half a million copies, and those numbers were dropping precipitously.

Radio had a lot of advantages over records: A 78-rpm disc could hold only three minutes of music per side, and then one had to get up and turn it over or put on another record, but radio could broadcast full concerts. In the early days, radio also sounded better, with a clean electric signal instead of a scratchily revolving acoustic disc. And once you had bought a radio, the music was free. *Talking Machine Journal* stopped carrying music news by the end of the 1920s, because the business had shifted overwhelmingly to radios and, unlike a phonograph dealer, a radio dealer didn't have to think about what his or her customers wanted to hear.

Radio broadcasts could include news, theater, or sports events, but music—and in particular pop music—accounted for the vast bulk of programming. In 1928 Charles Merz, later the editorial page editor of the *New York Times*, wrote that over the course of a week ten typical small stations had devoted 26 percent of their time to "serious and part-way serious music" and 10 percent to talk, with the remaining 64 percent taken up by "syncopation," and that ten larger stations had given fully three-quarters of their time to popular tunes. "The predominance which jazz enjoys is even more impressive than those figures show," he added. "For at all the larger stations the usual procedure is to get the serious part of the program done with fairly early in the day, so as to have the evening free for sheer enjoyment.... The saxophones begin at seven."[14]

Those saxophones Merz was hearing would have been in radio studios or transmitted by telephone lines from local ballrooms, since at the time he was writing the vast majority of music programming consisted of live performances. Once again, this makes it hard for us to recapture the sounds of that era. By the late 1920s, it is likely that more people were hearing music on radio broadcasts than in any other way, and radio remained a dominant form for the next several decades, but virtually no musical broadcasts survive from the early period and only a tiny fraction from later years.

Until the mid-1920s, the only way to play records over the air was by putting a microphone in front of a phonograph horn, and even after it became possible to run a direct electronic connection from the phonograph needle to the amplifiers, the sound quality still was not comparable to a live broadcast; so only a few small stations resorted to canned music. In the early years of broadcasting, plenty of musicians were willing to perform for free, either for the fun of it or as a way of publicizing their gigs, and as the business got more professional the airwaves were deluged with sponsored bands: the A&P Gypsies, the Ipana Troubadors, the Cliquot Club Eskimos, the Moxie Minute Men, and May and Tag, the Washing Machine Twins.

Many bandleaders were wary of the new form, figuring that it would hurt their recording and concert revenues if people could hear their music at home for nothing; but others leapt at the opportunity to bring their music to millions of new fans, and within a few years radio had transformed the music business in ways that records never had. A few bands in New York had established widespread reputations through recordings, but live broadcasts provided performers all over the country with large regional fan bases. Before 1928 there were no regular national hookups, so a station in Kansas City or Los Angeles would run wires from a local hotel or dance hall, and in those days of strong signals and empty airspace, the bands could be heard for hundreds or even thousands of miles. When letters poured in demanding personal appearances, groups bought buses and began crisscrossing large sections of the country on strings of one-nighters.

This meant that, for the first time, dance bands all over the country were developing unique identities and becoming famous. Record buyers had bought individual hits, but radio listeners tuned in to the weekly or nightly broadcasts by their favorite orchestras. Guy Lombardo credited his whole success to radio: The Royal Canadians arrived in Chicago in the fall of 1927 and played their first couple of months at the Granada Café to an almost empty room. Then Lombardo and the Granada's owner split the cost of a fifteen-minute nightly broadcast on a new local station. After the first fifteen minutes, the station called to ask if the band could keep playing, and in the end it stayed on the air until one in the morning, by which time the Café was packed with customers. By the next afternoon, Lombardo had commercial sponsors for two weekly programs—a shoe manufacturer and a chewing gum company—and, as he later recalled, "in a few weeks, the combination of our unpaid broadcasts from the Granada and the Florsheim and Wrigley programs made us not only the most celebrated band in Chicago, but probably in the whole country."[15] As a result, they also had one of that season's best-selling records, "Charmaine!" but Lombardo did not consider this worth mentioning in his autobiography. It must have earned him some money and attracted a few additional fans, but that was irrelevant compared with being the most popular dance orchestra in Chicago and a radio star.

Lombardo's story was exceptional only in that he would go on to be the biggest-selling orchestra leader of the century. In its basic pattern, it was duplicated by dozens—perhaps hundreds—of other groups, from largely forgotten "territory bands" like the Coon-Sanders Orchestra, which never hit New York but was one of the most successful dance outfits between the coasts, to household names like Benny Goodman and Duke Ellington. For a band, getting a gig at a venue that had a regular radio hookup was more important than signing a record contract with a major label, because the record contract would follow automatically if the radio audience liked them and in any case there was more money to be made from live appearances than from record sales. As radio became a national industry with major sponsors, it also began to provide solid incomes for its stars. By 1934, Fred Waring and his Pennsylvanians had beaten Whiteman's live salary record by earning $10,000 for a week in a Broadway theater, but that was just a pleasant addition to the band's regular weekly stipend of $12,500 for presenting the hour-long *Ford Dealers Program*.[16]

Those were astronomical sums in the midst of the Depression, and they testify to the way radio had transformed the dance band market. Ten years earlier, fans had tuned in to broadcasts from local or regional ballrooms and heard whichever bands were playing there, much as dancers patronized favorite venues in their area regardless of which group the venue had hired that night. By the 1930s, radio was a national medium and listeners across the country were tuning in to Waring's Ford broadcasts and Whiteman's *Kraft Music Hall*. Ballroom hookups continued to be standard fare as well, but they aired later in the evening—NBC and CBS carried dance band remotes from 11 p.m. to 1 a.m., and the Mutual Broadcasting Network from 11 to 2—and they did not pay huge fees. These remotes were valued by bandleaders for their advertising value: In some cases, bands even accepted gigs for reduced wages at venues with wires in return for the exposure.[17]

Radio also changed the music that dance bands played, by creating a demand for singers. Before microphones and electronic amplification, a singer couldn't have been heard over a full orchestra in a large ballroom full of shuffling feet, and in any

case vocals were unnecessary, because dancers were concentrating on their partners and the band was just accompaniment. So singers performed in theaters and
nightclubs, and dance orchestras played instrumental music. Radio broke down
that barrier, putting Rudy Vallée's soft crooning in the same venue as the loudest
dance band, and it gave both singing stars and orchestras a reason to mix infectious rhythms with romantic lyrics. Whiteman's Crosby and Bailey became models
for hundreds of young band crooners and canaries, and although some orchestra
leaders took a while to adjust to the idea, by the 1930s most had accepted that they
would have to pack a microphone and amplifier along with the instruments.

The new generation of singers was quite different from any previous group of
vocal stars. Instead of having to project their voices with lung power and technique,
the radio crooners were murmuring to listeners in living rooms, and most band
singers followed this model. At first they tended to be considered window dress-
ing for what were still principally instrumental outfits, so neither their musical nor
their performing skills needed to be of the quality required for a vaudeville star, and
many were hired as much for their looks as for their vocal abilities. At live gigs, they
would be brought on to sing a chorus now and then, but they spent much of the evening sitting on the sidelines and typically were paid a fraction of what the musicians
earned, as well as being expected to do additional jobs such as taking care of the
music library. On records, it became standard for arrangements of popular songs
to include a vocal interlude, but the singers were rarely identified. Some eventually became famous, helped by film appearances and fan magazine profiles, but the
average band singer remained as anonymous as the average brass or reed soloist.

The melding of popular songs and dance music set a pattern that continued
for most of the century, but it was by no means greeted with universal enthusiasm. Though most songwriters and publishers at first welcomed radio plugs as a
new form of advertising, many came to see the medium as threatening their pro-
fessions. "Our songs don't live anymore," Irving Berlin lamented, in a cry echoed
throughout the industry. "Al Jolson sang the same song for years until it meant
something.... Today, Paul Whiteman plays a song hit once or twice or a Hollywood
hero sings them once in the films and the radio runs them ragged for a couple of
weeks—then they're dead."[18]

Bands were faced with a similar problem. Before radio, they had played the
same arrangements month after month and even year after year, and the fact that
someone had already heard a particular arrangement on a record just made it more
familiar and appealing. As radio stars, they were expected to have fresh material
every week. Whiteman, who had at first been hesitant about broadcasting because
he feared it would cut into concert and record revenues, signed on for a weekly,
hour-long program sponsored by Old Gold cigarettes in 1929, and immediately
brought William Grant Still into his organization to help with the new arranging
burden. Still's work with Whiteman is a perfect example of how badly the surviving

examples of this era's music represent what was available at the time: He wrote roughly a hundred arrangements for the band, which were heard by millions of people from coast to coast, but only two were recorded.

Between records and radio, by the 1930s the whole idea of a dance orchestra had changed. The result would be what is generally known as the Big Band era, but this was less a shift in the bands' music or their function than a matter of the public becoming aware of them as individual entities. Dance, restaurant, and theater orchestras had always provided the country's popular music, but, like cooks or set designers, they had remained largely in the background. People went to dances to dance, to restaurants to eat, and to theaters to see acts with a strong visual appeal, and the musicians were just employees who provided accompaniments. Many orchestras did not even exist except on an ad hoc basis, with their personnel on any given night consisting of whoever was hired for that gig, and theater bands sat invisibly in a pit in front of the stage and did not travel—the same house band that backed Sophie Tucker when she came through Cleveland also backed the Marx Brothers and whatever acrobatic troupes, magicians, or dancers were on the program.

Records and radio separated sound from visual presentation and particular situations, and attached names to the music. Even if you bought a record simply because you wanted the new hit song, you saw that it was by Whiteman, Bernie, or Waring, and if it turned out to be a favorite record, you were tempted to buy something by the same artist next time even if he was based in New York and you lived in Omaha. And when you got home from a dance in Omaha, tuned in a broadcast by the Coon-Sanders Orchestra from a ballroom in Kansas City, and noticed that it sounded better than the band you had been dancing to, that made you want the local hall to bring in the out-of-town outfit.

As bandleaders developed their own public, they began to emphasize their unique characteristics and look for signature sounds, from Lombardo's murmuring saxophones to Shep Fields's blowing bubbles in a water glass. (Fields was one of the most successful bandleaders of the 1930s, and the bubble-blowing introductions made listeners aware that they were hearing his trademark "rippling rhythm.") Some, including Waring, Kay Kyser, and, most enduringly, Lawrence Welk, began to present their own variety shows with singers, dancers, and whatever else was needed to entertain their audience. These "name" orchestras were always just the tip of a much larger iceberg, and most bands remained local and relatively anonymous, but the 1930s and 1940s brought instrumental performers to the forefront of popular music in a way they never had been before and never would be again, and a lot of people still recall this period as a golden age of American music.

SONS OF WHITEMAN

We weren't out to change the world musically. We wanted to make a living and get as much self-satisfaction out of our work as we could.

DUKE ELLINGTON

It is often said that history is written by the victors, but in the case of pop music that is rarely true. The victors tend to be out dancing, while the historians sit at their desks, assiduously chronicling music they cannot hear on mainstream radio. And it is not just historians: The people who choose to write about popular music, even while it is happening, tend to be far from average consumers and partygoers and often despise the tastes and behavior of their more cheerful and numerous peers.

One example of this is that virtually all popular music history and criticism up to the 1980s—and the vast majority of it today—has been written by men, though most of the main pop trends have been driven by women. As Vincent Lopez, one of Paul Whiteman's closest rivals, wrote in 1924, "the success of the public ballroom depends on whether it is in favor with the women patrons."[1] The reason, as the blues singer Little Milton told me some seventy years later, is that if you appeal mainly to men you will only draw an audience of those men; but if you appeal to women, "basically, for every woman that comes, you can figure that she's going to have at least three men to follow that one woman. You're laughing, but from experience and observation, it's true." As a general thing, American women dance because they want to dance, while American men dance because they want to be around women. The result is that the most popular dance music will be whatever style the most women prefer. That doesn't hold up in every single case, but—if one leaves out gay subcultures—it holds overwhelmingly true throughout the country and across lines of age and ethnicity. Artie Shaw recalled that in his initiation to the life of a full-time musician, working Chinese restaurant gigs around Cleveland in the mid-1920s, "the early session was a kind of luncheon dance affair, mostly attended by office girls who, between bites of chow mein, used to dance with one another, so that the floor was filled with nothing but women, young and old."[2] The way to attract single men to a dance hall in the same period was to have a staff of female taxi dancers.

When I began looking at the music of the 1930s, I called a few friends who were old enough to remember the period clearly. The first was a woman in her eighties. When I asked her what she had listened to as a teenager, she said she and her friends used to go over to someone's house pretty much every day after school, turn on the radio, and dance. "It was just girls, of course," she added. "We danced with each other." As to which bands they preferred, she didn't have an answer. They just searched the dial until they found some music they liked.

Trying to get further back, I called a friend who is ten years older. Her recollection was identical. She and her girlfriends had started dancing regularly in their early teens, around 1929, again with no boys present. As to which bands they liked, the first she named was Benny Goodman's. Goodman didn't have a band until 1934, and his success a couple of years later is usually cited as the breakthrough that launched the swing and Big Band era, but my friend was unsurprised by the anachronism. "Oh, we didn't care," she said, laughing at my ignorance. "There were lots of other bands. And the music didn't change that much. They all played dance music."

That last sentence is the great fundamental truth of the 1930s: Whether remembered as jazz, swing, sweet, hot, novelty, corny, or "Mickey Mouse," all the bands played dance music, which meant that their primary duty was to get people out on the floor, not to provide a deeply fulfilling listening experience. This irritated some musicians and music devotees, and it became a cliché in the jazz community to denigrate female tastes in particular. As a writer in *Down Beat* put it: "There are two kinds of women, those who don't like jazz music and admit they don't, and those who don't like jazz music but say they do."[3]

The male experts didn't deny that women loved to dance and that all the big bands sought to please them, but they acceded to that idea with ill grace. "Oh, yeah, all the bands had to play some romantic tunes for the ladies," they grumbled. And that was true. The division between "sweet" and "hot" (or "swing") bands, which was commonly made at the time and is reflected in the separate popularity polls that appeared in the music magazines *Metronome* and *Down Beat*, was really a division between bands that built their whole careers on sweet music and bands that played sweet only some of the time. (Some bands, such as Tommy Dorsey's and Glenn Miller's, regularly made the top ten in both categories.) There were plenty of orchestras that never attempted to swing as hard as Basie or Goodman, but no orchestra that did not try to play as romantically as Lombardo. And it is likewise true that the romantic music appealed to women far more than it did to men, just as it is true that crooners like Vallée and Crosby (and later Sinatra) built their careers on making the ladies swoon.

But something can be true and still be misleading. Male dance band fans studied their heroes with a devotion that seems to have been rare among their female friends (if they had any), and in their reminiscences about the era one constantly comes across variations of the phrase "Kids talked big band personalities like they talked baseball players."[4] What that means is that a lot of kids knew every trumpeter and drummer by name, but the choice of simile points up the extent to which this knowledge was part of being in the boys' club. Dance band records were like baseball cards, and their collectors had the same contempt for girls who couldn't name the Casa Loma Orchestra's rhythm section that they had for girls who couldn't name the Dodgers' infield. As record collectors and music fanatics, they naturally gravitated toward bands that were innovative and unique, with inventive arrangements and outstanding soloists, and they naturally were upset that so many of their peers preferred slick commercial outfits that just provided a solid dance beat. But even such college-boy favorites as Casa Loma were kept alive not by the few fanatical admirers who crowded around the bandstand but by the hundreds of couples swirling in each other's arms or necking in the corners. And when the swing era brought faster, hotter rhythms to the fore, it was still generally the women who pulled their boyfriends onto the dance floor, just as they had done in the rambunctious days of the turkey trot and the Charleston—and the coterie of male record collectors and critics once again circled their rhetorical wagons, forming a new club of devotees to whom the big swing bands were a dilution of the pure New Orleans tradition or a straitjacket to be cast off by the prophets of bop. But now I'm getting ahead of myself.

At the turn of the 1930s, the Casa Loma Orchestra was the most successful white band specializing in what was then called "hot" music. Their trademark "killer dillers," "Casa Loma Stomp" and "White Jazz" (shortly followed by "Black Jazz" and "Blue Jazz"), were imitated by white and black bands alike and set the stage for Benny Goodman and the crossover success of black bandleaders like Jimmie Lunceford and Cab Calloway. Their theme song, though, was the achingly romantic "Smoke Rings," one of the great slow-dance tunes of the era, and this was far more typical of what the average young dancer was looking for. In 1931, a *Metronome* columnist declared that "soft and subdued melody" suited the calmer national mood: "That feverish decade following the world war, has come to an end.... People are tired of raucous jazz, hysteria, stark reality and other concomitants of the postwar age and are turning longing eyes toward the flowering and shady by-paths down which our forefathers strolled.... The 'flapper' has given way to a miss who while still retaining her freedom, is more decorous and alluringly feminine."[5]

As a trade journal for working musicians, *Metronome* tended to be conservative, asserting the eternal verities of waltzes, theater orchestras (sound movies were throwing tens of thousands of musicians out of work, but it assured its readers that audiences would soon rebel and demand live music again), classical training, and the finely crafted melodies of Tin Pan Alley in the days before the depredations of radio. If it was true that people were tired of "stark reality" in the early 1930s, it was not the reality of the postwar years—the flappers and their wild dance steps had always been considered a flight into fantasy—but rather of the Depression. In broad cultural terms the embrace of soft melody may have reflected some vague longing for the safe, stable world that had mythically existed before the World War and the collapse of Wall Street, but in musical terms fast, syncopated rhythms had been trendy since Sousa's day, and in retrospect the shift toward slow dances seems very much to have been tied to the present. It was certainly romantic, but hardly nostalgic. The economic situation was dire, and there were few entertainments cheaper than a dance and few possibilities more comforting than spending an evening in a close embrace.

Indeed, this may have been the only time in American history when young people chose gentler, less agitated dance rhythms than their parents had. As late as 1935, on the cusp of the swing era, a review of Hal Kemp's band noted that his "type of music is, for the most part, slow and dreamy—mostly cupped brass and sustaining clarinets with a minimum of rhythm" and that his audience was "almost entirely the young, collegiate bunch, whose moods and style of dancing are made to order for Kemp's type of dansapation, and vice versa."[6]

Today, Kemp is all but forgotten, but a tabulation of the best-selling recording artists of the 1930s puts him in the top ten. Tommy Dorsey and Benny Goodman are there as well, but their successes were in the latter half of the decade. For the opening years, the biggest names in the dance music field were Lombardo, Whiteman, Kemp, Eddy Duchin, and Leo Reisman, all among the sweetest of the sweet.[7]

There are interesting things to be said about some of those bandleaders, but first I want to take a more general look at what dance musicians were playing for a living—and to emphasize that, in those early Depression years, playing for a living was a victory. Looking at music as a pleasure or an art is appropriate in many contexts and leads us to celebrate the musicians whose work continues to please and excite us today, but it doesn't always help us to understand how and why that music was created. In retrospect, dance band work has been recalled by many jazz musicians as arduous and constricting, and it certainly was both those things. Bands often played for five or six hours at a stretch, night after night, with long bus rides and bad food in between, for pitifully little money, and few provided much room for personal expression. But, especially in the early 1930s, they gave a lot of people work that, even at its worst, beat the hell out of standing on breadlines or digging ditches. Even some middle-class collegians found that it was easier to take their student bands on the road than to find jobs as recent graduates in architecture or chemistry at a time when building and industry had all but ground to a halt. Most of them would not remain in music for the rest of their lives—there were a lot more people who played with big bands in their twenties before going on to other careers than people who graduated from the big bands to the jazz clubs—but in 1932 a life of wine, women, and song with a few bucks thrown in for rent was a pretty terrific thing.[8]

Even at the best of times, working musicians are not necessarily creative artists, nor do they necessarily yearn to be. A lot of them are like journalists: people who have found that they can make a living by doing something more interesting and fun than working an assembly line or a routine office job and are happy with that. Of course, plenty of newspaper writers are frustrated novelists, and plenty of band musicians were frustrated jazz soloists, and the world would be a poorer place if Bix Beiderbecke had spent his whole career playing third trumpet in the Whiteman orchestra or Ernest Hemingway had covered a beat for the *Kansas City Star*. But there is no reason to think that frustrated artists have ever made up a majority in either profession, and plenty of journeyman musicians and newspaper writers lived longer, happier lives than the tortured geniuses of the Jazz Age. In the great scheme of things, playing trumpet for Hal Kemp or being a columnist for the *Daily News* was a good, solid gig that allowed people to buy houses, raise families, and lead lives that a lot of other people envied. The journeymen are not remembered alongside Beiderbecke and Hemingway, nor is there any reason they should be, but they were still an elite compared with the general run of working stiffs—and they created most of what people danced to and read in the morning paper.

As for what most people were dancing to: By 1930, the skills of dance-band arrangers had evolved a long way from the pioneering days of Hickman and Whiteman, but not all orchestras showed much sign of that fact. Most dance orchestras were still using generic "stocks," and a lot of prominent society and hotel bands were still spending most of their time playing repetitive choruses, with few if any solos, breaks, or special arrangements. A review of a hotel gig by Al Kavelin's society band explained the reason:

> The dancers... were continually asking for their favorite tunes and Kavelin, smartly enough, continually played them their favorite tunes. This, of course, meant mostly choruses, which is the ideal delivery for an orchestra of this type. Arrangements would be pretty much out of order... because to the up-and-ups dance music is much more an incidental medium, and should, therefore, never predominate above the general medium of the room.[9]

Many of the era's most successful bandleaders—Meyer Davis is a prime example—are forgotten today for exactly this reason. Their specialty was unobtrusively supplying whatever their customers wanted, from waltzes of the gay '90s to fox-trots, tangos, Charlestons, rumbas, swing, and, in later years, the twist. This meant that they had to rely on unwritten "head" arrangements more often than even the looser hot orchestras did, because when a prominent banker or a railroad magnate's wife requested a tune that only one band member knew, everyone else was expected to be able to fake it as fast as he could hum it for them.

A lot of bands were also limited to repetitive choruses and stock arrangements because they were bands in name only. I just referred to Davis as a bandleader—and on a busy night he would sometimes conduct sets by three different bands, occasionally in different cities—but he actually functioned more as the owner of a musical temp agency. At his peak, there were some sixty Meyer Davis bands playing in hotels and nightclubs along the Eastern seaboard, and these were in addition to his main business of supplying orchestras for society soirées and debutante balls. A *New Yorker* profile explained:

> Mr. Davis has a list of three hundred musicians who specialize in what he calls "party work." Composed of men on the list, each Davis orchestra comes into being for a specific party and disbands after the party is over.... This system, which is also used by Mr. Davis's competitors, has several advantages. The size of orchestras in "party work" varies in accordance with the taste and means of the client, and therefore a unit which was a constant in numbers would be impractical. If Mr. Davis, moreover, had a regular orchestra, he would have to pay it regularly. As it is, his musicians are paid only when they perform.[10]

Less famous leaders played for dances in less elevated neighborhoods, but many of them likewise just hired whoever was free for a given night's work. These ad hoc bands probably accounted for the majority of dance jobs—at least in some areas and periods—but they obviously were not the groups that set new trends or produced the greatest music. They made up the iceberg of which the name bands were the tip, and provided a training ground and a source of paying work for a lot of players who are remembered in other contexts: The list of musicians who played in Davis's outfits would include many of the most famous stars of the swing era, as well as some who went on to careers in classical music and studio work.

As jazz historians have frequently pointed out, a lot of the name bands of the Depression years were hardly more musically interesting than these temporary ensembles. At the opposite end of the professional spectrum from Kavelin and Davis were nationally famous bandleaders like Fred Waring, who by the early 1930s was rarely playing for dancers at all. Instead, his Pennsylvanians were appearing in theaters and on the radio, and though they were expert instrumentalists perform-ing carefully tailored arrangements, Waring openly granted that this was not their main attraction. He told a reporter in 1930 that at one time he had dreamed of rival-ing Whiteman, but "I realized I couldn't compete with Whiteman's music.... So I became a salesman—selling tricks. My boys are all good musicians. But they don't try to sell music. They all sing, dance and play solos. We have tricks with mega-phones, chant cheers; make figures with lighted dominoes on a dark stage."[11]

Waring's success was such that a lot of other hotel and ballroom orchestras took to adding similar displays between the dance sets. A review of Horace Heidt and His Brigadiers, who imitated not only Waring's showmanship but also his trademark glee club, noted that as a straight dance orchestra "the aggregation could not rate in the higher brackets for too long a time," but they "are the greatest spectacle in dancebandom today.... They're all over the place. When they're not playing dance music, they're singing and playing harps and cocktail shakers. Any minute you expect one of them to come swooping down at you from the ceiling on a flying trapeze."[12]

Music critics tend to disparage bands that rely more on spectacle than on sound, and when we listen to the past on records, it is hard to give acts like Waring's and Heidt's their due. In a live context, though, good entertainment can be as satisfying as good music, and that is what these bands were providing. As Duke Ellington wrote in 1939:

> If [a musician] is trying to earn his living by attempting to intrigue and win the approbation of the public, he feels that criticism of his work should not be based upon the degree of sincerity involved in the music which he is presenting, since he is obviously not directing his efforts with this particular goal in view.... The critics, on the other hand, feel it is their duty to constantly "expose" all musicians attempting to earn their living in any other manner than a strictly musical one. It may be, and probably is justifiable, to accord the highest praise to the greatest standard of musicianship, but, on the other hand, it is unfair to condemn completely the lesser product whose aims are admittedly less exalted.[13]

Ellington could speak from personal experience. Though by the 1930s some critics were already hailing him as one of America's finest composers, many of his early masterpieces were written during his orchestra's five-year residency at Harlem's Cotton Club, where his job was to provide appropriate music for social dancing and gaudily risqué revues. Like Chicago's Plantation Café, which in a triple-barreled display of nostalgic antebellum nomenclature had featured King Oliver's Dixie Syncopators accompanying a revue titled "Minstrel Days," the Cotton Club, which presented Ellington's orchestra "on the porch of an old Southern mansion,"[14] was named with an eye to attracting a well-heeled white clientele that could imagine itself back in a mythical south of happy darkies singing in the cotton fields. That is a disturbing fact, even when balanced by Ellington's recollection that the club was "a classy spot" where "impeccable behavior was demanded" of the clientele.[15] This was the period when Harlem was famous as a playground for white merrymakers, and if Ellington's radio broadcasts from the Club made him the most popular black bandleader in America, they were also the only way most Harlemites could hear those performances.

Along with that racial divide, it is worth remembering that Ellington's music was not the main reason most customers came to the Cotton Club. They came for the show, and as Gunther Schuller has pointed out, one of the main things that made Ellington's work from this period so distinctive was that, while other black orchestras were devoting all their time to dance jobs, his position as the Club's musical director required him to explore a wide range of moods, tempos, and background accompaniments, including abstract, semiclassical styles.[16] The result was that he became known not only for hot rhythms but also for unique compositions like "Black and Tan Fantasy" and "Mood Indigo." His recordings of these innovative arrangements still thrill modern listeners, but in their original context they could have had a very different flavor. For instance, every jazz fan knows that his group's growling horn section earned it the soubriquet the "jungle band," but it is easy to forget how accurately that phrase could fit a Cotton Club performance:

> A light-skinned and magnificently muscled Negro burst through a papier-mâché jungle onto the dance floor clad in an aviator's helmet, goggles, and shorts. He had obviously "been forced down in darkest Africa," and in the center of the floor he came upon a "white" goddess clad in long tresses and being worshipped by a circle of cringing "blacks." Producing a bull whip from heaven knows where, the aviator rescued the blonde and they did an erotic dance. In the background, Bubber Miley, Tricky Sam Nanton, and other members of the Ellington Band growled, wheezed, and snorted obscenely.[17]

One can be horrified or fascinated by that description, but in either case only a very unusual spectator would have noticed that he or she was listening to the work of one of America's finest composers. Ellington was already a famous bandleader, and the dance act may have been created to capitalize on his jungle sound, but for the average customer his orchestra was primarily there to provide instrumental backing for dancing and a great floor show. A review of the Club singled him out for praise, saying that "in Duke Ellington's dance band, Harlem has reclaimed its own after Times Square accepted them for several seasons at the Club Kentucky. Ellington's jazzique is just too bad." (Apparently, "jazz classique" had by then been collapsed into a single word.) But those two sentences were the only mention of the band in a fifteen-paragraph article. The ballroom dance team of Henri and La Perl received roughly twice as much space, as did the dancing Berry Brothers, singer Ada Ward, and several other featured artists, as well as songwriters, a costume designer, and the somewhat surly waitstaff. More to the point, the reviewer stressed that all of these were merely lagniappe: "The big attraction, of course are the gals, 10 of 'em, the majority of whom in white company could pass for Caucasians. Possessed of the native jazz heritage, their hotsy-totsy performance if working sans wraps could never be parred by a white gal. The brownskins' shiveree is worth the $2 couvert alone."[18]

We are so used to thinking of Ellington as a jazz pioneer and to seeing him discussed alongside Fletcher Henderson and Count Basie that it is easy to forget that as a revue composer and music director he was also part of the older black New York show business tradition of Sissle and Blake and Ziegfeld's Will Vodery. The fact that he was equally capable in both these roles made him a unique figure in 1930, and he remained an anomaly for the rest of his life. That was in a large part due to his extraordinary talents, but it also owed something to the fact that during these formative years the Cotton Club residency and the powerful management of Irving Mills made him the only black bandleader who could attempt the range of music that white leaders such as Whiteman or Reisman took for granted. Though it virtually never turns up on present-day collections of his work, one of his most popular records of the early 1930s was "Three Little Words," with vocals by Whiteman's recently departed Rhythm Boys, which had been featured in *Check and Double Check*, a film vehicle for the blackface comedians Freeman Gosden and Charles Correll, better known as Amos and Andy. Ellington and his band appeared in the film, providing music for a white society party—though to maintain the color line his trumpet section mimed the Rhythm Boys' part, and, to be extra safe, light-skinned Barney Bigard and Juan Tizol were required to "black" their faces so they would not be mistaken for white players.[19]

This ballroom sequence highlights another curious fact about the period: Although the featured instrumental is a hot version of Ellington's "Old Man Blues," the white partygoers do not dance to it but just nod along appreciatively. When we see them dancing, it is to a far less exciting performance, a lilting fox-trot of the sort associated with Reisman and the sweet bands. This is an apt reminder that—at least for white audiences—the hottest tunes were often played for show rather than for dancing, and that dance music needs to fit the capabilities as well as the tastes of its clientele. Intricate rhythms, thrilling though they may be, are tricky for dancers who are not familiar with them. I came up against this problem in another context when I was covering Latin music in the 1990s: The most successful Latin promoter in the Boston area had become disappointed with the repetitive quality of the salsa and meringue bands that were coming through town and wanted to book a Cuban *timba* group, but he found that his audience wouldn't dance to it. The Puerto Ricans, Dominicans, and Colombians were used to hearing clearly defined beats, and the intricate Cuban polyrhythms confused them. For a lot of dancers in the early 1930s, the hotter black bands presented a similar problem. Fred Waring recalled that when he brought an agent he knew to hear Ellington's music at the Cotton Club, insisting that it would be the next big trend, the response was, "Fred, I can't tell you that I like it because I don't. I'm considered a pretty good two-by-four dancer, but I couldn't dance to that number."[20]

One sees this disparity over and over again in films of this period. Fred Astaire's movies often included small, hot jazz bands, but he tends to be the only person dancing to them. The nightclub and ballroom scenes are accompanied by string-heavy orchestras in the Reisman mold—Reisman accompanied Astaire on the hit records of "Night and Day" and "Cheek to Cheek," though the film sequences use studio orchestras—and the couples provide a good sample of the standard white dance style: a sedate, gliding fox-trot. The shift in popular music that came a few years later with the swing craze would not be fundamentally a matter of freer, more improvisatory solos, but rather was an effect of a new generation of white dancers becoming more comfortable with the rhythms that confused Waring's guest.

Reisman's work provides a good example of how mainstream bandleaders dealt with this situation, because he tried even harder than most to expand his musical boundaries while remaining within the basic white dance band framework. In the European concert-master tradition, Reisman had started his career as a classical violinist, making his debut in 1909 as a twelve-year-old prodigy, then playing first chair for the Baltimore Symphony. He switched to dance music in the late 'teens, and in 1919 began an extended residency at the Brunswick Hotel in Boston, where his Whitemanesque approach thrilled both the society and college sets—the student newspaper of the Massachusetts Institute of Technology described him as "one of the most artistic of dance orchestra conductors [who] has won the praises of many of America's most fastidious critics of music" and declared that at the college's 1929 winter prom his men "proved to be every bit as popular and 'hot' as they were reputed to be."[21] By that time, he was featuring Eddy Duchin, whose unique piano style—single-note solos played on the bass keys—was a notable departure from the rhythmic chording that had been standard for dance band players. Duchin's solos sound clunky to modern ears, but they were certainly unusual, and when he left Reisman in 1931 he became America's most famous pop pianist and, with his suave good looks, the prototypical society bandleader.

Reisman's decision to hire Duchin—like the long hair that he tossed around as he conducted or his habit of flopping on his back and directing the orchestra with his feet—was distinctive, but in hindsight his most impressive choice in this period was to feature Bubber Miley, the man whose growling trumpet and melodic imagination had helped to put Ellington on the road to stardom.[22] Reisman seems to have first hired Miley for a short film he made in 1929, leading an Ellingtonian performance of "The Mooche,"[23] and he used him regularly for records, radio performances, and theater shows from early in 1930 through the summer of 1931. This was five years before Benny Goodman attracted national attention by hiring the black pianist Teddy Wilson, and if Reisman's breakthrough is more rarely noted, that is due both to musical and nonmusical reasons. The film finessed the racial issue by showing the band only in silhouette for the numbers in which Miley appeared, and, at least for some concerts, Reisman had the trumpeter dress as an usher and come onstage from the floor as a special guest. Miley's performances on Reisman's recordings of "What Is This Thing Called Love" and "Puttin' On the

Ritz" undoubtedly added to the discs' appeal, but because soloists were not listed on the labels, few listeners would have imagined that they were hearing a racially mixed band. And, more to the point, Miley's trumpet is the only hot sound on those records. Like Duchin's piano, it added quirky character, but the orchestra's foundation remained a steady, unadventurous rhythm that would not have confused even the most stolid white fox-trotter.

Reisman did experiment with more intricate rhythms, but they were of quite another sort. The rumba hit New York in 1930, its success ensured by the many prominent socialites who had developed a taste for Cuban music while partying in Prohibition-free Havana. The spark was a song called "El Manisero (The Peanut Vendor)," which the Cuban singer Antonio Machín performed that spring at the RKO Palace Theater, dressed in white street peddler's garb and tossing bags of peanuts to the audience, then recorded with Don Azpiazu's Havana Casino Orchestra. By the end of the year, every band in town was playing the song, and though Azpiazu took his group back to Havana to work the tourist hotels, he first spent a few weeks entertaining dancers at Reisman's regular venue, the swanky Central Park Casino, and Reisman caught the bug. According to *Time* magazine (which was prone to printing unchecked press releases and may have exaggerated a bit):

> Reisman's drummer mastered the four complicated beats which Cuban orchestras emphasize with the bongo ... [and Reisman] went into Cuba's interior and studied the primitive rumba dance, a series of writhings and twistings too lewd for fastidious eyes. A modified version of the rumba, the danzon, is the craze in Havana, a potential craze in the U. S. . . . [and] Reisman returned from Havana with another sheaf of Cuban scores.[24]

The rumba joined the already familiar tango as a staple of upper-crust, East Coast dances, and mainstream pop musicians were quick to latch on to the trend. Nat Shilkret, the music director for Victor Records, and the banjoist Harry Reser rushed out recordings as the Havana Novelty Orchestra and the Cuban Rumba Orchestra, and the Spanish violinist Enric Madriguera used the craze to launch himself as one of the decade's most successful hotel bandleaders. The rumba also penetrated venues that the tango had missed, aided by professional instructors and exotically themed Hollywood musicals (including the aptly named *Rumba*). It was an easier step and closer to African-American dance styles, and whereas there were very few Argentines in the United States, many port cities had substantial populations of Caribbean immigrants. This is not to say that the rumba danced in most American venues bore much relation to what was seen in Havana. As with jazz, the rhythms were adapted and simplified to attract the broadest possible audience: "American people are not becoming too conscious of the rumba as a rumba," Duchin explained after replacing Reisman at the Casino toward the end of 1931. "The different instruments brought into play attract by their unusualness in the playing of these rhythms. However, the only way in which the American leader can overcome this is to play these in the same tempo as the American fox-trot."[25]

That prosaic fox-trot would continue to be the essential American step as long as the mainstream dance bands survived. So it is appropriate to end this chapter with a look at the most enduringly popular dance orchestra of all, Guy Lombardo and His Royal Canadians. Like the other sweet bandleaders, Lombardo named Whiteman as his main inspiration, but he consistently played for dancers and never attempted to expand his musical horizons or add any showy tricks. Nonetheless, unlike the typical society bands, he did not have an anonymous, generic sound. The Royal Canadians were easily recognizable for their choir of silkily undulating saxophones, gently insistent rhythm—despite drums so subtle as often to be inaudible—and unadorned melodies, a combination they advertised as "the sweetest music this side of heaven."

Because virtually all the writing on the Big Band era has been done by people who love hot jazz, and because Lombardo's work was the antithesis of that approach, he has tended to be either ignored or reviled, but his fellow musicians understood the strengths that made him one of the most consistent record sellers of the century. As Benny Goodman noted at the height of the swing era:

> There's a lot to admire in Guy's way of doing things. His band has been prominent now for eight or nine years, and all that time he has gone along doing things in the same way, playing music the way *he* feels it. His band doesn't cut up on the stand or do comedy, just tends to its business of playing. It plays the melodies almost always in the right tempo—which I think is the most important thing of all—and their public doesn't seem to get tired of it.[26]

Lombardo became a national sensation in the late 1920s, and by the 1930s his sound was being imitated by virtually everyone, at least on live dates, and some of the most successful new bands—Jan Garber's, for example—were little more than Lombardo clones. Nor was that true only of white bands: Louis Armstrong consistently named the Royal Canadians as his favorite orchestra and took them as his model when he became popular enough to hire a saxophone section, and the Lombardo influence can also be heard in the cooing saxophones of Ellington's "Black and Tan Fantasy" and McKinney's Cotton Pickers' "Cherry," a reworking of the Canadians' "Little Coquette."[27] And if those are exceptional examples, that has more to do with recording patterns than with day-to-day playing styles. One of Fletcher Henderson's trademark numbers was a medley of waltzes with "Rose" in their titles—during his residency at Roseland, he also wore rose-colored suits and had his car painted to match—but it was never recorded, and he and Andy Kirk both lamented that the record companies let them cut only hot discs for the "Race" market, ignoring their broad repertoires of sweet material. "All the time we were making race records we were playing our pop tunes, romantic ballads, and waltzes for the dancing public," Kirk recalled. "But the people who controlled the output and distribution for Brunswick and Vocalion never gave a thought to that side of our band.... It was all part of the racial setup and climate of the times."[28]

Armstrong, Ellington, Henderson, and Kirk all did their best-paying work for white dancers, and such jobs necessarily had an effect on their musical decisions. But there were also plenty of black dancers who liked soft, soothing music. This is easy to forget, because the hot-versus-sweet debate has so often been framed as a battle between African-American and European-American rhythms and tastes. The average black dancers of the 1920s, 1930s, and beyond were comfortable with rhythms that baffled many of their white counterparts, but that does not mean that they loved those rhythms exclusively. Ella Fitzgerald, who got her start in the mid-1930s singing with Chick Webb's powerhouse band at the Savoy Ballroom, lamented in later years that "now everything is so fast and you hardly ever hear a waltz.... That's such a beautiful dance. Remember how they used to dance it up at the Savoy?"[29]

I have been unable to find even one other reference to waltzes at the Savoy, but that is not surprising. What set the Harlem ballroom apart from other dance venues was the acrobatic skill of its Lindy hoppers, so it was natural for people to recall it as hosting the hottest music in America. But even as Webb's orchestra was whipping all comers in battles for the swing crown, the Savoy also presented a relief band headed by the old-time, Ted Lewis–style clarinetist Fess Williams, and one visitor recalls that "there was a rule in the ballroom that he had to play slow and sad music, so Chick's boys could come on in a blaze of glory."[30] The contrast undoubtedly highlighted Webb's strengths, but Williams's sets would also have provided some older and more sedate dancers with a chance to take their turn on the floor. And, though they don't turn up in the history books, those more sedate dancers must have been pretty numerous: In 1930, a Savoy attendance record of 3,716 paid customers was set during a rare appearance by, of all people, Guy Lombardo.[31]

Once again, we have to consider not just the extraordinary bands and dancers but the ordinary desires of people who had finished a hard day at work and wanted to relax and enjoy themselves. Or, to put it differently, we have to remember that what has tended to fascinate white people—including music historians—about black culture is the ways in which it differs from the white mainstream, but that should not mislead us into confusing its most distinctive traits with its own mainstream. Black customers were buying a lot of Fletcher Henderson records at a time when most white music fans were barely aware of Henderson's name, but a collector combing Harlem for rare discs in the 1930s reported that he still found more by Lombardo than by Henderson.[32] And why not? As Panama Francis, who played drums in the Savoy's house band for a half-dozen years, recalled, "Guy Lombardo had a helluva beat! It didn't swing, but it had rhythm." Or as *Metronome* critic

George Simon wrote, Lombardo "knows how to select tunes that create a mood, an intimate, cozy mood.... [He] produces a succession of steady, unobtrusive beats that make it a pleasure to take your girl out on the floor and move around to the best of your ability. If you can dance at all, you can dance to Lombardo's music."[33] And for most people, regardless of race, that was what music was all about.

SWING THAT MUSIC

The other night I spent a few hours at the radio, listening to dance bands. I heard 458 chromatic runs on accordions, 911 "Telegraph ticker" brass figures, 78 sliding trombones, 4 sliding violas, 45 burps into a straw, 91 bands that played the same arrangement on every tune, and 11,006 imitations of Benny Goodman.

GORDON JENKINS, 1937

On December 5, 1933, Utah became the thirty-sixth state to ratify the Twenty-first Amendment, ending Prohibition. Newspapers were quick to announce the result:

> From East, West, North and South, from Boston to Los Angeles, from New Orleans to Chicago, from big places and little places, the call is coming through to New York and other key cities that provide the nation's entertainment: "Give us more music, more singers, more dancers. Let us have fun."
>
> More than for anything else the call is being broadcast throughout the land for orchestras. Hotels which formerly employed one to play for a chaste dinner hour are now hiring two to play throughout the entire evening; restaurants which never had music are today advertising their bands and band leaders; night clubs, cafés, beer gardens are sprouting up all over the country, and each in its way is calling in an awakened patronage to the tune of jazz, "blues" and "Ach Du Lieber, Augustine."[1]

For some musicians, at least, the worst of the Depression was over. Repeal gave a boost to all kinds of bands, from sweet orchestras to polka outfits, as well as rejuvenating the record business with the coin-operated tavern machines that became known as jukeboxes. And soon it would spark a new wave of bands playing the hotter, more African-American-influenced style known as swing.

Some fans of both earlier and later jazz styles have portrayed swing as an overarranged, relatively conservative form and its era as a time when innovative soloists were trapped in big, commercially oriented orchestras that only occasionally let them break loose and reach the heights of their abilities. Big band arrangements certainly limited improvisation, but this portrayal involves a confusing linguistic shift, because what people meant by "swing" in the early and mid-1930s was precisely the loose improvising and phenomenal rhythmic expertise that are the most celebrated hallmarks of hot jazz. Louis Armstrong's *Swing That Music*, the first autobiography of a black jazz star, appeared in 1936, and in it he recalled that "the swing idea of free improvisation by the players was at the core of jazz when it started back there in New Orleans thirty years ago...[but] this idea got lost when jazz swept over the country." He blamed music publishers, who discouraged improvisation on the theory that it was easier to sell sheet music when songs were performed the way they were written, and he portrayed the swing players as a brave band of outcasts, keeping true jazz alive in an age of conservative sweetness:

> Some of the boys stuck along and just wouldn't follow scoring, it wasn't in 'em, and some of the boys that didn't learn to read music went on swinging the way they had learned to love. Very few of them ever made much money, but playing in small clubs and dives they kept swing alive for many years. Then there was another group of the boys who took a straddle and I think they were the smartest and that they have probably done more to bring swing into its own than anybody. They were the swing-men who went into the commercial field, joined big conventional bands, played the game as it was dished out to them and made their money, and yet who loved swing so much that they kept it up outside of their regular jobs. They did it through the jam sessions held late at night after their work was done. It makes me think of the way the early Christians would hold their meetings in the catacombs under Rome.[2]

It is not clear that those were really Armstrong's words—though he was a prolific writer, his first book was substantially ghostwritten—but they expressed the feelings of a clique of musicians and record collectors that surfaced in the early 1930s on both sides of the Atlantic. The "hot clubs" and "rhythm clubs" that formed in France, Britain, and the United States met in apartments, living rooms, and college dormitories to listen to records of Armstrong's Hot Five, the New Orleans Rhythm Kings, and any small group that included Bix Beiderbecke, as well as to new releases that followed that loosely organized, improvisation-driven model.

A lot of those small-band releases were made by groups that were pulled together just for an afternoon's recording. A famous example was the interracial octet that cut two songs in 1929 as the Mound City Blue Blowers: Leader Red McKenzie, who played the "blue blower" that gave the group its name (it was a comb covered with strips of newspaper, which made a buzzing sound when he hummed into it), led small, rowdy novelty bands for New York society parties—though in the early 1930s he also spent a year singing with Paul Whiteman. Guitarist Jack Bland was McKenzie's regular party accompanist. Banjoist Eddie Condon, drummer Gene Krupa, and clarinetist Pee Wee Russell had recently arrived from Chicago to back the vaudeville song-and-dance star Bee Palmer—who had also been featured with Whiteman—but now were scuffling for gigs with middling-hot bands including the Red Nichols and Ben Pollack orchestras. (Condon described their lifestyle as "from hand to mouth and it was somebody else's hand."[3]) The two African-American players had the most steady employment: Coleman Hawkins was the saxophone star of Fletcher Henderson's band, and bassist Pops Foster was in the Luis Russell Orchestra. As for trombonist Glenn Miller—still ten years away from becoming America's most popular bandleader—he had spent the last year working as musical director for Pollack, playing in a Broadway pit orchestra, and arranging and recording with Nichols and the Dorsey Brothers.

Miller and the Dorseys, along with such future swing stars as Benny Goodman, Bunny Berigan, and Artie Shaw, were part of an elite clique of high-end, all-around New York players who worked everything from Meyer Davis dance gigs to jobs with radio and recording orchestras. Their first love was hot jazz, but they were expert readers and straddled a baffling variety of musical worlds: Shaw came east from California with Irving Aaronson's Commanders, a Waring-style group whose members devoted so much of their energy to singing and comedy routines that he would later write that, with a couple of exceptions, "there were no musicians in that band." When he sought extracurricular inspiration at after-hours sessions, his coworkers thought he was nuts: "They would see me grab my horn and tear off to start playing at an hour when they were only too glad to be finished for the night." In Chicago, Shaw often sat in with the Earl Hines band, but he also recalled jamming at a dance marathon where "while all this subtle and intricate musical stuff was going on...those pooped-out, broken-down Marathon Dance contestants...shuffled like the walking dead." After settling in New York and joining the CBS studio crew, he played everything from dance music to symphonic selections, working with musicians who would go on to prominent careers with the Boston Symphony Orchestra and the New York Philharmonic. Meanwhile, he was playing late-night gigs with Willie "The Lion" Smith in Harlem, spending so much time there that he claimed he "eventually came to feel more like a colored man myself than an 'ofay'—Harlemese for 'white man.'"[4]

Shaw's African-American peers were also playing a wide variety of styles, but they did not have the same freedom to cross the color line. So if some of the era's top white musicians were working in formal orchestras and sweet bands while dreaming of jam sessions where they could cut loose and play hot jazz, their black compatriots' fantasies were as likely to be of a job at CBS or of the salaries that the Whiteman band was getting. Benny Carter, another future swing bandleader, who in this period was sitting with Hawkins in the Henderson reed section, recalled:

Radio staff and studio orchestras were closed to us and these were steadier jobs paying hundreds of dollars weekly at a time when the union scale at places like the Savoy was thirty-three dollars....Of course many white musicians, making more than we did, came to listen to us and play with us. We welcomed them and enjoyed the jamming. But we couldn't go downtown to join them. We learned from each other and we didn't much blame the white musicians—we did envy them, though.[5]

The disparate opportunities for black and white musicians had far-reaching effects, some of which have received relatively little attention. Both Carter and his other neighbor in the Henderson reeds, Buster Bailey, had hoped to play classical music but were forced to give up those dreams: "Sure, we played concerts and overtures and numbers like that in the theaters, but when I started you couldn't even think, if you were a Negro, of making symphony orchestras," Bailey recalled, adding, "I guess you could say the only regret I have is that I didn't have a chance to make it in symphony music."[6] Looking back, jazz writers tend to celebrate the hottest bands and often assume that when black orchestras played sedate, semiclassical arrangements they were kowtowing to white tastes, but it was not that simple: While some big band musicians dreamed of after-hours jam sessions, others were dreaming of wearing tuxes and playing in Carnegie Hall.

That said, the next major development in the dance band business was a shift toward hot rhythms, and the interracial sessions of the late 1920s and early 1930s bred friendships that helped shape the course of American music. Over the next decade, Shaw would hire Billie Holiday, Hot Lips Page, and Roy Eldridge; Eldridge would also work in Krupa's orchestra; Jimmy Dorsey would feature the black vocalist June Richmond; and Condon would organize numerous mixed concerts and record dates. The man who gets most credit in that department, though, is Benny Goodman, and it is worth revisiting his oft-told saga, not only because of his importance but also because of what it reveals about the broader trends that both inspired and constrained him.

Goodman had grown up in Chicago, home to the 1920s' most dedicated assemblage of young white jazz devotees, but whereas most of the teenage hot music hounds who would be remembered as the "Austin High gang" were middle-class kids who played for fun, Goodman was from a poor family, and in 1923, at age fourteen, he dropped out of school to be a full-time clarinetist. Three years later he made his first recordings with Pollack's band (his brother Harry and Glenn Miller were also members), and in 1928 Pollack brought him to New York. Goodman was a quick reader and versatile soloist, and he soon found jobs in studio and pit orchestras as well as with hot recording groups whose work appeared under *noms de disque* including the Louisiana Rhythm Kings and the Charleston Chasers. Personnel varied from date to date, and the Chasers are best remembered for a 1931 recording of "Basin Street Blues" that featured Goodman, Krupa, Miller, and the Teagarden brothers, for which Miller wrote an introduction that invited listeners to travel down the Mississippi "to New Orleans, the land of dreams." As the band names and lyrics indicate, these records were intended for the jazz fans of Armstrong's catacombs, true believers who still loved the rowdy, small-band style that was beginning to be called Dixieland.

Goodman and his record-mates shared many of those true believers' tastes, but they were also professional musicians trying to make a living, so they could not afford to be purists. They took whatever work they could find, although they tried to stick together and get each other into bands or onto studio dates—Goodman recalled one Beiderbecke session that included three clarinetists (himself, Russell, and Jimmy Dorsey) because "all three of us were around town, and he didn't want to hurt anybody's feelings."[7]

As the Depression deepened, there were fewer of those dates, and Goodman's energies went into paying the bills for himself and his mother, who had moved east with him. He devoted himself to radio and dance orchestra work, and as John Hammond later recalled, became a "fairly slick professional musician…who had lost hope and interest in jazz."[8] Hammond was a scion of the Vanderbilt family and the most influential hot music fan of the era, producing sessions, writing criticism, and forcing radio programmers, record executives, writers, and bandleaders to listen to the artists who excited him. He was drawn to Goodman both musically and as a person (Goodman later married Hammond's sister), and in 1933 he organized the clarinetist's first date as a leader in over two years: a hot recording session for the English subsidiary of Columbia Records. Goodman was initially hesitant, thinking that the craze for hot music was over, but as it turned out Columbia decided to release the records in the United States as well, and signed him to a contract.

Hammond's musical agenda was intertwined with broader social concerns, in particular an active engagement in the civil rights struggle, and he saw jazz as not only a great art form but also a wedge with which to topple racial barriers. Once he had established Goodman as a Columbia artist, he insisted that they break with the usual hiring practices and use some African-American artists on Goodman's dates: first Billie Holiday, then Coleman Hawkins and the pianist Teddy Wilson. Holiday and Wilson were particular favorites of Hammond's, and he also arranged for them to do a series of sessions together on which Goodman sometimes appeared as the lone white player.

The Columbia contract gave Goodman a new outlook on his musical future, and when he received an offer to join Whiteman in 1934 he turned it down and instead formed his own orchestra. This decision was sparked in part by a lucky opportunity: His brother Harry, who was working with Pollack at the Casino de Paree, came home one day with the news that the Casino's manager, Billy Rose, was planning to open another room and would be auditioning bands. Figuring that Casa Loma's success might have whetted dancers' appetites for a hotter style of music, Goodman pulled together a group of eager young players and, after several auditions, got the debut gig at Rose's Music Hall. The job paid only union scale, but along with the live exposure it offered a local radio hookup several times a week, making it an ideal showcase for a new sort of band.

Goodman was adamant that his outfit *was* a new sort: "No white band had yet gotten together a good rhythm section that would kick out, or jump, or rock, or swing," he later wrote, "using arrangements that...would give the men a chance to play solos and express the music in their own individual way."[9] He bought some charts from Benny Carter, and his men did their best to play with the verve of the best black orchestras. Goodman was pleased, but the Music Hall's management was dubious: "Some people who came in stood around the bandstand to listen, and while we thought that was fine Rose got the impression we weren't getting across because everybody wasn't dancing."[10] That gap in perception between musicians and ballroom managers would persist through the swing years, and its immediate result was that when Rose went on a European talent search, the new manager sent Goodman packing.

At that point Hammond came up with another idea: He wanted Goodman to front the first fully integrated orchestra and take it to England and France, where hot records had created an eager audience. Goodman agreed, but the bookings never got settled, so he was still in New York when his major break came. Actually, it was two breaks: A young agent named Willard Alexander at MCA, the largest booking office in the country, was a longtime fan of Goodman's playing and felt his band could be a hit with college audiences. At the same time, the National Biscuit Company had decided to sponsor a radio program called *Let's Dance*, which would be broadcast on fifty-three stations from coast to coast every Saturday night. The idea was to feature three different bands in revolving half-hour sets, and the trio eventually chosen was Kel Murray's sweet orchestra, Xavier Cugat's Latin band, and Goodman's group.[11]

Let's Dance not only gave Goodman national exposure but also specifically required him to play hot jazz, which Nabisco hoped would draw collegiate listeners. It also provided a budget for eight new arrangements per week, and he immediately commissioned charts both from white studio pros (including George Bassman and Gordon Jenkins, who respectively provided his opening and closing themes, "Let's Dance" and "Goodbye") and from several black arrangers: Jimmy Mundy from Earl Hines's band, Edgar Sampson from Chick Webb's, and Fletcher Henderson.

It was Henderson's charts that shaped what would become recognized as the Goodman sound. Over the next few years he provided Goodman with more than 225 arrangements, building on the style he and Don Redman had worked out over the previous decade with his own orchestra. As outlined by Henderson's biographer, Jeffrey Magee, this style included brass and reed section parts that mimicked the way individual instruments interacted in the smaller hot ensembles, with space for soloists to come in at key moments and goose those sections to new heights. Henderson also perfected a pattern of call-and-response riffs that built to climactic finishes, exemplified by an arrangement of "King Porter Stomp" that became Goodman's defining flag-waver. Jelly Roll Morton had written "King Porter" back in the first decade of the century as a four-part piano rag, but Henderson cut it to its bare essentials, paring the first part down to a single chorus, dumping the second entirely, then setting the band loose on a half-dozen variations of the third before rising to a churchy call-and-response on the "stomp" finale.[12]

Goodman's success with the Henderson charts would lead other white band-leaders to hire black arrangers who could provide them with their own hot styles—Tommy Dorsey, for example, hired the Jimmie Lunceford Orchestra's Sy Oliver—and points up the extent to which arrangements rather than individual players were responsible for the distinctive sound of swing. Of course, it also points up the degree to which the white swing bands were built on a foundation of segregation. Henderson's orchestra had been the country's premier black band and a staple at Manhattan's most popular dance venues since 1924, and in a different world he—or Lunceford or Redman or Ellington—could have gotten the *Let's Dance* gig instead of being the wizard behind the curtain. Goodman's breakthrough led to a new level of acclaim for black players and bands, just as Elvis Presley's success would do wonders for the careers of Chuck Berry and Little Richard, but white artists and aggregations that sounded sufficiently black could almost always get better jobs and more money than their African-American counterparts.

In that first year, though, the fact that the Goodman band sounded like a hot black orchestra also caused some problems. *Let's Dance* ran for twenty-six weeks, until May 1935, and toward the end of that run MCA arranged for the band to play a residency in the Grill Room of Manhattan's Roosevelt Hotel. The Roosevelt was Lombardo territory, and the booking was a disaster for all concerned. Clients complained that the band played too loud and too fast, the management was unhappy, and Goodman was left wondering if any venue was ready for his style. Those doubts grew over the summer, as MCA sent him on tour to California via a series of Midwestern one-nighters and a four-week engagement in Denver. The Midwestern shows went okay, but the Denver date was a repeat of the Roosevelt debacle. The band was booked in an old-fashioned dance hall called Elitch's Gardens, and after the first half hour the manager came over to ask, "What's the matter—can't you boys play any waltzes?" Not only were they playing too many hot tunes, but they were also playing each for too long: The Gardens charged ten cents for three dances and was used to earning about a penny a minute per couple, but when Goodman's soloists got going they routinely stretched a single song to six minutes, cutting the profits in half. The manager complained to MCA, MCA read Goodman the riot act, and in the end the band kept the gig only by buying a hundred stock dance arrangements and playing them in three-minute chunks.

Even in its toned-down form the band did lousy business, drawing barely fifty couples on the weekends and far fewer during the week. Meanwhile, Kay Kyser's sweet orchestra was packing huge crowds into a more expensive pavilion across town. Kyser would remain one of the country's most popular bandleaders through the 1940s, thanks to a combination of well-honed musicianship, sprightly novelty tunes, and an audience participation segment known as the Kollege of Musical Knowledge. Goodman went over to catch his act and, though the music was not to his taste, noted that Kyser "certainly put it across, and maybe for a minute I wished I could do it too."[13]

After three weeks in Denver, the Goodman gang moved on, wending its way to the West Coast. Some gigs were better than others, but by the time the tour ended at the Palomar Ballroom in Los Angeles, Goodman was utterly discouraged. Opening night the band drew a decent crowd and its first two sets of sedate dance music went over okay, but having his own orchestra was bringing more headaches than acclaim, and he was ready to quit. So, because it might be the group's last show together, he decided to at least have some fun, and for the third set he pulled out several of the hottest Henderson arrangements. The musicians took off like racehorses leaving the paddock, and rather than protesting, the audience went wild. Apparently, young Angelenos had come to hear the hot band they knew from *Let's Dance* and were just waiting for it to cut loose: "To our complete amazement, half of the crowd stopped dancing and came surging around the stand," Goodman recalled. "After traveling three thousand miles, we finally found people who were up on what we were trying to do, prepared to take our music the way we wanted to play it."[14]

That night was Goodman's turning point, and August 21, 1935, has gone down in history as the birth date of the swing era. A few months later he got a residency at Chicago's Congress Hotel, where "for the first time we were booked as a 'swing' band—with the words printed just that way, as if it was something in a foreign language."[15] The orchestra also gave their first formal jazz concerts there, sponsored by the Chicago Rhythm Club, and *Down Beat* magazine reported that the audience behaved in a quite new way: Although the first show was advertised as a "tea dance," the few couples who tried some steps were "instantly booed" by those who "preferred to listen and watch." Unadulterated dance music, without novelty specialities, catchy choreography, or symphonic pretensions was for the first time being treated as a serious concert style.[16] Then, at the third Rhythm Club event, the concert organizer and jazz critic Helen Oakley suggested that Teddy Wilson play an intermission set with Goodman and Krupa sitting in. The positive reception led to this trio becoming a regular feature at Goodman's gigs: Twice a night the dance floor would be cleared for sets of what was essentially a chamber jazz group, as well as being the first full-time integrated ensemble of the swing era, and soon the trio was expanded to a quartet with the addition of vibraphonist Lionel Hampton.

I do not have space to tell the whole Goodman story, but in 1936 he got another national radio show—replacing the Casa Loma Orchestra on *Camel Caravan*—and a featured spot in a movie, and the *Metronome* readers' poll named his group "Best Swing Band," handily beating Casa Loma and distantly trailed by Jimmy Dorsey,

Lunceford, and Ellington. They were also voted "Favorite Band of All," with Casa Loma in hot pursuit but far outpacing Ray Noble, Whiteman, and Hal Kemp. (Noble, an English bandleader fronting an orchestra organized and directed by Glenn Miller, won the "Best Sweet Band" category.) *Metronome* was still primarily read by musicians, which is probably the reason that swing bands topped the "favorite" category and that Ellington and Lunceford made decent showings in the "swing" department. As the swing era picked up steam and the magazine acquired more nonprofessional readers, black bands dropped lower year by year, till by 1940—with Goodman still in the top spot—Count Basie was the only black artist in the top ten.[17]

That pattern would be replicated in the rise of rock 'n' roll, and before moving on I want to look at one more aspect of Goodman's rise that also presaged that later revolution: his appearances at New York's Paramount Theater. The Paramount was a movie theater that had added bands during the Depression to help fill its 3,664 seats.[18] For the bands it was a source of extra income, as they would typically work there in the daytime before playing their regular dance gigs at night. It was a grueling schedule: For a while Goodman was doing five daily Paramount shows, then playing from 7:30 p.m. to 1:30 a.m. in the Hotel Pennsylvania's Madhattan Room, rushing back and forth between the two venues for the early evening, as well as rehearsing new arrangements and doing the weekly *Camel Caravan* broadcast.

The unusual thing about the Paramount shows was the age and behavior of the audience. The word "teenager" was just coming into use in the late 1930s, and when the *New York Times* reported on a near-riot at Goodman's second opening there, in January 1938, it described the fans as a horde of "adolescent exhibitionists" who began lining up well before dawn. The management had to open the doors early and call the police to do crowd control, and once inside, Goodman's "legion of 'teenish admirers . . . jumped up and down . . . danced in the aisles, clambered upon the stage, waggled their hands, shook their shoulders, whinnied, whistled, clapped and sang." The movie—a late Mae West feature—was ignored, and the *Times* film critic noted that two weeks earlier, when he had watched Goodman on screen in *Hollywood Hotel*, the fans "weren't even willing to accept the non-Goodman parts of the picture in patience. . . . When Mr. G. & Co. weren't actually out there swinging, his public was matching notes in the balcony, marveling over the steel-brush strokes of the drummer and the way his hair kept falling over his eyes."[19] Though Goodman's look of spectacled reserve made him an odd teen idol, Krupa was a natural for the job, and his wayward hair and gum chewing attracted almost as much comment as his flashy, powerhouse drumming.

The screaming teens were not at all the audience Goodman had expected, and he seems to have been rather bemused by his new kingdom. Nor was his band typical of the orchestras that would dominate what was soon being called the Swing Era. He opened the way for other dedicated hot players, both black and white, some of whom seized the opportunity to cut loose and play their favorite music with a minimum of showbiz and pop balladry—Count Basie, Woody Herman, and Charlie Barnet are prime examples. But most bands, even if they were led by experienced "hot men," saw the value of compromise, and the rowdier, more improvisatory swing approach was streamlined and refined by commercially savvy leaders like Tommy Dorsey and, most famously, Glenn Miller.

For one thing, there was the issue of pleasing dancers. As his band's early problems suggested, Goodman always found this something of a burden. At Billy Rose's Music Hall he had apparently messed up the accompaniments to the floor show out of a belief that "the dancers and acts were supposed to follow *us*," and in general he insisted that "it's always been a fact that styles in dancing follow the styles in music."[20] In fact, the opposite tended to be true. New music did spawn new dances, but even the hottest, most innovative bands were expected to play whatever the customers wanted, which typically meant a mix of old and new, fast and slow, fox-trots, waltzes, and Latin numbers. Many of Goodman's arrangements were supremely danceable, with the swinging, four-to-the-bar beat that had been established in the late 1920s in a give-and-take between black bands and young black dancers at ballrooms like the Savoy. But those bands had also continued to play other rhythms: Fletcher Henderson would not have had to send out for stocks when the Denverites demanded waltzes, because he had several dozen of them in his own book.

Likewise, in the late 1930s, Tommy Dorsey was always careful to mix his swing tunes with plenty of other material, with the result that by 1939 *Metronome*'s readers were voting his group both America's number three swing band and the number two sweet band. And the sweet material was not there just to attract older dancers: *Billboard* began doing surveys of college students in 1938, and although Goodman topped the list of favorite bands that year, right below him were Dorsey and three sweet leaders: Kemp, Lombardo, and Kyser. Lombardo's campus popularity quickly declined, but the next three polls found Dorsey and Kyser both outscoring Goodman.[21]

Of course, such polls do not tell the full story, nor was Goodman necessarily interested in poll rankings. One of the reasons he is respected by jazz historians is that he was genuinely torn between his desire for success and his devotion to playing music that excited him, and once he was assured of a decent living and a chance to keep the band together, he did not see much need for further compromises. Dorsey and Kyser, by contrast, behaved like showmen. Dorsey was a good deal hipper than Kyser, as well as being a superb instrumentalist in his own right, but along with producing creditable swing records, he also gave the world Frank Sinatra and Jo Stafford—who could never have formed their styles or achieved similar popularity in the Goodman band—and his theme was the achingly romantic "I'm Getting Sentimental over You."

To the extent that swing existed as a stylistic movement, it was often torn between the musicians' personal tastes and what they had to do to please a mass audience—the demands of art and commerce—not that the two were necessarily contradictory. It was also torn between the past and the future: The facts that Goodman and Dorsey had both been Charleston Chasers and that Goodman's first showstopper was a Jelly Roll Morton composition indicate swing's connection to the Dixieland revival, which likewise attracted both somber acolytes and carefree dilettantes. Milt Gabler's Commodore record shop in Manhattan had become a jazz collectors' Mecca, with Gabler first selling old records—exhibited with cards that informed buyers of the personnel of each band, a detail the original issuers had considered irrelevant—then reissuing discs the majors had dropped, and finally sponsoring and recording regular interracial jam sessions. Gabler and his friends believed that jazz was a precious art form that should be respected on a par with European concert music, and after a while the larger record companies caught on to this new and potentially lucrative market. In 1936, when Victor released the first record set ever devoted to a nonclassical artist, it was *The Bix Beiderbecke Memorial Album*. Beiderbecke had died in 1931, little known except to his fellow musicians, but he now became a legend, helped along by a romantic 1938 novel, *Young Man with a Horn*, which traced the life of a doomed, Bixian genius.

Meanwhile, on New York's 52nd Street, bars were finding that they could draw customers with good-time, Dixieland-flavored bands that provided improvising musicians with a freedom they didn't have in the big dance orchestras. Red McKenzie had a club there for a while, and Eddie Condon played at Red's and other joints along the strip before moving downtown to a bar called Nick's in Greenwich Village. Condon also organized the jam sessions at Commodore and presented more formal concerts at Town Hall, but although these gigs were aimed at serious jazz lovers, he had no illusions about the bulk of his audience. Drummer Dave Tough memorably described the crowd at Nick's as middle-aged businessmen who "like to think it's still Prohibition and they're wild young cats up from Princeton for a hot time. All they need is a volume of F. Scott Fitzgerald sticking out of their pockets."[22] As Condon recalled:

> We did a lot of Dixieland numbers because the customers identified them with our music and asked for them; we could have played the most recent popular hits, giving them our interpretation, but many of the listeners would not have believed they were hearing jazz. Decca, for instance, asked us to make an album of tunes which Bix had played on records.... I wondered, as we were cutting the sides, how many of the tunes Bix would have been playing were he alive.[23]

The most popular acts on 52nd Street were extroverted entertainers like the jive-talking violinist Stuff Smith, the effervescent New Orleans trumpeter Louis Prima, and the Riley-Farley Orchestra, whose "The Music Goes Round and Round" was not only the biggest hit of 1935–1936 but also by some reports the best-selling record since the 1920s.[24] These musicians didn't care if critics called their music Dixieland or swing as long as the customers showed up and bought drinks, and their most successful tunes were quickly picked up by the bigger outfits: Riley-Farley's hit was covered by Kemp's and Frank Froeba's orchestras, as well as by small groups headed by Tommy Dorsey and Wingy Manone. A few of the most popular big bands—Bob Crosby's in particular, but Jimmy Dorsey ran him a close second—revived the old two-beat rhythm, advertised their music as Dixieland, and reworked New Orleans standards to fit their larger format. As for Goodman, although his music rarely sound much like anything played in the 'teens, one of his biggest early hits was the nostalgic "That Dixieland Band."[25]

As I will discuss in the next chapter, jukeboxes were becoming a factor as well, and in that market small bands could challenge the orchestras. Along with the 52nd Street combos, many orchestra leaders created pocket counterparts to their full ensembles: Crosby's Bobcats and Tommy Dorsey's Clambake Seven (a "clambake" was musicians' slang for a jam session) were modern variants on the old Charleston Chasers, largely devoted to recording nostalgic, good-time Dixieland. Meanwhile, Artie Shaw's Gramercy Five and Goodman's small groups used the small format to explore the possibilities of a sort of hot chamber music, with Shaw underlining this analogy by using harpsichord instead of piano.

Whether fun or serious, these small groups were intended more for listening than dancing, and were part of a drift that would continue from the swing era on—most obviously in later jazz, but also in popular music as a whole. The swing era has been remembered as a golden age of social dancing, and the swing orchestras got most of their jobs in ballrooms and tried to develop rhythm sections that would get people out on the floor. Nonetheless, as in the early 1930s, many dancers had trouble keeping up with the hottest styles, and although some young jitterbugs were ebullient exceptions, this problem never disappeared. Older European Americans were particularly slow to pick up the swing beat, but there were also plenty of African Americans who continued to enjoy slower and more varied dance programs. And while thousands of young couples of all races got together after school or work to rehearse intricate turns and throws, they were always substantially outnumbered by their less ambitious peers. It is astonishing to watch films of the Savoy's most athletic denizens tossing their partners over their heads and between their legs, but that was never something the average couple did on a Saturday night, and when the most spectacular dancers hit the floor, it was a signal for a lot of other people to move to the sidelines. As a result, the rise of swing meant that customers were dancing less and listening more, and nondancers became a major dance hall phenomenon. By 1938, *Billboard* was reporting:

In yesteryears it was only a dozen or two hep musicians that crowded the floor space around a bandshell. Now it is not unusual to find that of 1,000 crowded into a ballroom only 100 or so are actually dancing, while the others jam the floor and render themselves hysterical by the gymnastics of the hot horns getting in a groove.[26]

Goodman's recollection that when he first got hot at the Palomar "half of the crowd stopped dancing" was typical, and a reporter who covered that gig felt confused as to "whether he was attending a dance in a ballroom or some new and weird type of orchestral recital in a music hall."[27] Any rock fan, given a time machine, could have told him that he was just getting a glimpse of the future in which very few live pop music venues would encourage dancing, but at the time this was an astonishing departure.

A clique of hardcore jazz devotees and record collectors had always believed that their favorite styles should be treated as something better than dance music, and they were thrilled by the change: "Swing's for Listeners—Not for Dancers!" trumpeted a 1939 *Metronome* headline, over an article announcing that "real fans are beginning to realize that swing is appreciated more by those who listen and watch than the ones who attempt to dance to its music." Of a recent Count Basie gig, it noted that "much to the dismay of the ickies [ignorant swing fans], the torrid rhythms of the Count's swing numbers were much too fast for all but the most frantic jitterbugs, which made the evening wonderful for those who really knew their swing."[28]

Ballroom owners saw things rather differently. As *Billboard* put it, "the vet op [veteran ballroom operator]…always appealed to his patronage on the strength of a whirl around his hardwood floors with occasional relaxation in a Wiener waltz or a two-step." The most reliable customers had been couples who came to dance rather than to hear a particular band, and although the rise of name bands since World War I had meant that some orchestras could draw an added audience of fans, it had still been taken for granted that any band's primary job was to please the core clientele. Now, the more dedicated swing outfits were playing purely for their fans, and "as a result, the regular dancing crowds are staying at home when a band of beater-outers is booked."[29]

Meanwhile, the young swing fans were proving to be mediocre customers: They came out only when their favorite bands were booked and were famous for spending virtually no money, sometimes nursing a single Coke for the whole evening. As if that were not enough, they were rowdy and took up too much room. The head of the Iowa Ballroom Owners Association complained of "wide area dances where one couple can fill up space ordinarily occupied by [a] half dozen pairs of terpsters dancing the legit way," and a proprietor in Green Bay, Wisconsin, reported "constant complaints from other dancers on the floor of kicks in the shins, even in the teeth, of leg bruises and scratches and of feminine hosiery torn." In several Midwestern states, ballroom owners imposed bans on jitterbugs—whether dancing wildly or crowding around the bandstand—and similar controls were attempted in some Eastern hotels and even on college campuses.[30]

Swing was definitely the big news of the day, but its mixed reception on the dance floor explains why old-time orchestras such as Lombardo's and Lawrence Welk's remained in high demand and would continue to do good business twenty years after the collapse of the swing era. Welk recalled that in the late 1930s he almost quit a residency on the Santa Monica pier because he didn't think he could stand up to the competition of Tommy Dorsey's nationally famous band, but stayed on after a fan assured him that "the ones who love to dance will go in and listen to the other band for a while, but then they'll come over to your place before the evening is over." As it turned out, that was exactly what happened, and Dorsey's visit actually improved Welk's business. Welk himself was a Louis Armstrong fan and would later take pride in recording with Ellington's star sax player, Johnny Hodges, but he knew his business: "Though we had often been tempted into playing fancy or technically brilliant musical arrangements, we always pulled the biggest, and happiest, crowds when we stuck to what we did best and what they wanted most— playing the most danceable music around."[31]

I don't want to overemphasize the split between swing and dancing. For plenty of people swing *was* the most danceable music around, and they would recall the late 1930s and early 1940s as a golden age. Welk and Lombardo were not the only bandleaders who survived professionally into the 1960s, and if Duke Ellington and Count Basie were playing more concerts and festivals and making their best money on the coasts, they also continued to draw dance crowds in the middle of the country. But the swing years marked the beginning of a trend that continued for the next three decades, in which—at least for white fans—dance music would become less and less closely linked to actual dancing. The jitterbugs who yelled and twitched to Krupa's drum solos were direct ancestors of rock's headbangers, and the teenagers who screamed through Beatles shows were following a trail blazed by those who made "so much deafening noise... that one had to strain to hear the subtle passages" at Goodman concerts.[32]

So in some ways swing was already sowing the seeds of the rock 'n' roll revolution. A lot of white jitterbugs were trying not only to dance like black dancers but also to dress like them, to use their slang, and even, in some cases, to hang out with them socially, and Lionel Hampton's "Flying Home," Tommy Dorsey's "Boogie Woogie," and countless Basie hits were setting patterns that would be imitated and emulated by everyone from Bill Haley to James Brown. There were obviously plenty of differences as well, but I can't resist ending this chapter with a lyric recorded in 1937 by a young Ella Fitzgerald with Chick Webb's Savoy Ballroom orchestra:

It came to town, a new kind of rhythm,
Spread around, sort of set you sizzlin'
Now I'm all through with symphony,
Oh, rock it for me....
It's true that once upon a time, the opera was the thing.
But today the rage is rhythm and rhyme,
So won't you satisfy my soul with that rock and roll![33]

And just to stretch this analogy to the breaking point, in 1939 Irene Castle devised a new dance that she felt could be a more graceful alternative to the jitterbug. Its name: the Castle Rock and Roll.[34]

10

TECHNOLOGY AND ITS DISCONTENTS

We are just cutting our own throats with this record business. In New York music comes out of the walls and ceiling all over town, but you never see a live musician.... We are scabbing on ourselves.

JAMES CAESAR PETRILLO, 1942

In the summer of 1941, a reviewer for *Metronome* caught a morning show by Vaughn Monroe at New York's Paramount Theater. Monroe was one of the popular vocal stars of the moment, an operatic baritone and romantic heartthrob who had topped the charts in 1940 with "There I Go" and would be remembered in later years for his hit versions of "Let It Snow, Let It Snow" and "Ghost Riders in the Sky." That is to say, we remember Monroe for his records—so it is interesting to find the reviewer mocking him for presenting himself as a recording artist:

> Vaughn let the lads and lassies know that he knew that their great acquaintance with his band came from records, so he confined the bulk of his show to his diskings, starting off with "Salud, Dinero y Amor." ... [He sang] another record arrangement, "There'll Be Some Changes Made." ... Vaughn didn't make any bones about the origin of "The Donkey Serenade," which he next sung and the band next played. "Our record of it, you know." The kids know.[1]

Within another couple of years no one would find it strange for performers to assume that their audiences were familiar with their records, and in the following decades it became standard for concerts by pop stars to consist largely of recapitulations of their recorded hits. At the dawn of the 1940s, though, this was still quite a new idea. Records had largely lost out to radio in the later 1920s, and what remained of the market had been crushed by the Depression. But the years after repeal brought the rise of the jukebox and the disc jockey, and in 1941 the music business was in the midst of a dispute between radio networks and publishers that made records more important than ever as a way of popularizing hits. These developments hastened a transition that was probably inevitable: Once a high-quality, permanent record of a performance could be made, it was natural that people would come to think of it as the definitive version of that performance.

For older audiences, the idea that a live performer would essentially go onstage as the touring version of his or her recordings was pretty strange, but younger fans took it for granted. So musicians now had a new responsibility: not only to play as well as they could and entertain the audience, but also to fulfill the expectations of fans who often knew their records better than they did. "One of the problems we had when the records became popular was that the guys wouldn't learn to play the same solo," recalled Sy Oliver, one of the key arrangers for the Jimmy Lunceford Orchestra. "We'd get in a dancehall where everybody knew all the solos on the records, and when they started playing something different, the people would be disappointed."[2] Because the particular solo that ended up on a record was often just one of several played at a session—not to mention all the versions that might have been improvised at live shows—when a record became a hit the musicians had to sit down with it and learn the variations they had happened to play that one time, often months in the past. Buddy DeFranco complained that his clarinet solo on the released take of Tommy Dorsey's "Opus #1" (a Sy Oliver composition) became a burden after Dorsey insisted that he play it exactly the same way every time they did the song, which sometimes meant several times a night. To him it was just the way he had played the piece on one occasion, but to fans who had fallen in love with the record it was the only one.[3]

The growing prominence of records was helped along by the rise of disc jockey programs and also by a drop in prices sparked by the success of the cut-rate Decca label. The main factor, though, seems to have been the newly ubiquitous jukeboxes. A 1940 *Newsweek* feature on Glenn Miller was headlined "King of the Jook Box," and the trade press of the time was full of discussions of hits—Artie Shaw's "Begin the Beguine" in 1938 and Will Glahé's "Beer Barrel Polka" the following year tended to be cited as pioneering examples—that had been made by jukebox rather than radio play.

Jukeboxes, per se, were nothing new; the first phonographs to attract any attention had been coin-operated nickelodeons. But those could play only a single record and could be listened to only through earphones. The technology improved significantly through the 'teens and '20s, but by that time the record market had shifted to home Victrolas. So it was only with repeal that the modern jukebox came into its own. The new machines had loud, clear electronic amplification and could hold twenty or more records, play both sides of each, and allow customers to choose multiple songs at a time. In 1933 there were some 20,000 to 25,000 of them spread across the United States; by the end of the decade there were 350,000 to 400,000.[4] Even more striking than those numbers is the extent to which they dominated the record market: By 1940, it was regularly estimated that nearly half of all the records sold in the United States went to supplying jukeboxes, and some tallies ran as high as 60 percent.

Though they were found in restaurants, soda fountains, and even beauty parlors, jukeboxes were particularly associated with the thousands of bars that had replaced the Prohibition-era speakeasies. The word "juke" (or "jook"—oral culture is not fussy about orthography) was Southern slang for a working-class tavern or dance venue. The music machine industry thought the word made their products sound vulgar, and they fought against its use throughout the 1940s, but most listeners were apparently happy with the association. Before Prohibition, pianos had been the standard barroom musical furniture, but the new establishments tended to get jukeboxes instead. From the clients' point of view, the machines could play a much broader range of music—a polka band following a sweet orchestra following a jump blues combo—performed by the biggest stars. For bar owners, the coin-operated machines had still greater advantages. Back in the days of mechanical player pianos, advertising fliers had already pointed out that a music machine "never gets tired, doesn't belong to the union, works overtime without extra pay, never gets sulky or dopey, has no bad habits and is always 'fit' and ready for business."[5] Not only that, but whereas bands had to be paid, jukeboxes paid the bar owner to give them space.

Pianos had at least required an initial investment, but jukeboxes were owned by "operators" who placed them in bars and other venues at no cost to the proprietors, paid those proprietors a percentage of the profits, and took full responsibility for keeping the boxes in good working order and stocked with the latest records. A typical operator owned over a hundred machines, bought records in bulk, and kept close tabs on which songs were pulling in the nickels, changing a couple of selections a week at each location. As a result, the machines functioned like tiny radio stations, playing a "Top 40" tailored to the tastes of each neighborhood and clientele. Of course, they differed from radio in a lot of ways—most obviously that customers had to pay a nickel per song—but both critics and bandleaders soon noticed that success on the boxes could translate into local or even national popularity. By 1940, Jimmy Dorsey was remarking that "thanks to the music machines phonograph recordings have become more important to the band leader than the radio."[6]

Meanwhile, the radio was also playing a lot of records, sometimes guided by reports of jukebox trends. The birth of the modern deejay is usually traced to *Make Believe Ballroom*, a New York program that debuted in 1935 with a smooth-talking host named Martin Block. Block had adopted both name and format from a Los Angeles host named Al Jarvis, and the concept reached back to the 1920s: to play records while creating the illusion of a live broadcast. This had been so common on smaller stations that in 1928 the Federal Radio Commission made a rule that any time a recording was played on the air it must be identified as such. Not all stations complied, and in the 1930s both Fred Waring and Paul Whiteman, backed by the newly formed National Association of Performing Artists, went to court to prevent radio[8] play of their discs. Waring was particularly vehement on this point. He was earning over $10,000 a show for his radio broadcasts, and it seemed obvious to him that he would not be able to keep making those wages if broadcasters could buy a dozen of his records for $10 and put on roughly the same program. His solution was to have Victor print "Not licensed for radio broadcast" on his record labels, and in 1935 he brought suit against a Philadelphia station for playing these recordings without permission.

The Pennsylvania Supreme Court upheld Waring's complaint and also accepted the argument that his interpretations of popular songs showed "such novel and artistic creation...[as to] elevate interpretation to the realm of independent works of art."[7] This was a potentially earthshaking decision for the whole field of popular music. Pretty much everyone had accepted that written songs were the basic articles of musical commerce, and standard royalties for performances—whether live or recorded—had been paid only to composers, lyricists, and publishers. The Waring decision seemed to put records on the same level as sheet music and to give performers the same rights as songwriters. This threatened to open a very messy can of worms, because in a band made up of a dozen or more musicians plus an arranger it would be virtually impossible to sort out who was making what original contribution—a matter Waring prepared for by incorporating his orchestra, thus making anything it did his property. But it was not to be. Whiteman's similar suit lost in the New York court, leaving the Waring decision valid only in Pennsylvania, and that particular line of attack was soon abandoned. Waring kept up his personal fight by ceasing to make any recordings (he relented only in the 1940s), but most bandleaders came around to the idea that radio play would help them more than it hurt.

Other people in the music business were less sanguine, and the later 1930s and 1940s were marked by dozens of legal proceedings, labor actions, and legislative bills designed to rescue income and job security for musicians and composers threatened by the success of jukeboxes and deejays. In retrospect, most historians have set these actions on a par with King Canute's attempt to hold back the ocean tides, and many have even argued that they hurt exactly the artists and interests they were meant to protect, but at the time they reflected a real sense of desperation.[8] Tens of thousands of musicians and songwriters had seen their livelihoods shrink or disappear over the previous two decades, wiped out by successive new technologies—records, sound films, radio, and coin machines—as well as by Prohibition and the Depression. Census figures give a rough idea of the situation: From 1910 to 1940, the population of the United States grew by 43 percent, but the number of professional musicians, singers, and music teachers fell by 7 percent— and that decline does not take into account all the people who still considered themselves musicians but could not find work. A survey in 1933 found that of fifteen thousand musicians registered with the union in New York, twelve thousand were currently unemployed.[9]

The struggle to preserve some kind of livelihood for music makers was led by two main organizations: the American Society of Composers, Authors and Publishers (ASCAP) and the American Federation of Musicians (AFM). These groups were in quite different positions, with different goals and challenges, but both were acutely conscious that although the music business was expanding at a ferocious pace, their members were not necessarily gaining in the process. For example, record sales were skyrocketing, but the composing and publishing royalties received for each record were less than a tenth of what was earned from a printed sheet of music. And in an uncertain legal market, even more drastic changes were looming. One implication of the Waring decision was that a musician who preserved his or her ideas on records might be considered a new kind of composer and that record companies might take over the role of publishers, forcing a complete overhaul of the existing systems for tabulating and distributing royalties. As it happened, there was enough precedent on ASCAP's side to protect them from that particular threat, but they had plenty of reason to be nervous. Jukeboxes, for example, paid no royalties whatsoever—bar owners who hired bands or played records for their customers had to pay a set fee for the public performance of ASCAP tunes, but, in a holdover from nickelodeon times, the law considered each person who put a nickel in a jukebox to be playing a song for his or her personal entertainment, so it did not count as a public performance.

Radio broadcasters did pay for the use of ASCAP material, at least on live broadcasts, but those fees could not make up for all the income being lost with plummeting sheet music sales. In 1932, the Society protested that "not long ago a man who wrote a hit song could not only buy that house in the country but all that went with it.... Now a man who writes a hit song is lucky if he gets his last year's overcoat out of hock with the proceeds."[10] By the end of the decade, matters had come to a head. ASCAP presented a contract to the major networks asking for a higher royalty rate of 7½ percent on all commercial advertising revenue and also for these royalties to be paid directly by the networks rather than having to be collected from the myriad local affiliates. The networks responded by forming a parallel organization, Broadcast Music, Incorporated (BMI), and announcing that as of December 31, 1940, they would cease to use any ASCAP material.

ASCAP was not particularly worried. The Society represented some 1,450 songwriters and 138 publishers and controlled a catalog of over 1,250,000 songs, including virtually all the important hits and hitmakers of the previous four decades. In 1932 its president, Gene Buck, had responded to a similar threat by saying "All right.... Give the public 'Nellie Gray' and 'The Little Brown Jug.' If you quit broadcasting our music, maybe the public will open the parlor piano. Maybe we can sell a little sheet music again."[11]

The networks felt similarly secure. Not only could they fall back on old, out-of-copyright favorites such as Stephen Foster's melodies and the songs Buck mentioned—as it happened, one of Glenn Miller's biggest hits of 1939 was a revival of "Little Brown Jug"—but they had already signed up a couple of major publishers who were disgruntled with ASCAP: Edward B. Marks, one of the deans of Tin Pan Alley, and Ralph Peer's Southern Music, which among other things had the U.S. rights to pretty much every song published in Latin America. They could also count on new songwriters to leap into the breach, spurred by the opportunity to be recorded by bands and singers desperate for radio-friendly material.

The ASCAP ban was big news in the industry, but, judging by surviving press reports, most radio listeners barely noticed it. A couple of particularly hit-oriented programs—notably *Your Hit Parade*—lost some listeners, but overall the struggle excited relatively little comment. Nor did it last all that long: The Mutual Broadcasting Network settled with ASCAP in May, and by late October NBC, CBS, and most local affiliates had signed new contracts. The Society accepted a much lower royalty rate than it had wanted ($2\frac{1}{4}$–$2\frac{3}{4}$ percent), while the networks agreed to be responsible for making the payments. Nonetheless, the ban had some far-reaching consequences: For almost a year, two of the main radio networks that blanketed the United States had been unable to play most of the pop repertoire that had been built up over the previous forty years or songs published by most of the established companies. This was a boon for Latin bands—Xavier Cugat became the new host of *Camel Caravan*—and also pushed non-Latin artists to explore more exotic tunes: Jimmy Dorsey topped the charts with four south-of-the-border items, "Amapola," "Maria Elena," "Green Eyes (*Aquellos Ojos Verdes*)," and "Yours (*Quiéreme Mucho*)," and Artie Shaw's Mexican medley "Frenesí," which had been on and off the record charts since the pre-ban summer of 1940, shot to the top of the *Hit Parade* countdown. Other bandleaders wandered still further afield, Glenn Miller getting one of the biggest hits of the year with the Russian "Song of the Volga Boatmen" and Freddy Martin, Horace Heidt, and the King Sisters going head-to-head with a nutty Swedish novelty, "The Hut-Sut Song." Martin also topped the charts with Tchaikovsky's *Piano Concerto in B Flat* (which reappeared with lyrics a few months later as "Tonight We Love"), and Guy Lombardo matched him with "Intermezzo (*Souvenir de Vienne*)." Meanwhile, the ban produced some rather odd side effects: For the first time, sports announcers were isolated in soundproof booths, for fear that the bands at college games might play an ASCAP tune and subject the broadcaster to fines; and the networks banned all improvising in jazz performances, lest a solo inadvertently quote a snatch of forbidden melody.[12]

The clear winners in the ASCAP fight were neither the Society nor the networks but BMI and the jukebox industry. BMI shortly became independent of the radio czars who had established it—antimonopoly laws made that imperative—and it has been ASCAP's main competition ever since. It changed the industry somewhat by accepting hillbilly and blues songwriters whom ASCAP had disdained and by collecting royalties not only on live broadcasts but also on deejay programs, which

ASCAP would not do until the 1950s.[13] On the whole, though, the main thing the ban proved was that songwriting and publishing were not really threatened by new technologies; they just needed to iron out the fine points of royalty payments, then could continue business more or less as usual.

Musicians were in a very different position. Major headliners like Whiteman and Bing Crosby could insist on contracts that gave them royalty payments for their recordings, and thus could make their peace with changing technologies much as the songwriters did. But most musicians had never gotten royalties and never would. They were not in the business of producing "novel and artistic creations"; they were playing second violin in a hotel, theater, or radio orchestra or working in a polka band or in the pool of journeymen who performed at local parties, picnics, and parades in Omaha or Atlanta or some midsize town in Maine or New Mexico. Not only did they not have much in common with the hit songwriters and name bandleaders but most of them did not even have much in common with the anonymous sidemen in the touring dance orchestras. They were local service professionals, accustomed to working fairly regular hours, getting fairly regular paychecks, teaching some students on the side, and going home to their families every night. By 1934, thanks to Prohibition, sound movies, and the Depression, half the musicians who had been lucky enough to have full-time employment were out of work.[14] Of the jobs that remained, many were at radio stations or in bars and nightclubs, and with deejay shows and jukeboxes, those seemed likely to disappear as well in the near future. So the journeymen had good reason to worry, and, because they were the core constituency of the AFM, the union's actions have to be understood in that context. It was not primarily fighting for a better deal for people like Goodman, Lombardo, or even the men in their bands; it was fighting for the basic survival of people threatened by the fact that when their neighbors wanted to listen or dance to the latest hits, those neighbors were now listening and dancing to recordings of Goodman and Lombardo.

Of course, musicians were not unique in this respect. Throughout the industrial age people have lost their jobs to new technologies. So the AFM at first fought back with the tactics being used in other industries: Through threats of strikes and other direct action, it forced theaters and radio stations to keep a minimum number of musicians on their payrolls, and in some areas it managed to get wages for union "standby" players even when recorded or remote broadcasts provided the actual music. Chicago's Local 10 won particularly strong protections, forcing stations that played records to hire union musicians as "platter-turners," to pay an equal number of local standbys whenever they broadcast music from elsewhere, and to destroy any records they used after a single play.[15]

The president of Local 10 was James Caesar Petrillo, and these victories helped to make him the most popular and powerful figure in the AFM. As a result, when the Federation's president, Joseph Weber, retired in 1940, Petrillo was unanimously chosen as his replacement. Petrillo was acutely conscious of the challenges his constituency faced, but he was also convinced that it had a unique power. When weavers had been thrown out of work by textile mills, the cloth had been produced without their labor—just as icemen, to cite a favorite Petrillo example, were not needed to build refrigerators—but the records that were replacing live music could not be made without musicians. In his words, "the living musician must be consulted and his services utilized … or else the machine will be silent."[16]

In 1937, Petrillo put this theory into practice in Chicago, imposing a restriction on all recording for a year. In 1942, he applied the same tactic nationally, declaring that as of August 1 no union musician would play on any kind of recording, whether for public sale or broadcast. He admitted that this was a drastic move but noted that there were virtually no musicians who derived the majority of their income from records, and in any case he saw no other choice. As he told the Federal Communications Commission, which was considering whether his tactic could be construed as an illegal "secondary boycott"—that is, a boycott imposed on the record companies but in fact intended to wrest concessions from radio networks—his constituency felt assaulted from every side. "Ninety-five percent of the music in the United States and Canada is canned music. Only five percent is left for the poor professional musician who studied all his life so that he might make a living for his family. This is … a question of a large group of men fighting for their very existence."[17]

The response from Petrillo's opponents just confirmed the accuracy of this statement. Neville Miller, president of the National Association of Broadcasters, in an affidavit arguing that the AFM was indeed violating antitrust laws, pointed out that "before the phonograph record, only persons who could pay to go to the large concert halls in the large cities could hear the great symphony orchestras, and only the persons who could afford to go to fashionable restaurants and hotels could hear the best dance orchestras.… [The AFM] cannot expect the American public to stop listening to the artists whom they have learned to enjoy, and listen to the small aggregations of part-time non-professional musicians who are available for employment in the small communities."[18]

Plenty of full-time professional musicians were losing their livelihoods along with the semiamateurs Miller deprecated, but essentially his description of the situation matched Petrillo's. What the AFM was fighting for was indeed that people be forced to hire local musicians rather than throwing them over for canned importations, good as the canned produce might be. At first, Petrillo did not even provide a basis for negotiations, but simply said that no more recordings would be made. This was at least in part a cagey tactic based on antitrust laws and on wartime wage and price controls that would have made it illegal to give new royalties to recording artists. When he did come up with terms, though, they reflected not only a clever end-run around the legislative obstacles but also a keen sense of his broader constituency: Rather than asking the record companies to pay a standard royalty to the relatively small group of musicians who had recording careers, he asked that they pay those royalties into a fund that would sponsor union musicians all over the country to give concerts in their own communities. Petrillo was no angel, and recording artists would charge that this tactic hurt their incomes and provided him with a slush fund that he could use to reward his cronies, but in the context of the moment it provided both good public relations and a neat path through the legal thicket.

Although Petrillo had to claim otherwise for legal reasons, the recording strike was unquestionably aimed at radio broadcasters at least as much as at record companies. An FCC survey in 1942 showed that, although music programs accounted for three-quarters of broadcast time on network-affiliated stations, more than half of those programs used prerecorded music—either from commercial records or special transcriptions—and that the proportion went up to four-fifths for programs on unaffiliated stations.[19] Two of the three major record companies, Columbia and RCA Victor, were connected to broadcasting corporations and displayed no dismay at those numbers, but Decca had no broadcasting wing and found the situation as irritating as Petrillo did. Indeed, in 1940 Decca's Jack Kapp had imposed his own ban on radio play, arguing that the growing popularity of deejay shows was hurting sales because they allowed people to hear the latest releases for free, and *Billboard* suggested that this ban was responsible for Glahé's original version of "Beer Barrel Polka" outselling the Decca cover by the Andrews Sisters. When it came to jukeboxes, though, Kapp and the musicians diverged: Decca had captured a disproportionate share of the jukebox market on its arrival in 1934, thanks to its practice of issuing 35-cent discs of top stars such as Crosby and Lombardo when other companies were reserving their low-priced lines for Race, hillbilly, and no-name acts, and by 1940 the company accounted for some two-thirds of all jukebox offerings.[20] By contrast, the AFM estimated that by the early 1940s jukeboxes had cost their members at least eight thousand jobs.[21]

The AFM recording ban dragged on for more than two years, in part because of the stubbornness of all parties concerned but also because it overlapped the peak years of World War II. As *Billboard* explained, the war had a devastating effect on the whole music business:

> The band biz finds itself reeling.... The draft cut into agency rosters in a way that left gaping holes that couldn't be filled. Many more leaders are expecting to be called to arms. Sidemen to the tune of 10,000 to 15,000 have departed, complicating the problems of remaining maestri. Rationing of gas and rubber has finally struck in a manner that has virtually brought traveling bands to a halt. The dozen-or-so exempt names in a position to mop up everything in sight were brought up short by a $25,000 ceiling on their net earnings.[22]

Female musicians filled some of the jobs the men had left, but aside from a few outstanding outfits (most famously the International Sweethearts of Rhythm), the industry did not regard them as adequate substitutes—the subheading of the quoted *Billboard* piece lamented that "skirts and A.K.'s flop," a flip way of dismissing the women and older musicians (*alte kakers*, Yiddish for "old farts") who tried to pick up the slack. Female string players were an exception, and one result of the wartime situation was that some of the remaining bands added batteries of violins, cellos, and harps. The $25,000 salary cap applied to bandleaders, because they were classified as employees of the establishments where they played rather than as employers, and some concluded that if they couldn't pocket their income they might as well plow it back into their orchestras. The rage for "sweet swing" outfits like Tommy Dorsey's and Glenn Miller's, which were equally at home with hot rhythms and dreamy ballads, had overflowed into classical pastiches during the ASCAP ban, Harry James hitting with "Trumpet Rhapsody" and Artie Shaw with "Concerto for Clarinet." Now Shaw assembled a thirty-two-piece orchestra with thirteen strings and a wind quartet, and when he joined the Navy in 1942 Dorsey took over his strings and added a harp, eventually expanding the section to nineteen members, all of them women. Even Earl Hines, whose most famous wartime orchestra included Charlie Parker and Dizzy Gillespie, fronted a group in 1943 that included women playing violins, cello, and harp, as well as bass and guitar.[23]

Meanwhile, the record companies were facing their own wartime shortage: In April 1942, four months before the AFM ban went into effect, the War Production Board cut the industry's supply of shellac (a vital ingredient in phonograph discs) by 70 percent. As a result, ban or no ban, the companies could not have kept up their standard production of new releases, and that made the AFM's action a good deal less painful for them than it would have been under normal conditions, especially as the manufacture of jukeboxes and radios for civilian use was likewise halted for the duration of the war.

Amidst all this confusion, the ban took a while to show results. Petrillo had given the companies advance notice, and they had worked their most popular artists around the clock in the weeks before it took effect; so for about six months they continued to issue new recordings and it is unlikely that many buyers noticed the difference. By 1943, though, the supply of unreleased masters had dried up and the record companies were looking for alternatives. One obvious move was to dig out older recordings that the public might have missed or forgotten: When *Casablanca* became one of the most popular movies of 1943, Victor topped the charts with Rudy Vallée's twelve-year-old version of "As Time Goes By;" and Columbia had similar success when the release of MGM's *Cabin in the Sky* gave new impetus to Benny Goodman's "Taking a Chance on Love," recorded to capitalize on the show's Broadway run three years earlier. Then someone at Columbia remembered that back in 1939, when Harry James was not yet a major bandleader, he had recorded a song called "All or Nothing At All" featuring a then-unknown singer named Frank Sinatra. Sinatra had recently quit his career-building stint as Tommy Dorsey's male vocalist, and when Columbia reissued the old James recording under his name, it became his first number one hit as a solo artist.

Sinatra's success presented Columbia with a problem: They had the country's hottest new vocalist under contract, but they could not maintain his sales momentum by mining old Harry James recordings—especially since, in February of 1943, he had taken over as the main singer on *Your Hit Parade* and could be heard every Saturday evening performing the top current material. Their solution was to rush him into the studio with a series of choirs—singers were not musicians by AFM standards—to cut a cappella versions of his *Hit Parade* winners: "You'll Never Know," "Sunday, Monday, or Always," and a pair of songs from the new Broadway smash, *Oklahoma!*: "Oh, What a Beautiful Morning" and "People Will Say We're in Love." Decca was doing the same with Bing Crosby: "Sunday, Monday, or Always" came from his new film, *Dixie*, but whereas the movie version featured a full band, his record was accompanied by the Ken Darby Singers, and the Sportsmen Glee Club provided the backing for his versions of the *Oklahoma!* hits. Meanwhile, Dick Haymes, Sinatra's rival for the affections of swooning bobby-soxers, cut the biggest selling version of "You'll Never Know," backed by the Song Spinners. Petrillo was unhappy about these vocal discs and ordered union arrangers not to work on them, as well as getting statements of support from the singers, but they continued to appear through the rest of the year.

Old recordings and choral arrangements were temporary stopgaps, but everyone knew that they would not be enough to keep the phonograph business going, and under normal conditions the labels almost certainly would not have held out as long as they did. Their recalcitrance was encouraged by the legal possibilities of the wartime situation: Strikes had been generally prohibited as harming the war effort, and there were numerous attempts to have the AFM censured and ordered back to work by the courts or the executive branch. Petrillo stood firm through it all, winning the legal battles and countering attacks on the union's patriotism by pointing out that members were playing in Service bands, giving free shows at camps and bases, and recording V-discs—V for Victory—for the troops overseas.

In the end, Decca was the first company to crack. Jack Kapp had always seen himself as a scrappy little guy who could outmaneuver the big corporations, and, unlike RCA and Columbia, he did not have to worry about setting a precedent that might adversely affect a radio empire. So at the end of September 1943 he signed a four-year contract with the AFM, agreeing to pay royalties to the union fund on all records he pressed. Within a month, twenty-two smaller record and transcription companies signed a slightly modified version of the same contract, and over the next year Decca cemented its already strong position against Victor and Columbia: Of the seventeen number-one hits tabulated from *Billboard* for 1944, fifteen were

Decca releases—the only exceptions being Columbia's reissue of a Harry James recording from 1941 and an RCA choral disc featuring Dinah Shore.[24]

Decca was not the only winner. There had been plenty of small labels before the ban, but they had been just local and specialty outfits. Now, with jukebox operators clamoring for product and two of the three majors out of the running for new material, the minor players were in a very different position, and they were quickly joined by a host of new names. Some, such as Cincinnati's King and New York's Apollo, specialized in hillbilly or Race material; others simply waxed cheap versions of current hits for the jukebox market using no-name bands or big-band sidemen. The most prominent newcomer was the Los Angeles–based Capitol Records, formed by a trio of music business pros that included the singer-lyricist Johnny Mercer, which boasted a lineup including Mercer, Nat King Cole, Jo Stafford, and the Pied Pipers (as well as Whiteman with Billie Holiday). Capitol began getting national hits virtually from its first release and would remain a prominent player from then on.

Nonetheless, Columbia and Victor stuck to their guns for another thirteen months. Then the government relaxed controls on shellac, allowing the contract signers to resume full production, and the classical virtuoso Jascha Heifetz switched from Victor to Decca because he was tired of waiting for a settlement. Facing a potential flood of big-name abdications, the two remaining majors gave in and agreed to pay their royalties along with everyone else, and in November 1944 the recording ban was over. There would be another ban in 1948—the original contract ran for only four years—but it was less long, less influential, and ended with the same basic terms.

For Petrillo it had been a victory, and today there are still musicians giving live performances paid for by the AFM's Music Performance Fund.[25] But if the battle had been won, the war was inevitably going to be lost. The kind of generic dance, theater, and radio work that had been the mainstay of working musicians across the country would continue to lose ground to canned substitutes, and, as Petrillo had pointed out at the start, record royalties could not make up for the loss of gigs.

Meanwhile, for the record companies it was back to business as usual: Victor's first new release beat Columbia by a few days, and it was a version of "The Trolley Song" from the new MGM picture *Meet Me in St. Louis*, sung by that unabashed record promoter Vaughn Monroe.

11

WALKING FLOORS AND JUMPIN' JIVE

Bob Wills, who was from Texas and played the fiddle, said to me, "Pee Wee, how in the hell can a Polish boy from Wisconsin play the accordion, write 'The Tennessee Waltz'... and lead the country's most popular western swing band? It just doesn't add up."

I said, "Bob, all you got to do is please the people and sell records."

PEE WEE KING

In some ways the early 1940s was the most mixed-up, disorganized, and exciting period in American popular music. It was a time when Ernest Tubb, a rawboned Texas guitar strummer and bar singer accompanied by a whining electric lead guitar and a bass could hit with a honky-tonk lament called "Walking the Floor Over You" and go head to head with a brassy Dixieland version of the same number by Bing Crosby with the Bob Crosby Orchestra. And Cab Calloway, the sharpest cat in Harlem, could hit with a mess of uptown patois called "Jumpin' Jive" and see it reworked into a cheerily lightweight harmony number by three Greek-Norwegian-American sisters named Andrews.

Bing and the Andrews Sisters, separately and together, waxed a repertoire that touched all the extremes of the era. Crosby had established himself simultaneously as a hip jazz singer and an exemplar of homespun Americana, and he ranged with legendary insouciance from slangy novelties to sentimental cowboy ballads. The Andrewses came on the scene in 1938 with "Bei Mir Bist Du Schoen," an English-language version of a song some Jewish music mavens had heard a black duo sing in Yiddish at Harlem's Apollo Theater, then scored the following year with a cover of an import from Nazi Germany—though the irony was not noted at the time—the "Beer Barrel Polka." A few months after that, they and Crosby collaborated on both an Italian song, "Ciri-biribin," and the bizarrely self-explanatory "Yodelin' Jive." Their biggest record in between was a number called "Hold Tight (I Want Some Seafood Mama)," the first top-ten pop hit about oral sex—the sisters insisted they had no idea, but Fats Waller's gleeful original left no doubt that he was hep—and by 1940 they had also scored with the Russian "Pross-Tchai," the Cuban "Say 'Sí, Sí' (*Para Vigo Me Voy*)," and another of the era's oddball fusions, the "Rhumboogie" (rumba and boogie-woogie).

The main impulse for this peripatetic genre-hopping was the growing importance of records, especially on jukeboxes, but also at parties, in homes, in schools, on army bases, and on the radio. Crosby and the Andrewses were stars in the Decca firmament, and the label's head, Jack Kapp, was an assiduous marketer both to jukeboxes—hence the attempt to touch every ethnic base with perky Andrews harmonies—and to home users through the new medium of albums, which at that point were often thematic collections such as Crosby's sets of cowboy and Hawaiian numbers. Crosby had one of the most popular music-centered shows on radio, but records gave him a chance to address niche audiences in a way that a national radio broadcast could not. Meanwhile, barroom music machines leveled the playing field to a point where Tubb's and Calloway's recordings were more popular than the Crosby and Andrews covers, something that would never have been possible in the days when live radio performances were the motivating force behind the national pop scene.

The ASCAP-BMI and AFM battles, the shellac shortage, and the dislocations and population shifts of World War II all had roles in breaking up the big dance orchestras' dominance of popular music, but most of the records I just mentioned were made in the last couple of years of the 1930s, so the trend was under way before any of those events became factors. Nonetheless, the musical shifts were immeasurably accelerated by the battles at home and abroad. One result of the war was the most drastic internal population shift in American history, first with the mobilization of millions of men and women into the armed forces, but more important with the permanent transfer of a huge proportion of the civilian labor force from rural areas, mostly in the South, to cities—Los Angeles, Oakland, Chicago, Detroit, Cleveland, Baltimore—that had wartime industries. Not only did many millions of people move to new areas, but the overwhelming majority of them were young and got relatively decent-paying jobs, which meant that they were open to new musical styles and had the money to make their tastes count.

This young audience fueled two apparently opposite trends: one for rural and ethnic styles, such as hillbilly and polka, and the other for African-American hipster jive, blues, and boogie-woogie. In musical and cultural terms these styles were poles apart, but a lot of people enjoyed both, and it makes sense to see them as flip sides of the same coin. The young dancers and record buyers arriving in the cities wanted to hear sounds that connected them with the homes they had left behind, and also to celebrate their new social and economic freedom. Hence titles like "Yodelin' Jive" and Spade Cooley's "Jive on the Range"—not a major hit, but a phrase that neatly conjures up the odd hybrid known as Western Swing.

The labor struggles and shellac shortage provided new opportunities for nonmainstream artists to reach these young listeners. The ASCAP-BMI fight encouraged radio programmers to use hillbilly and cowboy—and to a lesser extent African-American—material, and more enduringly BMI gave songwriters in these previously disrespected fields a new reason to keep at it, providing them with royalties and access to mainstream stars. The AFM ban helped to cement these gains. For one thing, jukebox operators found that hillbilly records not only did well in a lot of regions in which they had not expected such success but also had a much longer life than pop hits. Mournful barroom ballads like Ted Daffan's "Born to Lose" kept earning nickels for months at a time and could even be removed from a box and successfully reinstated a year or two later. At a time when new records were at a premium, this made the hillbilly hits doubly valuable.

Despite rumors to the contrary, virtually no hillbilly or Race artists were recorded in defiance of the ban, but like the mainstream stars many of them had laid in a backlog of recordings that were slowly released over the dry span. For example, Al Dexter, a Texas-born, Los Angeles–based honky-tonk singer, had cut a song called "Pistol Packin' Mama" that became a sensational hit on jukeboxes all across the country when it was released early in 1943. In normal times, Dexter's record might never have reached beyond the Southern audience that typically pitched its nickels to play hillbilly tracks, as it would have been competing with a stronger field of mainstream pop hits and, if it had broken into the broader market, would instantly have been covered by a half-dozen pop vocalists. In 1943, though, Dexter had the song to himself—at least on records—from the time it entered the national charts in June until Decca signed the AFM contract in September. The first new disc Decca waxed was a cover of "PPM" (by then the trade press just used the song's initials) by Crosby and the Andrews Sisters, and by the beginning of 1944 their version was outselling Dexter's even in places like Fort Worth. In the interim, though, he had established himself as a national star, and four of the twelve records that reached number one on *Billboard*'s new "Most Played Juke Box Folk Records" chart in the next year were his. (Within the industry, "folk" was the preferred term at this point for everything from Appalachian fiddle tunes to Western Swing and sometimes even blues and boogie-woogie. A lot of people considered "hillbilly"— which was far more commonly used—to be an insult, and the more descriptive and value-neutral "country and western" did not catch on until *Billboard* adopted it as a chart heading in 1949.)

"Pistol Packin' Mama" was a new kind of hillbilly hit. Pretty much the only rural-flavored songs that had traveled out of the South before that point—minstrelsy aside—had been sentimental paeans to cowboy life such as "The Last Round-Up," a major hit of 1933 that was recorded by everyone from Gene Autry to Crosby and the Royal Canadians. Thanks to a string of singing-cowboy movies, Autry was by far the best-known specialist in this kind of material, and he had established himself as a national archetype of prairie virtue. Dexter, by contrast, came across as a wry honky-tonk hell-raiser—his "Honky Tonk Blues" in 1936 was the first country record to capitalize on that term—and his song was an earthy, three-chord melodrama of cheating and booze: "Drinkin' beer in a cabaret and was I havin' fun / Until one night she caught me right and now I'm on the run. / Lay that pistol down, babe...." This was not to everyone's taste, and *Your Hit Parade*, which supposedly showcased each week's ten most popular songs, refused to include "PPM" until the publisher took the producers to court. *Life* magazine speculated that the censorship order might have come either from the show's notoriously conservative sponsor—American Tobacco Company president George Washington Hill, who also objected to jazz improvisation—or from Frank Sinatra, the program's reigning star. Sinatra was notoriously contemptuous of hillbilly music, but if he was the motivating force in this case, the punishment fit the crime: After "PPM" was added to the *Hit Parade* lineup in October 1943, he had to sing it on fourteen subsequent episodes.[1]

Aside from its lyric, there was another odd thing about Dexter's disc: Although it was classified as a hillbilly record, its only instrumental solos were on trumpet and accordion. Like the electric guitar, a new invention that had made only rare appearances on record before the honky-tonkers and Western bands made it ubiquitous, these were not typical instruments in hillside cabins or on the open range, but they were common in small barroom combos, in which their volume made up for the lack of a larger ensemble. This is an important thing to understand about the rurally identified styles that nudged their way into the mainstream in this period: They reminded recently arrived urbanites of home, but were not the sort of old-time music that their parents had heard or that Uncle Dave Macon and Roy Acuff were playing on the Grand Ole Opry. Acuff, a staunch traditionalist who never used electric instruments, accordion, or drums, may have been the most popular singer in the hillbilly field—Hank Williams said that "for drawing power in the South, it was Roy Acuff, then God," and even outside his core region he set a record of 11,130 listeners at a 1944 Los Angeles ballroom appearance[2]—but his style never reached beyond that market, nor were his songs much covered by mainstream artists.

That's where the accordion came into play: The instrument can be heard on two-thirds of the hillbilly records that reached the top of the *Billboard* folk chart in the mid-1940s—and of the remaining third, half were Western Swing hits by Bob Wills and the Texas Playboys, whose horn section and piano gave them an obvious crossover appeal.[3] Like the swing arrangements, the accordion provided a bridge to a broader audience: not the pop mainstream but all the listeners who had grown up around ethnic waltz and polka bands. This may seem an odd connection, but when the *Los Angeles Times* did a feature piece on the hillbilly music boom in 1940, it singled out "Beer Barrel Polka" as the biggest hit in the genre—and, as it happened, Will Glahé's German recording featured both an accordion and an electric steel guitar, the most distinctive instrument of the Western bands.[4]

This connection did not escape Dexter, who cut a "Guitar Polka" that was one of the biggest country hits of 1946, nor Elton Britt, another of the top Texan honky-tonkers, who did a "Yodel Polka." Spade Cooley, Bob Wills's main rival as King of Western Swing, also recorded a "Yodellin' Polka" and often featured not one but two accordions in his big band (as well as a harp), and the Kentucky singer Red Foley made the top of the folk chart in a collaboration with Lawrence Welk, the ultimate purveyor of polka to the pop mainstream. The clearest beneficiary of this trend was Pee Wee King, a Polish accordionist from Milwaukee, Wisconsin, whose original name was Frank Kuczynski. King left Milwaukee in 1934 to work with Autry and, after forming his own band, the Golden West Cowboys, hired a young singer named Eddy Arnold, who would become the dominant voice of the Nashville mainstream from the mid-1940s through the 1960s. King is best remembered as the coauthor and original performer of "Tennessee Waltz," which he followed with "Tennessee Polka," a hit for both him and Foley in 1949.

This may seem like a peculiar digression, but country and western styles would remain an influential part of the American popular music mainstream into the 1970s and beyond, and their appeal was based on a contrasting blend of myth and reality. The myth was of a rural, hardworking, Anglo-Saxon past in which Appalachian mountain folk and cowboys had preserved a British ballad tradition while carving a new life out of the frontier. This was a comforting and inspiring image, perfectly suited to a nation mobilizing to send its young men abroad to fight the forces of evil, and country songwriters understood their role. The biggest hillbilly hit in the year before "Pistol Packin' Mama" was Britt's "There's a Star-Spangled Banner Waving Somewhere," and critics in this period regularly noted that though Tin Pan Alley had provided the soundtrack to World War I, the current demand for patriotic numbers was being met by Southern troubadours. The sacrifices of war were eulogized in Tubb's "Soldier's Last Letter" and Wills's "White Cross on Okinawa," and its passions were stoked with Wills's "Stars and Stripes on Iwo Jima" and the immensely popular "Smoke on the Water," recorded by both Foley and Wills, which was patriotic to the point of genocide: "There'll be nothing left but vultures to inhabit all that land / When our modern ships and bombers make a graveyard of Japan."

If the new folk hits conjured images of an all-American heartland of "singing cowboys and musical mountaineers"—to quote the title of Bill C. Malone's exploration of this mythology[5]—they also reflected the more complex realities of rural settlement. The Appalachians had been settled by German as well as Scots-Irish immigrants, and the plains and prairies west of the Mississippi were full of Central Europeans and Scandinavians. The evolving music of the cattle ranges, whether sung in English or Spanish, routinely fell into waltz or polka time, and the French and Italian populations spread around the hill and farming regions also used accordions and many of the same rhythms. These people had been listening to each other and adopting other musical fashions, from the sentimental ditties of Tin Pan Alley to minstrel comedy, Alpine yodeling, and Hawaiian guitars. The Western

Swing bandleader Adolph Hofner grew up in Texas speaking Czech and continued to record in that language throughout his career, modeled his vocal style on Bing Crosby's, started out playing ukulele in a Hawaiian trio, and got his first hit with the Spanish "Maria Elena." All of which is to say that from its inception country and western was as mongrelized a style as any on earth, and the breadth of its influences had a lot to do with the breadth of its appeal. It was no accident that accordion-flavored bands and mellow crooners were the biggest sellers on the folk charts: Eddy Arnold and Lawrence Welk shared a largely overlapping audience, and that overlap kept both artists at the top of the entertainment business long after most of their early peers had vanished.

I have no space here to give even a capsule history of country music and am only trying to provide some sense of how it intersected and influenced the pop mainstream and to point out that one of the keys to its appeal was that it drew on just as varied and changing a hodgepodge of influences as the more overtly urban styles did. Autry came to New York not to be a cowboy singer but to follow in the footsteps of crooners like Rudy Vallée and Gene Austin, even adopting a new first name in emulation of the latter.[6] And though the national press tended to portray Western Swing as a hillbilly style with jazz influences, the people who played it tended to consider themselves jazz musicians with a sideline in fiddle tunes. Most of the English-speaking population of the Southwest had arrived relatively recently and did not have any deep regional traditions. Cooley, born in Oklahoma and one-quarter Cherokee, got his start in music by playing classical cello in the orchestra of the Chemawa Indian School in Oregon.[7] Drew Page, another Oklahoman who went on to play saxophone with Harry James—himself a musical product of Beaumont, Texas—left home in response to an ad in *Billboard* for oil-field workers who could double as band musicians.[8] The Western Swing players might wear cowboy hats for publicity purposes, but essentially they were dance band professionals satisfying the varied musical tastes of their particular region. And with the influx of war workers from Texas, Oklahoma, New Mexico, Arkansas, and Louisiana, even swing bands that had no cowboy associations had to pick up some of that repertoire. A 1943 *Billboard* article headlined "Coast Orks Go 'Billy" reported that with the influx of Southern immigrants to Los Angeles, "dance bands, as a result, are being forced to insert in their books hillbilly, mountain music and to some extent race ballads to comply with requests of dancers." The bands it referred to were not Cooley's or Dexter's—although both were Los Angeles ballroom fixtures—but Woody Herman's swing outfit, Freddy Martin's society orchestra, and the Casa Loma crew.[9]

As for that reference to "race ballads," a glance at the repertoires of the Western Swing and honky-tonk stars shows numerous songs learned from the records of blues-oriented singer-guitarists like Kokomo Arnold and Memphis Minnie, who until then had rarely been covered by white hitmakers. With hindsight it is easy to link these borrowings to the later hillbilly-blues fusions of Elvis Presley and his peers, but at the time—and indeed in Presley's day as well—they were a common aspect of rural taste. White and black Southerners had been trading tunes for centuries, the European fiddle blending with the African banjo, and artists like Arnold and Minnie always sold to a lot of the same people who loved Tubb and Jimmie Rodgers. One result of this overlap was that the same period that saw a growing interest in hillbilly styles brought a rise in blues recordings by everyone from Herman's orchestra (known as "The Band That Plays the Blues") and Dinah Shore (whose defining hit was "Blues in the Night") to the electric guitar pioneer T-Bone Walker, the smooth Nat King Cole, and the ebullient Louis Jordan.

The swing craze fundamentally reshaped white America's relationship to black music. Swing hit as an interracial style, in which black and white musicians, though they generally worked in separate bands, were seen as part of a single movement, jamming together, wearing the same kinds of clothes, and using the same slang. This inspired a generation of white fans to think of themselves as members of a sort of insiders' club, taking Harlem fashions as their guide not only for music and dance but for clothing, language, and attitude. By 1938 this club had become so visible that the generally staid *New York Times* published a guide to hep terminology and even signaled its awareness that such guides were by their nature "unhep," noting that its lexicon was "offered with the admonition that one-quarter of the swing-lingo rolled naturally from the tongue of the Negro swing musician, that the rest is the lucubration of press agents, and that all of it is used only by the ickie." ("Ickie" was defined as "One whose enthusiasm for swing is exceeded only by his ignorance of it.")[10]

The war years saw the ranks of aspiring hepcats—ickie or not—spread beyond the confines of the jazz world. On radio and in films, it became common to hear established stars like George Burns and Gracie Allen trying out phrases like "Gimme some skin, Jack. Lock it, sock it, and put it in your pocket."[11] For the first time, Americans of all backgrounds and skin tints adopted black fashions as the sine qua non of urban modernity. The Andrews Sisters' oeuvre shows how mainstream jive had become. Unlike their models, the Boswell Sisters, whose New Orleans roots and phenomenal sense of time and phrasing made them the most innovative harmony group in jazz, the Andrewses had little if any connection to the improvisatory, musically challenging aspects of swing. Their hot inspiration was Glenn Miller, whose orchestra swung like a well-oiled and precisely calibrated machine, and unlike the Boswells they could never have been mistaken for a black group. And yet, in a 1941 Abbott and Costello comedy called *In the Navy*, the bumbling stars wander into a dance hall just in time to catch the Sisters slapping each other five as they sing, "If you want to shake my hand like they do it in Harlem / Stick your hand right out and shout, 'Gimme some skin, my friend.'" Three years later, when Bing and the Sisters topped the charts with "There'll Be a Hot Time in the Town of Berlin," they were still on the same kick, singing, "They're gonna take a hike through

Hitler's Reich / And change the '*heil*' to 'gimme some skin.'" Nor was that phrase an isolated example, though it seems to have cropped up a lot in this paragraph. The sisters made a subspecialty of jive numbers, and in 1944 had jukebox hits covering both Louis Jordan's "Is You Is or Is You Ain't (Ma Baby)?" and the King Cole Trio's "Straighten Up and Fly Right."

This was not just a new kind of minstrelsy; the white hipsters were emulating black people rather than mocking them. But neither was it necessarily a sign of racial harmony. Swing was certainly a factor in the racial integration of American culture, but most white swing fans, despite their expertise in Harlem slang, rarely found themselves in close proximity to any black people, nor did they necessarily want to. Swing dances by and large remained segregated: Some bands routinely booked two dates back to back at key venues, playing a white night and a black night, and if both races were admitted to the same show, there would be separate seating areas and a rope down the middle of the dance floor to prevent any mixing. (In some regions there were further complications with Latino and Native American dancers, but these are less well documented.) Even when there was mixing, no one could ignore the racial power relationship: The more daring white fans might attend black dances or slip under the ropes to dance on the black side at mixed events, but black fans did not have the same freedom to visit white territory.

The war created further mixing, and with it some further complications. A lot of people found themselves meeting members of another race at close quarters for the first time in army camps and wartime industrial jobs, and in some cases their minds were broadened by the experience. But the idea of black men being armed and sent abroad to shoot at white men—not to mention possibly sleeping with white women—brought extreme reactions from white racists. The fact that the Nazis were notorious for their racist ideology made the hypocrisy of American racism easier to confront and harder to defend, but that didn't keep the enemies of race-mixing from doing their damnedest. The Savoy Ballroom, long a haven not only for black dancers but also for daring white swing aficionados, was closed by a New York police commissioner in 1943, supposedly because some servicemen had caught venereal diseases from prostitutes they met there—but the same commissioner had previously demanded a crackdown on mixed dancing and forbidden the club to hire white bands or advertise in white newspapers.[12] The same year, authorities in Little Rock, Arkansas, temporarily banned all black dances after a near riot at a local hall, and in Los Angeles some clubs stopped booking black bands to avoid racial tensions.[13] Meanwhile, Jimmie Lunceford prematurely ended his residency at Los Angeles's Trianon Ballroom after two members of the Basie Orchestra were refused admittance to his show, and Lena Horne quit a USO tour of Southern army camps in protest over the treatment of black servicemen.[14]

A *Billboard* article headlined "The Negro Makes Advances" gave the encouraging news that "Negro performers are being presented with more dignity, their employment opportunities have increased [for example, in radio, recording, and even some Hollywood studio orchestras], their race is being portrayed more sympathetically in films, radio and stage, and they are getting publicity in publications hitherto closed to them." But it also stressed the limits of these advances: Announcers on commercial network radio shows were forbidden to introduce black artists "with the appellation of Mr., Mrs. or Miss preceding his or her name"—though Bing Crosby had recently broken this rule when presenting Paul Robeson—and "the role of the American Negro in the war effort cannot be mentioned in a sponsored program."[15]

In this climate, it is easy to understand why African-American artists did not produce a lot of records like "There's a Star-Spangled Banner Waving Somewhere." There were some patriotic hits from black bands—the most successful seems to have been Duke Ellington's jive-talking "A Slip of the Lip (Might Sink a Ship)"—but other war-related tunes on the Race market included the King Cole Trio's "Gone with the Draft," in which the skinny, flatfooted protagonist boasts that since the fitter boys have been shipped overseas he's making fine time with the ladies; Louis Jordan's "Ration Blues," about the tribulations of wartime shortages; and "GI Jive," a comic hipster plaint about army life that was a huge hit for both Jordan and its author, Johnny Mercer.

Meanwhile swing was hitting harder than ever thanks to the most prosperous generation of teenagers in twenty years, and the country was also being swept by a craze for the pounding rhythm called boogie-woogie. Tommy Dorsey had set things off in 1938 with "Boogie Woogie," an orchestral reworking of a ten-year-old Race hit by the black pianist Pine Top Smith, and a further push came from the success of three black keyboard masters, Albert Ammons, Meade Lux Lewis, and Pete Johnson, at John Hammond's "From Spirituals to Swing" concert that year at Carnegie Hall. Then Will Bradley, a white trombone player who had been a big-band and studio stalwart since the early 1930s, hit with a boogie anthem, "Beat Me Daddy, Eight to the Bar," which was quickly covered by Glenn Miller and the Andrews Sisters, and pretty soon everyone from swanky hotel bands to hillbilly guitarists was cutting boogie-woogie discs.

Both jive and boogie-woogie were ideal styles for small bands: The cool humor of the former was better suited to a club-size combo than to a ballroom orchestra, and the pounding rhythms of the latter required no more than a piano, with maybe a couple of sidemen to add flavor. So it is not surprising that the biggest black stars to emerge in this period, Louis Jordan and Nat King Cole, though poles apart in virtually every other respect, were both noted for their stripped-down instrumental lineups.

Born in 1908, Jordan was a decade older than Cole, and he had learned show business from the ground up: Starting out with his father, a minstrel troupe musician in Arkansas, he worked his way from gigs with local bands to jobs in New York, and by the mid-1930s was playing alto sax in Chick Webb's Savoy Ballroom orchestra. His trademark style, urban jive rooted in Southern blues and boogie-woogie, would become the model for generations of hard-rocking R&B combos (James Brown was still recycling his arrangements in the 1960s[16]), and his presentation mixed the impeccably rehearsed show-band choreography of Fred Waring and Jimmie Lunceford with the rowdy comedy of Fats Waller and Louis Armstrong. His hits included the hip "Knock Me a Kiss" and "Jack, You're Dead," but also the quasi-minstrelsy of "Ain't Nobody Here but Us Chickens" and the down-home blues of "I'm Gonna Move to the Outskirts of Town." And he made a conscious effort to target both white and black audiences, aided by Decca, which in 1945 teamed him with Crosby and moved his records from its "Sepia" line to its pop series. His aim was to be the most popular black entertainer in America, and for a couple of years he managed to be just that, appearing in movies—mainstream Hollywood features, his own starring vehicles, and over a dozen of the short jukebox films called "soundies"—and guesting on network radio shows that rarely included other African-American performers.

Like Glenn Miller, who by the early 1940s had become the country's most popular bandleader, Jordan streamlined the energy of the hot swing orchestras into a precise routine that could be replicated night after night, no matter how tired or grumpy his musicians might be. Bill Doggett, who worked as his piano player for several years before going solo and becoming one of the biggest-selling R&B artists of the 1950s, recalled Jordan telling the band, "Don't play anything you can't play twice. Because if I like it you've got to keep it in.... If you're experimenting with your solos, some nights you're not going to be able to invent and we're going to have a sad show. But if you play the same thing all of the time it will always sound right."[17]

Jordan also avoided fancy arrangements and complex harmonies. During the 1940s many jazz soloists and bandleaders were trying to extend the music's language in the explorations known as bebop, but although Jordan admired Charlie Parker's inspired virtuosity, he had no interest in starving for his art. "I wanted to play for the people," he later explained. "For millions, not just a few hep cats."[18] He prided himself on offering the best wages in the black band business, paying his sidemen almost $300 a week at a time when a job with the Ellington orchestra paid barely a third of that.[19]

Jordan could pay so well because he was filling the same halls as Ellington and Basie but with a fraction of the personnel and transportation costs. When he formed his own group in 1939, his dream was to be able to get the power and energy of a big band with a small outfit—despite its name, his Tympany Five usually had six or seven members, but that was still tiny by ballroom standards—and he made up for his group's size by playing music that went right for the gut: 12-bar blues, boogie-woogie, and "rhythm changes" (the chords of "I Got Rhythm") backed by a driving shuffle beat. Inspired by Jordan's success and the realities of the wartime market—record companies desperate for jukebox product and a shortage of men—similar combos sprang up all across the country, and by the end of the decade his style had provided a new appellation for *Billboard*'s Race chart: rhythm and blues.

The King Cole Trio represented a still more dramatic departure from the big-band style. With Nat Cole on piano, Oscar Moore on electric guitar, and a couple of different bass players, the trio was not designed for dance halls or theaters. It was, in the parlance of the times, a cocktail combo—and that in itself was startling for a black act. Piano and guitar duos had become a staple of the Race record market in the late 1920s, and Cole's group owed a clear debt to Leroy Carr, the trendsetting blues crooner and composer of that time; but Carr's music had been associated with working-class bars and rent parties, not cocktail lounges. In Los Angeles, though, a newly arrived, young, and relatively prosperous black population faced a more relaxed color line than in other parts of the country, and a new kind of blues and saloon act was emerging. The pioneer was a tall, cool character with movie-star looks named Slim Gaillard, who had become the toast of Hollywood in the late 1930s playing piano and electric guitar and singing suave comic collations like "Flat Foot Floogie" and "Vol Vist Du Gaily Star." Cole formed his trio about a year after Gaillard's, at the request of a Hollywood nightclub owner, and for the first few years he specialized in similar hipster shtick, writing lightly boppish rhythm numbers including "Hit That Jive, Jack" and "I Like to Riff," as well as the moody blues hit, "That Ain't Right."

Cole was a mellower and more soulful singer than Gaillard, as well as a far more accomplished musician—Gaillard was a competent and entertaining player, but Cole was among the greatest pianists of the era—and his group set the pattern for a decade of intimate, immaculate West Coast lounge combos, from Johnny Moore's Three Blazers to Ray Charles's Maxim Trio. Musicianship aside, the new focus on small ensembles was due to economics and technology. Since repeal, smaller clubs were making enough money to hire name acts, and the wartime shortage of musicians gave further impetus for them to replace the big ballrooms of the Prohibition years. Meanwhile, amplification and the new prominence of records meant that a group that hit in those small clubs could go on to reach as large an audience as the biggest orchestra. Cole's murmured vocals and Moore's supple guitar lines were perfectly suited to the new era, and Johnny Mercer, one of the trio's local fans, made them the first stars of the new Capitol label, breaking precedent by marketing them as a mainstream pop act rather than in a separate Race catalog. Cole had the perfect combination of talents to capitalize on this opportunity: His pianistic ability earned the respect of jazz connoisseurs, his whispery phrasing on romantic ballads like "Sweet Lorraine" and "(I Love You) For Sentimental Reasons" satisfied the women and slow dancers, and the hip humor of "Straighten Up and Fly Right"—his first major pop hit—got the men in the army camps and the neighborhood bars. As far as Cole's own career went, the trio gigs were just a beginning, but the style they established survived long after he graduated to lush string sections.

Between the white honky-tonkers and the hip black combos, the jukeboxes, radio shows, and record hops that made them national figures, and the trend toward small clubs and lounges, the world of ballrooms and orchestras was becoming more and more a thing of the past. Their day was not yet over, by any means: There were still plenty of older dancers, and well into the 1960s it was common for teenagers to prepare for high school proms and coming-out parties by learning to fox-trot, waltz, and rumba, then dress up in tuxes and gowns and dance to a band that sounded a lot like Freddie Martin's or Sammy Kaye's. Still, that was in large part because the proms and debutante balls were seen as an introduction to adulthood, and such orchestras bore little resemblance to the music most youngsters were dancing to every week at parties or sock hops. The less formal styles varied from year to year and region to region, but whether live or on records, they tended to be played by small bands using amplified instruments, and the songs were as likely to come from Nashville or Los Angeles as from Tin Pan Alley. Meanwhile, a lot of people were enjoying their music at home and not listening to bands at all. A new invention called television invited the most famous stars into any living room, and like parlor visitors of previous eras, they arrived alone or in couples, their musicians as unobtrusively invisible as the murmur of a movie soundtrack.

12

SELLING THE AMERICAN BALLAD

Before Mitch [Miller] came along, pop music was vestigial, strings-behind-potted-palms; he changed all that. He threw out the 32-bar form; he used bastard instruments. He was the first great record producer in history.

JERRY WEXLER

By August 1945 the war was over, and the United States was ready to return to normal—or not return, exactly, as most Americans had no experience of a period they could consider normal. The previous three decades had included World War I, Prohibition, the Depression, and another world war. At a more personal level, most Americans were relatively recent immigrants or descendents of recent immigrants, some from other countries, some from rural areas to cities that in many ways were as foreign as another country. So for most of them, "normal" did not mean a life that they recalled from before the war or that their parents had lived. It meant an idealized life: a decent job, a house on a quiet street, a loving spouse, and a happy, stable family.

A lot of them got that life, too, or at least something that for a few years felt like it. There were stresses in the immediate postwar years, but in general the following decade and a half would be a period of unprecedented prosperity. The United States was the only major industrial nation that had not been damaged by the war—indeed, the war had spurred an increase in production—and New Deal economic programs insured that the wealth was spread more evenly than ever before or since. The GI Bill and other federal programs helped returning soldiers go to college and buy houses, and many of the people who had stayed home had found good jobs, or at least better jobs than their parents had held. The combination of this prosperity and the baby boom that began with the war's end meant that couples were marrying at younger ages and settling down to a life centered on homes and families, and a postwar housing shortage was soon balanced by a building boom in the suburbs that spread like prosperous ripples around every city.

Of course, there were still a lot of people living relatively unchanged lives in both country and city, and many of them were poor or single or otherwise failed to fit the demographic trends or share the dominant dreams. If the suburbs were a solution for some, they were a source of frustration for others: William Levitt, the most prominent developer of prefabricated suburban communities, famously said, "We can solve a housing problem, or we can try to solve a racial problem. But we cannot combine the two." So by 1960 the 82,000 residents of Long Island's Levittown still did not include a single black family, while Harlem was blacker than ever before.[1] One result of this division was to cement the association of African-American culture with urban life. Another was a split in popular music: During the swing era, however segregated the orchestras and dance halls had been, black and white dancers had favored roughly the same sorts of bands. Now the era of the dance orchestras was over, and black pop music got a stripped-down, heavier beat, while white pop music got perky, dreamy, and reassuring.

The pop mainstream in the eight or nine years between the end of the war and the arrival of Elvis Presley has tended to be disparaged by both jazz and rock historians. The former lament the replacement of swing bands, large and small, by studio pop confections, while the latter see Elvis and Little Richard as rescuing America from a decade of bland conformity. But the swing bands died a natural death for which the stars of the next era were not to blame, and the rockers owed a greater debt to their pop predecessors than most of their fans care to admit. As always, there was change mixed with continuity, and while some musicians were upset or thrilled by new sounds, others just tried to go about their business.

The failure of large swing orchestras to snap back after the war startled a lot of people, and the most startled were the bandleaders themselves. In hindsight, though, the surprising thing is that hundreds of touring dance orchestras had been able to flourish for so long. Prohibition had pushed the ballroom business into larger venues, and the combined shocks of sound films and the Depression had flooded the market with musicians who were willing to work for almost nothing, so for about twenty years big bands were in demand and easy to staff. Now audiences were shrinking, amplification had made small combos viable even in large rooms, and music-business wages had to compete with better wages in more stable industries. The end of wartime price controls meant that gasoline, hotel, and food prices all shot skyward, making it hard to keep a band on the road. And the customers were not coming out dancing in anything like their prewar or wartime numbers. Summer had always been the best time for touring, but in the summer of 1946 bands and dance halls were struggling to break even, and by November *Billboard* reported that "some locations have dropped band policy completely, while others have concentrated on half-week and week-end biz."[2]

Halls could save money by shutting down on slow days, but touring bands did not have that option. Their payroll, food, and lodging costs were the same whether they played or not, and the only thing that had made them viable was unbroken chains of one-nighters. With summer over and no relief in sight, Benny Goodman, Tommy Dorsey, Harry James, Woody Herman, Benny Carter, Les Brown, Charlie Ventura, and Jack Teagarden all disbanded their orchestras, and Duke Ellington followed a few months later. To some extent this was a momentary panic, and Ellington and Dorsey soon had big bands working again, but for the rest of their careers they would be exceptional figures rather than the leaders of a mass popular style.

Of course, swing outfits were not the only orchestras around, and the list of failures notably lacked such names as Lawrence Welk, Guy Lombardo, and Sammy Kaye. Indeed, a *Metronome* article headlined "Hats Off…to Sweet" reported that "schmaltz bands" were in such demand that three of the main New York hotel ballrooms were supporting two alternating aggregations each, seven evenings a week.[3] Hotel groups did not have to worry about touring costs, and rather than depending on fickle young fans, they relied on a regular clientele that came to dine and dance. So plenty of schmaltz bands comfortably survived the end of the swing era and would hang on as "easy listening" orchestras through the heyday of rock 'n' roll.

What changed was that dance orchestras were now just dance orchestras, and no longer played a central role in popular music. For the previous twenty years, bandleaders had been functioning as hosts and ringmasters of what amounted to touring variety shows, including solo vocalists, trios, glee clubs, small instrumental groups, and often dancers and comedy routines. On tour the most important function of any band was to provide dance music, but for records, radio, and theater appearances they also needed to produce hits that would enthrall seated audiences. That meant using singers, because most listeners like to hear words as well as melodies and to have the direct, personal communication of a human voice. So, like it or not—and the common musician's perception is evident in a *Metronome* headline, "Casa Loma Gives In: Takes Girl Singer"[4]—the bands all featured vocalists, and most of them had both a male and a female soloist and some kind of vocal group.

Through the mid-1930s, these singers had been as anonymous as the instrumental soloists—that is, they would be introduced at live shows and on the radio, and the fans might know their names, but record labels tended just to have the name of the orchestra, and even when vocalists were listed most listeners thought of them as part of the larger group. In 1940, an article highlighting the success of Tommy Dorsey's new record, "I'll Never Smile Again," described it as "90 per cent vocal, played and sung softly, slowly, and highlighted by the silver Dorsey trombone and the almost classical celeste touches." The names of Dorsey's singers were apparently considered irrelevant, although they were printed on the record's label: the Pied Pipers and Frank Sinatra.[5]

Two years later, when Sinatra left Dorsey to embark on a solo career, a lot of people thought he was crazy. The only pop vocalist to have stayed on top of the market without a band was Bing Crosby—Eddie Cantor and Al Jolson were huge on radio and in theaters but hadn't had a hit in years—and Crosby's success was based not only on vocal chops but on his exceptional wit and charm, displayed in a string of movies and as host of the top musical show on network radio. Nonetheless, Sinatra was supremely confident, and he would later say that Crosby's uniqueness was exactly what prompted his decision:

> Crosby was Number One, way up on top of the pile. In the open field, you might say, were some awfully good singers with the orchestras. Bob Eberly (with Jimmy Dorsey) was a fabulous vocalist. Mr. Como (with Ted Weems) is such a wonderful singer. I thought, If I don't make a move out of this and try to do it on my own soon, one of those guys will do it, and I'll have to fight all three of them to get a position.[6]

So in August 1942, at age twenty-six, Sinatra went solo, and for a few months it looked as if he had made a bad mistake. He had a few records out under his own name, and a lot of young fans knew him, but he no longer had the power of the Dorsey organization behind him, and no one was offering him a network show or a booking in a major nightclub. Then the manager of New York's Paramount Theater hired him as an "extra added attraction" on a New Year's program featuring Benny Goodman's orchestra and the new Crosby movie. In an oft-told story, Goodman was not expecting anything special, and when Sinatra stepped onstage and was greeted by the screams of a house packed with adoring bobby-soxers, the bandleader's response was, "What the fuck is that?!"[7]

Goodman's question was soon being echoed across the country. Sinatra's blend of natural gifts and technical mastery earned him the nickname "the Voice," and his style would influence generations of pop balladeers, but he was also the first modern teenybopper idol. In February, CBS added him as the featured vocalist on *Your Hit Parade*, providing a national platform from which he sang the top hits each week—a particularly important setting during the AFM recording ban—and the reissued disc of his pre-Dorsey "All or Nothing at All" reached the top of the charts in June. In October he came back to the Paramount as a headliner on Columbus Day. Schools were closed for the holiday, and thirty thousand kids surrounded the theater clamoring for tickets, while the lucky three and a half thousand who had seats hunkered down and stayed through five shows and hundreds of police had to be diverted from the Columbus Day parade to keep order.

Sinatra was the musical news of the moment, but as with Presley a dozen years later, a lot of people treated him as a joke. It did not help that his press agent made an open secret of having encouraged girls to scream and faint at his concerts. Nor that some regular fans were as well rehearsed as the ringers: "We loved to swoon," a Boston bobby-soxer recalled thirty years later. "We would gather behind locked bedroom doors, in rooms where rosebud wallpaper was plastered over with pictures of The Voice, to practice swooning. We would take off our saddle shoes, put on his records and stand around groaning for a while. Then the song would end and we would all fall down on the floor."[8] It helped still less that "the frail lad from Hoboken," as the *New York Times* called him, was attracting all this feminine attention at a time when his fitter peers were off fighting the war.[9] Sinatra was classified 4-F because of a punctured eardrum, but it was no accident that during these years his wimpy physique was a running joke—his habit of holding onto the mike stand while he sang provoked comments that it was all that kept him from falling over, and a thirteen-year-old Elizabeth Taylor, appearing opposite him on a radio broadcast and invited to touch his chest, responded, "Would you mind pointing it out to me?"[10] The cracks were backed with real resentment, and a headline from 1944 gives a sense of his reputation: "Found: Male with Some Kind Words for Frank Sinatra."[11]

Of course there were plenty of men who liked Sinatra's work, including soldiers who heard him on Armed Forces broadcasts and the voters who put him on top of the *Down Beat* and *Metronome* polls, but there were also many who very vocally did not, and by the end of the decade his career was on the skids. In 1946 he was still the most-played male vocalist on disc jockey shows—perhaps reflecting the personal tastes of platter spinners but certainly helped by requests from members of his more than seven hundred fan clubs—but when it came to sales, both at the record counters and on jukeboxes, he was behind Perry Como and Crosby. By 1948 none of those charts even included him in their year-end tallies, while Crosby was number one on the retail and juke charts and number three with the jocks.[12]

Crosby's enduring success was not just a matter of charm, talent, and name recognition. Though he was twelve years older than Sinatra, he was more in tune with the current direction of popular music. Sinatra would always remain committed to Tin Pan Alley compositions backed by big bands and string orchestras, but Crosby had never been principally a Broadway or band singer. He was comfortable in that milieu, as he was everywhere, but even in his Whiteman days he had been part of a stand-alone trio, and his first million-selling record was 1937's "Sweet Leilani" with a Hawaiian ensemble. A small-town boy from Spokane, Washington, he was at home with rural material as well as jazz, and when Gene Autry made ersatz cowboy ballads a cinema and radio staple he responded by getting a huge hit with "I'm an Old Cowhand," then went on to cover numerous country-folk records and to issue albums of cowboy songs.

Most of the singers who dominated the pop charts over the next few years shared Crosby's willingness to present a broad range of material, and especially songs with country, folk, or western tinges. Most had been band singers and, left to their own devices, tended to share Sinatra's tastes, but few had his single-minded focus. "I like to sing the songs I feel like singing," Patti Page assured the musically sophisticated readers of *Metronome*. "But there are more people that aren't hip than those that are, so you've got to please those that aren't. You've got to please the people who get up at eight o'clock in the morning."[13]

It was not just a matter of pleasing the working stiffs. Sinatra was from Hobo-ken, New Jersey, but many of the up-and-coming vocal stars hailed from areas where country and western styles were as familiar as pop tunes: Page was from Oklahoma, Dinah Shore from Tennessee, Rosemary Clooney from Kentucky, and Johnnie Ray from small-town Oregon. Jo Stafford, Sinatra's female counterpart in the Dorsey band, had been raised in Southern California by a mother from rural Tennessee who sang her to sleep with traditional ballads. She went solo in 1944, and three years later, encouraged by the success of the New York café folk singers Susan Reed, Josh White, and Burl Ives, began mingling the pop hits she sang on NBC's weekly *Supper Club* with "Barbara Allen" and "Black Is the Color of My True Love's Hair." An article in the *New York Times* noted that although this material already had a devoted cult of listeners, it "had a specialized and limited appeal [and] Jo's purpose was to widen that appeal to those who were not hobby-ists in this field, perhaps even to her juke box-set fans."[14] To that end, early in 1948 Stafford released a three-disc album titled *American Folk Songs*. It had orchestral arrangements by Paul Weston, an ex-Dorsey arranger whom she would shortly marry, and the liner notes promised that "purists may object strenuously to the presentation of these songs with any accompaniment other than the traditional guitar, but after hearing the records, the listener will agree that the simplicity and loveliness can be preserved and even enhanced by the tasteful use of strings and woodwinds."

Traditional folk music had developed a radio and album presence during the New Deal years, thanks in a large part to the efforts of Alan Lomax, a strong Roosevelt supporter who argued that it was the true sound of the American peo-ple. Lomax ran the Folk Music Archive of the Library of Congress, produced sev-eral radio series for CBS (introducing not only Ives and White but also such rawer talents as Woody Guthrie and Huddie "Lead Belly" Ledbetter), and in the postwar years compiled a series of albums for Decca that ranged from old hillbilly and blues reissues to new recordings by White and Richard Dyer-Bennett. Due to his many years as a field collector and his preference for nonprofessional rural artists, Lomax is usually remembered as a folk purist, but he was well aware that mainstream per-formers and arrangements could bring a wider audience into the fold, and he wel-comed Stafford's efforts: The playlists for his late-1940s deejay show, *Your Ballad Man*, which was carried nationally on the Mutual Broadcasting Network, include her records more regularly than any other artist's.[15]

Lomax had himself worked with orchestras in the early 1940s, using settings of traditional tunes by Aaron Copland and Ruth Crawford Seeger on his broadcasts for the *Columbia School of the Air*.[16] As it happened, one of the musicians in that radio orchestra was an oboe virtuoso named Mitch Miller, and Miller would become the most influential record producer of the early 1950s by, among other things, rework-ing folk and country material for the pop audience.

Record producers, or as they were then called, "A&R men" (for artists and repertoire), took on a new importance in the postwar years. As long as bands had been the main force in popular music, it was the bandleaders who hired arrangers, assigned instrumental soloists and singers, and worked with the record and publishing companies to select material. For a Crosby or an Andrews session, Decca's owner, Jack Kapp, might do much of that work himself, but other labels still relied on bands for most of their hits. As the entertainment industry's focus shifted from live performances to recordings, though, the record companies began to notice that vocalists were easier to handle than bandleaders. For one thing, they tended to be cheaper: Bandleaders were used to managing a large payroll and thought in tens of thousands of dollars, whereas vocalists had been on salary and thought in hundreds. For another, they were used to being pushed around. Singers had always had their material and arrangements selected by the bandleaders, so taking orders from A&R men was nothing new for them. *Billboard* summed up the new attitude: "Why hold onto batoneers who want too much dough or make trouble on the tune selection?" As Eli Oberstein, the head of pop A&R for RCA Victor put it, "We're in the record biz, not the band biz."[17]

It was natural that the shift from orchestras with fixed personnel to producers supervising one-off record dates would broaden the range of material that was recorded, especially given the growing prominence of country music. Having proven their jukebox strength during the war years, country performers were now showing a similar power on the road: "In the face of a generally poor national box office for name ork [orchestra] attractions, almost all hillbilly and Western performers working one-nighters and locations have been coming out healthy," *Billboard* wrote at the end of 1947.

> When a Bob Wills holds better than three-quarters of all West Coast one-nighter gross records—and not a Harry James, Stan Kenton or Tommy Dorsey—the band offices can take a hint....No one in the band biz today could have equaled the $20,000 one-nighter gross racked up by hillbilly Eddy Arnold in the Washington Municipal Auditorium a couple of weeks ago. The sole attraction was Arnold with his guitar, without an ork or other surrounding bill.[18]

In the later 1950s it became common to draw sharp distinctions between the folk market (largely urban and middle class) and the country and western market (largely rural, Southern, and working class), but in this period the terms overlapped as substitutes for the more derogatory "hillbilly." Ernest Tubb claimed that he came up with the "country and western" rubric as a heading that would encompass both southeastern acts like Roy Acuff and Westerners like himself, Wills, and Autry. But when he opened his Nashville record shop in 1947, he advertised it as "Folk Music Headquarters."[19]

These lines were further blurred by songwriters in New York and Los Angeles who saw no reason why all the hillbilly material should be collected by folklorists or written by people like Tubb and Dave Dexter. As early as 1943, *Billboard* had noted both that a "widening circle of folk music addicts" was forcing bands to come up with arrangements of folk tunes and that "even when actual folk tunes are not taken over bodily, there is a clear tendency on the part of the pop field to satisfy an increasing desire for tunes that closely approach the country type."[20] Along with blackface minstrelsy, there was a vaudeville tradition of comic "rube" numbers, and just as Louis Jordan leavened his blues with songs about chicken stealing, the folk and country songs were mixed with pseudo-Appalachian confections like two numbers Stafford took to the top ten the year before her *Folk Songs* album: "Tim-Tayshun," a nasal backwoods novelty for which she was billed as Cinderella G. Stump, and "Feudin' and Fightin'," which featured a backing group listed with tongue in cheek as Paul Weston's Mountain Boys.

As for the western end of the spectrum, the next decade would be a golden age for Hollywood cowboys. In 1949 John Wayne appeared for the first time among the ten top-grossing movie stars, and for the next eight years he was consistently in the top three. By the mid-1950s Westerns dominated prime-time television, reaching a high point of thirty weekly series. And in suburban backyards, pint-sized cowboys (and a few cowgirls) filled the air with the snap of their cap pistols.

Hollywood's cowboy songs bore roughly the same relationship to the songs of working cowboys that suburban yards bore to the open range, and had a similarly broad appeal. They combined a sense of freedom with a wholesome, old-fashioned security and were the perfect antidote to a modern world haunted by nuclear bombs and Communist spies. Before the war Crosby had been pretty much the only mainstream pop singer regularly mining this lode, but in 1948 Vaughn Monroe got into the act, joining the Sons of the Pioneers for a new version of their classic "Cool Water," and the following year he topped the pop charts with both "Riders in the Sky," a hollering hunk of cow-camp fantasy that had originally hit for Burl Ives, and "Someday," from a recent Autry feature. This tendency toward things western caught the attention of Abe Lyman, who had been Los Angeles's ruling sweet orchestra leader since the 1920s and now was doubling as a B-movie producer, and he signed Monroe to star in a screen version of Max Brand's novel *Singing Guns*. The film was soon forgotten, but one of the songs Monroe performed in it became the runaway craze of the year: a clip-clopping novelty titled "Mule Train."

Monroe's record of "Mule Train" reached the top ten, but the version that really took off came from an even less likely source than the big-band baritone: the team of Mitch Miller and a thirty-four-year-old nightclub singer named Frankie Laine. Born Francesco LoVecchio in Detroit, Laine had been singing professionally since the 1930s. His first record, 1945's "Melancholy Madeline," was with a black group, the Three Blazers (which for that session included the King Cole Trio's Oscar Moore), and he had such a bluesy sound that *Billboard* listed his breakthrough hit, 1947's "That's My Desire," in its Race chart. Typically he would have followed up with a similar selection, but toward the end of that year Mercury Records hired Miller as its new A&R director, and Miller persuaded Laine to record "That Lucky Old Sun," a rural-flavored lament reminiscent of "Ol' Man River," which shot to the top of the pop charts.

A native of Rochester, New York, Miller had made his reputation as one of Manhattan's first-call oboe and English horn players, working in the CBS orchestra and as a concert artist under the batons of Leopold Stokowski and Sir Thomas Beecham. Along with his A&R duties at Mercury he was one of the principal players on Charlie Parker's bop classique album, *Bird with Strings*, and as a sideline he organized accompaniments for Simon and Schuster's Little Golden children's records with his Eastman School of Music classmate Alec Wilder. A pointed beard and thick moustache gave him the air of a Renaissance count or mountebank, and over the next few years he would be credited with an alchemical gift for transmuting esoteric instrumentation and unlikely song choices into musical gold.

"Mule Train" was a perfect example. Laine recalled that when Miller played it for him over the phone, his response was, "Jesus Christ, you can't expect me to do a *cowboy song*! I'll lose all my jazz fans. I'll lose everybody who ever loved 'That's My Desire.'"[21]

It was a reasonable attitude for a bluesy singer who had spent his life in clubs and dance halls, but Miller's natural habitat was the studio, and he had become the highest paid oboist in America by expertly executing whatever was placed in front of him, from Bach to schlock. So he appealed to Laine's professionalism, and eventually Laine agreed to try a few takes of "Mule Train" and even to mimic the shouts of a wagon driver. Miller backed him with guitars, accordion, a clicking drum, and a vocal group doubling the bass line, dubbed in a cracking bullwhip, and the team had their first million-seller. They followed up with "The Cry of the Wild Goose," a pastoral pastiche by a West Coast folk singer named Terry Gilkyson, and over the next few years would move from Mercury to Columbia (another of Miller's Eastman classmates, Goddard Lieberson, was the larger label's executive vice president) and hit with country, polka, Spanish, South African, and Dixieland tunes.

While still at Mercury, Miller also produced Patti Page's first records, on which they used the new technology of overdubbing to create one-woman duets and quartets. It was after he left in 1950, though, that Page recorded one of the two defining records of the country-folk-pop boom (which were also that year's two biggest hits)—an auto-duet version of "Tennessee Waltz." The other key recording came from Decca, where the growing interest in folk styles had inspired an arranger named Gordon Jenkins to craft orchestral backings for a quartet of Greenwich Village folk singers named the Weavers. And in a coincidence that perfectly illustrates the mongrel oddity of American music, both Page and the Weavers were singing romantic waltzes they had learned from African-American performers. In the Weavers' case, this is common knowledge, because the song was Lead Belly's "Goodnight Irene." As for Page, it is usually assumed that her inspiration was Pee Wee King's two-year-old hillbilly hit, but in fact she was covering a recent R&B recording by the swing bandleader Erskine Hawkins.[22]

This confluence of a quartet of urban folk revivalists, a veteran orchestra arranger, a Polish-American hillbilly accordionist, an Oklahoman pop singer using a new studio gimmick, and a black jazz musician was a foretaste of fusions to come. And while the Weavers tend to be remembered as forerunners of the later folk revival rather than as central figures in a pop trend, they were part of the same movement as Stafford, Miller, and Burl Ives. (Ives had teamed with the Andrews Sisters on "Blue Tail Fly" in 1948 and would get his only top ten showing for this period with a cover of the Weavers-Gilkyson version of "On Top of Old Smoky.") The flip side of "Irene" was an Israeli hora called "Tzena, Tzena, Tzena," which reached number two on the *Billboard* pop chart, trailed at number three by Miller's version on Columbia—his first hit under his own name—and "Irene" went to number nine for Stafford on Capitol and to number five for Sinatra with the Mitch Miller Singers. (Meanwhile, Ernest Tubb and Red Foley took a duet version of "Irene" to number ten, the biggest crossover hit of Tubb's career, and topped the country and western chart.)

Sinatra's appearance in the "Irene" sweepstakes might seem to contradict my previous comments about his taste, but in fact it just confirms the extent to which record producers considered singers' tastes to be irrelevant. By 1950 his career was in trouble, so he was obeying orders—his previous top ten record had been a cover of Foley's "Chattanooga Shoe-Shine Boy"—and when he mentioned the Lead Belly song in a backstage interview, his discomfort was evident: "We've got a new one that's moving pretty good called, you'll excuse the expression, 'Goodnight Irene.'"

The interviewer, clearly startled, responded, "Hey, that's a nice tune."

"You wanna bet?" Sinatra snapped, then paused and added, "Naw, it's really cute." But when the interviewer suggested that he should do more songs like it, his response was, "Don't hold your breath."[23]

To urban jazz fans of Sinatra's generation, country music was the lowest style imaginable, representing not only inept musicianship but also the archaic redneck attitudes that classed blacks, Jews, and Italians as less than full Americans. For them, as for the big bandleaders and the Tin Pan Alley publishers, songs like "Mule Train," "Irene," and "Tennessee Waltz" were the beginning of a cultural decline that would reach its logical conclusion with the arrival of Elvis Presley.

But if Sinatra didn't want to go along with the program, there were plenty of other singers who would. Miller chose to follow "Irene" with a cover of the Weavers' next hit, a seafaring ballad called "The Roving Kind," and when the Voice refused to cut it, he tapped a young fellow named Albert Cernik, whom he rechristened Guy Mitchell. Mitchell had worked as a cowboy and sung Western Swing before turning to pop, so he was comfortable with folk-oriented material, and when Miller handed him "The Roving Kind" and "My Heart Cries for You"—another Sinatra reject—and surrounded him with a quartet of French horns, Columbia had another hitmaker in its stable. Around the same time, Miller lured Stafford away from Capitol and got her a double-sided hit with "Tennessee Waltz" and Lefty Frizzell's honky-tonk hell-raiser, "If You've Got the Money, I've Got the Time," both featuring a blend of clarinet and steel guitar. And a few months later he got a number one hit for Tony Bennett with Hank Williams's "Cold, Cold Heart."

Like his *paesani* Sinatra and Laine, Bennett (born Benedetto) was not wild about cutting a country number, but he gave in after Miller persuaded him to listen to the lyric and cushioned his vocal in a lush setting by the Percy Faith Orchestra. Five decades later, with Williams enshrined as a legend, Bennett recalled the record with affection and added that the country singer was equally pleased: "Hank's friends told me how much he loved my recording and said that whenever he passed a jukebox, he'd put a nickel in and play my version."[24]

Williams, Tubb, and Foley might have seemed like hicks to the New York studio crowd, but they were all adept professionals and saw which way the wind was blowing. Williams's publisher, Acuff-Rose, followed up Bennett's success by agreeing to give Miller advance copies of the songwriter's future singles, and Columbia hit with seven of them in the next three years: Mitchell did "I Can't Help It If I'm Still In Love with You," Rosemary Clooney did "Half as Much," Laine did "Your Cheatin' Heart," Stafford did "Jambalaya" and teamed with Laine on "Hey, Good Lookin'" and "Settin' the Woods on Fire" (with blazing steel guitar by L.A. session man Speedy West), and Bennett was back in 1954 with "There'll Be No Teardrops Tonight."

Miller's quest for unlikely pop material also took him further afield. The success of "Tzena," like the earlier Andrews Sisters excursions, had proved that upbeat ethnic material could please a broad audience, and in 1951 he latched onto a song by Ross Bagdasarian (later to mastermind Alvin and the Chipmunks) and the playwright William Saroyan, which paraphrased some lines from Christopher Marlowe's *Dido Queen of Carthage* in comical Armenian dialect and matched them with an old folk-dance tune. Miller thought this novelty would be perfect for Rosemary Clooney, a jazz singer he had previously taken to number eleven with a country ballad. Clooney was more than dubious: She took one glance at the opening lines, "Come on-a my house-a, my house / I'm gonna give-a you candy..." and turned down the session, telling Miller, "I don't think so."

"Know what I think?" he replied. "I think you'll show up because otherwise you will be fired."[25]

Miller was no longer a novice A&R man at Mercury; he was the king of pop at Columbia. So Clooney sang "Come On-A My House," accompanied by a honky-tonk harpsichord, it stayed at number one for eight weeks, and over the next year and a half Miller took Clooney and the harpsichord to the top twenty with pop ballads, country novelties, a duet with Marlene Dietrich, and an Italian dialect number, "Botch-A-Me." Meanwhile, Laine was hitting with the ferocious "Jezebel," backed by flamenco guitars and tambourine, and a French tango, "Jalousie." Then Miller signed up Marais and Miranda, a South African duo who had been singing songs of the Veldt for New York café society, handed their most audience-friendly material to Stafford, Laine, Doris Day, and Johnnie Ray, and shortly had his house quartet, four lads from Canada known as the Four Lads, cover a Rhodesian record by the Bulawayo Rhythm Boys called "Skokiaan."

All in all, major-label hits were coming from a broader range of sources than ever before and probably ever since. A lot of the material—for example, the Lads' lyrics about going off to "happy, happy Africa"—might be dismissed as kitsch, but it was steering both listeners and musicians in interesting directions. The Rhythm Boys' original recording of "Skokiaan" followed the Lads' cover onto the pop charts—the first African record ever to do so—as did several big band versions, including one by Louis Armstrong and one by Perez Prado's mambo orchestra. Soon there would be a full-scale mambo craze, as well as a vogue for calypso and Polynesian exotica. In 1952, the year's number-one pop hits included two tangos, a Brazilian *choro* (Percy Faith's Miller-produced "Delicado," again with harpsichord), and "Auf Wiedersehn Sweetheart," a German ballad by the English songbird Vera Lynn.

If the range of material was impressive, though, the range of performers was pretty narrow. The gusher of regional and ethnic music that had blown sky high in the war years had been capped, and the crude styles refined for easy home consumption. Miller was envied and emulated but also denounced for creating the musical equivalent of Automat cuisine—cheap, uniform, easily accessible, and essentially tasteless. At times, he seemed to concur, stressing that his Columbia productions also included recordings of Duke Ellington and Sarah Vaughan and dismissing his pop hits. "I wouldn't buy that stuff for myself," he told *Time* magazine in 1951. "There's no real artistic satisfaction in this job. I satisfy my musical ego elsewhere."[26] But a year later he struck a more defiant note: "Musical snobbishness is one of the curses of the music business," he told *Down Beat*. "Many of the most eloquent things have been said very simply and the simple things are the hardest things to say well."[27] And with thirty years of hindsight he would add, "Most people then were concerned with what category a song belonged in, but I just looked at them as plain good songs.... There's an art to everything. A great mystery writer *is* a great writer. It's like saying that Richard Rodgers is not Beethoven or Bach. And that's right, but there's room for both."[28]

Miller took a craftsman's pride in doing the best job possible with the materials at hand. He would compare himself to Atlantic Records' legendary R&B producer,

Jerry Wexler—they were friends, and Wexler had turned him on to Hank Williams—pointing out that whereas Wexler took groups of street-corner doo-woppers and spent weeks rehearsing them, the Columbia recipe used professionals who could come into the studio cold and cut four songs in three hours. A top-flight studio player understands what will work in a given situation, can instantly generate new licks to suit a changing arrangement, and executes them flawlessly. Personal taste is irrelevant, and in some cases it may even interfere with the job at hand. Miller's job as a pop producer was not to create enduring art, it was to cut hits; and his triumph was that under his guidance Columbia became the country's top pop label, dominating the singles charts from 1951 through 1954.

Miller and the producers who followed his model were creating a new sort of pop record. Instead of capturing the sound of live groups, they were making three-minute musicals, matching singers to songs in the same way that movie producers matched stars to film roles. As Miller told *Time* magazine in 1951, "Every singer has certain sounds he makes better than others. Frankie Laine is sweat and hard words—he's a guy beating the pillow, a purveyor of basic emotions. Guy Mitchell is better with happy-go-lucky songs; he's a virile young singer, gives people a vicarious lift. Clooney is a barrelhouse dame, a hillbilly at heart."[29] It was a way of thinking perfectly suited to the new market in which vocalists were creating unique identities and hit songs were performed as television skits.

Along with finding interesting material and matching it to appropriate singers, the new producers looked for instrumental and sonic touches that would make people stop and pay attention to a record and instantly recognize it the next time they heard it. As with the adoption of folk and country songs, this reflected a broader trend: Electric instruments were not only louder than their acoustic predecessors but also provided a previously unavailable range of sounds. Steel guitar, the first obviously electric instrument to hit, had been followed by electric organ and early synthesizers such as the Novachord, "the instrument that reproduces the tone of a dozen instruments." (Not everyone was thrilled by this description: Ferde Grofé attempted to introduce the Novachord at the 1939 New York World's Fair, only to have it barred by the AFM as a threat to jobs.[30]) The ultimate wizard of sonic surprise was Les Paul, who racked up over three dozen hits between 1948 and 1953 with high-tech collages that combined the multitracked voice of his wife, Mary Ford, with his overdubbed, speed-shifted, and electronically modified guitar. And it was not just a matter of new technologies: Whiteman had attracted early buyers with a slide whistle, and as the market moved away from swing bands, there was an ever greater need for instruments and combinations that would give a record a distinctive flavor. Harmonica orchestras had a brief rage during the AFM ban—the union did not consider harmonicas to be instruments—and the Three Suns became a top-selling instrumental combo with their trademark mix of organ, accordion, and electric guitar.

Miller admired Paul's work, but he preferred odd instrumental juxtapositions to studio gimmickry. He was convinced that the best records came from groups of singers and musicians in one room, listening to one another and energized by the knowledge that if anyone messed up they'd have to do the whole thing over again. "How can an artist work with a [recorded] background and the headset in his ear?" he would ask rhetorically in later years. "When you were in a studio and the musicians were in there and you knew that that was it, there was an interaction that went on. You couldn't explain it; you only knew when it wasn't there."[31]

So Miller got his version of the Paul sound by using a half-dozen guitarists simultaneously, created instrumental signatures for his regular singers—Clooney's harpsichord, Mitchell's quartet of French horns—and put together some of the oddest combos in history: A *New Yorker* reporter described a Laine session that included piano, bass, organ, steel guitar, electric guitar, celeste, vibraphone, harp, and sax.[32] Not all the experiments worked—even Miller granted that backing Dinah Shore with bagpipes was a mistake—but his imagination and eagerness to try new approaches would inspire generations of studio innovators.

This new style of record making fitted the new patterns of music listening. Miller's confections were intended to be heard at home, on radios, phonographs, and television. The breakthrough moments for previous generations of stars had tended to be concerts: Whiteman at Aeolian Hall, Goodman at the Palomar, Sinatra at the Paramount. But Clooney's breakthrough was with a record that bore no relation to anything she had performed live—or, indeed, could perform live, except in special circumstances, since she was not going to tour with a harpsichord. For the singers, this presented a problem. Bennett complained that "Mitch and Percy Faith insisted on using their guys, who were great, but I was building up a rapport with my trio that's hard to duplicate with studio musicians." On the one hand, that meant that Bennett was unhappy with his records, and on the potentially more important hand, it meant that audiences at live shows were not hearing the music that had attracted them to the new stars in the first place. The result was that when Bennett tried to break into the next level of venues, he found that his generation of singers was not considered strong enough to hold a sophisticated crowd: "Vegas generally took its booking cues from the Copa then," he recalled. "And at first neither venue was too keen on what they called 'record acts,' which they figured were a bunch of fly-by-nighters who wouldn't bring in the right type of customer. They preferred old-line show business legends like Sophie Tucker."[33]

Bennett overcame that reluctance and became a major draw both at the Copacabana and in Las Vegas—indeed, he was one of the few singers who would still be able to carry a full orchestra on the road in later decades. But most of the top hitmakers of this period failed to build the sort of enduring live audience that the stars of previous eras had commanded, and this was at least in part because their style came not from their own tastes and working groups but from the new studio system. One of the appeals of the rock 'n' roll acts that appeared in the mid-1950s would be that many of them were self-contained bands with a unique sound that they could recreate onstage.

Of course, the rock 'n' rollers also had other strengths that distinguished them from their pop predecessors, and before we move on it is worth looking at a Miller-produced star who presaged that next wave. In 1951 Columbia's R&B subsidiary, OKeh, put out a record called "Whiskey and Gin Blues," by a singer at the Flame Show Bar, Detroit's foremost black nightclub. The voice sounded a lot like Dinah Washington's, but the singer was a young, half-deaf, gay white man named Johnnie Ray. "I look back now and say that it was probably the very first rock and roll record," Miller would tell Ray's biographer,[34] and though to modern ears "Whiskey and Gin" sounds more like 1940s café blues, the disc Miller produced as a follow-up clearly fits that bill. The song was "Cry," which had first been recorded by a black singer named Ruth Casey on a small New York R&B label. Miller added a glockenspiel and back-up harmonies by the Four Lads, but it was the emotional fervor of Ray's performance that took it to number one for eleven weeks at the beginning of 1952.

Ray had an eerie, vulnerable voice, with neither the relaxed warmth of the crooners nor the operatic power of Monroe or Laine, and it reached across lines of color and genre. "Cry" topped the R&B charts, and Hank Williams singled Ray out as an exception in the pop world, comparing him to Roy Acuff: "He's sincere and shows he's sincere. That's the reason he's popular—he sounds to me like he means it."[35]

Ray was also quickly recognized as more than just a "record act." His shows were the nightclub equivalent of what Marlon Brando was doing in *Streetcar Named Desire*, their raw passion a jarring contrast to the theatrical sexiness of previous stars. When he got a booking at the Copacabana, it was to some degree as a novelty act: Clooney recalled him displaying "the kinds of antics rock stars would pick up later ... everyone waited for him to fall down on his knees and cry and do all the outlandish things that people had never seen done on the Copa stage before."[36]

Ray understood the ambiguity of his appeal. "They come out to see what the freak is like," he told the *Saturday Evening Post*. "They want to know what this cat has got. I know what it is. I make them feel, I reach in and grab one of their controlled emotions, the deeply buried stuff, and yank it to the surface."[37]

Miller made Ray a star, but their work also showed the limitations of his production style. "I didn't want Johnnie to be noted just for his black inspired singing," he recalled,[38] and he soon had Ray hitting with lightly swinging standards, hokey ragtime, and a pair of country-folk duets with Doris Day. Ray seems to have been happy with this range of material—he was the son of a square-dance fiddler and had grown up on swing records—but the later choices rarely played to his unique strengths. Even when he covered an R&B tune, the Prisonaires' "Just Walking in the Rain" in 1956, Miller paired him with a whistler who gave the disc an insouciant, Gene Kelly flavor rather than the lonesome soulfulness of the original.

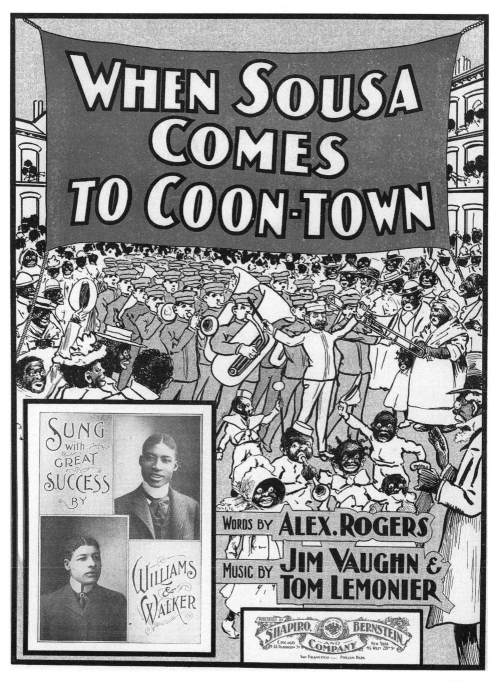

Ragtime and race: sheet music for a song celebrating America's most popular bandleader, portraying an African-American neighborhood in the stereotyped style of the era, and crediting the country's most successful black song and dance team, who performed the piece in their 1903 Broadway show, *In Dahomey*. (Courtesy of Duke University Rare Book, Manuscript, and Special Collections Library)

ABOVE James Reese Europe (with baton) and his Society Orchestra, c. 1916, with drums, bass, cello and three different sizes of banjos. (Courtesy of the Maryland Historical Society)

JAMES REESE EUROPE
SUPERIOR COLORED MUSICIANS
67-69 WEST 131st STREET
NEW YORK

RIGHT A sample of Europe's letterhead.

FACING PAGE Vernon and Irene Castle demonstrate some of their distinctive steps, and her distinctive fashions. (From their book *Modern Dancing*, World Syndicate, 1914)

The Promenade

The Step Out

The Castle Walk

The Tango of Today

Innovation

The Spin

The Polka Skip

The Skating Step

New Victor Records
Jass Band and other
Dance Selections

The Original Dixieland Jass Band

SPELL it Jass, Jas, Jaz or Jazz—nothing can spoil a Jass band. Some say the Jass band originated in Chicago. Chicago says it comes from San Francisco—San Francisco being away off across the continent. Anyway, a Jass band is the newest thing in the cabarets, adding greatly to the hilarity thereof.

They say the first instrument of the first Jass band was an empty lard can, by humming into which, sounds were produced resembling those of a saxophone with the croup. Since then the Jass band has grown in size and ferocity, and only

ABOVE Paul Whiteman is crowned King of Jazz by Jeanne Gordon of the Metropolitan Opera, the obvious person to present this honor. (From *Jazz*, by Whiteman and Mary Margaret McBride, J.H. Sears, 1926, the first book published about the new musical style)

FACING PAGE Jazz—or Jass, Jas, or Jaz—arrives in New York courtesy of a white band from New Orleans, via Chicago (or should that be San Francisco?). Note the foxtrotting dancers sporting the latest high society styles. (Victor advertising flyer, courtesy of the Hogan Jazz Archive, Tulane University)

75

ABOVE The early cylinder phonographs both played and recorded: This advertising photo shows a middle-class family making a record in the comfort of their parlor. (Courtesy of U.S. Department of the Interior, National Park Service, Edison National Historic Site)

LEFT By the 1920s phonograph merchandisers were offering to install their "instruments" in dance halls and theaters and to provide "talking machine concerts," saving customers the cost of hiring live musicians. (*Talking Machine Journal,* July 1926)

*"—I went to the Canned Goods Fair,
The prunes and the tunes were there"*

Have you, too, heard the Cannery racket—the little tin-clad "Sound" operas and jazz numbers so joyously welcomed here by the delicatessen set?

To some theatre interests this is a heart-warming clamor. It means economy for them, hence greater profits.

To persons of sound musical taste, it is ludicrous and impudent—an affront to the intelligence and taste of the theatre-going public. They see in the talkies no excuse for resort to Canned Music.

If you, dear reader, are one of those who recognize that machine-made sound cannot take the place of living orchestras and organists in the theatre . . . if you deplore corruption of musical appreciation and discouragement of musical talent . . . if you see no reason why you should forego the pleasure of real music in the theatre to enable an economy whose benefits you do not share, TREAT YOURSELF TO A SIGH OF RELIEF. SIGN THE COUPON BELOW. Then mail it!

THE AMERICAN FEDERATION OF MUSICIANS

Comprising 140,000 professional musicians in the United States and Canada

JOSEPH N. WEBER, President. 1440 Broadway, New York, N. Y.

The arrival of sound movies put hundreds of thousands of musicians out of work. The musicians' union considered calling a strike against the theaters, but instead decided to take their message to the public, which they hoped could be persuaded to demand live over "canned" music. (*The Metronome*, March 1930)

Gem O' My Heart

Featured by

GUY LOMBARDO

AND HIS RADIO FOLLIES ORCHESTRA

in the

RADIO FOLLIES

HOUR

Coming to you from the New York Studios
of the Columbia Broadcasting System.

GUY LOMBARDO and his
RADIO FOLLIES ORCHESTRA

Words and Music by
AL SHERMAN
and
AL LEWIS

Sincerely Yours
Guy Lombardo

Thru the Courtesy of
KAPPEL'S
109 Sixth St.
6103 Penn Ave.
PITTSBURGH'S LARGEST
JEWELERS

IT DON'T MEAN A THING
(IF IT AIN'T GOT THE SWING)
Words by IRVING MILLS Music by DUKE ELLINGTON

ABOVE Guy Lombardo was the most popular
"sweet" orchestra leader following Whiteman's
model, and defined the dance band mainstream
for decades — as well as the jazz world's notion of
squareness (as in the comic on the facing page).

RIGHT Duke Ellington wrote the anthem of
swing, but he was also inspired by Whiteman and
created some superbly sweet arrangements.
(Courtesy of the Tom Morgan Collection)

Highlights of the Benny Goodman saga, from *Picture News*, March 1946. The comic book's cover drawing showed Frank Sinatra knocking out "the biggest bully of them all," a burly figure representing "racial bigotry," watched by an admiring quartet of teenaged bobby-soxers. As for the "famed Goodman Sextet," this particular lineup seems to have existed only in the cartoonist's imagination.

Country music comes to town: **TOP** A 1947 RCA Victor ad joins Vaughn Monroe, Louis Armstrong, Tommy Dorsey and Pee Wee King. **BOTTOM** Gene Autry, the Andrews Sisters, and that ol' cowhand Bing Crosby. (Courtesy of and © the Autry Qualified Interest Trust and the Autry Foundation.)

Folk music without cowboy hats: Jo Stafford and Frank Sinatra had been the female and male vocal stars of the Tommy Dorsey Orchestra before going solo. Stafford, with Dorsey arranger Paul Weston, produced the first major pop-folk album in 1947. Three years later, "Goodnight, Irene" was the number one song in the United States, with top ten versions by the Weavers, Stafford, and a less-than-thrilled Sinatra.

down beat

May 1, 1958 35c

'58 Disc Jockey
Poll Results

Tony Bennett
Sings and Swings

ABOVE Mitch Miller coaches Tony Bennett at a recording session.

LEFT Harry Belafonte in 1954, about to become America's most popular folksinger. (Photo: Carl Van Vechten, courtesy of the Library of Congress, Prints & Photographs Division, Carl Van Vechten Collection)

Alan Freed souvenir program, c. 1956. The artists range from old-line pop stars Kay Starr and the McGuire Sisters to LaVern Baker, Fats Domino, Bill Haley, two doo-wop groups, and the new rockabilly stars Elvis Presley and Carl Perkins, while an inside photo showed Freed with the swing bandleader Count Basie. (Courtesy of www.alanfreed.com)

May 19, 1954

THE NEW

DOWN BEAT

Miller Reunion
Concert Weak
(See Page 1)

'I'm Lazy'—
Gerry Mulligan
(See Page 2)

New C&W
Wax Ratings
(See Page 13)

Les Elgart
Hits Road
(See Page 1)

RECORDS
HIGH-FIDELITY
INSTRUMENTS
FILMLAND UP BEAT
RADIO • TV

25 CENTS

CANADA 30c
FOREIGN 35c

EVERYTHING IN THE WORLD ABOUT THE WORLD OF MUSIC

A Young
Man With
A Horn
See Page 3

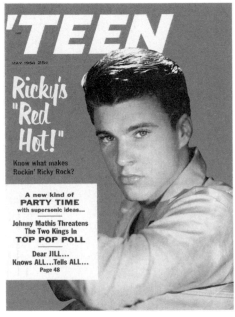

'TEEN

MAY 1958 25c

Ricky's
"Red
Hot!"

Know what makes
Rockin' Ricky Rock?

A new kind of
PARTY TIME
with supersonic ideas...

Johnny Mathis Threatens
The Two Kings In
TOP POP POLL

Dear JILL...
Knows ALL...Tells ALL...
Page 48

FACING PAGE Charlie Gracie onstage with Buddy Johnson's Orchestra (Courtesy of www.charliegracie.com); Frankie Avalon as a fourteen-year-old jazz prodigy; Ricky Nelson as every teenage girl's dream. (Courtesy of Browne Popular Culture Library, Bowling Green State University)

THIS PAGE From Los Angeles in 1955, *Dig* magazine gives a taste of solo dance styles to come (Courtesy of Browne Popular Culture Library); Chubby Checker and a friend do the twist. (Courtesy of Getty Archive)

THE SUPREMES
A BIT OF LIVERPOOL

A HARD DAYS NIGHT
HOUSE OF THE RISING SUN
BITS AND PIECES
I WANT TO HOLD YOUR HAND
CAN'T BUY ME LOVE
YOU'VE REALLY GOT A HOLD ON ME
YOU CAN'T DO THAT
DO YOU LOVE ME
HOW DO YOU DO IT
WORLD WITHOUT LOVE
BECAUSE

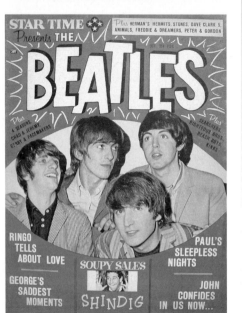

STAR TIME Presents THE BEATLES

Plus HERMAN'S HERMITS, STONES, DAVE CLARK 5, ANIMALS, FREDDIE & DREAMERS, PETER & GORDON

Plus A SEASONS, CHAD & JEREMY, GERRY & PACEMAKERS

Plus SEARCHERS, RIGHTEOUS BROS, BEACH BOYS, KINKS

RINGO TELLS ABOUT LOVE

PAUL'S SLEEPLESS NIGHTS

GEORGE'S SADDEST MOMENTS

SOUPY SALES SHINDIG

JOHN CONFIDES IN US NOW...

2. "We heard Paul and Ringo are going steady, so could we turn these in on a couple of Rolling Stones?"

TOP Motown joins the British Invasion.
LEFT A typical Beatles fan mag cover.
ABOVE A cartoon from *16 Magazine* suggests the fickle nature of teen fans and the interchangeability of British rockers.

To Miller, the unbridled passion that distinguished a lot of R&B (and, shortly, rock 'n' roll) performances was always suspect: "Emotion never makes you a hit," he said. "I always tell this to singers: Emotion is not something *you* feel. It's something you make the listener feel. And you have to be very cool and know what you're doing. You get a little tear in your voice, you put it there if the lyric calls for it—and little things like that. That's where a good producer comes in."[39]

As always, Miller thought like a studio pro. And for all his openness to unlikely songs and instrumental blends, he shared his generation's basic concept of "good music." Their standards had been formed through music lessons, at classical concerts, and by working with the consummate professionals who staffed and directed both concert orchestras and big bands. When they were attracted to folk songs, country songs, and blues, it was in much the same way an haute cuisine chef appreciates fresh meat and vegetables: as raw materials waiting to be improved by some educated sautéing, a little cream for smoothness and a touch of rosemary.

It was still more or less the Whiteman approach. Only thirty years had passed since Whiteman made a lady out of jazz, and the people now ruling the music world had been formed in that era. When Miller and Laine set the pattern for dozens of future Western movie themes with their hit version of "High Noon (Do Not Forsake Me)," the song's composer was Dimitri Tiomkin, a Russian émigré who had first won fame by organizing and playing piano at the European premiere of *Rhapsody in Blue*. It is an odd irony that, in a period when cowboys were seen as the apotheosis of American virtue and Russia as America's most fearsome enemy, the paradigmatic Western soundtracks were composed by a man who loved the plains because they reminded him of the steppes.[40] Or perhaps it was in keeping with James Reese Europe's notion that only the Negro and the Russian had true peasant souls.

In any case, the ways in which people were hearing and experiencing music were changing dramatically, but the ways in which most of them thought about it were still framed by an earlier world. If Eddie Fisher, the premier teen idol of the early 1950s, had emerged not from a band but from a broadcast talent show, he was still routinely compared to Sinatra and claimed Jolson as his vocal model. If Perry Como had become the most familiar voice in America through fifteen-minute video visits to millions of living rooms, he was still seen as another Crosby. There were a few more Southern accents in the pop mainstream, but they belonged to Dinah Shore and Kay Starr, not to Kitty Wells or Hank Williams (though Eddy Arnold was smooth enough to host Como's show for a couple of weeks in the summer of 1952). And though Nat King Cole had become one of the country's favorite romantic balladeers, black faces were notable rarities on the nation's television screens.

At a time when unprecedented prosperity was balanced by unprecedented fears, the pop mainstream was aiming for the same appeal as the suburbs: a modern, cosmopolitan future with all the comfort and security of an idyllic, small-town past.

13

ROCK THE JOINT

They've called it a lot of things since King Oliver brought it up the Mississippi from New Orleans—this peculiarly American music that moved from the levees to Carnegie Hall. Mostly, I guess, it's been called jazz, but there were those days of the early 30s when the term was swing. Today they tell me the music of this half-century decade is known as rhythm and blues.

THE LOS ANGELES TIMES, 1954

On Monday, July 14, 1952, Paul Whiteman was presenting his *TV Teen Club*, a weekly amateur contest on Philadelphia's ABC television affiliate. It was more than thirty years since the erstwhile King of Jazz had swept the country with his dance orchestrations, and he had weathered the decades better than most of his peers. He had bailed out of the touring band business toward the end of 1942 and taken over as director of music for NBC's Blue Network, which shortly became the American Broadcasting Company. In 1947, he became one of the first coast-to-coast disc jockeys as host of the *Paul Whiteman Club*,[1] and in 1948, when ABC expanded into television, he conducted a performance of *Rhapsody in Blue* on the inaugural telecast, then began hosting the *TV Teen Club* the following spring.

The *Teen Club* was a weekly talent contest: One surviving show includes a jazz clarinetist, a kid soloing on ocarina, a tap dancer, a gymnast, and a gangly guitarist in cowboy duds, and the audience picked a winner with the aid of an applause meter. This particular afternoon, after a little banter with his female cohost, Whiteman yielded the stage to a local sixteen-year-old named Charlie Gracie. Gracie played an introductory riff on electric guitar, hit a stop-time chord, and began to sing:

> We're gonna tear down the mailbox, rip up the floor,
> Beat down the windows, and knock down the door,
> We're gonna rock, baby, rock this joint!
> We're gonna rock, yes, rock this joint!
> We're gonna rock, we're gonna rock this joint tonight![2]

In hindsight, it seems like a classic culture clash—the old king hearing the shock of the new. And to add to the sense of foreshadowed revolution, the *Teen Club*'s announcer was an ex-country and western deejay from upstate New York named Dick Clark, who in a few years would become television's biggest promoter of rock 'n' roll.[3]

But if Gracie heralded a new era, he was also connected to the old. His father, an Italian immigrant who worked at the local Stetson hat factory, was a swing fan—Louis Prima, a fellow Sicilian, was a particular favorite—and his guitar teacher was a relative of Joe Venuti, the Whiteman orchestra's one-time violin star, who taught him the standard skills of a band guitarist. His mother preferred country and western music, and he had picked up "Rock the Joint" a few months earlier after the family went to a country show in nearby Quakertown. The group onstage was called Bill Haley and the Saddlemen, and Gracie recalls that "they had cowboy outfits on, the hats and so forth. But they were playing country music with a drum, which was unheard of in those days, with a backbeat."[4]

Haley had grown up in Chester, Pennsylvania, about twenty miles from Philadelphia, a shy boy, blind in one eye, who idolized Gene Autry and taught himself to play a few chords on guitar and yodel. At first he just sang at the local auction mart, but when the World War II draft brought a shortage of male performers, he landed a job as lead vocalist for a Midwestern hillbilly act, and by the end of 1947 he was back in Chester working as a singing cowboy on radio station WPWA. The next year his Four Aces of Western Swing recorded their first sides for a local outfit called Cowboy Records. Soon they would change their name to the Saddlemen—there was already an R&B group in the region called the Four Aces—and over the next four years they recorded for six different small labels.

The Saddlemen's instrumental lineup was guitar, bass, steel guitar, and a keyboard player who doubled on piano and accordion, and a surviving ad calls them "the Most Versatile Band in the Land," featuring "Modern Cowboy Swing and Jive."[5] Haley's radio program followed an R&B record show called *Judge Rhythm's Court*, so he was keeping up with the current black styles, and "Rock the Joint" was Judge Rhythm's theme song, a rowdy dance number that had been recorded in 1949 by two local rhythm and blues bands. "It was strictly a Race record," Haley later recalled. "I started to sing and hum the tune, and I started to use it in the show, and every time I would do it I would see this tremendous reaction. So I rewrote some of the lyrics, released the record and it became a big smash hit for us."[6]

In the postwar years, black music had been going through an evolution that in some ways paralleled what was happening in the white pop world: *Billboard*'s rhythm and blues columnist noted in 1952 that one of the most important developments in the genre was the new prominence of "the country or southern style blues and country style singer."

At one time there was a wide gulf between the sophisticated big city blues and rocking novelties waxed for the northern market, and the country or delta blues that were popular in the southern regions. Gradually the two forms intermingled and the country blues tune, now dressed up in arrangements palatable to both northern and southern tastes, have been appearing on disks of all r.&b. labels.... The sophisticated item is still more important, but... many diskings have the country tinge. Along with this country kick, some exclusively country artists have achieved popularity of late, including Howlin' Wolf, B. B. King, Muddy Waters and others.[7]

As in the pop world, this shift was driven in part by wartime migration—which in the case of African Americans just sped up an ongoing diaspora—and also reflected the basic appeal of direct lyrics and simple tunes. There was nothing new about average Americans preferring a solid beat and songs that were easy to sing, and though both classical and jazz boosters had hoped to improve these plebian tastes, the democratizing force of the jukebox had proved their endurance. Nor was the emphasis on such performances just a matter of country versus city. The honking saxophones that drove so many R&B records at the turn of the 1950s had their root in Illinois Jacquet's 1942 solo from "Flying Home," recorded with Lionel Hampton's swing orchestra. As Hampton wrote at that time, "When my tenor man takes off with a string of choruses, then reaches the point where he grabs one note and repeats it, two to the bar, for sixteen bars, the jitterbugs usually work themselves up into a terrific panic of excitement, as if the repeated note were the greatest or most difficult thing in the whole solo." Those sixteen bars inspired a generation of exuberant minimalists, including Joe Houston, Willis "Gator Tail" Jackson, Gil Bernal, Big Jay McNeely, Sam "The Man" Taylor, and Big Al Sears. Some of them were capable of playing swing and bop, but they made their names as raw honkers with rhythmic drive, and the headline of Hampton's piece reflected the mixed feelings a lot of jazz fans would express with more vehemence a dozen years later: "The Public Is Square—But It Rocks."[8]

I suggested a connection between swing and rock 'n' roll a few chapters back, and though there were immense differences as well, Hampton and Haley both provided direct links. Haley consistently hired musicians with swing backgrounds: Art Ryerson, the guitarist on his first nationally charted hits, had spent two years in the Whiteman orchestra, and by the mid-1950s his regular band, now called the Comets, included Rudy Pompilli, a saxophonist who had apprenticed in Ralph Marterie's big band, and Franny Beecher, a guitarist who had worked with Benny Goodman.[9] Haley's group became the defining rock 'n' roll band when his recording of "Rock around the Clock" was used as the opening music for 1955's *Blackboard Jungle*, and the film famously emphasized the generational conflict between his music and jazz with a scene in which the rowdy, rock-loving high school students smash their teacher's collection of Dixieland 78s—but in real life, Haley's record had been produced by Milt Gabler, the same man who sponsored the first Dixieland reissues back in the 1930s. Gabler had also produced Louis Jordan's hits, and he recalled that the Comets' sound was based directly on Jordan's style: "I'd sing Jordan riffs to the group that would be picked up by the electric guitars and tenor sax.... They got a sound that had the drive of the Tympany Five and the color of country and western."[10]

Not only had a lot of R&B and rock 'n' roll musicians served apprenticeships in swing orchestras, but those orchestras continued to be a key part of the evolving musical mix. When Alan Freed premiered his *Camel Rock and Roll Party* in 1956—the first national radio show to feature the new trend and, from the sponsor's point of view, heir to Casa Loma, Goodman, Xavier Cugat, and Vaughn Monroe—the house band was the Count Basie Orchestra, which also received an on-air award from *Cash Box* as the country's "best rock 'n' roll band."[11] That partnership did not last long, but when Freed hosted a multiact revue at the Paramount Theater in 1957, he still had a twenty-piece big band backing and alternating with the shouters, doo-woppers, and rockabillies and explained to the *New York Times* that "rock 'n' roll is really swing with a modern name." Echoing the pronouncements of history-minded bandleaders since Whiteman's time, he added, "It began on the levees and plantations, took in folk songs, and features blues and rhythm. It's the rhythm that gets the kids. They are starved for music they can dance to, after all those years of crooners."[12] Basie concurred, saying, "Rock 'n' roll started the kids dancing again—that's certainly a blessing for us."[13]

Admittedly, such statements need not be taken at face value. Freed's Paramount engagement came at a moment when stripped-down R&B rhythms were under attack for encouraging juvenile delinquency, and the theater's accompanying movie, which featured Haley and Little Richard, was defensively titled *Don't Knock the Rock*. Freed enjoyed telling reporters that Goodman and Whiteman had invited him "to compare scrapbooks" showing that critics had similarly claimed their music "corrupted the youth of their day."[14] So although he was a longtime jazz fan—he had led a high school dance band called the Sultans of Swing—Freed's comparisons of rock 'n' roll to earlier styles were also meant to reassure the older generation. Likewise, it was natural for Basie and Hampton (who was featured in the fictionalized 1957 Freed biopic, *Mister Rock and Roll*) to try to associate their style with a young audience.

Nonetheless, rock 'n' roll dancing looked a lot like the Lindy hop and jitterbug, and many of the key black jazz outfits, from King Oliver to Basie, had based their core repertoire on the same Southern blues styles that were now hitting the mainstream as a hot new trend. It is a paradox of twentieth-century American music that although black audiences consistently pioneered and adopted new styles faster than white ones did, they also stayed closer to rural styles. The buffer between country and city was much thinner in African-American culture, because whatever their tastes or successes, segregation meant that longtime black city dwellers were crowded together with their newly arrived country cousins, and economic discrimination meant that they were often stuck in the same jobs. What is more, the sheer number of Southern immigrants relative to the older urban population was very different than in white communities. And the musical shift was made easier by the fact that black country musicians tended to be hipper than their white neighbors—they were looking toward Chicago and Harlem long before the war—and black urban bands remained in touch with Southern rural trends in a way that their white counterparts generally did not. After all, most of the black city musicians were only a generation out of Mississippi, Texas, or the Carolinas, while the white city musicians were as likely to be a generation out of Italy, Ireland, or Eastern Europe.

When the white pop scene shifted away from jazz and began adopting more country and western flavors in the postwar years, it had seemed like a move away from urban and black styles, but it also opened a door for Haley and the raft of honky-tonk blues cats who hit the mainstream in the second half of the 1950s with the fusion dubbed "rockabilly."[15] This confused a lot of rhythm and blues fans at the time, because they considered themselves urban hipsters. By 1958, Freed would be describing Elvis Presley as "the only white man who can really sing the blues. He's got a real feeling for it. It comes from the contact he had as a child with Negroes in Tennessee." But when Presley first hit, Freed argued that rather than being a genuine rock 'n' roller, "he really sings hill-billy or country-and-western style."[16] The early Presley movies presented him as a country singer who only gradually adopted rock 'n' roll mannerisms, and though there was some truth to this portrayal, it also made him seem safer, less like the juvenile delinquents of *Blackboard Jungle* and more like a natural extension of Jo Stafford and Frankie Laine.

The story of early rock 'n' roll has been told often and well, so there is no need for me to revisit all the familiar themes, but I do want to touch on some of them briefly and complicate matters a little. For one thing, as with jazz, the style was not defined in musical terms. There were clear rhythmic differences between the way Haley's Comets played "Shake, Rattle and Roll" and the way it was played by the black rhythm and blues veterans who backed Big Joe Turner's version of the song, and I have no problem with historians who consider those differences a musical dividing line between R&B and rock 'n' roll. But that semantic distinction was not made in the 1950s. In 1953, "Shake, Rattle and Roll" was considered a rhythm and blues song, and both Haley's and Turner's versions were included in that category. And in 1956, when "rock 'n' roll" had become a common phrase, it was also used for both artists, as well as for gospel-flavored vocal groups, hiccuping hillbilly singers, and airbrushed teen idols. Freed had popularized the new term while still a local deejay in Cleveland, and as the *New York Post* reported, he "played only R&B records on his show, although he christened the style Rock and Roll to avoid the racial stigma of the old classification."[17]

In the 1950s, as in the ragtime and swing eras, a lot of white teenagers were drawn to black music, and if that fact excited more attention this time around and more emphasis was placed on the music's racial lineage, that is at least in part because African Americans were now in the news every day demanding a share of the American dream. In 1954, "Sh-Boom" became one of the first black teen hits to cross over to the pop charts and the Supreme Court handed down its decision in *Brown v. Board of Education*. In 1955, Martin Luther King Jr. came to national attention as a leader of the Montgomery bus boycott and a *Billboard* headline declared it "The Year R.&B. Took Over [the] Pop Field."[18] As Mitch Miller suggested in the *New York Times*, "There is a steady—and healthy—breaking down of color barriers in the United States; perhaps the rhythm-and-blues rage ... is another expression of it."[19]

The idea that rock 'n' roll served as a racial meeting point and helped transform American society is obviously attractive to rock historians, but we need to remember that at the time it also made a lot of white people nervous, and some of the music's pioneers felt a need to reassure them. A Freed concert program noted that he had twice received "brotherhood" awards from the black-owned *Pittsburgh Courier* but added that "he firmly resists any suggestion that he is a do-gooder in the field of race relations" and quoted him as saying, "I'm no champion of the Negro people just because they are Negroes.... Of Negro music, yes. Because it's honest, not because it's Negro."[20]

I reprint that quotation not to discredit Freed's accomplishments or paint him as a racist but simply as a reminder that there was a lot of ambiguity in the era's racial overlaps. White Northerners regularly decried Southern segregation, but the black comedian Dick Gregory pointed out an uncomfortable parallel: "Down South they don't care how close I get as long as I don't get too big; and up North they don't care how big I get as long as I don't get too close."[21] In the case of music, that meant that although white Southern teenagers went to segregated schools and some of them were willing to fight to keep it that way, they were also dancing to black rhythm and blues records at a time when their Northern peers still tended to be listening to Eddie Fisher and the McGuire Sisters. Of course, attitudes varied from region to region and neighborhood to neighborhood and often were very different for teenagers and their parents. Charlie Gracie recalls that some African-American deejays who heard his early records assumed he was black (a common recollection of early white rockers) and he used to joke with them that "Sicily's only twenty-eight miles from Africa; we're the original soul brothers." His biological brother went to school with Chubby Checker, and he says that "my black brothers used to come home and have lunch with me; we never had any problem in South Philadelphia." But he adds that those "brothers" did not appear in the *Bandstand* audience, because the producers "thought it best to keep only white kids on the screen."

The standard cliché about television was that suburban families were inviting the stars into their living rooms, and that had a nasty corollary when it came to black entertainers. Television was both the most centralized and the most conservative mass medium America had ever known. Until 1951, when the completion of a chain of microwave transmission towers made national broadcasts possible, most television programs were purely local creations, but the medium did not develop in the haphazard way that radio had. In 1948, when there were still only about a hundred stations in the country, the FCC declared a freeze on new license applications in order to sort out interference problems, and due to the Korean War the freeze lasted into 1952. The result was that, although New York and Los Angeles had seven stations each, most areas had no television until the end of that period, and by the time it reached them it was already in the hands of the national networks.[22] Network programming decisions reflected New York advertising agencies' notion of middle American tastes, which at the height of the McCarthy era were assumed to be homogeneously conservative. The target audience was white middle-class viewers, as they were the most coveted consumers, and suburbanites in particular, as they were presumed to have few other entertainment options.

Television presented a special challenge for the music business. The other established radio formats—comedy, variety, drama, and quiz shows—might need some tweaking and new performers but were inherently suited to a visual medium. Music, though, flourished on radio in large part by providing a background for people's daily lives, and the disc jockey shows that by now accounted for most musical programming were profoundly unsuited to seated, attentive viewing. In the early, local years, before network offerings were available for afternoon and late-night time slots, many TV stations did feature deejay shows, often augmented with odd visual effects: Philadelphia's *Whirligig* had "a combination electronic and optical device which transforms musical sounds instantaneously into myriads of constantly moving geometric patterns of light." Detroit's *Pat 'n' Johnny Show* displayed "parakeets, canaries, hamsters, rabbits, guinea pigs, tropical fish and other animals while records spin."[23]

But with a couple of notable exceptions, the record format did not translate to television. Viewers wanted to watch the singers they were hearing, and in those early days the most successful musical shows were either short and friendly or featured a mix of singers with other acts. Perry Como and Dinah Shore became enduring favorites through fifteen-minute shows that opened with a mention of their sponsors' products and some brief, innocuous remarks, included three or four songs interspersed with low-key chit-chat, and ended with an invitation to drop in again soon. Arthur Godfrey, who hosted *Arthur Godfrey's Talent Scouts* and *Arthur Godfrey and His Friends*, was appreciated for his casual, folksy manner, telling stories, delivering commercials that sounded like neighborly cooking tips, strumming a tune on his ukulele, then introducing some fresh-faced young singers and dancers.

In the broadcast season of 1952–1953, Godfrey's shows were the second- and third-rated evening television programs, right behind *I Love Lucy*. Not coincidentally, some of his regular performers—the Chordettes, the McGuire Sisters, and Pat Boone—were among the biggest-selling recording artists of the decade. Godfrey's male vocal quartet, the Mariners, did not have much success on records but was notable for another reason: It was the only interracial group making regular television appearances, and included two of the very few black faces seen on the networks.

Although segregation had long been an established practice in record marketing and radio, some performances had managed to slip by. As Paul Robi of the Platters recalled, "When our first two records hit, 'Only You' and 'The Great Pretender,' it was like we were getting away with murder because people in the South did not know we were black"—a situation paralleling Laine's and Gracie's memories of "passing" in the other direction.[24] Television did not allow such invisible crossovers, so although Ed Sullivan presented the Platters in 1956 and had previously invited a Harlem disc jockey, Dr. Jive, to host a fifteen-minute R&B revue, the black guests on network shows tended to be such established, older artists as Nat King Cole, Pearl Bailey, and the Mills Brothers, and even they appeared only occasionally compared with their Caucasian counterparts.[25] Both TV and radio made their money from advertisers buying an audience, rather than from listeners and viewers buying entertainment, and the advertisers were very wary about having their products associated with black performers, no matter how popular those performers might be. When Cole got his own network show in 1956, viewers tuned in to it in droves and within a year it had been extended to a half-hour and was rated alongside the wildly popular *$64,000 Question*; but no regular sponsors signed on, and after a year and a half Cole had to give up, wryly noting, "Madison Avenue is afraid of the dark."[26]

Meanwhile, when television went national it drew away most of the big corporate sponsorships that had supported network radio programs, and radio became more dependent than ever on recorded music. Staff orchestras and live dance-band remotes, already in decline by the mid-1940s, essentially vanished from the airwaves—Lawrence Welk was one of the few bandleaders to find a home in the video medium—and the typical modern radio station, rather than having a studio with room for a stage and a live audience, had a couple of cubbyholes from which a lone deejay and a lone engineer signaled to each other through a double pane of soundproof glass.

The demise of national radio broadcasting was a tragedy for some big stars and a couple of thousand staff musicians, but it was a boon for fans of classical, country, jazz, and ethnic styles, who now found programmers clamoring for their attention.[27] As television monopolized the mass-market accounts, radio had to concentrate on local sponsors and advertisers hawking products aimed at niche audiences: hair relaxers, for example, or acne creams, or rhythm and blues records.

Independent record labels flourished in the new broadcast climate, and much of the shift in popular music over the course of the 1950s can be traced to the interlocking agendas of local disc jockeys and "indies." The major labels were concentrating on mainstream pop acts who could appear on Godfrey's shows and Ed Sullivan's *Toast of the Town* or be guests of Como and Shore. Meanwhile, indie promoters were chatting up the deejays. Some were already friends and drinking buddies—everybody in a local music scene tended to know everybody else—and in unfamiliar territory the indie owners had a direct, personal stake in their records and would do whatever was necessary to make friends and get airplay: take a jock out to dinner, fix him up with a female companion, cut him in for a share of publishing and songwriting royalties, or hand him a stack of free records or a wad of cash. Dale Hawkins, Chess Records' entry in the rockabilly sweepstakes, recalled promotional trips with Leonard Chess that would start with the label owner filling his car trunk with alligator shoes:

> We'd be driving through some town that had a station that would play the music, and we'd go in to talk to the deejay, and ol' Leonard would say, "What size shoes you wear?"
>
> He'd say "eleven," "twelve," whatever, and Leonard would give me a sign, and I'd go out and get them shoes and that guy'd put 'em on there—and you talk about playing a record! We'd listen all the way out of town, as far as we could pick it up. We'd just go town to town, station to station, and those fifty-thousand-watters could bust a record wide open.[28]

There were all kinds of deejays and all kinds of indies: Baroque music, Latin styles, folk songs, and modern jazz all found wider audiences in the 1950s, to a great extent because there were small labels willing to record them and local programmers looking for something different to put on the air. But, at least in terms of the hit parade, by far the most significant new force was rhythm and blues. As was natural in a diffuse, small-budget market, R&B hits were often local: Haley's "Rock the Joint" was the third version of the song by a Philadelphia band, and none of them ever appeared on a national chart, but there is no reason to doubt his recollection that it was "a big smash hit" in the Delaware Valley area. And the fact that records broke regionally meant that a lot of different indies could get pieces of a single song, covering each other's releases and working to get their versions played by the local jocks. Of course, that also meant that a major label could cover a local hit before most of the country was even aware of it: Johnnie Ray's "Cry" was the only version of the song to appear on national rhythm and blues charts, though Ruth Casey had recorded the original on New York's Cadillac label (which coincidentally was recording Gracie's first discs around the same time) and at least three indie versions were available before Ray and Columbia got into the act.

This duplication is another reminder that songs, rather than records, were still widely considered to be the main currency of popular music. There were fourteen versions of "Cry" on the market by the time Ray's reached number one, and through the mid-1950s that was par for the course.[29] In 1955 "The Ballad of Davy Crockett" became the fastest-selling song in American history, helped along by versions on twenty different labels, and most pop hits were still charting in at least two versions with a half-dozen less successful competitors in tow.[30] That would change over the next few years, though, and some sectors of the industry were already preparing for the future. Songwriting contracts had included a standard reversion clause saying that a publishing company forfeited all rights if it did not make sheet music available within a year, but in 1955 the publishers moved to strike this clause, arguing that due to "the disk-based nature of the industry today . . . even click waxings often do not lead to sheet publication if the material is in the current rhythm and blues trend and the beat and arrangement are paramount to the words."[31]

Though the publishers did not mention it, that observation had a logical corollary: If the beat and arrangement were what made a hit, then when a record took off and other companies wanted a share of its sales, they not only had to cover the song but also had to clone the performance. And that became more and more true as rhythm and blues garnered a larger share of the pop audience. In 1952 "Cry" was an anomaly on the pop charts, but by March 1955 *Billboard* was reporting that thirteen of the thirty songs currently listed as pop best-sellers fell into the R&B category, and that meant not only that they had first been recorded by R&B artists but also that pop producers were trying to capture the flavor of the originals. The magazine's current "Honor Roll of Hits" included "Sincerely," "Tweedle Dee," "Ko Ko Mo," "Earth Angel," and "Hearts of Stone," all originally done by black singers on indies but getting their biggest sales in versions by the McGuire Sisters, Georgia Gibbs, Perry Como, the Crew Cuts (a quartet of young Canadians inspired by the Four Lads), and Como's TV trio, the Fontane Sisters. Some labels were devoting the bulk of their catalogs to reverse carbon copies of rhythm and blues hits—Decca's Coral subsidiary had white covers available for five of the seven top discs on the magazine's R&B chart.[32]

The degree of imitation varied from label to label and artist to artist—no one was going to mistake Como for an R&B singer, whatever material he was doing—but imitating a hit record was still quite different from simply doing a version of a hit song. Jimmie Haskell, an arranger for Imperial Records, recalled that the label's owner, Lew Chudd, would bring him another company's single and demand a chart of exactly what was being played:

> I'd listen to the record, take it down, and maybe improve it a little. Lew would say, "What are you doing?"
>
> I'd say, "I'm improving it."
>
> And he'd scream, "Don't improve it. Copy it."[33]

Mercury went Imperial one better, not only copying the arrangement of Atlantic's "Tweedle Dee" but also hiring the same backup vocalists to remake their parts.[34]

To a lot of music business veterans, this was outright theft. Benny Goodman had played Fletcher Henderson arrangements, but he had credited and paid Henderson for them. In the 1950s, no such accommodations were being made, and in February 1955 LaVern Baker, the original singer of "Tweedle Dee," sent a public letter to her congressman requesting that the copyright act be amended to protect arrangements. Baker was no naïve ingénue: She had been schooled by her aunt Merline Johnson, a popular 1920s blues queen known as the Yas Yas Girl; had worked with Henderson's orchestra; and had been singing in nightclubs for almost ten years, billed as "Little Miss Sharecropper." She had also been a friend and mentor to Johnnie Ray while they were appearing together at the Flame Show Bar, and by the mid-1950s she felt that she should be able to drop the stereotyped moniker and pick up some of Ray's white audience. So she was particularly incensed when the Mercury A&R team, Hugo Peretti and Luigi Creatore, not only brought in Atlantic's backup singers but also apparently coached big-band belter Georgia Gibbs to imitate every nuance of Baker's vocal phrasing.

Baker was careful to distinguish what had happened with "Tweedle Dee" from the normal process of making cover records. As she wrote, "It's not that I mind anyone singing a song that I write, or have written for me by someone, but I bitterly resent their arrogance in thefting my music note for note."[35] Nor was she alone in drawing this distinction. A few months after Baker raised the issue, New York's WINS announced that it would no longer play "copy" records and similarly added that this did not imply any criticism of "the release and spinning of cover disks—which is an integral part of the disk business and which is regarded as completely ethical by all."[36]

The distinction between covers and copies made sense, but in hindsight it was beside the point. Although this controversy is usually explored as a matter of white singers covering black originals and major labels covering indies, on a broader level the most significant thing was that covering was no longer a foregone conclusion. As long as the pop scene had been driven by live performances, it was assumed that any band would play the current hits and that some people would prefer one band's version, others another, and most would be happy dancing to whoever was on the bandstand. But once pop fans were getting most of their music on records, everyone could listen to the same performance, so there was no reason that it should not be the only performance.

Or, rather, there were lots of reasons, but now they needed to be explained. Some of the explanations were economic (multiple labels and distributors wanted a share of the action on current hits), some were social (white parents objected to their children listening to black singers), and in both cases they were often rephrased to seem like aesthetic judgments (black groups sang off-pitch, and indie pressings had mediocre sound). The easiest and most reasonable explanation was still that different versions suited different tastes: When "Cold, Cold Heart" hit on the pop, C&W, and R&B charts in versions by Tony Bennett, Hank Williams, and Dinah Washington, they were clearly very different records, suited to different audiences and aesthetics. But that explanation became harder to make as the charts converged. In 1956, *Billboard* reported that "one out of every three records that made the rhythm and blues chart also made the pop retail chart"[37]—a very different thing from songs crossing over in cover versions—and Baker's anger was fueled by the fact that her own recording of "Tweedle Dee" showed up on the pop jukebox and best seller charts and presumably could have gone a good deal higher without Mercury's sound-alike competition.

At that time, pop radio playlists were still lagging behind consumer tastes. Baker's song did not dent the pop jockey chart, and that discrepancy would continue through the next few years: Rock 'n' roll records consistently scored higher on the pop sales chart than on the jockey chart, while mainstream singles scored higher with the jocks than with buyers.[38] (Once again, "mainstream" is not just a synonym for white: Cole's patterns were similar to Sinatra's.) Still, radio was opening up in terms of both race and music, and after RCA signed Elvis Presley in 1956, more than a dozen of his records hit the top ten on all three charts of all three genres. Of course, there were also plenty of artists who remained in one genre or another—Carl Perkins's record of "Blue Suede Shoes" reached the top in all three but also spawned covers by Pee Wee King in C&W, Sam "The Man" Taylor in R&B, and Lawrence Welk in pop.

In April 1955 Victor became the first major label to announce that it would no longer make covers and also that in the future it would demand exclusive rights to any new songs it planned to record. *Billboard* doubted that this commitment would last, pointing out that the label's distributors would continue to demand "a share of the local action on any breaking tune,[39] and, though its covering slowed down, Victor did not remain immune to temptation. But the music world had changed. That fall, the magazine noted that mainstream disc jockeys were increasingly shunning covers: "The pop boys played Fats Domino, Lavern Baker, Nappy Brown, Al Hibbler, the Platters, etc., because there is strong sentiment growing everywhere for the 'original,' the creator, as opposed to the copyist."[40] That October, Chuck Berry's "Maybellene" became the first black rock 'n' roll hit to reach the pop charts solely in its original version. The situation was still in flux, but records rather than songs were clearly coming to define the pop mainstream: More than fifty years later, we continue to think of the hits of the 1930s and 1940s as "standards," performed by jazz and pop artists around the world, but of the hits of the 1950s as "oldies," usually heard on recordings by the original artists.

The fact that single, unique recordings were replacing multiple performances of songs meant that record companies were becoming more interested in quirky, one-off records and less dependent on reliable studio performers—which is to say it encouraged the deprofessionalization of pop music. A street-corner doo-wop group could get a top ten hit while still in high school without making any professional appearances, knowing more than a handful of songs, or understanding the intricacies of union regulations, record royalties, or publishing contracts. So a lot of the resistance to rock 'n' roll within the music business can be traced to professional musicians, songwriters, and arrangers worrying about their future in a world that was being taken over by amateurs. Gracie's father had bought him a guitar and lessons with the idea that a trained musician could always find work, but that would become less and less true over the following decades. Popular music would come to be seen less as a trade than as a lottery in which young aspirants either got lucky or went into a more solid business, and it is no accident that whereas virtually all the artists who topped the charts in the 1930s and 1940s—including "one-hit wonders"—performed professionally for many years, a lot of the people who had hits in the 1950s were working outside music by the time they were in their twenties.

In 1952, *Time* magazine had described Jo Stafford as being comfortable with everything "from ballads to bop, from hillbilly tunes to hymns," and quoted her saying, "I don't want to be typed.... Once you get typed, you lose value."[41] Some show-biz-savvy rockers attempted a similar versatility, but a lot of them were just teenagers who had figured out how to do a few songs in an exciting way. Gracie, who got his only top ten hit in 1957 with "Butterfly," says, "I only had ten minutes of fame in my life, but the difference between me and a lot of the other guys was I was a musician. I was taught the proper way—I can sight-read music, and I still can play anything. So even when things were rough, I went out and I worked the joints, five hours a night, five nights a week, got my pay and went home. And now I'm 71 years old, and I've never had a day job."

Gracie was not unique, but he was no longer the norm, and critics were quick to deplore the amateurism of the rock 'n' roll trend. Dinah Washington complained that the teen vocal groups "sound terrible.... They don't rehearse. They just start hollerin'."[42] The cultural pundit Dwight MacDonald staked out a particularly elevated position, writing that rock 'n' roll was "even less interesting musically than the insipid ballads that Crosby and Sinatra crooned to earlier generations of adolescents." He singled out the young rockabilly singer Jimmie Rodgers "who a year or so ago was getting hamburger money by collecting Coke bottles in the back alleys of Los Angeles, and who now is making about two hundred thousand dollars a year."

> He has a pleasant voice, a good sense of rhythm, and average skill with the guitar; unable to read music, he started out by memorizing songs as they came over his car radio. One imagines an even less musically literate troubadour preparing his

repertoire by sitting in *his* car and listening to Mr. Rodgers coming over the airwaves, and so on, like that unsettling baking-powder label with a picture of the can on it, which bears the picture of another can, et cetera ad infinitum.[43]

Personally, I tend to find the 1950s R&B hits more consistently exciting than any previous national pop style. I would rather listen to Chuck Berry and the Coasters than to big bands or pop crooners, and when Ray Charles starts hitting, I feel that virtue is finally triumphant. So I understand why rock historians treat the 1950s as a period of much-needed musical revolution. Nonetheless, the attacks on rock 'n' roll were not all driven by racial and cultural prejudices or parental conservatism. It is easy for rock historians to tar the old guard with such prejudices and single out the silliest pop covers as typical, but Pat Boone's crew-necked crooning of Little Richard's Pentecostal boogies and Gibbs's stiff simulacrums of Baker and Etta James are dredged up over and over again not because they were the best of a bad bunch but because they are easy targets. Both singers made those particular records at the behest of their producers and were openly uncomfortable with the material, and Boone went on to greater success with ballads like the hugely popular "Love Letters in the Sand" and "April Love," which earned him second place to Presley as a '50s hitmaker. Less damning examples of white mainstream cover records might include the Crew Cuts' "Sh-Boom," a perky performance that is still enjoyed by oldies fans, or the McGuires' "Sincerely," which, although less soulful than the Moonglows' original, is warm and utterly sincere. They benefited from a racist system, but on their own merits they are perfectly satisfying and far superior to a lot of the teen hits that followed. Likewise, although Teresa Brewer's "Pledging My Love" was not as powerful as Johnny Ace's version, it is an excellent reminder that the jazz-schooled singers of the previous generation had skills that their younger colleagues lacked.

From the beginning, though, one of the appeals of rock 'n' roll was its air of authenticity, the idea, in Freed's words, that there was something "honest" about the voices of young black urbanites or rural Southerners that was missing from the polished studio hits that Mitch Miller and his peers were producing. This was, after all, the era of Marlon Brando and James Dean, who moved young fans with the sincerity of their moody, inarticulate performances. When Miller argued that singers should project passion with technical expertise rather than feeling it personally, he was taking the same position as older actors who disdained the emotion-driven "method," and teenagers preferred Elvis to the mainstream pop singers for much the same reasons they preferred Dean to the more traditionally glamorous movie stars. But there are many kinds of authenticity. Once the pop mainstream began drawing on country and R&B material, it was natural that some listeners would choose to hear that material in its original, rawer form, and that choice was not just a teen craze: In the early 1950s *Down Beat* annoyed some of its jazz-oriented subscribers by adding rhythm and blues and country music columns. But artists like Hank Williams and B. B. King were every bit as professional and studied as Miller's crew, albeit in more regional or ethnically rooted styles. And if, as Freed suggested, white teens were attracted to R&B for its honesty rather than its racial roots, it was natural that a lot of them would be even more captivated by the unsophisticated honesty of teenage rock 'n' rollers who looked and sounded like their friends and neighbors. As Miller noted to his chagrin, "The kids don't want recognized stars doing *their* music. They don't want real professionals. They want faceless young people doing it in order to retain the feeling that it's their own."[44]

In the second half of the 1950s, a lot of white teenagers were not only listening to rhythm and blues but also playing it, and they were no longer just producing copies of black records. Presley's version of "Hound Dog" can be traced back to an earlier hit by Big Mama Thornton, but it had a different lyric, melody, and rhythm, and its flip side, "Don't Be Cruel," was the first recording of a new composition by the black songwriter Otis Blackwell. As a result, Presley's hits were played both on pop programs and by Freed and the other R&B deejays. And as Presley was joined by artists like Carl Perkins, who not only had their own styles but also wrote their own material, it ceased to be possible to describe the scene simply in terms of black originators and white imitators.

Segregation was still the rule on television and at some concerts, but there were a lot more mixed shows than in previous eras, and if in some ways the racial overlap on the early rock scene resembled what had happened in the swing era, there were also significant differences. For one thing, the overall racial climate was changing, and for another the music industry was much less centralized. The rhythm and blues scene had its own record labels, radio stations, and touring and promotional networks. By 1956, though, it was becoming less and less clear what "rhythm and blues" meant: The term had been invented as a marketing category for African-American music directed at an African-American audience, but the success of Presley and his peers threw that easy equivalence into question. When "Hound Dog" and "Don't Be Cruel" simultaneously topped all three *Billboard* charts in September 1956, it was the first record by a white artist to reach the number one R&B spot since Johnnie Ray's "Cry" almost five years earlier. Yet between September 1957 and October 1958, sixteen of the top-ranked records on what had once been the magazine's Race chart were by white performers and only twelve by black, and in the year-end listing for 1958 whites accounted for more than half the top fifty R&B hits. (There was also one entry by the Cuban bandleader Perez Prado.)[45]

Rock historians tend to interpret those numbers as reflecting a confluence of black and white teen tastes[46]—and indeed there were ten records by black artists in that year's pop top fifty, making 70 percent of the pop and R&B lists identical. But the R&B side of that equation owed at least as much to the confusion of the chart makers as it did to a genuine racial convergence. Some black teens certainly enjoyed Elvis and the other white rockers, but a more significant factor was that deejays and stores that had previously served an overwhelmingly black clientele were now serving a huge audience of white teens while continuing to report their playlists and sales as part of the R&B market. That meant that, whatever the real degree of overlap, a number one teen-pop record like Jimmie Rodgers's "Honeycomb" could reach the top of the R&B chart without necessarily attracting many black fans.

Meanwhile, rhythm and blues artists whose work was not geared to white teenagers—for example, B. B. King, Bobby Bland, and Ray Charles—were still selling well to black listeners but were not showing up on any chart at all. And that, in turn, was hurting them with the deejays and jukebox ops. As one record promoter complained, "You can turn out the greatest, authentic, Deep South blues and never get near the r.&b. charts today. The stores that once sold strictly r.&b. traditional stuff are trying to be all things to all buyers, pop, country and western and rhythm and blues alike. The rockabillies are taking over everywhere."[47]

This would always be a tricky side effect of integration: "Separate but equal" was never equal, but when barriers came down a lot of businesses that had survived in a restricted environment were wiped out by larger, richer, and more powerful competitors. Unlike any previous R&B star, Elvis had RCA, network television, and Hollywood films supporting his records, and there were also many more white record buyers than black ones. Some performers who had built their careers in the segregated R&B market welcomed the rise of an interracial rock 'n' roll scene as a way of reaching that larger audience, but others saw their success slipping away with the old, race-based rubric, and they were joined by country music promoters who were similarly scared by the way young Southern fans were clamoring for Elvis and the Everly Brothers. Faced with this problem, *Billboard* announced in October 1958 that henceforth the R&B and C&W charts would be tabulated differently, with a focus on each style's core constituency.[48] Within a month King and Bland were back in the R&B top ten, Charles followed two months later, and 1959's year-end listing of the top fifty R&B sides included only four records by white performers, a level of representation that would remain fairly steady for the next three years. Meanwhile, the pop chart continued to trace a growing racial overlap: The magazine's fifty "Top Sides of 1959" included twelve records by black artists, including two of the top ten, and those numbers would mount steadily through 1962.[49]

If that story suggests some of the complexities of the relationship between American racial and musical attitudes, it is also an apt reminder that the record charts were created for particular purposes and never simply measured musical tastes. The lists in *Billboard* and *Cash Box* often provide the best evidence we have of consumer preferences during key periods, but they were limited both by subjective genre definitions and by irregular reporting of figures by deejays, stores, and record companies. Their results were to a great extent self-perpetuating, as chart rankings affected radio play and store promotions, and in that sense they were important even when their accuracy is questionable. But it is always worth remembering that they were intended specifically to serve the needs of the record and radio industries, and at best measured only selected markets. The charts of pop, R&B, and C&W hits were never meant to be lists of people's favorite performers or songs; they were lists of favorite—or most-played, or best-selling—singles.

Until the 1950s, singles were pretty much the only records that mattered in the popular music market, so they provide a fairly representative picture of the field. But by the time rock 'n' roll hit, the musical styles directed at older and more financially secure buyers were appearing primarily on long-playing albums. This meant that to an increasing degree the singles and radio charts were measuring teen and minority tastes rather than overall music listening. Nor were they even a reliable guide to those audiences, since stars like Sinatra and Doris Day were reaching fans through movies and television, and plenty of young and minority listeners were getting into album-friendly styles like folk songs and modern jazz. So the fact that rock 'n' roll was winning a huge share of the singles market did not necessarily mean that it was taking over the music business or even winning the allegiance of all the kids. This was particularly true when it came to the rowdier, rawer styles. As in the jazz world, the most mainstream, pop-oriented rock 'n' rollers tended to reach the broadest audience, but the music's critics and historians have typically sought to distinguish the music they love from the mediocre pap that surrounded it. As a result, virtually all rock histories portray Pat Boone and Connie Francis in much the same way that jazz histories portray Guy Lombardo and Rudy Vallée, and in both cases this reflects the fact that the people who grow up to be music critics tend to have very different tastes than the majority of their peers—and, in particular, than the majority of their female peers.

Charlie Gracie's high school buddies preferred Little Richard to Boone, but when I asked him what the other kids thought, he said, "If the record had it in the groove, as we said in those days, and the kids liked it, they went out and they bought it. Pat Boone was a young, good-looking guy, you know. He didn't have the sex appeal that Elvis had, because Elvis always had that sneer—and of course when they put him in Hollywood, they fixed his face and made him prettier. But Pat Boone was still very famous and popular." He added that when he started making records it was a big deal with his schoolmates, but "even more so with the guys than the girls, because, you know, rock 'n' roll was set by the males."

As with all such comments, Gracie's reflects a particular definition of rock 'n' roll, but in the music's early years few people would have disagreed. In 1956, a poll of nearly ten thousand high school students in the New York area found that girls and boys both chose Elvis as their favorite male singer, but while the boys chose rock 'n' roll as their favorite style, the girls chose pop vocals, and their favorite female singer was Doris Day. Meanwhile, a companion survey of more than five thousand college teens reported that both genders preferred pop, and the favorite male singers were Como for the girls and Sinatra for the boys—and when it came to which artist they actually bought on records, three out of the four groups named Harry Belafonte.[50] Such polls are not necessarily a reliable guide to national tastes, but they are a reminder that although rock 'n' roll was the news of the moment, it still faced a lot of competition even among young listeners. And when it came to older folks, the teenagers of the swing era were not yet in their forties and they were still buying a lot of records.

14

BIG RECORDS FOR ADULTS

I feel romantic and the record changer's automatic…baby.…

"MAKE YOURSELF COMFORTABLE," #6
POP HIT FOR SARAH VAUGHAN, 1955

Everyone sing the chorus—including intellectuals!

HARRY BELAFONTE, AT THE RIVIERA THEATER,
DETROIT, 1957

In the spring of 1957, *Time* magazine ran a feature on the "music rooms" that were taking the place of New York City's classier nightclubs. Such rooms had no cover charge and simply presented a jazz combo or cocktail trio rather than a full show with dancers, comedians, and singers. Their appearance reflected the new realities of urban nightlife: Fewer people were interested in going out and paying for the full nightclub experience, and many club owners were lamenting "that spectacular TV has satiated the public's appetite for shows, or that people simply do not dance any more." Other explanations included the federal cabaret tax, which added a 20 percent surcharge to checks in clubs that had dancing or a floor show but not those that just had music. The Village Vanguard's Max Gordon highlighted suburban flight, saying, "My old customers have been lost to Great Neck." And a Broadway producer singled out the appearance of long-playing phonograph records: "When you had the 78s, you had to get up and change the damned things every few minutes, so you got bored and went out."[1] Now, people could put a stack of albums on the hi-fi and enjoy a couple of hours of uninterrupted music in the comfort of their living rooms.

It may seem odd to accuse LPs of destroying café society, but it was certainly true that the new format not only changed the phonograph business but in some ways affected the broader conception of popular music. By 1955, seven years after they were introduced, long-playing albums accounted for half of all record revenues,[2] in large part because of performers and styles that had barely been acknowledged by record producers before their introduction. And while rock 'n' roll was making big news on the teen market, the vast majority of LP buyers were adults—including the sort of people who had supported ballrooms and cabarets.

Like other new technologies, LPs were initially regarded as simply an improvement on what had gone before. In June of 1948, when Columbia Records held a press conference to announce the new format, they displayed a fifteen-inch stack of 33 1/3-rpm discs and contrasted it with an eight-foot stack of 78-rpm albums of the same music. Along with being more compact, LPs were made of unbreakable vinyl and had less surface noise, but even today we refer to them as "albums," a semantic survival of the bound sets of 78s that preceded them. In fact, the word reflects an even earlier idea: Like stamp or photo albums, most 78-rpm record albums were not even sets of records. They were simply storage volumes, and as late as 1945 Columbia's only Frank Sinatra album was a set of four empty pockets with his picture on the cover, in which a bobby-soxer could keep her favorite discs.[3]

That had always been standard on the pop scene. The first prefilled record album was a four-disc set of Tchaikovsky's *Nutcracker Suite*, issued by German Odeon in 1909, and such packaged sets had continued to be associated with the upscale classical market. The late 1920s and 1930s brought a few nonclassical sets, including albums of Broadway musicals, memorial tributes to Bix Beiderbecke and Bessie Smith, and some small-label offerings devoted to the compositions of Gershwin and Cole Porter and the folk songs of Lead Belly and Josh White. But these were still largely aimed at the sort of middle-class, educated listeners who also bought classical music. By 1941, though, Bing Crosby had produced sets of cowboy, Hawaiian, and children's songs, and *Billboard* wrote that although albums had previously been "bought only by nuts and jazz hounds . . . the advent of the moderate-priced phono-radio combinations, plus new showmanship production methods for albums, has now brought packaged records out of the new-pants stage and into their own alongside of the Brahms, Strauss, and other classical albums."[4] Nonetheless, the article noted that all the major companies still gave dealers the option of splitting up pop sets for customers who wanted only one record, and also that Victor was not going along with the fad and would continue to just sell empty storage albums. Victor joined its competitors during the AFM ban, embracing multidisc collections as a way of repackaging older recordings, and by 1944 *Billboard* was referring to an "album craze,"[5] but in truth the form did not have much to offer the average pop fan. As with present-day downloaders, buyers confronted with a choice between picking the songs they wanted or buying a set compiled by a record company tended to choose the former, unless they were getting the original cast album of *Oklahoma!*

Many customers continued to buy their music on a song-by-song basis even after the arrival of the LP. Although Columbia's new albums provided fifteen or twenty minutes of uninterrupted listening per side, the last years of the 1940s found them locked in what was known as "the battle of the speeds," competing not only with 78s but with RCA's small, light and durable 45-rpm singles—which, because they were easier to ship than 78s, were also favored by the hit-oriented indie labels. There were also plenty of customers who didn't see the need to buy music in any form. Although record sales were climbing, radio was still the primary music source in most homes, and for a while the competing formats scared off new buyers who didn't know which kind of phonograph to get. Over the next few years, though, manufacturers began producing machines that could play all three speeds, and as radio gave way to television, long-playing albums provided an ever-larger share of domestic background music.

Through the first decade and a half of the LP era, soundtracks and original cast recordings would continue to lead the long-format record market. The Broadway version of *South Pacific* was the best-selling album of 1949, 1950, and 1951 and remained strong through 1953, and a tabulation of the *Billboard* charts from 1955 to 1965 finds five show discs among the ten top sellers. That figure gets even more impressive if one looks at their longevity. Though no later set managed to duplicate the original *South Pacific*'s three-year run at the top, the cast albums of *My Fair Lady* and *The Sound of Music* and the movie soundtracks of the 1958 *South Pacific* and 1961's *West Side Story* each held the number-one spot for from fifteen to fifty-four weeks, and all remained on the charts for several years. (*My Fair Lady* held on for more than nine years, setting a record beaten only by Johnny Mathis's *Greatest Hits* and, two decades later, Pink Floyd's *Dark Side of the Moon*.)[6]

The popularity of show collections demonstrated a degree of continuity with the 78-rpm album era, but in other ways the new form encouraged new approaches. One was "mood" music, which would have made little sense without long-playing discs, because its whole raison d'être was to create a lingering, romantic ambiance. Paul Weston, Jo Stafford's husband and arranger, is usually credited with recording the first explicit mood album, *Music for Dreaming*, which as it happens was originally released as a set of 78s in 1945. But it was with the advent of LPs that mood became a genre, its status heralded by Weston's *Mood Music*, released as a ten-inch LP in 1953. That year's most popular album was Jackie Gleason's *Music for Lovers Only*, which was joined in 1954 by Gleason's *Music, Martinis and Memories* and *Music to Make You Misty*—as well as his ballet score *Tawny*—giving the television comedian (who neither played nor arranged any of the music but acted as a combined producer and celebrity figurehead for the projects) four of that year's ten best-selling LPs, and proving the widespread attraction of string-drenched standards with a hint of jazz. In part, these records fed nostalgia for disappearing dance-band styles and went along with the parallel popularity of Dixieland discs. Gleason's star instrumentalist was the trumpeter Bobby Hackett, who had played the solo on Glenn Miller's "String of Pearls," and two of the LPs that shared the top ten with him were the soundtrack of *The Glenn Miller Story* and an anthology of old Miller recordings of the songs used in that movie. (Though Miller himself had disappeared over the English Channel in 1944, his orchestra had re-formed in 1946 under the leadership of saxman-vocalist Tex Beneke, and by the early 1950s there were several sound-alike outfits purveying his brand of tightly arranged swing.)

Though the music was nostalgic, the packaging was not. In 1954, *Time* pointed out that whereas "once upon a time...popular recordings were stacked in bins, and hardly anybody thought to dignify them by collecting them in albums," now pop albums were "almost as common as paperback novels. And more and more, they are packaged with the same kind of half-dressed jacket heroines." Examples included Weston's *Dream Time Music*, a collection of string-drenched standards adorned with "a disheveled, shirtless brunette striding through a misty landscape" and Les Baxter's "*The Passions*, with subthemes entitled 'Despair,' 'Ecstasy,' 'Hate,' 'Lust,' 'Terror,' 'Jealousy' and 'Joy.' On the jacket: the picture of a lush young woman lost in a mixture of subthemes."[7]

If Weston was the father of mood, Baxter was the father of exotica. A popular Hollywood orchestra leader, Baxter was credited with the accompaniment to two of Nat King Cole's defining hits, "Too Young" and "Mona Lisa" (though both arrangements were in fact ghosted by Nelson Riddle), and he had his first exotic hit with 1947's *Music Out of the Moon*, a 78-rpm album featuring spacey theremin sounds. Over the next twenty-plus years, Baxter transported his listeners from distant planets to tropical jungles, most famously with Yma Sumac's Inca orchestral debut, *Voice of the Xtabay*, the number three album of 1951, and the same year's *Ritual of the Savage*, which included the frequently covered "Quiet Village." The latter album's liner notes provided a neat encapsulation of the fantasy that launched a thousand imitations:

> Do the mysteries of native rituals intrigue you...does the haunting beat of savage drums fascinate you?...This original and exotic music by Les Baxter was conceived by blending his creative ideas with the ritualistic melodies and seductive rhythms of the natives of distant jungles and tropical ports to capture all the color and fervor so expressive of the emotions of these people.[8]

Without devoting too much space to a form documented in loving detail on dozens of Internet sites, it is worth pointing out how intimately mood and exotica LPs intertwined with the sweet swing orchestras of the past, the mainstream of adult pop through the 1960s, and the cool wing of progressive jazz. Weston had been an arranger for the Tommy Dorsey band and insisted that even his most string-drenched records had a swing that other easy listening orchestras lacked, but this was a matter of degree and few fans were likely to make the same distinction. Likewise, George Shearing was an innovative jazz pianist and composer, but album titles such as *Velvet Carpet* and *Black Satin* show the degree to which he was marketed as a mood musician, and his thick chording and neoclassical harmonies were echoed both in Riddle's arrangements for Frank Sinatra and in Martin Denny's *Exotica*, which, thanks to some well-placed bird calls, spent five weeks at number one in 1959.

The attraction of jungle sound effects in music that in other ways was just an update of Whiteman's jazz classique may seem curious to a lot of readers, but makes more sense if one thinks of these albums as aural scenery, transforming the comfortable middle-class living room—or "den"—into a corner of suburban Eden. As Keir Keightley has pointed out, there was also the attraction of high-fidelity recording techniques, joined in the later 1950s by stereo, which put those birds right in the room with you. *HiFi & Music Review*—one of many popular magazines devoted to audio technologies—wrote in 1958 that "some hi-fiers, rather than immerse themselves in operatic or chamber music, or even rock 'n' roll, listen for the joy of just 'hearing' sounds not likely to be found in the average living room."[9] At one extreme that could mean listening to sound effects records, at another it could mean treating Bartók's string quartets or Brubeck's modern jazz as if they were sound effects. (Not that one necessarily had to make a choice: The first stereo LP, issued by the Audio Fidelity label in 1957, had the Dukes of Dixieland on one side and a selection of train sounds on the other.) A female correspondent to *Saturday Review* wrote, "There is no question of *listening* to music when two or more men gather around a phonograph, except as the recording serves to illustrate some point of discussion."[10]

That quotation also highlights the extent to which hi-fi was seen as a male craze. "Wives Sing Stereo Living Room Blues" and "Les Gals Don't Dig," wrote *Billboard*, heading a column on how stereo speakers and wiring cluttered up family rooms,[11] and one of the distinctive things about the album market in this period was how much of its advertising was targeted at adult men. This was reflected both in the emphasis on recording technologies—RCA's "New Orthophonic," Capitol's "Duophonic," and Mercury's "Perfect Presence Sound" processes—and in the scantily clad models who graced the album jackets. *Playboy* magazine, which made its debut in 1953, devoted nearly as much space to audio components as it did to its "playmates," and modern fans often refer to the mood albums of this period as "space-age bachelor-pad" music. Of course, that phrase implies not only a male consumer but specifically one who was creating a seductive atmosphere, which in turn implies that although men might buy the records, women were expected to enjoy them. As Mitch Miller's new discovery, Johnny Mathis, eloquently put it, "Since other media cannot be controlled to give a continuous flow of relaxing songs at the exact time that people choose to cuddle up on their sofas or bearskin rugs, phonograph records become a catalyst to generate sensuous vibrations that induce the closest form of love-making."[12]

Mathis's caressing voice and relaxing tempos were assumed to appeal primarily to women, and though he is not usually classified alongside Weston and Denny, his discs certainly turned up in a lot of the same collections and remind us not to overemphasize the gender gap among mood-record buyers. From Shearing's discs and Erroll Garner's *Concert by the Sea* to the sinuous stylings of Dakota Staton, many of the 1950s' most popular jazz albums soothed the tensions and warmed the emotions of males and females alike—as did the lilting, light-classical effusions of

Andre Kostelanetz and Mantovani and the passionate romanticism of Van Cliburn. (Cliburn's 1958 recording of Tchaikovsky's *Piano Concerto No. 1* was the first classical album to sell over a million copies.) The tropical ambience of Baxter, Denny, and Arthur Lyman evoked romantic Asian and Pacific Island cultures recalled by GIs who had fantasized about local damsels during World War II and the Korean conflict, but that same romanticism also fueled female-oriented fare such as the decade's most popular film soundtrack, *South Pacific*, and Elvis's *Blue Hawaii* a few years later, as well as the popularity of their own fantasy island mate, Harry Belafonte.

And then there was Sinatra. The story of Sinatra's mid-fifties comeback as an icon of hard-bitten male independence is one of the classic dramas in American entertainment. Divorced, raked over the coals by Ava Gardner, his voice shot, his career in ruins, the washed-up teen fave was driven to the brink of suicide, then snapped back after undergoing a ritual beating in *From Here to Eternity*—yet another Pacific Island fantasy, albeit a more serious one—to win an Academy Award and become one of America's richest and most admired singers. What is less often emphasized is the extent to which Sinatra's albums fit the broader mood-music trend. *In the Wee Small Hours* invited close listening in a way that *Black Satin* and the Weston discs did not, but Riddle's arrangements were very much in the Weston-Shearing tradition—his solo releases included *Sea of Dreams*, with a cover photo of a comely nude adrift in the deep—and the intent was explicitly to create a late-night ambiance. It was hardly coincidental that Sinatra's first Capitol album, released while Gleason's *Music for Lovers Only* was at its peak, was titled *Songs for Young Lovers*: Though his recordings have proved far more enduring, they were directed at the same audience.

Sinatra had been one of the first people to realize that LPs could be more than just a collection of songs. As early as 1949, *Billboard* found him arguing that "much of the production thought that has gone into LP has derived from conventional 78 production methods and thinking," but the time had come "to pioneer in the use of script material in conjunction with music, the presentation of musical sketches, commentary, narrative and mood music."[13] As it happened, he would not have the chance to program his own albums for another five years, and by that time he had apparently figured out that if LPs were not just longer 78s, they also were not a kind of frozen radio show. For people who wanted to sit still and be entertained, television was providing the sketches and narrative, so albums' main job was to create a sonic background.

I do not mean to suggest that Sinatra listeners, or jazz or classical listeners, or the people buying *My Fair Lady* and Doris Day only wanted audio wallpaper. Obviously, the longer-playing format made it possible to record extended jazz improvisations and full symphonies, and all sorts of listeners gave their full attention to their favorite records. But the people who were paying serious attention had also paid serious attention to 78s during the decades when the most common home music machine was the radio. The LP format didn't force anyone to use records as background music for housework or romance, but it made such uses possible, and once possible they quickly became common.

At the same time, the long-play format gave popular music a new level of seriousness. Consumers—even the most intellectual or independent consumers—develop habits. My grandparents were classical music listeners, and they bought only albums. That included a few popular albums, or at least Paul Robeson's *Ballad for Americans* and the *Songs of the Spanish Civil War*, but it never seems to have occurred to them to buy an unpackaged 78 in any genre. By contrast, most R&B fans right through the 1950s seem to have bought only singles and never bothered to look in the album racks—indeed, though teenagers famously favored 45s, a lot of older fans stuck with their existing phonographs, and as late as 1955 three-quarters of R&B sales were still on 78s.[14] The association of albums with classical and intellectual tastes carried over into the LP era, as did the idea that pop hits came on singles: Even in the 1970s, I don't remember an LP track ever being played for dancing at a high school party. By that time, though, virtually all the biggest-selling albums featured hit songs that were also available as 45s, whereas in the 1950s there was minimal overlap between the two markets. In 1955, the year Sinatra released *In the Wee Small Hours*, he also released a doo-wop-flavored single, "Two Hearts, Two Kisses," and it seems safe to assume that he didn't expect any of the same people to buy both. That is a particularly drastic contrast, but it exemplifies a broader pattern: Although Sinatra placed nine albums in the top two chart positions between 1955 and 1960 and had six top-ten singles in the same period, they included no overlapping tracks. Even a song as iconic as "One for My Baby (and One More for the Road)" was strictly an album track, and though Capitol also released compilations of his singles, those packages never did as well as single-less sets like *Come Fly with Me* and *Only the Lonely*.

The album-single dichotomy is even more obvious in the work of other performers. Most modern fans are familiar with Sarah Vaughan from her albums and are startled if they come across her pop singles of the later 1950s, which range from R&B to calypso to Mitch Miller-style pseudo-country, complete with steel guitar. Vaughan embraced this side of her career when she signed with Columbia in 1949, saying "I wanted to prove that I could sing the pops as well as anybody could."[15] It was after she switched to Mercury in 1954, though, that her recordings became truly polarized, and the label reinforced the divide by releasing her singles on the parent label and her LPs on its EmArcy jazz subsidiary. She apparently saw this not only as a musical split but also as a line between art and commerce, telling reporters, "My contract with Mercury is for pops, and my contract with EmArcy is for me."[16] Such divisions between single and album fare remained common into the mid-1960s: Everyone from Sinatra to Doris Day was expected to cut hits for the teen market, but this aspect of their work tended to be carefully segregated from their LP careers. Meanwhile, teen idols like Pat Boone and Connie Francis used albums to prove their appeal to older fans—both released compilation albums of their hits, but Boone's most successful long-format disc was a collection of older pop standards titled *Star Dust* and Francis's were two sets of Italian favorites. Elvis was the only artist to be equally successful in both formats without specifically tailoring his LPs to the adult market—of the nine teen-oriented albums that managed to reach the top of the *Billboard* charts before the Beatles era, seven were his, with seventeen-year-old Ricky Nelson and twelve-year-old Stevie Wonder providing the only competition.

The idea that a whole segment of the pop music market—and, by the latter half of the 1950s, the most lucrative segment—was directed primarily at adults was in some ways even more revolutionary than the discovery of the teen market. Young people had always been assumed to be the main pop trendsetters: When older dancers made news in the ragtime era, the reason was that they were jumping in alongside their youthful offspring. By contrast, albums might feature absurd jungle scenes or pneumatic blondes on their covers, but they were being bought overwhelmingly by grown-ups or by young people who wished to seem mature. Polls of college students regularly found them dismissing rock 'n' roll as kid's music, and album acts like Dave Brubeck and, a few years later, the Kingston Trio were specifically associated with college listeners—a group that had grown to unprecedented size thanks to the boom in higher education following World War II.

Numerous researchers have pointed out that it was in roughly this period that the idea of "good music" expanded to include jazz, folk, and some varieties of adult pop along with classical styles.[17] Sinatra is often made exhibit A for this argument, and he certainly brought a new level of seriousness to pop singing, as well as underlining the classical connection with frequent comments on opera and occasional recordings for which he served as conductor rather than vocalist. In jazz, Brubeck's name was regularly linked with Bartók's, due both to the tempting alliteration and to the fact that both exemplified a highbrow modernist aesthetic—one of the funniest scenes in *Jailhouse Rock* finds Elvis exploding in sullen fury when a group of college professors and their wives solicit his opinion of Brubeck's new release. The Modern Jazz Quartet appeared in formal concert attire, with a printed program listing each evening's selections, and Miles Davis and Charles Mingus made a point of not entertaining their audiences but rather demanding that listeners treat them with a respect and attention previously reserved for classical performers. All also used the album format to create extended works—a significant departure from anything that had been done in the past. Whiteman and Ellington had pioneered the idea of composing jazz rhapsodies and suites, but until LPs arrived there was no way to preserve long-form improvisations. Now, just as Jackson Pollock's "action paintings" defined a new era of high art, jazz made the same point with action compositions.

In Brubeck's words, "composers have all year to think about the next note. We have to decide in a second."[18] Jazz album covers often emphasized the connection to modernist painting, with the Neil Fujita canvas that adorned Brubeck's 1959 *Time Out*—the first million-selling jazz LP—serving as a prime example.

Sinatra's albums also had painted covers, but *Only the Lonely*'s Grammy-winning depiction of a crying clown indicates the extent to which his work mixed highbrow aspirations with middlebrow kitsch. The idea of "popular culture" in the modern sense, with doctoral dissertations being written on Elvis, Madonna, and Tupac Shakur, had not yet arrived. Jazz was touted as a modern classical music in part because it had ceased to be pleasantly tuneful or danceable—it demanded more effort and attention from its listeners, and hence was considered more serious. And Sinatra's seriousness, though sneered at by many intellectuals, was similarly integral to his new identity as an adult artist. Where once he had been a smiling, curly-haired youth, he now was pictured with an introspective frown, lonely beneath a lamp post or wearing glasses as he examined the music for a recording session. Glasses or not, though, he remained an accessible, mainstream entertainer, glad-handing other pros on television and kidding the ringside customers at the Copacabana or his home away from home, the Sands Hotel in Vegas. He was a tougher nut than Crosby, but still from the same tree.

Brubeck and Cliburn were more surprising stars, but in some ways they too had a familiar appeal. Brubeck was the new Benny Goodman—the jazzman in glasses who could go toe to toe with the classical cats—and there had always been a few classical virtuosos who were household names to radio listeners. At a time when intellectualism tended to be linked to pink politics, they also provided their respective genres with a healthy dose of the rugged American west. *Time* made much of Cliburn's Texas drawl and Brubeck's background as a ranch hand who "grew up among the green Western hills" and could "rope, brand and vaccinate cattle."[19] In a way, they were bridging the same gap as Faulkner's Mississippi modernism or Agnes de Mille's cowboy ballet in *Oklahoma*—proving that the United States no longer need look to Europe for its high art.

That all-American appeal was also integral to the folk music boom. The Weavers' Communist associations wiped them off the hit parade, but their songs and style were carried on by less controversial figures. When Eddy Arnold, the biggest star in country music, made his first 12-inch LP in 1955, it was a collection of traditional ballads that had been popularized for urban audiences by the Weavers, Burl Ives, and Josh White, and took its title song, *Wanderin'*, from Carl Sandburg's *American Songbag*. To some extent this may have been a way of connecting Arnold's updated country style with older traditions, but it was also an attempt to reach the urban and college audiences who sneered at hillbilly hits but appreciated folk music as the unspoiled art of the countryside, much as audiences in Elizabethan London had loved the songs of Shakespeare's carefree shepherds.

On college campuses, in particular, there were also a lot of folk fans who accepted and even demanded some political controversy with their music. Pete Seeger was appreciated by folk audiences for his adept banjo playing and devotion to unadorned rural styles and by anti-McCarthyites for his unique defiance of the House Committee on Un-American Activities—while other leftists took the Fifth Amendment, in effect admitting that their testimony might be incriminating, Seeger relied on the First Amendment, arguing that freedom of speech included the freedom not to trot out one's political views for congressional committees. The result was that he was blacklisted from commercial television until the late 1960s but was a hugely popular concert artist in college towns across the country.

Of all the political battles of that time, the fight to end Southern racial segregation drew the broadest support among young people, particularly in the urban north and west. Even conservative politicians were wary of seeming like Nazis, and it was relatively hard to Red-bait a movement that was largely led by ministers, so although the civil rights struggle faced bitter and sometimes lethal opposition, it was less controversial than other left-wing causes. And there was no easier way to express one's racial liberalism than by (figuratively, at least) embracing black entertainers. Rhythm and blues might be associated with juvenile delinquency and condemned as "jungle music," but Nat King Cole had opened the way for a wave of African-American pop singers, some of whom were more successful with white audiences than with black ones. Mathis became one of the country's biggest-selling black stars with albums of tenderly color-blind ballads. Vaughan had over thirty entries in *Billboard*'s pop charts and four in the album listings before 1959, when the doo-wop-flavored "Broken-Hearted Melody" became her first R&B hit. Sammy Davis Jr. never appeared on the R&B charts, but he had two top-ten albums in 1955, one of which stayed at number one for six weeks, and was a member of the Las Vegas "Rat Pack" with Sinatra and Dean Martin. But the defining black LP artist was America's most popular folk singer, Harry Belafonte.

Belafonte combined all the appeals of the adult album market: He was exotic, erotic, intellectual, artistic, and folkloric. Trained as an actor, he had started out in the nightclub world in the late 1940s singing jazz and standards, but he gave up after a few months and joined some friends to open a small restaurant in Greenwich Village. The Village was a hotbed of bohemianism and international folk song, and in October 1951 the *New Yorker* reported that "Shoshana Damari, the Israeli nightingale" would be replaced at the Village Vanguard by "Harry Belafonte, now a folk minstrel, making his debut in his new calling."[20] The Vanguard was still a full-scale cabaret, and the bill included comedian Phil Leeds, the Clarence Williams Trio, and a black chanteuse named Royce Wallace, who in a sidebar to the Belafonte story would make news five years later by marrying the scion of one of Bermuda's ruling white families.

That sidebar may seem terribly tangential, but the theme of interracial marriage and tropical islands would come up again and again in this period. There was *South Pacific*, with its theme of intermarriage bedeviled by prejudice and its antibigotry sermon, "You've Got to Be Carefully Taught," and a less didactic example was available weekly on America's most popular television show, in which Lucille Ball was keeping house with a Cuban conga drummer. Social limits were being stretched in some interesting directions, and Belafonte's breakthrough overlapped both the first wave of rock 'n' roll and a new Latin music craze. As R&B got teens dancing, the mambo tempted a lot of their parents away from the living room television, and the two trends frequently converged. The record that "Rock around the Clock" displaced at the top of *Billboard*'s best-sellers chart was Perez Prado's "Cherry Pink and Apple Blossom White," Bill Haley had reached the top twenty four months earlier with "Mambo Rock," and the movie *Rock around the Clock* showed Haley's Comets and Tony Martinez's mambo band both busting loose from the conservative tastes of the adults supervising a college dance. Meanwhile, Machito's Cuban orchestra was outdrawing Count Basie's in Catskill resorts and New York ballrooms, and though Tommy Dorsey had died in 1956, two years later his band reached the top ten with "Tea for Two Cha Cha." On the rock 'n' roll side, a Los Angeles R&B singer named Richard Berry had made a local hit with a cha-cha-chá called "Louie, Louie," which would resurface as one of the genre's enduring standards, and the hits of 1958 included the Champs' fabulously popular "Tequila" and Johnny Otis's "Willie and the Hand Jive," which recycled a rhythm popularized over the previous three years by Bo Diddley and described by him as combining "blues, an' Latin-American, an' some hillbilly, a little spiritual, a little African, an' a little West Indian calypso."[21]

With calypso, we come back to Belafonte and the romantic race angle. The singer's most popular movie, 1957's *Island in the Sun*, explored the same turf as *South Pacific*, though he never quite kissed his white costar, Joan Fontaine. But even conservative *Time* magazine pointed out that the film's racial attitudes were specific to the United States and bore no relation to the realities of the Caribbean, where both of Belafonte's parents were the fruit of racially mixed marriages. Closer to home, Josephine Premice, the daughter of Haitian immigrants, had been New York's first nightclub calypso singer in the 1940s and preceded Wallace and Belafonte into the Vanguard by several years, and she also married a white millionaire. And to tie up the string of coincidences, in the fall of 1951 Premice was appearing in London with Josh White, the main model for Belafonte's folk act. Belafonte was opening his shows with one of White's trademark numbers, "Timber," and on his first album both he and his guitar accompanist mimicked White's style. Nor was it just a matter of music; Premice recalled how the first black man to sing folk songs with a sexy laugh and an open-necked shirt had affected New York's café society: "From age eight to eighty, women were all in love with Josh White. They just swarmed around him like bees to honey . . . and they were not black ladies, they were white."[22]

Belafonte was younger than White, he blended blues and folk with calypso and international material, and he took full advantage of his acting skills. He also was not saddled with any cold war political baggage: White had been one of the first civil-rights singers, but now was blacklisted by the right for his old Communist connections and reviled by the left for having renounced those connections in a voluntary appearance before the Un-American Activities Committee. Belafonte was politically active—a *Life* photo spread from 1957 showed him deep in discussion with Martin Luther King Jr.—but he was young enough to have missed overt Communist sponsorship. So although his views undoubtedly kept him off some television shows, they also added to the air of seriousness that was one of his greatest assets. His first big write-up in the *New York Times* was headlined, "A Folk Singer's Style: Personality and Integrity Worth More than Cultivated Voice to Belafonte," and spoke of the "simple, moving...dignity" of his performance and "a ferocity in his singing of the tragic ballads of his people," balanced by "a vivacity that is delightful" in the calypso numbers.[23]

That was in 1954, when Belafonte was on Broadway in a variety showcase called *Almanac*. He was still regarded as a relative newcomer, despite having signed with RCA in 1952 and scoring a minor hit with the Japanese "Gomen Nasai," appearing successfully in Vegas (where, like all black performers, he was barred from the casino, dining room, and swimming pool of the hotel where he was working), and playing roles in two all-black films, *The Bright Road* and *Carmen Jones*. He had even managed a few television appearances as a singer and actor. But 1956 was the year he became a superstar. His first album, *Mark Twain*, had appeared without much fanfare two years earlier, but in January 1956 it hit the *Billboard* album chart, climbing to number three, and a month later his *Belafonte* album arrived, reaching number one and staying there for six weeks. In June he released *Calypso*, by some counts the first million-selling album by a solo performer, which remained at number one for thirty-one weeks; and that same month he sang to 25,000 fans at New York's Lewisohn Stadium, with thousands more turned away for lack of space, and with a symphony orchestra as his opening act.[24]

Historians often kid the calypso craze, because when it hit a lot of commentators hailed it as the successor to rock 'n' roll. A typical article, surveying female teen tastes, noted, "The most avant-garde of this group think Harry Belafonte is a 'doll'; alas, poor Presley"—which in retrospect seems more amusing than insightful.[25] But the craze had fairly deep roots, and its effects reverberated well beyond the first rush of bongo buyers. In the 1940s, "Rum and Coca Cola" had been followed by other island-flavored hits, including Louis Jordan's "Run, Joe" and his duet with Ella Fitzgerald on "Stone Cold Dead in the Market." The songs were smart and funny, attracting the college crowd with their social commentary, exotica fans with their tropical flavor, and dancers with a rhythm that with a bit of effort could be matched to a mambo or cha-cha-chá. As Danny and the Juniors sang on *American Bandstand*, "When the records start spinning, you cha-lypso and you chicken at the hop." Purists complained that Belafonte was singing an adulterated pop variation rather than real calypso, but his success brought new attention to genuine calypsonians like Lord Beginner, Lord Melody, and Lord Flea, and Belafonte himself was always clear that he was presenting a theatrical reworking of Caribbean styles. His orchestra leader, Tony Scott, compared his approach to Glenn Miller's adaptation of jazz, and he likewise inspired a flock of imitators: College campuses across the country became spawning grounds for exuberant folk singers in Hawaiian shirts.[26] Terry Gilkyson got his only top-ten hit in this period with "Marianne" ("All day, all night, Marianne / Down by the sea-side, sifting sand"), which did even better for the Hilltoppers, a collegiate quartet from Kentucky. The Tarriers, an outgrowth of the Weavers, took off with "The Banana Boat Song," their version of Belafonte's "Day-O," which also made the pop charts in versions by the Fontane Sisters and Sarah Vaughan. The list could go on—Robert Mitchum's calypso LP being one of the odder entries—but suffice it to add that the Kingston Trio, who became the most popular college-style folk act of all time and the most successful album-oriented singing group before the Beatles, got together in 1957 and named themselves after the town immortalized in Belafonte's "Jamaica Farewell."

Belafonte also inspired a generation of black entertainers who combined strong politics with a broad appeal to white audiences—Nina Simone and Oscar Brown are obvious examples—helped several young artists, including the South African singer Miriam Makeba, and even left echoes in the work of some major R&B stars. (Check out Sam Cooke's "Everybody sing!" interpolation in "Another Saturday Night.") But for the purposes of this chapter, his most distinctive contribution was his insistence on being seen as a serious and independent artist rather than as a pop star. Historians have often credited Sinatra with establishing that persona, and the connections between the two singers do not end with their Italian surnames. Like Sinatra, Belafonte took control not only of his music but also of his business—he was not dubbed "the Chairman of the Board," but by 1959 the *New York Times* was calling him "a corporate enterprise ... [functioning] not only as a singer and an actor, but as a song publisher, a concert bureau, and a producer of motion pictures and TV shows."[27] Both disliked rock 'n' roll: Sinatra called it "brutal, ugly, phony, and false," and Belafonte dubbed it "musical rot."[28] Both were political liberals and took strong stands against racial prejudice: In 1945 Sinatra made a widely seen short film, *The House I Live In*, to combat discrimination (though it failed to include any non-European characters and pictured Americans standing together against the "Japs"), and he was famous for punching people who used nasty epithets for blacks or Jews. And both were routinely singled out as representing the kinds of music teenage rock 'n' roll fans would come to prefer as they matured and went on to college or family life.   ·

But Sinatra was also the epitome of a mainstream adult pop star, celebrating the values of what was coming to be known as the "American songbook," the masterpieces of the great Broadway songsmiths and the Big Band era, while a lot of Belafonte's fans, like Brubeck's and Pete Seeger's, equated that music with middlebrow commercialism and corporate conformity. In interviews, Belafonte explained that he had spent weeks in the Library of Congress studying field recordings of rural singers, and his devotion to folk styles was expressed as a sort of sacred trust. He insisted that he was not a musical purist, and took pride in turning old songs into modern theatrical presentations, but there was an air of moral purity and asceticism to his work, an oft-stated dedication to songs that had "something more to offer than a thirty-two-bar musical comedy."[29] In a way, his Carnegie Hall concerts and the resulting albums were realizations of James Reese Europe's dream to bring black folk art to the concert hall, harnessing the orchestral and theatrical trappings of European high art while preserving the music's primitive soul—a phrase that jars on modern sensibilities, but which Europe would have meant with the fullest respect to both traditions.

One of the lasting effects of long-playing records was that, by making it possible to create one's own musical environment, they made the pop music world more segmented than ever before. When *South Pacific* hit on Broadway in 1949, seven different performers put versions of "Some Enchanted Evening" on the *Billboard* pop charts. When the movie hit in 1958, its soundtrack album was the most popular LP of the year, but not a single version of the song cracked the charts—and that was not because the current singing stars were all rock 'n' rollers: Perry Como, the McGuire sisters, Domenico Modugno, and the Platters had number-one hits that year and all could have been very comfortable singing "Some Enchanted Evening." But show tunes were now their own genre rather than being raw material for singing stars; people who wanted to hear their favorite musical just bought the cast recording.

Pop radio still smoothed over musical divides: I find it hard to imagine a single listener buying "Volare," "Tom Dooley," "Purple People Eater," "At the Hop," and Perez Prado's "Patricia," but everyone listening to pop radio in 1958 heard all of those songs many times.[30] A number one hit on the album charts did not imply similar ubiquity: Along with *South Pacific*, that year's offerings included debut LPs from the Kingston Trio and Ricky Nelson, Cliburn's Tchaikovsky, two Sinatra albums, and two Mitch Miller *Sing Along* sets—"Yellow Rose of Texas" had sparked a solo career in which the bearded producer led living room song sessions with the lyrics printed on the album jackets—and there were plenty of people who adored one or several of those albums without even hearing some of the others. There were also millions of listeners who bought none of those albums and still considered themselves on the cutting edge of what was happening in popular music, and people who were buying albums that sold in the millions but expressed a disdain for anything called "pop."

I am about to get back to teenagers and rock 'n' roll, but these new worlds of album buyers have to be kept in mind as we enter the 1960s. For one thing, by the end of the 1950s LPs were surpassing singles in consumer sales and accounted for about three-quarters of overall record revenues, so over the next few years more and more young, rock-oriented artists would try to find ways to enter that market.[31] For another, the prestige of jazz and folk albums, especially among college listeners, would lead to the growing prestige of R&B and rock 'n' roll as artists associated with those styles turned more of their attention to album projects. Ray Charles had been getting R&B chart hits since 1949 without showing any sign of crossing over to white buyers, but in 1957 Atlantic Records released an eponymous LP collecting his singles and also an album of new recordings (*The Great Ray Charles*) aimed at the jazz market. The next year brought *Belafonte Sings the Blues*, which drew half its selections from that first Charles collection, interspersing them with folk material learned from Lead Belly and John Lomax field recordings, along with "One for My Baby," a song usually associated with Sinatra, but which Josh White had recently done on a folk-blues album. The idea that R&B singles could be repackaged for folk fans was unprecedented, but it would be taken up with a vengeance in the 1960s, when Chess Records issued albums of old cuts by Muddy Waters, Howlin' Wolf, and others as *The Real Folk Blues*.

Charles himself did not dent the album charts until the 1960s, but his jazz LPs brought him a level of critical credibility that no other R&B star could match. Intellectuals and college students were a limited market, but their approval carried a certain cachet. Just as the embrace of "folk art" by academic modernists had opened fine arts museums to African and pre-Columbian sculpture, the academic embrace of musical styles that had previously been associated with bars and juke boxes would create a new audience that considered itself too mature for Elvis and too progressive for Sinatra.

15

TEEN IDYLL

I like to sing ballads the way Eddie Fisher does and the way Perry Como does. But the way I'm singing now is what makes the money. Would you change if you was me?

ELVIS PRESLEY, 1956

History is often written as a series of conflicts, whether the wars are between nations or artistic styles. Battles tend to be more exciting to read about than marketplaces, though cultures have met far more frequently in trade than in war and there are always more countries coexisting than fighting. In the 1950s, old-guard pop music fans recoiled in horror from the evils of rock 'n' roll, and when rock 'n' roll fans began writing their side of the story, they countered with equally vituperous condemnations of old-line pop. So it is easy to forget that a lot of listeners enjoyed both styles. Dick Clark regularly pointed out that more than half the audience for *American Bandstand* was over twenty-one, and polls of teenagers tended to show that plenty of them liked Doris Day and Perry Como.[1] Likewise, although rock historians generally draw a sharp line between the teen idols of the 1950s, with Pat Boone a symbol of the insipid mainstream and Elvis Presley the standard-bearer for the revolution, most teenagers seem to have had no problem enjoying both, along with Day, Como, the Drifters, Harry Belafonte, and Connie Francis.

Presley is a particularly ambiguous example, because he was so many things to so many people. In some ways he typified the latest trends; in some ways he was unlike any other performer. One way in which he exemplified the modern scene was his initial focus on recording. All the artists I have covered up to now built their reputations by playing in clubs or at dances, or at least on live radio shows. Elvis did none of that until after his first record became a hit around Memphis. He would sing and play guitar for friends at parties and picnics and had auditioned unsuccessfully for the gospel quartet in his church, but his only gesture toward making a career in music was to haunt Sam Phillips's Memphis Recording Service, the home of Sun Records. In a familiar story, he first went there in August 1953 to record a couple of romantic pop ballads as a birthday present for his mother, and over the next few months he stopped by the studio a few times to chat and recorded another pair of equally sentimental songs. In the process, he attracted Phillips's interest, and in July the label owner put him together with Scotty Moore and Bill Black, a guitarist and bass player who worked together at the Firestone tire plant and in a band called the Starlite Wranglers. At their first session the trio recorded a rhythm and blues song called "That's All Right Mama" and a hopped-up version of a country waltz, "Blue Moon of Kentucky," and the eighteen-year-old would-be balladeer was reborn as "the hillbilly cat."

In the early 1950s, "cat" had a special meaning in parts of the South. White Southerners had always danced and listened to a lot of black music—not just ragtime and jazz, but rural fiddle tunes and down-home blues—and in 1939 a jukebox operator in Beaumont, Texas, wrote to *Billboard* that "when we get a Race number that proves a hit we just leave it on the machine until it wears out. They don't get old and lose play like other records."[2] By the 1950s, young white listeners in much of the South were calling the stripped-down R&B dance hits "cat music." (The term "cat," for a male musician or fan, had been common in jazz parlance since at least the 1930s.[3]) The hipper pop marketers were well aware of this, and the Chords' original version of "Sh-Boom" appeared on an Atlantic subsidiary called Cat Records. (Along the coast of Georgia and the Carolinas, the same records were—and still are—called "beach music.")

Because their audiences included people who were listening to these records, a lot of hillbilly singers and musicians played their own versions of cat music. The Starlite Wranglers' name had the country and western ring of Hank Williams's Drifting Cowboys, but on that first session Black and Moore sound as comfortable as Elvis does with the jump blues style. They were also capable of backing him on songs drawn from the Ink Spots or Billy Eckstine, though Phillips wisely steered them in other directions, as there was no chance that they—or Elvis, at this point, whatever his personal tastes—would have attracted much attention doing mainstream pop. As Sonny Burgess, who was fronting a bar band in Arkansas and would shortly follow Elvis to Sun, recalls, "Back then, if you played clubs you did pop music. You did stuff like 'Stardust,' 'Harlem Nocturne,' Tommy Dorsey's 'Boogie Woogie,' and you did country and some rhythm and blues." He adds that there were also musicians who just played country or blues, "but if you worked the clubs like we did, you had to play different types of music."[4]

Live music was holding on better in the South than in most other regions. In part, that was an effect of the climate: Before homes were air conditioned, nobody wanted to stay indoors on hot days, so when a lot of Northerners were home listening to records, Southerners were still going out. Partly it was that honky-tonk and blues bands, which in the South could draw older audiences as well as youngsters, didn't have the overhead of the large dance orchestras that older Northerners preferred. The South was also a relatively compact market, so bands could tour without having to make the huge jumps that were necessary for any Northern group that worked off the East Coast. And partly it was just a matter of custom: Forty years after partner dancing disappeared from all but a few specialized clubs up north, a lot of white Southerners still dance two-steps, waltzes, and versions of the Lindy and jitterbug.

Some older country fans found Presley's style abrasive, but not enough to keep him from becoming the hot new name on the scene. Bill Monroe, the father of blue-grass and composer of "Blue Moon of Kentucky," produced a new recording of the song by the Stanley Brothers based on Elvis's version, and in October 1954, Elvis, Scotty, and Bill made their debut on Nashville's *Grand Ole Opry*—though they were too wild to get a return engagement—then got a regular spot on Shreveport's *Louisiana Hayride*, the show that had introduced Hank Williams to a mass Southern audience. Both *Billboard* and *Cash Box* chose Presley as the most promising new country and western act of 1955, and the following year, when he managed the unequaled trifecta of putting five records in *Billboard*'s annual C&W, R&B, and pop top fifties, he had an additional four records that made only the country listing.[5] (As previously noted, not everyone was pleased by this: *Billboard*'s editor reported getting calls from Nashville executives demanding that Presley's name be removed because "he was not truly representative of the country field."[6])

Some historians date the dawn of the rock 'n' roll era to that year, when Elvis left Sun for RCA, appeared on almost a dozen national television broadcasts, signed a movie contract with Paramount Pictures, and took the record business by storm. In its way, this makes as much sense as dating the dawn of jazz to 1916 and the first Original Dixieland Jazz Band records. Like the ODJB, Elvis reached a wide audience that had not heard anything like him before and opened the pop scene to a flood of similar-sounding artists, many of whom sounded similar only because he had hit and they wanted a piece of the action. Like the ODJB, he was playing a wild-sounding Southern style based on black dance music that a lot of older musicians dismissed as disorganized noise. And, like the ODJB's small-combo, unwritten jazz, within a few years that style had been tamed and absorbed into the mainstream. By 1959, *Billboard* was reporting that "the man who was among the first to light the fuse on the rock and roll explosion, Sam Phillips, is now talking about it in the past tense.... Perhaps never again, says Phillips, will pop music be so dominated by a single style of sound. But the kids 'got tired of the ruckus' and we are moving into a period of greater variety in taste." Phillips added that he thought this was a good thing, because after being shaken up and improved by the rock 'n' roll revolution, the music business was finding a new equilibrium: "It took artists like Perry Como to show how to marry the old and the new. Now a deejay can pace a show with out-and-out rock and roll, the old standards, a lot of stuff in between, and still have a modern sound all the way thru."[7]

If it seems odd that the man who shaped Elvis's early success would single out Como as bridging the gap between new and old, it reminds us that although a lot of people in the mainstream pop world attacked rock 'n' roll as an abomination and a lot of young rockers sneered at their elders' tastes, Como and Presley did not consider themselves to be leaders of warring camps. When Presley first topped the *Billboard* pop chart with "Heartbreak Hotel" in the spring of 1956, the record that replaced it after eight weeks was Como's "Hot Diggity"—and the juxtaposition of those titles is an apt reminder that whatever rock 'n' roll did, it hardly caused a dumbing down of pop lyrics. Nor were Como's fans universally older than Presley's. A poll of high school students in 1957 and 1958 found more than 10 percent choosing him as their favorite singer, and although that put him behind Boone, Presley, and Belafonte, it was almost double the number that chose Sinatra.[8] The kids were not asked the reasons for their choices, but Sinatra was a serious, introspective artist who openly despised the new styles, while Como—like Boone, who topped the poll with over 40 percent of the votes—was a relaxed balladeer who seemed genuinely to enjoy bopping around to a rock 'n' roll beat.

Both Boone and Como also had their own television shows, and it is impossible to understand their appeal without watching them. Como's records tend to sound utterly lightweight, but on screen that casual, offhand manner was immensely appealing. He always stayed cool, whether he was singing a love song or goofing around on a novelty number, and his unflappable ease won him a very broad range of fans, from Phillips and Presley to a young African-American singer named Marvin Gaye. "Perry had a great attitude," Gaye would recall. "When I finally got some money together over at Motown in the sixties, I used to sport Perry Como's sweaters. I always felt like my personality and Perry's had a lot in common."[9]

The shift from bands to singers put that kind of personal identification at the center of popular music, and shifted the balance from virtuosity to communication. Sinatra was acclaimed for approaching every song as an actor, making his listeners believe that he was feeling the emotions in the lyrics. But the fact that this made him an exception in the world of big-band vocalists points up one reason that style was losing out to country, blues, and rock 'n' roll. The dry Texas drawl of Ernest Tubb, Ruth Brown's rough growl, and now the callow wistfulness of a teenage Paul Anka or Frankie Avalon all gave listeners the sense that they were hearing someone speaking honestly and directly to them and for them. Television made it possible for singers to create that sort of intimacy in other ways as well: Over and over again, people who recall how Elvis changed their lives refer not to hearing him for the first time on radio but to seeing him bursting off their TV screens.

Elvis's appeal was the opposite of Como's—nervous heat rather than relaxed cool—but both captured their audiences as much with their manner as with their music. And just as Como made obvious attempts to reach the younger generation, Elvis was soon reaching out to older listeners. By the end of 1956 he had appeared in his first movie, *Love Me Tender*, and the title song did not have the faintest touch of rock 'n' roll: Set to a melody from the mid-nineteenth century, it was crooned in a warm baritone over a gently strummed acoustic guitar on the front porch of a Southern farmhouse on a tranquil evening, as his on-screen mother smiled at him from her rocking chair. This was a very different image from the greasy rebel who ground his pelvis as he growled and shouted his way through "Hound Dog," and it is not the image favored by the fans who put him in a rockabilly pantheon alongside Carl Perkins and Jerry Lee Lewis. But it helps explain why he had not only sixteen number one singles in six years but also seven number one LPs, would star in thirty movies, was welcomed back from his army stint with a guest appearance on a Frank Sinatra television special, and in later years, when his peers were doing oldies shows, became king of Las Vegas.

Both Presley and Phillips were always clear that it was the producer rather than the singer who steered their collaboration toward rhythm and blues. Elvis had an encyclopedic knowledge and keen grasp of the hotter black styles, and he obviously enjoyed getting loose and wild, but he was equally at home with the music of Dean Martin, Eddy Arnold, and black balladeers like Roy Hamilton and the Ink Spots' Bill Kenny. When a reporter covering the "Love Me Tender" record session expressed surprise at his gently old-fashioned performance, he told her, "People think all I can do is belt, [but] I used to sing nothing but ballads before I went professional."[10] Nor was that just adept public relations: Throughout his career, when Presley was asked about his favorite music, he always mentioned romantic songs and gospel.

To his devoted fans, this was common knowledge. The fact that the sneering, sideburned rock 'n' roll pose concealed a shy, sensitive young man who was devoted to his mother was a staple of magazine profiles—and this was a moment when teen-oriented magazines were cropping up in unprecedented numbers. "Fan mags as we knew them in the old days featured the top movie stars and were snapped up by chubby matrons who drooled over the contents whilst ensconced on a downy couch munching bon-bons," a *Billboard* writer recalled in 1958. "Now the fan mags concentrate on young disk talent...Ricky Nelson, the Everly Brothers, Frankie Avalon, and, of course, Elvis."[11] The writer might have added that the two fields frequently overlapped: Elvis, Nelson, Avalon, and other teen singing idols were quickly tapped for movie roles, and young movie and television actors like Sal Mineo and Edd Byrnes were rushed into recording studios to wax disc hits.

In the preceding chapter I dealt with LPs as an adult medium, but along with their longer playing time and higher fidelity, they also had a visual component that made them attractive to the same kids who poured over fanzines. Bobby-soxers in 1945 had been willing to buy a Frank Sinatra album even though it had no records in it, and one reason that Elvis's LPs sold so well was that, along with a disc of music, they provided a twelve-by-twelve-inch portrait of the new matinee idol. The only rock 'n' roll offerings to make the top thirty in *Billboard*'s year-end LP tally for 1957 were three Elvis albums and one each by Boone, Nelson, and Tommy Sands (who shot to national fame that year in an Elvis-inspired TV movie, *The Singing Idol*).[12] For the next few years, it would continue to be teen heartthrobs rather than the most musically exciting hitmakers who reliably sold long-playing discs to the youth market: Fabian managed only three hit singles but had two top ten albums, while Chuck Berry put five singles in the top ten but failed to reach the LP charts.

Which is to say that, as ever, female fans were a huge part of the equation. As a raw rock 'n' roller, Presley appealed to both sexes, but the fact that his tough exterior concealed a sensitive balladeer gave him the deeper romantic appeal of a James Dean or Montgomery Clift. Fabian, a good-looking teenager who had trouble carrying a tune and never thought of becoming a singer until a talent scout tapped him as a potential Presley clone, recalled how girls would flock backstage to talk with him:

> What guys like me represented was a fantasy boyfriend. That's how they would deal with, maybe, a boyfriend they did not have, or one they thought they wanted.... They would express that they're not doing much in their lives, and talk about how their mothers treated them, or a boyfriend treated them. A lot of them didn't like the way they were being treated. They would express all this to a guy like me, because that's the way they envisioned their life—wanting to be with someone like that.[13]

I don't mean to suggest that girls or women were attracted to Elvis only because he was sappy, any more than women liked the Casa Loma Orchestra or Glenn Miller just because they played dreamy slow dances. Plenty of women loved the big bands for their propulsive rhythms and expert soloists, and plenty of women loved Elvis as a rocking rebel. But, as with the dance bands, what made Elvis a star was only in part the talents celebrated by music critics and historians, and although he was the archetypal rock 'n' roll icon, his appeal transcended the appeal of rock 'n' roll.

Or perhaps it is more accurate to say that rock 'n' roll's appeal was broader and deeper than it first appeared to be. Though it was overwhelmingly greeted as the sound of youth and rebellion, in some ways the music was distinctly old-fashioned. When Elvis first appeared on the Milton Berle Show, Harry James and Buddy Rich were also on the program, and Berle recalled that "he started to strum on the guitar, and I caught a glimpse of James and Buddy Rich looking at each other. Rich made a square sign with his fingers and pointed at Elvis."[14] From the rock point of view, it is easy to dismiss the big-band men as old-timers who were out of touch with what was happening in front of them. But James and Rich were not just musical conservatives reacting to Presley as a symbol of juvenile delinquency and cultural revolution; they were hip jazz musicians sneering at him as a square.

The relationship between jazz and rock 'n' roll in this period was complex. Quite a few films about juvenile delinquents used jazz rather than rock on their soundtracks—part of a broader crime movie trend—so, in 1953, Marlon Brando rode into town to the music of an all-star band of West Coast jazzmen, and seven years later Jack Nicholson and his hot-rod buddies in *The Wild Ride* were still doing their rock 'n' roll steps to a cool post-bop beat. Meanwhile, much of the jazz world was locked in a struggle between modernists and traditionalists, and some of the old guard seized on rock 'n' roll as proof that the blues-based styles they loved were hipper than the overintellectualized experiments of Brubeck and Stan Kenton. Roger Pryor Dodge described Presley's style as "healthy" and "refreshing," and Rudi Blesh wrote a new afterword to his history of early jazz in which he praised Elvis as "a young folk singer...[whose 'Heartbreak Hotel' and 'Money Honey' are] blues of the same primitive quality...as archaic in form as Ma Rainey's 'Shave 'Em Dry.'"[15]

It would be easy to dismiss those quotations as old men's attempts to seem contemporary, but the best of Presley's movies, *King Creole*, found him singing with a couple of New Orleans jazz bands and, although the result did not sound like Ma Rainey, it did sound like a natural meeting of related styles. Presley's affinity for blues was not what separated him from the previous generation of pop singers: Frankie Laine would complain, "It irks me a little nowadays to hear Elvis Presley touted as 'the first white man who sang black.' I had to scuffle for seventeen years because I 'sang black.'"[16] But in some ways Presley's style did reach back to an earlier, more rurally rooted variety of blues, untouched by the rhythmic and harmonic innovations of Count Basie and Billie Holiday, much less any hint of Charlie Parker. When Rich and James dismissed him as a square, they were reacting in the same way that urban jazz fans, white or black, tended to react to down-home bluesmen like Muddy Waters. And it was not just jazz fans: Doc Pomus, a big-band blues shouter who wrote hits for the Drifters, Ray Charles, and Presley, recalled that "My group of people—Joe Turner, King Curtis, Mickey Baker—used to laugh at all the country blues singers who were backwards musically. John Lee Hooker and Lightnin' Hopkins sang out of meter—we couldn't respect them."[17]

This is a tricky subject, because although it is a simple fact that different standards will produce widely divergent opinions, that does not mean that it is easy to hear a performer one loves get slammed for not meeting standards one considers unfair or inappropriate. But to understand any group of artists or any audience, one has to understand its standards—which means accepting that although one's own critical criteria may be more rigorous, more heartfelt, more fair, or more intelligent, they are not the only ones possible. From the viewpoint of musicians trained in classical conservatories and swing orchestras, virtually all rock 'n' roll performers and composers seemed like musical incompetents, and what distinguished Elvis from Fabian was less notable than their shared noisy amateurism. Likewise, from the viewpoint of the fans who watched *American Bandstand* every afternoon to hear songs and performers that made them want to dance and expressed their feelings and their dreams, the older pop world's standards of competence were irrelevant and out of touch.

No performer exemplifies this split better than Frankie Avalon. In 1954, at age fourteen, Avalon was on the cover of *Down Beat*, America's most influential jazz magazine, hailed as "a trumpet-playing bandleader...[who has] won a Paul Whiteman TV show contest; has guested with Tommy Dorsey, Louis Prima, and Harry James, and is a protégé of Ray Anthony."[18] In the spring of 1957 he was playing trumpet with a group of fellow teenagers from Philadelphia, Rocco and the Saints, when a songwriter and indie record producer named Bob Marcucci came by to check out the band's lead singer. Avalon sang only one number that evening, but Marcucci was struck by his charismatic presence and told him they should make a record. Avalon protested, "I'm not a singer, I'm a trumpet player." But within a few months he had a record out, Marcucci had joined Dick Clark to produce a movie called *Jamboree,* and Avalon was singing in it, billed at the bottom of a lineup that included Perkins, Lewis, Charlie Gracie, Fats Domino, and Count Basie.[19] He was still backed by Rocco and the Saints, but there wasn't a trumpet in sight: Instead, Avalon appeared as a slim kid with a sexy smile and Elvis moves, bopping his way through a song about how he didn't want to be a "Teacher's Pet." Watching the film, one can't help noticing that virtually all the male singers are being sold as variations on the Elvis model. (Though with the usual admixture of anachronisms: The Texas rockabilly Buddy Knox sings a Tin Pan Alley Hawaiian number from 1911, "My Hula Hula Love," which he took to that year's pop top ten.) The most striking exception is the film's male lead, a callow youth named Paul Carr, who is presented as "the new Sinatra."

If Avalon's career had been based on his personal tastes, he might have aspired to that title himself. Connie Francis, who had made her debut on the *Ted Mack Amateur Hour* at age eleven playing accordion and singing "St. Louis Blues," recalled that when she met Avalon, his first question was, "Do you like Frank Sinatra?"

Her response: "Are you kidding? I'm crazy about Frank Sinatra! For my birthday, I buy myself nothing but Sinatra albums."[20]

Frankie Avallone and Concetta Franconero were Italian-American show-biz kids, and they would have been at least as happy playing the pop music of another era as they were singing their variety of rock 'n' roll. Like Francis's sometime boyfriend, Bobby Darin (né Cassotto), they were in a tradition that reached back long before Sinatra to whatever nice-looking ingénue was singing the current love songs in vaudeville and the Broadway boîtes of the preradio era. Nor were they contemptuous of the pop styles that immediately preceded them: Francis's first number one record, "Everybody's Somebody's Fool," had been written as a slow R&B waltz with LaVern Baker in mind but was transformed into a jaunty, upbeat hit after Francis suggested modeling her version on Mitch Miller's recent C&W pastiche for Guy Mitchell, "Heartaches by the Number."

It is no accident that Francis is the first young female singer to be mentioned in this chapter. The shift to rock 'n' roll and teen idols brought a low point for female artists on the pop charts. In 1956, there were ten records by women in *Billboard*'s year-end pop top fifty, including three of the top ten. In 1958, when Francis broke out with a rock-flavored remake of a thirty-five-year-old standard, "Who's Sorry Now," it was one of only three records by women to make the annual tally, none of them in the top twenty-five—and the other two were by old-timers, the Chordettes and the McGuire Sisters.[21] Francis later recalled that, as far as the teen scene went, "It was a totally male-dominated market. The majority of the people who bought records were girls. And their idols were boys. So they bought records by boys. I was really a fluke."[22] She was also explicitly marketed as chubby and unglamorous, so her success affirmed her fans rather than threatening them, and this aspect of her appeal was shared by many of her successors. As Brenda Lee, the first teen queen to challenge Francis's dominance, would put it: "My image wasn't one of a heart-breaker...I was the little fat girl your mother didn't mind you playing with."[23]

The country charts had never included many women, and the rural blues market was no better, so the trend toward male singers was in some ways just a logical extension of the new prominence of those types of music—but in terms of pop stardom, Francis's explanation was more relevant. The New York music business treated rock 'n' roll as revolutionary, and the shift in styles posed a serious threat to older songwriters and musicians, but to a great extent the eternal verities were being maintained. Although records and television had replaced sheet music and vaudeville, and a few performers—Perkins, Berry, Anka—composed their own material, most of the tunesmiths churning out teen-themed songs for Avalon and Francis were still haunting the old publishers' offices in the Brill Building and very consciously walking in the footsteps of Irving Berlin. (While the young Northeastern singers were disproportionately Italian, the young songwriters—Jerry Leiber, Mike Stoller, Neil Sedaka, Carole King, Gerry Goffin, Barry Mann—were overwhelmingly Jewish.) Tin Pan Alley still hummed with scuffling "cleffers" and fly-by-night publishers ready to jump on every trend, and song pluggers still hustled to get their products recorded by name artists and featured in the new equivalents of the old vaudeville variety bills: *American Bandstand*, *The Ed Sullivan Show*, *Pat Boone's Chevy Showroom*, and teen-oriented movies like *Jamboree*. One of the silliest sideshows of the next few years would be the payola scandal, in which, like Claude Raines's police captain in *Casablanca*, the barons of Broadway expressed their shock that song pluggers were paying people to play their product—a process that was already old news in the 'teens.

There had been huge changes in both music and technology, but as live bands gave way to record hops, the deejays and television hosts took on many of the attributes of the old-time orchestra leaders. Alan Freed and, most prominently, Dick Clark had replaced Whiteman, Kay Kyser, and Tommy Dorsey, and as in the old days, the nationally known names inspired a still larger number of regional imitators. An ex-bandleader named Ted Steele started a show in New

York called *Teen Bandstand*, and there was also a *Detroit Bandstand*, a *Connecticut Bandstand*, and Chicago's *Bandstand Matinee*. Like the bandleaders, the television and radio personalities acted as ringmasters and quality controllers for a shifting mix of dance instrumentals, solo performers, and vocal groups, serving an audience that was happy to applaud a different hit and another nice-looking singer the following week. The late 1950s and early 1960s were a peak period for "one-hit wonders," acts that reached the top ten once and never repeated the feat. The enduring figures in listeners' lives were the hosts, and in *Bandstand*'s case, the regular dancers. Reading through *16 Magazine*, which in its early years functioned largely as a fanzine for the Philadelphia TV show, singers and television actors tend to be pictured on the covers, but few if any record makers are written about as often as the teenage dancers—Arlene Sullivan, Kenny Rossi, Justine Carrelli, and Bob Clayton were the most popular—who appeared every week and received tens of thousands of letters from fans who regarded them as personal friends.

Except for *Bandstand*, the national music and variety shows mostly came out of New York: the Arthur Godfrey and Milton Berle programs, the *Ed Sullivan Show*, the Steve Allen–hosted *Tonight Show*, the short-lived Alan Freed and Dorsey Brothers shows, and even the Saturday evening *Dick Clark Show*. So despite all the changes, it was easy for New York publishers, record companies, and entertainers to feel that they were still at the center of the universe. There were a lot of satellites, though, which were growing more important every day. When *Billboard* compared the state of the music industry in 1959 with the situation twenty years earlier, it found that although the number of hit songs had stayed roughly even, the seventy songs that scored in 1939 had come from twenty-two New York-based publishers, and almost all had been written by New York songwriters, whereas the seventy-two songs in 1959 had come from sixty-nine publishers in eight states, and their writers were based in seventeen states and the District of Columbia. The expansion of hit-producing record companies was even more dramatic: from three New York labels to thirty-nine labels in ten states.[24]

Ricky Nelson, California's main contribution to the rock 'n' roll boom, was a prominent symbol of the new era and in some ways the archetypal teen idol. Even more than Boone, Como, and *Bandstand* favorites like Avalon and Fabian, Nelson was a creation of television, known to millions of viewers as the younger son on *The Adventures of Ozzie and Harriet* before he ever picked up a guitar. Ozzie Nelson had been a successful bandleader in the 1930s, Harriet had been his vocalist, and they started their sitcom as a radio serial in 1944. It shifted to television in 1952, when Ricky was thirteen and his brother David was sixteen, and by the time Ricky sang his first song on the air in the spring of 1957, viewers felt as though they were watching a member of their own family. As a teenage fan in Kansas told a *Life* magazine reporter, "It's like he was Elvis and my brother at the same time."[25]

That familiarity was the key to Nelson's appeal. He made his musical debut with Fats Domino's "I'm Walkin'," and in typically self-deprecating fashion recalled that he chose it because "it was the only song I knew at the time . . . [and] it had about three chords, so I could play it on guitar."[26] He was a rank amateur, lifted to musical stardom only because he was already a TV star—but his passion was genuine and caught the spirit of the time. To kids who loved rock 'n' roll, he was neither a distant icon like Elvis nor a packaged show-biz commodity; he was one of them who just happened to be on television. A teenage loner named Bob Zimmerman in Hibbing, Minnesota, later wrote, "We were about the same age, probably liked the same things. . . . I felt like we had a lot in common."[27] Nelson could barely play his instrument, and his singing had far more sincerity than technique, but unlike the *Bandstand* idols or even Elvis, he believed in rock 'n' roll as something very different from his parents' music, purer and more rooted in his own hopes and experiences. For both him and his listeners, it was a way of fighting free for a moment from suburban normalcy, and despite his background and national fame, he reacted to it in a way that did not fit the old show-biz paradigms.

Ozzie Nelson showed a rare grasp of the situation by encouraging his son's unusual path. With a hugely popular TV show, they could easily have gotten a contract with a major record label, but instead they stuck to smaller outfits based in Los Angeles: "I'm Walkin'" appeared on Verve, an independent label that specialized in jazz. (Guitarist Barney Kessell produced the session, with Merle Travis on guitar and Earl Palmer, who had played on the original Fats Domino record, on drums.) And after the song's success they shifted to Domino's label, Imperial, which had never had a white pop hit. The song selection was equally surprising: Nelson's debut album, *Ricky*, which was the best-selling rock 'n' roll LP of 1958, included two songs by Carl Perkins—neither of them the ubiquitous "Blue Suede Shoes"—and he continued to cover obscure Southern rockabilly records, including Sonny Burgess's "My Bucket's Got a Hole in It," which he took to the top twenty.[28]

Nelson not only loved country and rockabilly music but also chose players and performers from those fields as his closest friends and collaborators. The flip side of "Bucket" was a song by Johnny and Dorsey Burnette, who had been two-thirds of a Memphis band called the Rock and Roll Trio, and the lead guitarist was James Burton, fresh from playing on Dale Hawkins's "Susie-Q" and working in the house band of the *Louisiana Hayride*. Nor were those artists just brought in as hired guns: The Burnettes made their own connection by buying a "star map" of Hollywood, driving over to the Nelson house, ringing the bell, and playing a few songs for Ricky in the driveway when he got home from the television studio; over the next two years he took four of their compositions to the top twenty. As for Burton, Ricky happened to hear him auditioning for Imperial with the Texas singer Bob Luman and invited him to come down to the TV show and meet Ozzie. Soon he was not only playing in Ricky's band but also living in the Nelsons' home and jamming late into the night.

There was a casual feel to the L.A. music scene—perhaps because it was so over-shadowed by the movie industry—and ever since World War II it had been a major center for both country and blues performers. The surreal way in which Ricky's TV life overlapped his daily life made him a kind of video avatar for kids in suburban or rural communities across the country. He fell for a girl he had seen on a local country and western television show, Lorrie Collins, who worked with her younger brother in a hot rockabilly duo called the Collins Kids, got her phone number through a mutual high school friend, called her, and they began going steady—both offscreen and on the show, on which she became his TV girlfriend. His first num-ber one hit was written by another local teenager, Sharon Sheeley, who met him by driving with her sister to the Nelsons' weekend home near Laguna Beach and pretending their car had broken down. As Sheeley recalled, "Ricky Nelson walked out tossing a football, just like on *Ozzie and Harriet*," and after a brief chat he invited the girls to come in and listen to some Jerry Lee Lewis and Everly Brothers records. Shortly thereafter, Sheeley began a long-distance romance with Don Everly, and when she found he was married, she compensated for the disappointment by writ-ing "Poor Little Fool," which Nelson took to the top of the charts in August 1958.[29]

Nelson's bizarre juxtaposition of ordinariness and stardom made even Elvis Presley, his musical idol, react like a normal teenager: When Nelson showed up at one of his concerts, Elvis's first question was, "How's your mommy and daddy? Did David come too?"[30] But there was nothing normal about the reaction when Nelson appeared onstage. Bruce Belland, a high school friend of David's who sometimes appeared on the TV show and also sang with a quartet called the Four Preps, recalled that the first time Ricky performed live was when the Preps played at a local school assembly. It was a typical show until one of the singers mentioned that they might be able to "coax a pal of ours out to sing a couple of songs . . . Rick Nelson":

> Well, you know the place exploded—*arghhh*—just at the mention of his name. Rick, I see him kind of looking around. He straps his guitar on . . . takes a deep breath, and walks out onstage. He hits the stage. Chaos. Fucking chaos. We're singing, and I'm looking at Rick. It's so loud we can hardly hear ourselves. Then, something I never saw before or since in any assembly in any high school, they left their seats and came rushing down to the front. It was forty or fifty deep up each aisle of girls, just screaming.[31]

If that sounds like the Sinatra story all over again, there was one big difference: Sinatra had attracted screaming teens, but he was also an established big-band vocalist challenging Bing Crosby for the throne of mainstream pop. By contrast, the idols of Nelson's generation were teenagers themselves, fantasy friends who were appreciated as much for their normalcy as for their talents, and no one but their most adoring fans thought they were in the Sinatra or Crosby class. Ricky was having fun playing rock 'n' roll, but the TV scripts always made it clear that his older brother preferred classical music, jazz, and show tunes—with the implied assumption that Ricky, too, would grow to appreciate more mature styles—and those styles still constituted the mainstream for most music consumers.

What is more, although high school kids dominated the singles market and their buying habits were also reflected in the growing Top 40 radio format, they couldn't go to nightclubs or keep the dance halls running. Teen bands proliferated, but most were made up of amateurs and part-timers, and the high-paying live gigs were still largely played for adults, or at least in adult styles. Even the teenagers danced to old-fashioned orchestras at special events like coming out parties and graduations. In his television life, Ricky Nelson took fox-trot lessons before going to a dance at the local country club, and by 1962 the Midwestern swing band leader Preston Love recalled that pretty much the only gigs that paid well were at high school and college proms.[32]

When the new rock 'n' roll stars appeared in concert, the format was typically similar to their television appearances: Whether in special, deejay-sponsored concerts or as part of one-nighter touring packages, they were grouped in multiact programs on which each act sang just two or three songs. Nor were those all-star packages necessarily successful. In 1958, *Billboard* reported that most were losing money, and though Dick Clark's annual Caravan of Stars did good business for several more summers, it wasn't making its performers rich. Clark recalled that his top star would get about $1,200 for fourteen shows a week, but most acts were getting less than half that and "it didn't matter if there were twelve people of the band.... Once they got paid their $500 or $600 they divided the money among themselves, took off 10 percent for their agent, 10 percent for their manager, put some aside to pay their taxes, paid for their room and board on the tour—they were lucky if they had $20 a week to play with."[33]

In any case, most performers did not get invited on a Dick Clark tour, and even for those few, the gig lasted for only two or three months in the summer. Clark, whose blandly cheerful persona concealed a relentless focus on the bottom line, recalled a conversation on the tour bus with the young bass player for the Caravan band: "He told me about the exhilaration he got from travel, the joy he got from performing. I told him I thought he was foolish to follow it as a career—that most of the money was back down the road with the promoter."[34]

Most rock 'n' roll singers still didn't have their own bands, and the ones who did were essentially working as stripped-down, underpaid equivalents of the old dance orchestras. Conway Twitty, who would reemerge in the mid-1960s as a country star but in the late 1950s was hitting as a big-voiced Presley clone, traveled with his own combo, and he told *Billboard* that what worked at gigs was very different from what clicked on record. Though he had recently topped the pop chart with a soaring proto-power-ballad, "It's Only Make Believe," at dances he was filling requests for "cha-chas and the swinging rock and roll items."[35] Likewise, though Dale Hawkins made his name in 1957 with a guitar-driven rockabilly record, "Susie-Q," the band that kept him working up and down the Eastern Seaboard through the early 1960s had three horn players and tended toward R&B dance hits.[36]

As ever, name acts like Twitty and Hawkins were the tip of a huge iceberg of similar bandleaders, most of whom never cracked the record charts. Rock 'n' roll had put a new emphasis on distinctive stylists, but that just meant that the standard pop band not only was required to play all the current hits but had to be able to play them in the styles of the current hitmakers—that is, generic dance orchestras were being replaced by generic cover bands. Big Al Downing, a black pianist and singer from Oklahoma who, like Twitty, would later reemerge as a country artist, had some regional success with a rockabilly single, "Down on the Farm," but recalled that when he got his first East Coast club booking, the owner was a Fats Domino fan and insisted that he play all of Domino's hits: "He even put a big sign in front of the window, saying 'Big Al Domino.' I said, 'My name is Downing.' He says, 'No, it's Domino.'"[37]

Known or unknown, live performers were expected to play what the owner and the audience wanted to hear, which meant not only mastering the range of styles and dance rhythms that were hitting at any given moment but also being able to please older customers who weren't keeping up. Danny and the Juniors might sing "Rock and Roll Is Here to Stay," but no one really believed it, and, with the possible exception of Elvis, no teen idol was earning anything resembling the income of Sinatra or Crosby, nor was there any sign that they might in the future. So the performers who hoped to stick with music as their life's work did their best to prove that they were not limited to teen styles. The rockabilly guys could always go back to country music, but urban rock 'n' rollers who aspired to enduring careers, from Connie Francis and Frankie Avalon to Sam Cooke, James Brown, and the Supremes, recorded albums of standards and tried to establish an appeal to grown-up nightclub audiences. As Motown founder Berry Gordy would explain, the Supremes did not particularly like the pop tunes he selected for them, nor did their usual audience care for those recordings, but "I knew those standards were the key to taking our people to the next level of show business—top nightclubs around the country."[38] Having a number-one single was a thrill, but as Buddy Miles would say, "Hit records are like Bic pens; they only last so long."[39]

16

TWISTING GIRLS CHANGE THE WORLD

The Twist, superseding the Hula Hoop, burst upon the scene like a nuclear explosion, sending its fallout of rhythm into the Minds and Bodies of the people....They came from every
level of society, writhing pitifully though gamely about the floor, feeling exhilarating and
soothing new sensations, release from some unknown prison in which their Bodies had been
encased, a sense of freedom they had never known before.

ELDRIDGE CLEAVER, MINISTER OF INFORMATION

OF THE BLACK PANTHER PARTY, 1968

At the dawn of the 1960s the basic American dance was still the fox-trot, with its
more exuberant offspring, the Lindy or jitterbug, which in some quarters had been
renamed the rock 'n' roll. Horn and reed sections were giving way to honking saxes
and electric guitars, but teenagers were still paired up in one another's arms doing
pretty much the same range of steps that their parents—or at least their parents'
friskier peers—had done. In some areas, though, the old patterns were beginning
to break. The popularity of black and Southern musical styles was a spur to new
ways of moving, and as a 1958 book called *Dance, Teens* put it:

> The rock 'n' roll danced in Shreveport, La. or San Antonio, Texas (where the "shine"
> or solo position is stressed) differs in certain aspects from the rock 'n' roll danced
> in Brooklyn, N.Y. or Los Angeles, Calif. (where the "closed" or together position is
> stressed). However, more and more teens prefer to dance SOLO because it prevents
> them from stepping on each other's feet ("Ouch!")....While dancing SOLO, the
> boy's and girl's footwork will often vary. This is no cause for worry since *the footwork
> doesn't have to coincide!* It's this correct difference that appeals and automatically
> rules out the old answers, "I can't dance your way," or "You're too good for me," or
> "Ouch!"[1]

It was not just a matter of solo dances; there were also group dances, line dances,
and just plain silly dances. Television had made it possible to spread a new dance as
quickly as a new song, and by 1957 Dick Clark had realized that one of his show's
greatest appeals was that it instantly provided teens across the country with the
latest steps. The first *American Bandstand* dance contest was held that year and
drew almost 750,000 letters, and soon each televised competition was getting

over a million mailed-in votes for favorite couples. The most popular new dances included the bop, the cha-lypso, the stroll, the strand, and all sorts of variations of the old couples styles. Clark and the teenage regulars confirmed in later interviews that most of the steps were developed by black kids, but on *Bandstand* they were danced by white kids, often with the sexier motions eliminated.[2] And the most famous and influential of these new dances was, of course, the twist.

The story of the twist begins with Jo Jo Wallace and Bill Woodruff of the Sensational Nightingales, one of the most popular quartets on the black gospel circuit, and the dance craze it inspired owed a notable debt to black churchgoers. Just as the fervent singing styles and complex rhythms of Clyde McPhatter, Ray Charles, James Brown, and the Motown stars were to a great extent adapted from gospel artists, steps that looked a lot like the mashed potato and the pony had been commonplace for decades in the less sedate black churches, where congregants seized by the spirit kicked out in footwork that the go-go dancers of the 1960s could only envy. This was not a connection most church folk were eager to acknowledge, though, so when Wallace and Woodruff came up with a secular dance number, rather than trying to record it themselves they began shopping it to R&B singers. In 1956 or '57 they sang their version of "The Twist" for Hank Ballard, the leader and songwriter of the Midnighters, who were still riding high on the Southern circuit on the strength of their naughty "Annie" songs: "Work with Me Annie," "Annie Had a Baby (Can't Work No More)," and "Annie's Aunt Fannie."

Ballard rewrote "The Twist"—how much is not clear, but when it was published he was listed as the sole composer—and recorded it for Cincinnati's King label in November 1958. King didn't see much potential in the tune and just put it out as the B side of a ballad, "Teardrops on Your Letter," and the charts seemed to back up that decision, since "Teardrops" took the Midnighters to the R&B top ten for the first time in several years and also broke the pop Hot 100. Some deejays were turning the record over to the dance side, though, and its chart success was probably helped by buyers following suit. In any case, Ballard followed with another dance disc using virtually the same tune, "Finger Poppin' Time," and this time hit the jackpot. Clark played the record on his show, it got a good response, and the Midnighters were invited on *Bandstand* in June 1960, after which it took off, reaching the pop top ten by August. The downside of this was that Clark had simultaneously developed a taste for "The Twist," and he wasn't about to promote two Ballard tunes in a row.[3] The Midnighters were clearly not teenagers, they sounded very black, and they had a reputation for being one of the dirtiest groups in R&B thanks to stage antics that included pulling a doll from between the legs of a cross-dressing back-up singer during "Annie Had a Baby." Clark's success was built on his wholesome image, and in 1960 he was being particularly careful in the wake of the payola scandal, so it had been a stretch for him to have them on at all.

Clark's first thought was to have a new version of "The Twist" cut by a white singer, Freddie Cannon, but Cannon declined because he was getting good airplay with another record, a remake of the Dixieland standard "Way Down Yonder in New Orleans." So Clark went to his pals at Philadelphia's Cameo label, Bernard Lowe (né Lowenthal), who had played piano with Meyer Davis and Lester Lanin and been the bandleader for Whiteman's *TV Teen Club*, and Kal Mann (né Kalman Cohen), who had joined Lowe to write Charlie Gracie's "Butterfly." They gave the song to Ernest Evans, a young black singer with a gift for mimicry who had recorded a minor hit titled "The Class," on which he sang "Mary Had a Little Lamb" in the styles of Fats Domino, the Coasters, Elvis Presley, Cozy Cole, and the Chipmunks. Who better to record a sound-alike cover of Ballard's dance hit? Evans was a cheerful, light-skinned teenager, and Clark's wife dubbed him Chubby Checker, a play on Domino's name that made him seem particularly cute and unthreatening. Checker's version of "The Twist" was so close to the original that Ballard recalled hearing it on Miami's main pop station and thinking, "Wow, I'm finally getting some white airplay. I'm gonna be a superstar.'...I thought it was me, so help me God, until almost the end of the record. And it was Chubby Checker."[4] Ballard's initial disappointment was soothed by the songwriting royalties from a number one hit: "It's one of the best copyrights I have," he would say in the 1970s. "Dick Clark did me a favor; otherwise the song would never have been heard."[5] Along with collecting royalties, Ballard saw his original recording come back and rise to number twenty-eight, and he quickly followed up with another dance hit, "Let's Go, Let's Go, Let's Go."

If Checker's record was just a sound-alike cover of Ballard's, he can take somewhat more credit for the dance. Although the basic moves had been around for years, Checker reworked them and it was his version that shortly traveled around the world. On August 6, 1960, he appeared on the Saturday night *Dick Clark Show* and combined his lip-synched performance with a one-sentence dance lesson that would be frequently recycled in the next few years: "Just pretend you're wiping your bottom with a towel as you get out of the shower, and putting out a cigarette with both feet."[6]

It really was as simple as that, and though detractors howled that it was just "a gimmick turned into a dance,"[7] that simplicity was its charm. At first Checker saw the twist mainly as a springboard to further dances: He followed it with the pony (its namesake record, "Pony Time," actually outlasted "The Twist" at *Billboard*'s top spot) and the mess-around, and the next summer he was back in the top ten with "Let's Twist Again (Like We Did Last Summer)" and "The Fly"—a particularly silly dance invented by a pair of *Bandstand* regulars, which consisted of flapping your hands around as if chasing a fly.[8] In hindsight, though, this was all an extended preamble. In September 1961, the New York *Journal-American*'s society gossip columnist, Cholly Knickerbocker, visited a ratty bar called the Peppermint Lounge, saw the regulars gyrating to the house band, Joey Dee and the Starliters, and wrote in his "Smart Set" column that "the Twist is the new teenage dance craze. But you don't have to be a teenager to do the Twist." And shazzam! It was the Castles and the turkey trot all over again.

Throughout this book I have stressed the continuity and connections between pop eras, and by now some readers are probably rolling their eyes when I drag fifty-year-old trends back into the story. But this time it really isn't my fault. Within the next year and a half, a black teenager named Little Eva would follow her number one hit, "The Loco-Motion," with a top-twenty tune called "Let's Turkey Trot," in which—after the backup singers set the stage by repeating "gobble-diddley, gobble-gobble diddley"—she sang, "My grandmother taught this dance to me / She did it at the turn of the century / Yeah, yeah, yeah, yeah."[9] And Irene Castle weighed in on "the twist and so forth" in the *New York Times*, sounding exactly as she had in 1914: "I don't mind so much what they're doing with their fannies these days. . . . That's not nearly so awful as what they do with their arms and heads. All this jerky, jerky jerking around. It's so unbecoming."[10]

Writers noted that a version of the twist had surfaced in the first dance craze, citing 1912's "Messin' Around" and 1913's "Ballin' the Jack," and Checker cemented their argument by recording the latter song in 1962, giving new impetus to its instructions to "twist around, twist around with all your might."[11] As in the 'teens, the big news as far as the press was concerned was that the crazy new styles were being danced not only by kids but also by adults, including the cream of New York high society. The twist could be made to fit virtually any music, and one of the oddities in films of this period is seeing rooms of well-dressed grown-ups twisting to everything from electric guitar bands to full orchestras and avant-garde jazz groups.[12]

Duke Ellington, who had recorded his "East St. Louis Toodle-oo" as "Harlem Twist" back in 1928, must have been amused to see his upscale white fans doing moves that had once been reserved for Cotton Club chorus girls, but as their audiences started gyrating like teenagers, old-guard musicians began to make their own stabs at the style. Count Basie recorded the "Basie Twist," and Frank Sinatra dented the Hot 100 with "Everybody's Twistin'," a rewrite of 1935's "Truckin'." The society bandleaders jumped in with a vengeance: Paul Whiteman's old rival Vincent Lopez, now leading his orchestra nightly at Manhattan's Hotel Taft, proved his familiarity with current trends by explaining that "the Twist is a mixture of the shimmy, the hula, the Charleston, and rock 'n' roll. . . . It is totally unlike the pony, the Bristol stomp, and the slop."[13] Lester Lanin made *Billboard*'s LP chart with *Twistin' in High Society*. And Louis Simon, who had been working around New York since the 1940s, called on his son Paul (yes, that Paul Simon) and Paul's buddy Al Kooper to add teen appeal at dance appearances, strumming electric guitars that were unamplified for most of the show, then jumping up to play a few minutes of rock 'n' roll.[14]

"Habitues of Meyer Davis Land Dance the Twist," blared the *Times* headline over a story noting that Greta Garbo, Noel Coward, Elsa Maxwell, and Tennessee Williams "vie with sailors, leather-jacketed drifters and girls in toreador pants for admission to the Peppermint's garish interior.... Café society has not gone slumming with such energy since its forays into Harlem in the Twenties."[15] As it happened, the society folk were also going up to Harlem, where Wilt Chamberlain had taken over Smalls' Paradise and welcomed them with King Curtis's band and a team of dancers dubbed the "World's Greatest Twisters." Nor was Davis's name taken in vain: The king of orchestra contractors recorded a twist album for Cameo, and labelmate Checker welcomed him to the genre, exulting to the *Chicago Defender* that "I figure I'll be playing the White House soon.... When he goes to the White House, I go. Just think of it—me, Chubby Checker, in the White House."[16] (Sadly, it was not to be: Lanin rather than Davis had the honor of backing the first twisters at the presidential residence.)

All of this might be discounted as an amusing fad, but in retrospect it signaled a sea change in popular music. In 1961, *Billboard*'s year-end list of the top fifty LPs had not included a single rock 'n' roll dance record, but in 1962 there were six: Joey Dee's *Doin' the Twist at the Peppermint Lounge, Do the Twist with Ray Charles* (a collection of old recordings that happened to be in the appropriate tempo), and four Checker entries: *Your Twist Party, The Twist, For Twisters Only,* and *Let's Twist Again.* There were also two other Charles LPs (though one was of country and western songs) and rock-related hit collections from Paul Anka, Dion, Buddy Holly, and the Platters. The Platters, in particular, had been successful album sellers in the past, but the field was growing. It was also proving to have an unexpected reverence for its own history: At number nineteen was a three-year-old album of songs that most people had already considered passé at that time, *Oldies But Goodies.*

What all of this signified was that adults were becoming a substantial part of the rock 'n' roll market, and although some of them were middle-aged ballroom dancers twisting for a lark, many were twenty-somethings who had grown up in the early rock era and were holding onto their teenage tastes. Already in 1960, *Billboard* had noted that Checker's remake of "The Twist" was an example of the pop world's growing fascination with older R&B. The week Checker reached number one, the Hot 100 chart also included the Everly Brothers' version of Little Richard's "Lucille" from 1957, Bobby Vee's cover of the Clovers' "Devil or Angel" from 1956, and the black New Orleans duo Shirley and Lee remaking their own 1956 hit "Let the Good Times Roll."[17] The latter disc is particularly noteworthy, because the duo's original recording had been reissued a year earlier on the *Oldies But Goodies* anthology and the new version made the pop top fifty without denting the R&B charts. That is, its revival was largely driven by white nostalgia for music—and especially black music—of the recent past. (Two of the other songs on the *Oldies* album, the Five Satins' "In the Still of the Night" and the Mello Kings' "Tonite,

Tonite" also reappeared in the *Billboard* pop chart in 1960–1961 in their original versions, and a third, "Earth Angel," was reported to have sold an additional four million copies since its original release.[18])

The idea of repackaging black R&B singles on LPs aimed at white consumers had been around since 1956, when Atlantic Records edged an anthology of hits by Joe Turner, LaVern Baker, the Drifters, and others onto the album charts thanks to a cover featuring a white female dancer and the prescient title *Rock & Roll For Ever*. At the time, though, this was more a dream than a prediction. Atlantic's Jerry Wexler suggested in *Down Beat* that a day might come when record collectors would seek out old Fats Domino singles the way they were currently hunting up old King Oliver 78s, but the year he imagined this happening was 1993, and he put forward his hypothesis to support the contention that R&B was the new mainstream of jazz.[19]

Nonetheless, as more and more white dancers became aware of the current black styles, a lot of them began wondering what they had been missing, and deejays discovered that they could recycle old R&B hits for a new audience. Art Laboe, who was hosting a nightly deejay show from a Los Angeles drive-in restaurant, found that his most popular selections included a lot of older songs, and it occurred to him that he could cheaply license some out-of-print hits and put out an LP. He issued *Oldies But Goodies* on his own Original Sound label, and it exceeded his wildest expectations by spending 183 weeks on the *Billboard* album charts and spawning not only a series of follow-up volumes—three of which reached the top twenty—but also a host of imitations with titles like *Goodies but Oldies*, *Golden Goodies*, and *Golden Oldies*. This trend was so influential that "oldies," which had been a common term in the music business since the 1930s,[20] has ever since been associated with this period, and it proved that rather than just being ephemeral music for teenagers, rock 'n' roll was creating enduring classics.

Although the twist and the oldies sets were news because they were attracting white adults, both were overwhelmingly reliant on black performers. All but one of the records on Laboe's first anthology were by black or mixed groups, and the twist craze was distinguished by being the first popular music movement—at least since James Reese Europe's reign in the early 'teens—in which African Americans were consistently the top sellers. Of the twelve songs with "twist" in their titles that reached *Billboard*'s top twenty-five between 1960 and 1963, ten were by black artists, and the other two were by Joey Dee, who fronted a mixed group and stressed that his music should be considered rhythm and blues rather than rock 'n' roll.[21]

This was a distinct shift from the way rock 'n' roll had reached most white listeners in the 1950s, and it signified a stronger emphasis on African rhythmic roots than in any previous period. Those roots were most often traced through the black church and Afro-Latin connections, but the exotica craze, for all its silliness and fakery, had also helped to create an audience for recordings of genuine African musicians. Guy Warren, who had been a well-known drummer in his native Ghana, recorded albums for both Decca and RCA in the 1950s; by 1958 the New York dee-jay Murray the K was using an African field recording as his opening theme; and in 1959 the Nigerian drummer Babatunde Olatunji appeared at Radio City Music Hall, then recorded a popular LP, *Drums of Passion*. Though the title suggested the usual exotic schlock, Olatunji was a champion of traditional West African styles and reached not only exotica and jazz listeners but also a broad audience that included the crowd for James Brown's *Live at the Apollo* recording.[22] Admittedly, the recognition of African roots could take odd forms: "The Twist has been going on for a long time," Checker told one early interviewer. "Take a look at some of those old TV shows like *Ramar of the Jungle*. Seems to me the natives have been doing something like The Twist for years."[23] *Ramar* was an adventure series from the early 1950s that followed a team of white scientists through African locales populated by elephants, lions, and scantily clad tribesmen, and Checker's comment is a reminder that the music that accompanied dances like the twist and, most obviously, the Watusi was not only connected to gospel, R&B, and Latin styles but also shared some of the romantic primitive allure of exotica and calypso.

The calypso craze had been limited by the fact that most Americans did not regard it as dance music, but the twist provided a solution to that problem, and several of the top twelve twist hits came out of the Belafonte songbook: Gary "U.S." Bonds's "Twist, Twist Senora" was "Jump in the Line" and led off an album titled *Twist Up Calypso*, and Jimmy Soul's "Twistin' Matilda" was a reworking of "Matilda," which Soul followed up with the number-one hit "If You Want to Be Happy," based on the calypso standard "Ugly Woman."[24] Checker himself made this connection in 1962, reaching *Billboard*'s number-two spot with "Limbo Rock," and by 1964 Atlantic Records had sent a recording team to Jamaica and edged the island's top bandleader, Byron Lee, onto the Hot 100 with "Jamaica Ska." (Lee, who had been introduced to international audiences in the first James Bond movie, 1962's *Dr. No*, was booked for the 1964 New York World's Fair, and the song's opening line was aimed directly at the U.S. market: "Not many people can cha-cha-chá, not everybody can do the twist. / But everybody can do the ska, it's a new dance you can't resist.") Meanwhile, the Cuban percussionist Mongo Santamaria latched onto the fad with a "Pachanga Twist" and reached the pop top ten in 1963 with a dance-friendly Afro-jazz hit, "Watermelon Man."

The mainstream bandleaders and musicians tried to keep up with these innovations—Arthur Murray sponsored a *Discotheque Dance Party* LP that had a studio group playing the "Jamaica Ska" and Victor Gerard and his Orchestra playing a "Universal Merengue"—but in a world in which rhythm was all, they were absurdly ill equipped. Murray tacitly acknowledged this when he produced *Arthur Murray's Music for Dancing the Twist*, going outside his usual range of accompanists to feature a band led by King Curtis, the man whose "Soul Twist" was the first hit title to employ the next rubric for black popular music. Curtis Ousley was a Texas-born saxophone player, familiar to millions of listeners from his solo on the Coasters' "Yackety Yak." Like most R&B studio musicians, he had started out playing jazz, and within the jazz world "soul" had taken on a new meaning during the 1950s as black players looked for ways to connect with Southern roots and young R&B fans and to counter the overly intellectual excursions of the white-dominated "cool" school. Even Ray Charles, widely seen as the defining soul singer, was first associated with the word through 1957's *Soul Brothers* and 1958's *Soul Meeting*, both duet albums with Milt Jackson of the Modern Jazz Quartet—and Jackson had previously made an album called *Plenty, Plenty Soul*.

It may surprise some readers that the use of "soul" as an expression of African-American pride reached R&B through jazz, but this is an apt reminder that what was happening on the dance floor was far from the only way in which black artists were reshaping their role in American culture. In later years, black and white pop styles would grow so far apart that it is easy to forget that in the late 1950s and early 1960s African-American entertainers were not yet exclusively—or even primarily—identified with urban dance rhythms or gospel-inflected passion. Along with all the artists who were crossing over from R&B to pop, there were also some very prominent black singers who had little if any connection to R&B. The successes of Nat King Cole, Sarah Vaughan, Lena Horne, Sammy Davis Jr., and Belafonte had opened the way for Dakota Staton, Nancy Wilson, and young singers like Leslie Uggams, who was featured on Mitch Miller's *Sing Along* show. Johnny Mathis placed thirty-six singles and twenty-six LPs on the *Billboard* pop charts between 1957 and 1964 (the only person with more LP entries was Sinatra), and *Ebony* magazine reported in 1962 that he was the entertainment business's only black millionaire—which helps explain why a lot of other black singers were recording string-laden ballads.[25]

I'll get to some of those ballads in a minute, but first want to wrap up my discussion of the twist with one more nod to black church traditions. I already mentioned that many of the new dance steps had church roots, and though I have tried to broaden the discussion to include jazz and Caribbean styles, the most influential rhythms and vocal techniques to enter the pop repertoire on the cusp of the 1960s came from the gospel world. Ray Charles and Sam Cooke are the artists who are typically cited in this context, and both reached a lot of new listeners through the twist boom, but the record that most faithfully captured the gospel style while firing up dance floors was the Isley Brothers' "Shout." In the more demonstrative black congregations, to "shout" is to be possessed by the spirit, losing control of your mind and body, flailing and jumping so that the people nearby have to protect you from hurting yourself, and the Isleys conveyed all the joy and power of that ecstatic experience. Recorded in 1959, "Shout" failed to register on *Billboard*'s R&B chart and reached only number forty-seven on the Hot 100, and today it is less familiar than the Isleys' Latin-flavored 1962 sequel, "Twist and Shout" (in a large part due to the Beatles' cover of the latter record). Nonetheless, as the appearance of a sequel three years after its arrival indicates, its influence belied the chart action. "Shout" was the era's defining dance-floor workout, with a relatively slack cover by Joey Dee reaching the top ten and versions by the Shangri-Las, the British singer Lulu, and the Beatles testifying to the breadth of its appeal. Asked what sort of music he played for club audiences in the early 1960s, Dale Hawkins simply answered, "Back then if you didn't play 'Shout' you might just as well stay home."[26] It was pure rhythmic energy with hardly any tune—which helps explain why the white covers fell far behind the Isleys' original—and its ferocious power and raw vocalizing pointed the way to James Brown's "Brand New Bag" and sounded the death knell for the old dance orchestras as surely as the twist killed off the fox-trot.

Those two deaths were intimately linked and almost totally unexpected. A lot of older bandleaders had hoped that rock 'n' roll would help them by getting a new generation out on the floor, and most of them cheerfully added the twist to their repertoires, but in the early 1960s young dancers were not just adopting new styles, they were abandoning the old ones. Considering how long couples had been dancing in each other's arms, it is startling how quickly that whole tradition disappeared, and it was that disappearance, more than all the evolutions of instrumental styles and rhythms, that signaled an irreparable break in popular music. By the end of the decade the average high school prom couldn't feature an old-style orchestra because the students not only didn't want to do fox-trots and waltzes, they didn't know how. There were regional exceptions, but for most of us the whole idea of formal steps and dance classes no longer existed. If we learned new dances at all, we learned them from television shows like *Shindig*, *Hullabaloo*, and the defining showcase of my high school years, *Soul Train*—or from girls who watched the shows, bought the records, then brought them to parties and taught the rest of us. But in general we didn't do particular dances; we just danced.

In the light of that change, the dance fads of the twist era can be seen as essentially exercises for the free-style solo dancing that has reigned ever since. Once people stopped holding onto their partners, there was no reason to do set steps, so the twist, frug, swim, surf, fish, fly, bug, dog, duck, chicken, bird, monkey, slop, Watusi, pony, shake, jerk, waddle, stomp, and mashed potato weren't dances in the way that a waltz, polka, or mambo was a dance. They were moves that could be mixed and matched as the dancers saw fit, and their most enduring effect was to help European Americans—as well as plenty of African Americans and other people all around the world—loosen up and explore new ways of using their bodies. As *The Hullabaloo Discothèque Dance Book* put it:

You don't do just one or two dances all evening, or even for the duration of one song, as you could with a fox trot. No matter how terrific you get at, say, the Frug, you can't get out on the dance floor till you've learned at least another couple of dances; you'll get bored, you'll bore your partner, you'll bore anybody who's watching. You've got to be able to go casually from one dance into another—and no matter what your partner does or doesn't do, you can go on to something else whenever you feel like it.[27]

Along with freeing bodies from old habits and teaching people new ways to shake their hips and move their arms, the new dancing drastically reshaped social interactions. The *Saturday Evening Post* mused that women "must have been swearing under their breath for years—led around, pushed around, held down. Now they can be as wild as they feel."[28] And a female dancer explained that it was not just a matter of getting wild: "In the old-fashioned style of dancing we may not feel particularly in a romantic mood and yet very often our partner would grab us and dance very close and hold us so closely, and I like this because, you know, we can completely keep at arms length and dance however we please."[29] Or as the writer Bruce Pollock recalled, with somewhat more ambivalence, "the concept of asking a girl to dance (and thus being accepted or horribly rejected) . . . lost meaning—any girl would accept a twist, because she didn't have to come within ten feet of you."[30]

Girls also could dance with each other, or alone—Peppermint Lounge manager Ralph Saggese ascribed the rapid rise of the new style to "the fact that it takes two to tango but only one to twist"[31]—or in groups of three, four, or however many cared to establish occasional eye contact while writhing and jumping around the floor. Of course, girls had always danced with each other, but this had generally been considered something one did only when there were no boys, or not enough boys, in the room. That remained true at most public events, at least in theory; but even if a girl ostensibly had a male partner, he was no longer holding onto her and controlling her movements—indeed, to the extent that there was any leading, it was now at least as common for the boys to imitate the girls—and she could easily catch the eye of a nearby friend and create a moment of girl space.

Once again, women were driving the course of popular music, and as it happens the rise of nontouch dancing coincided with a new wave of female singers and singing groups. Unlike their predecessors, who had built on the big-band "chick singer" tradition or been trios of wholesome sisters, the new wave—whose distinctive sound would come to be known as "girl group"—tended to come across as best friends who shared each other's secrets and desires. The song that perfectly presaged the new style was 1958's "I Met Him on a Sunday." Recorded by the Shirelles, a quartet of black teenagers from Passaic, New Jersey, it starts out with hand-claps and finger-snaps, then the singers trade lines about a boy met on Sunday, missed on Monday, found on Tuesday, dated on Wednesday, kissed on Thursday—but "he didn't come Friday," so "when he showed up Saturday, I said 'Bye-bye, baby'." It was pure girlfriend affirmation, and although the punctuating chorus of "doo-ronde-ronde-ronde-pa-pa" suggested a debt to earlier, male doo-wop ensembles, the clapping and the way the vocal lead bounced around the circle put the song squarely in the tradition of schoolgirl rhyme games. Indeed, the Shirelles made the song up by themselves and sang it to amuse their friends before they performed it for anyone in the music business.

"I Met Him on Sunday" only climbed halfway up the Hot 100, but it started the Shirelles on their way. By 1961 they were one of the most popular groups in the country, thanks to "Dedicated to the One I Love," "Mama Said," and the genre's most enduring standard, "Will You Love Me Tomorrow." And their style was imitated not only by hundreds of other young women but also by a lot of male groups: The Four Seasons were noted for their girl-group flavor, and the Beatles' first LP included two Shirelles covers. The group's precursors included the Bobbettes, who had pioneered a similar sound in 1957 with "Mr. Lee," and their name was adopted in emulation of the Chantels, who had hit in 1958 with "Maybe," a doo-wop ballad galvanized by Arlene Smith's gospel-inflected lead. But the Shirelles dominated the field until the fall of 1961, when the Marvelettes' "Please Mr. Postman" became the first number-one pop hit for a new family of labels a black entrepreneur named Berry Gordy was running out of an old house in Detroit—Motown would be the most famous, but the Marvelettes were on Tamla, which Berry had named after the title song and character of the 1957 Debbie Reynolds feature *Tammy and the Bachelor*.

To some extent the "girl group" rubric is misleading, because at first no one was thinking of the Shirelles, Chantels, Marvelettes, and their successors as forming a separate genre, but it highlights the inclusive feel that made their records so attractive. The problem Connie Francis had described—that female consumers saw female singers as competition—disappeared when instead of a single star the singers were a group of teenage pals. It was as if the most popular girls in the country were suddenly your best friends, sharing all your problems and anxieties, and it is common for women who grew up in this period to recall fantasies of being a Shirelle or a Supreme.

For a lot of boys, this trend was as annoying as the similarly girlish passion for squeaky-clean teen idols and sappy death ballads like "Teen Angel" and "Tell Laura I Love Her." Rock historians have routinely dismissed the early 1960s as a dismal period in American pop, and this can to a great extent be traced to the fact that the historians are male and the teen pop market wasn't geared to their tastes. Nor is that just hindsight; the opening paragraph of a 1963 article in *Time* magazine drips contempt for the young female music listener:

> There she sits, desperate, unhappy, twelve years old. She is cursed with the catastrophe of parents, and her boy friends complete her misery by being too young to drive. She sulks behind a screen of bobby pins, slapping at her baby fat, mourning the birth of her acne. She is a worried sixth-grader, an aging child, a frightened girl—and the queen of the $100 million-a-year popular record industry.[32]

Adolescent fears and unhappiness were certainly a common theme of teen records, but the emphasis on angst ignores the fact that these buyers were the same girls who were twisting up a storm at pajama parties. What is more, as with the twist trend, the girl-group craze was giving a new prominence to African-American performers. In 1958 *Billboard*'s year-end top fifty charts for pop and R&B had only three records each that featured female lead singers, but by 1961 the pop chart had seven and the R&B chart twelve; in 1962 the pop chart was up to fifteen and the R&B chart to eighteen; and the next year, though pop stayed even, the R&B chart counted twenty-two records with female leads.[33] Even in 1964, after the Beatles had hit, women held the number-one pop spot for a quarter of the year, and except for a week with the Shangri-Las, they were all black women: Mary Wells, the Dixie Cups, and the Supremes. Some listeners may not have been aware of that fact, since Gordy did not include artist photos on some early Tamla and Motown albums for fear of alienating potential white buyers, and the Dixie Cups' *Chapel of Love* and the Crystals' *He's a Rebel* were issued with pictures of a white bridal statue and a white motorcyclist, presumably for the same reason.[34] But anyone watching the TV teen shows was seeing a lot of black girls.

For young women, it was an exciting time. Critics might argue that the girl-group lyrics tended to reinforced old stereotypes of weakness and dependency—"Will You Love Me Tomorrow" and "I Will Follow Him" are obvious examples, along with the notorious "Johnny, Get Angry," in which Joanie Sommers begged her boyfriend to get mad at her for kissing another guy (though the record's chorus of kazoos suggested at least a hint of sarcasm).[35] But there were also some fierce declarations of autonomy and condemnations of male behavior. In a telling story, Calvin Carter, the head producer at Chicago's black-owned VeeJay label, recalled that he originally planned to record a song called "You're No Good" with a male singer, but "when I went to rehearsal with the tune, it was so negative. I said, 'Hey, guys, don't talk negative about girls, because girls are the record buyers.'"[36] Instead, he cut the song with Betty Everett, producing one of the most powerful performances of 1963 and an enduring classic: "Feeling better now that we're through / Feeling better 'cause I'm over you."[37]

The genre's most explicit feminist statement, at least in lyrical terms, was Lesley Gore's "You Don't Own Me," which spent three weeks at number two in 1964, failing to reach the top spot only because the Beatles were there with "I Want to Hold Your Hand." Gore had hit in 1963 with a two-song soap opera in which her boyfriend went off with a girl named Judy ("It's my party, and I'll cry if I want to"), then came back ("Judy's Turn to Cry"). Though Gore was a white seventeen-year-old aiming at the mainstream pop market, these recordings were produced for Mercury Records by the company's new head of A&R, Quincy Jones, the first African American to be in charge of anything but jazz or R&B at a major label. And less than a year after establishing herself as the new queen of teary teen melodrama,

Gore was singing a very different lyric: "Don't tell me what to do, don't tell me what to say / Please when I go out with you, don't put me on display / Cause you don't own me, don't try to change me in any way."[38]

Such explicit statements were rare, and lest the picture get too rosy, it must be added that if girl-group camaraderie gave even the most adoring and lovesick lyrics an affirming power for their audience, the singers themselves often found that their managers and record companies did own them and could change them on a whim. Very few teen singers were thinking about money and control when they made their first records; as Mary Wilson of the Supremes recalled, "It was just cool, you know? And if you are sixteen, cool is the meaning of life itself."[39] As a result, the girl groups were often mercilessly exploited. The old record business norm of cutting four songs in three hours was giving way to complex productions that could involve days of rehearsals followed by multiple recording and mixing sessions. Jerry Leiber and Mike Stoller's records for the Drifters made ornate string arrangements a hallmark of modern R&B, and the Shirelles' producers continued that approach and were joined by a generation of studio wizards who exercised a degree of control that made Mitch Miller seem positively hands-off: Phil Spector, the most famously extreme, buried his singers under a towering "wall of sound" and casually used the same group names for different sets of vocalists. And because recording costs were deducted from the artists' share of royalties, all the studio experimentation and instrumental overkill was paid for by the singers.

As a result, even a group as popular as the Shangri-Las could find that their share of the profits from their hits had been spent on symphonic backing tracks and studio overtime—along with vocal coaching, choreography, stage get-ups, travel, and other incidental expenses. And when they stopped hitting, the producers would just look for another group. As Gore noted, "Nobody in the business really took female performers too seriously.... If a man's career wasn't successful anymore, he could move into A&R or production, or into the company hierarchy—but we couldn't do that."[40] Plenty of black male artists were similarly exploited, as were lots of white ones, but Gore's comment is an apt reminder that some—Larry Williams, Smokey Robinson, Sam Cooke, and the Tokens leap to mind—did indeed move behind the controls, and aside from Sylvia Robinson of Mickey and Sylvia, it is hard to come up with any woman who made the same transition.

Nonetheless, for black and female performers the early 1960s felt very different from previous pop eras, and there were plenty of reasons to be optimistic about the future. Two black-owned labels, Motown and VeeJay, were among the most prominent new indies; and while Motown was having all its success with black performers, VeeJay also had one of the period's most popular white groups, the Four Seasons, and in 1964 issued the first American LP by the Beatles.[41] Meanwhile, girl-group singers were not the only women making their voices heard. In 1963, when *Billboard* tabulated the top-selling LP artists of the year, the top three included

Peter, Paul, and Mary and Joan Baez, who between them accounted for five of the year's top twenty-five albums, with two and three entries respectively. (The Kingston Trio were at number four, making Andy Williams, at number two, the only non-folk singer in the reigning quartet, and Ray Charles was at number five thanks to his two volumes of *Modern Sounds in Country & Western Music*. There were only two albums in the top twenty-five that were even vaguely rock-oriented: *Roy Orbison's Greatest Hits* at fourteen and the Beach Boys' *Surfin' USA* at twenty-five.)

Baez is not generally thought of as a pop star, much less as part of the girl-group era, but *Time* magazine's article on the dismal state of the girl-driven music industry saw fit to include her, noting that she "is a hit with teen-agers at least partly because of the gloomy songs she sings." The magazine had put her on its cover four months earlier, dubbing her "Sibyl with Guitar" and crowning her queen of a nationwide folk boom: "New York, Boston, Chicago, Minneapolis, Denver and San Francisco all have shoals of tiny coffee shops, all loud with basic sound—a pinched and studied wail that is intended to suggest flinty hills or clumpy prairies. Not even the smaller cities are immune." Indeed, there was a folk venue in Fort Wayne, Indiana, "where people squat on the floor and sip espresso by candlelight over doors that have been made into tables"; one in Joliet, Illinois; one in Council Bluffs, Iowa; and two in Omaha—and lest the point be missed, the writers concluded: "When something is that big in Omaha, Daddy, it can be said to have arrived."[42]

To old-line music business pros, Baez was an even more mystifying figure than Elvis had been. He was a raw, drawling hick, but at least had the sense to jump at a contract with RCA. By contrast, *Time* noted that when Baez became the sensation of the 1959 Newport Folk Festival, she brushed off the "record-company leg-and-fang men" who closed in on her:

> "Would you like to meet Mitch, Baby?" said a representative of Columbia Records, dropping the magic name of Mitch Miller, who is Columbia's top pop artists-and-repertory man when he isn't waving to his mother on TV.
>
> "Who's Mitch?" said Joan.

Instead of signing with a major label, Baez went with Vanguard, an album-only indie that had started with classical music, expanded into jazz with the help of John Hammond, then stood up to the anti-Communist blacklist by recording Paul Robeson and the Weavers. It was this latter stance that decided Baez. She had a passionate sense of right and wrong, and wanted to be with a company that would not try to make her do anything contrary to either her artistic or her social convictions. And that purity of purpose, though frequently sneered at both in the contemporary press and by later writers, made her a defining spirit of the new folk music movement. She was not a ethnographic purist striving to duplicate authentic rural inflections in the manner of the New Lost City Ramblers or even, in their first incarnation, the Rolling Stones, but neither was she a popularizer in the manner of the Weavers or Peter, Paul, and Mary, who sang traditional and political songs but were consciously aiming for a mass audience. She was a desperately sincere young woman singing songs that moved her personally and doing what she could to change the world around her, appearing at marches and rallies against the nuclear bomb, the Vietnam War, and racial segregation—all issues that united a lot of worried, sincere young Americans whose political interests had caught fire as grandfatherly, conservative Dwight Eisenhower was replaced by young Jack Kennedy.

I do not want either to overemphasize or to belittle the political sentiments of young people in these years—some were more committed than others, some more naïve, some sillier, some smarter—but just to point out that there were connections between listening to songs that expressed worries about whether your boyfriend would love you tomorrow and songs that expressed worries about whether there would be a tomorrow, and between marching for civil rights and dreaming of dancing with Chubby Checker or being a Shirelle. (Baez herself was half Mexican and felt cut off from her Anglo schoolmates by her dark skin, and her first performance experience was singing "Earth Angel" and Hank Ballard's "Annie" songs in her high school cafeteria.[43]) Most listeners probably did not make those connections, though, and at the time it was common for folk and rock fans to laugh at each other's tastes. Folk singers occasionally appeared in the teen mags: *Seventeen* published a couple of pieces on high school folk clubs, as well as guest columns by Pete Seeger, Josh White, and the teen protest star Janis Ian, and a *16 Magazine* feature on stars and their pets showed Patty Duke and her dog alongside Phil Ochs and his cat.[44] But the main folk audience was college students and twenty-somethings, and they regarded the music as an antidote to the childish superficiality of the pop scene. Peter, Paul, and Mary's first album included a note advising listeners that "it deserves your exclusive attention. No dancing, please."[45] So the high school kids who went in for folk songs did so with a sense of demonstrating their thoughtfulness and maturity. Meanwhile, the rebel image of rock 'n' roll had not yet melded with political rebellion, and as late as 1965 *Hit Parader* appended a patriotic put-down to its mention of Baez's appearance at an anti-Vietnam War march in London: "(You've got a nice voice Joan, but get lost)."[46] Nonetheless, the ease with which folk and rock merged in the next couple of years suggests that they were never as far apart as their more extreme exponents insisted.

Of course, there was a lot of other music around that I have not mentioned in this chapter. Old-line pop continued to dominate evening television and sell plenty of records, and in 1963 it acquired a new, young queen when the first two albums by twenty-one-year-old Barbra Streisand reached *Billboard*'s top ten. Jazz and classical styles also had much broader audiences than they would in later decades; through the mid-1960s, even *Seventeen* had a regular classical music column. Country and western was still considered primarily a rural and regional style, but the doors opened by Mitch Miller and Elvis were blown wide by Ray Charles, and 1963 found

Bill Anderson and Skeeter Davis in the upper echelons of the pop charts. Westerns also played a part in that crossover, priming audiences for a spate of cinematic ballads that included Marty Robbins's "El Paso," Jimmy Dean's "Big John," and Lorne Greene's "Ringo," a dolorous gunfighter recitation that topped the pop charts in 1964. (The song's success was due to Greene's starring role on *Bonanza*, and it had no connection to the Beatles' drummer—though the coincidence can't have hurt.)

There is also one more rock 'n' roll style that needs to be mentioned before we move on. By the end of 1963, *Billboard*'s tabulation of "Top Singles Artists" had the Beach Boys at number one; the year's best-selling instrumentals were "Pipeline" and "Wipe Out" (the previous year's had been pseudo-trad-jazz excursions, Mr. Acker Bilk's "Stranger on the Shore" and David Rose's "The Stripper," and 1961's had been Lawrence Welk's "Calcutta"); and the upper reaches of the charts included the Trashmen's "Surfin' Bird," the Rip Chords' "Hey Little Cobra," and Jan and Dean's "Drag City." Surf music and the related hot-rod rockers were unlike the other styles in this chapter in that the artists were uniformly white and the audience for all but the sweeter-sounding vocal groups was overwhelmingly male. One result was that, although it appealed to virtually no adults, the music sold well on LP: Boys tended to have more money than girls did, so instead of paying 95 cents for a single they could spend $3.95 for an album, and 1963's best-selling LPs included not only the Beach Boys' *Surfin' USA* but also *Shut Down*, an anthology of street-racing songs (including two by the Beach Boys), the Surfaris' *Wipe Out*, and the Ventures' *Surfing*.

The Beach Boys and the Ventures were by far the most successful bands to get caught up in the surf craze, but neither was exactly typical of the style. The Ventures had hit *Billboard*'s number-two spot in 1960 with a reverb-drenched instrumental called "Walk Don't Run," then turned their solid-body guitars and rock 'n' roll drumming loose on everything from Latin numbers to twist hits and Broadway show tunes. They were widely imitated by other surf bands, but their Seattle base, early arrival, and breadth of style prompted some fans to regard them as outside the genre. As for the Beach Boys, they emerged from the heart of the Southern California scene and had a rawer guitar sound—*Surfin' USA* included covers of two instrumentals by the original surf king, Dick Dale, and its title song was a straight steal from Chuck Berry—but they soon developed a vocal approach modeled on collegiate quartets like the Four Freshmen, and that sweet sophistication brought them a huge female audience that had little interest in instrumental rock or the rowdy sound of the aptly named Trashmen.

The more typical surf bands had their roots in instrumental combos such as Johnny and the Hurricanes, who had been playing teen dances since the mid-1950s, and Duane Eddy, the "twangy" guitarist who had been the most frequently played performer on *American Bandstand*. Eddy's work was anything but flashy, but that just made him a particularly tempting model for all the teenage boys across the country who were buying electric guitars. Both he and Dale had started out as country and western players, and although Dale developed a speedy, sledgehammer style that in retrospect points the way toward heavy metal, they kept the guitar-focused, unpolished feel of the honky-tonkers, supported by loud, thudding drums.

Most critics treated surf as a transitory craze, but it helped to form a new image of the rock 'n' roll band. For one thing it enthroned the electric guitar, which had previously been on an even footing with the saxophone and keyboards, as the music's dominant lead instrument, along with the electric bass guitar, which was transforming the sound and feel of both rock 'n' roll and R&B rhythm sections. For another, it provided a new model of teen machismo that mixed the open-air, rule-bending image of the wild west with the modern world of customized cars and bikinis, and helped to shape the boy- and guitar-focused aesthetic that is perfectly summed up in the term "garage rock." As Beach Boys paterfamilias Murry Wilson explained to *Billboard* in the halcyon summer of 1963, "Surfing music has to sound untrained with a certain rough flavor to appeal to the teenagers. As in the case of true c.&w., when the music gets too good, and too polished, it isn't considered the real thing."[47]

There is, as always, far more that could be said about this subject. Along with its roots in Western honky-tonks, the surf sound also overlapped crime jazz (Eddy made Henry Mancini's theme for *Peter Gunn* into a garage standard) and spy music (obvious examples include the guitar-driven James Bond theme and, later, "Secret Agent Man")—all male-oriented fantasy styles. And that was part of a broader process in which what had once been thought of as teen music was merging with adult and mainstream sounds. But time presses, so I will end this chapter by suggesting that the most enduring legacy of the surf craze may have been the creation of a rock 'n' roll utopia, removed from R&B, schoolyards, or gritty city streets. A mythic California, where young white men hung out in the sun, singing and playing guitars, not caring about money and surrounded by lovely girls, would remain one of rock's most popular escapist fantasies, reworked every few years to suit the changing times. In 1964, though, it was time for another fantasy: the buoyant insouciance of swinging London.

17

SAY YOU WANT A REVOLUTION...

[The Beatles] are leading an evolution in which the best of current post-rock sounds are becoming something that pop music has never been before: an art form.

TIME MAGAZINE, 1967

I'm sick and tired of British-accented youths ripping off black American artists and, because they're white, being accepted by the American audience.

MITCH MILLER

All of this happened a long time ago. A half century has passed since a group of young Liverpudlians got together and named themselves the Beatles, and their triumphant arrival in New York is now as distant from us as the arrival of the Original Dixieland Jazz Band was then. Those of us who grew up on their music may take pleasure in the fact that it is still widely heard, but we need to remember that our parents' and grandparents' music also held on through their lifetimes: In the first months of 1964, the record that pushed the Beatles off the top of the singles charts was Louis Armstrong's "Hello, Dolly!" and the album right below them on the LP charts was by the Dixieland revivalist Al Hirt. Armstrong was sixty-two years old— younger than Bob Dylan or Paul McCartney is now. And the youth of the 1960s was as familiar with older stars as kids are today. Dean Martin and Frank Sinatra were television and radio regulars, and although McCartney was joking when he referred to Sophie Tucker, whose career reached back to 1911, as "our favorite American group" at the 1963 Royal Variety Performance, he wasn't pulling her name from the distant past; she had been the highest-billed singer on the previous year's show.[1]

For the youth of the 1960s, the "generation gap" between our elders and us was an article of faith, and rock music was its most potent symbol. Even ten years seemed to us a cultural eternity, and it was typical that when John Lennon, in 1968, named Little Richard and Elvis Presley as influences, the interviewer responded by asking, "Anyone contemporary?"

Lennon, well aware of the difficulties of maintaining a place in the pop pantheon, coyly replied, "Are they dead?"[2]

The Beatles, along with Bob Dylan and a long list of other names, were hailed as spokesmen for a generation that was rebelling against the past, and that made it easy for their fans to see them as separate from that past. But it is telling that Lennon, while granting that the Beatles provided the soundtrack of their time, would say "I don't think they were more important than Glenn Miller or Woody Herman or Bessie Smith."[3] If one accepts the conventional wisdom that "the '60s" began around 1964 or 1965 and lasted into the early 1970s, the Beatles are an obvious symbol of that decade, and it was a unique and exciting time—for one thing, 1964 was the peak of the "baby boom," with 45 percent of the population under twenty-five and seventeen-year-olds the largest age group. But looking back from the vantage point of thirty years of hip-hop and rap, it makes as much sense to see the Beatles as signaling the end of a musical era as the beginning of one. Like the musicians before them, they had started out as a live band, playing covers of other people's songs for audiences of young dancers, and on their early records they simply went into the studio and performed the selections the same way they would do them onstage, as most bands had done since the 'teens. That was already a fairly old-fashioned approach in pop music terms, and by *Rubber Soul* and *Revolver* they were thinking like record makers rather than live performers, but they never lost their attachment to and affection for that past.

Indeed, one could see the early Beatles as a summation of all the trends of the previous few years wrapped in a particularly attractive package. "I Want to Hold Your Hand," their first hit in the United States, had the hand-claps of the girl groups, the melodic sophistication of the best Brill Building compositions, a rhythm perfectly suited to the new dances, and the loose energy of the surf bands—one reviewer tagged it "Surf on the Thames."[4] The fanzines quickly adopted the "fab four" as ideal boyfriends, with the advantage that readers didn't have to choose between buying records by Elvis, Ricky, Frankie, or one of the various Bobbys, because all tastes could be accommodated in one group. As Roy Orbison noted, "It's not completely a sexy thing either. Guys are interested, too. They might get a chance to chat with Ringo."[5] Older fans recognized a sophistication that the previous teen idols had lacked—not so much in the music, in those first months, but in the cool, absurdist intelligence of the press conferences and soon in the anarchic *nouvelle vague* artiness of *A Hard Day's Night*.

It all happened very fast: Beatlemania arrived before the Beatles did, primed by reports of mobs chasing them around England and the coup of getting booked for three appearances on the *Ed Sullivan Show* before having their first American hit—a happy accident, sparked by Sullivan's being delayed on a London airport runway by hordes of Beatle fans. When they made their U.S. debut in February 1964 the *New York Times* noted that they had "simply followed their fame across the Atlantic."[6] Capitol Records had initially passed on its option to release the group's recordings, allowing several other American labels to get early Beatles singles, but it now provided a barrage of publicity, and the fact that there were competing singles on five different labels meant that the radio was deluged with Beatles material. To the surprise of almost everyone, the band's talent lived up to this craziness, though at live shows that was more a matter of infectious energy than musical skill, as the screaming girls rendered them all but inaudible.

The startling thing was how quickly the Beatles transcended that initial image. It took Sinatra more than a dozen years to get over being typed as the bobby-soxers' dreamboat, but the Beatles managed the same feat almost instantaneously. It helped that they were British. Even if their remarks had been less witty, their accents would have made them seem smart and cosmopolitan to American ears, and they arrived at a particularly anglophilic moment. A year earlier, the New York Times had announced a "British invasion" of Broadway,[7] and their fellow acts on that first Ed Sullivan appearance included the British stars of The Girl Who Came to Supper and Oliver! (including future Monkee Davy Jones). It was also a moment when Americans desperately needed a dash of escapism: President Kennedy had been assassinated two months earlier, and though it is simplistic to talk of a "national mood," it is easy to understand how a bevy of cheery Brits contrasted with the way a lot of Americans were feeling.[8]

The mix of jangling guitars with jet-set sophistication fit neatly into the romance between rock 'n' roll and high society that had started with the twist, and the British Invasion overlapped the discothèque craze, which likewise was marketed as rock 'n' roll à l'européen. In May of 1964, Life magazine opened its feature on discothèques with a photo of young dancers at New Jimmy's in Paris doing the saint (it involved throwing your arms in the air as if at a revival meeting), followed by a shot of the club's owner, Regine, doing the surf with Omar Sharif, then "lively young aristocrats" in London doing the woodpecker. By page three the magazine was in Los Angeles, but the featured club was named for a Paris disco, the Whisky à Go-Go, and by 1965 there were Whisky (or Whiskey) à Go-Gos in Milwaukee, Chicago, Washington, San Francisco, and Atlanta, as well as a Frisky à Go-Go in San Antonio, a Champagne à Go-Go in Madison, Wisconsin, and so on.[9] As the liner notes to Arthur Murray's Discothèque Dance Party put it:

> Who but the frugal French would have hit on the idea that the fanciest dance joints don't really need a band. Play records instead. Gives you a wider choice of musical styles. Besides, a small place with just a phonograph is a lot more intime than a ballroom. So the most fashionable dancing places in Paris these days are Discothèques—tiny little spots with just a record player and lots of atmosphere.[10]

Both discothèques and guitar-based groups on the Beatles model succeeded in a large part for economic reasons. They were far cheaper than live music and larger bands, and earlier equivalents had been making inroads on the music scene for twenty years. But the appeal of London and Paris was quite different from the appeal of an R&B or rockabilly combo, a soda fountain jukebox or a deejayed sock hop, and the effort to associate discothèques with Continental chic was sometimes taken to ridiculous lengths. The producers of *Hullabaloo*, a prime-time network TV show that appeared early in 1965, claimed in their *Discothèque Dance Book* that "All the Discothèque Dances are imported, mostly from Europe," though its only steps with even faintly foreign roots were the bossa nova and the ska, and the rest were rehashes of old *Bandstand* favorites.[11]

One obvious effect of this European glamour was to separate rock 'n' roll from its associations with juvenile delinquency and, more enduringly, with black Americans. Another was to smooth the path to its acceptance as art. In the long run, the discothèque craze did not much influence either of those trends: Record-propelled dance clubs were relatively cheap to run, so they quickly lost their aristocratic, European associations, and black recording artists by and large held onto the dance-floor primacy they had won during the twist era. As for art, it seems to be a given that any music intended primarily for dancing is, ipso facto, not accepted as serious art.

By contrast, classical music—even mediocre classical music—is the quintessence of seriousness for most pop listeners, and by the fall of 1965 the number one song in the United States was "Yesterday," featuring Paul McCartney accompanied by a string quartet. Like Whiteman's first "jazz classique" discs, this did not excite the interest of many highbrow critics, but it was immediately greeted with enthusiasm by older pop musicians and Tin Pan Alley tunesmiths. The Beatles themselves had some ambivalence about this—McCartney recalled, "we didn't release 'Yesterday' as a single in England at all, because we were a little embarrassed about it; we were a rock 'n' roll band."[12] But with its romantically world-weary lyric, soothing melody, and mild variation of the conventional thirty-two-bar song structure, it was accepted as an olive branch across the generation gap.[13] The song was quickly covered by every old-line orchestra leader and vocalist who dreamed of being more than a nostalgia act, and by August 1966 *Billboard* proclaimed it a modern standard, noting that there were already over 175 versions on the market, including recordings by Lawrence Welk, Xavier Cugat, and Mantovani, as well as by country singers, cabaret artists, and the Supremes. The only comparably covered recent compositions were "The Girl from Ipanema," popularized by Stan Getz and Astrud Gilberto, and "A Taste of Honey," which had its greatest success in a pseudo-mariachi version by Herb Alpert.[14] The Beatles, as it happens, had recorded "A Taste of Honey" on their first album, an apt reminder that from the beginning they showed a breadth of taste that would allow them to capture not only young rock 'n' rollers but also the sort of listeners who enjoyed the perky trumpets of the Tijuana Brass and the gentle lilt of bossa nova.[15]

That breadth of appeal was what set the Beatles apart from their contemporaries. They got the teenage girls, the rock 'n' rollers, the easy listening fans, and a good part of the folk audience, and they soon were making inroads with devotees of jazz and classical music. It took a while, but as they followed the string quartet of

"Yesterday" with the string octet of "Eleanor Rigby," the brass, strings, and wood-winds of "Strawberry Fields" and "Penny Lane," and finally *Sgt. Pepper*, they found themselves hailed as kindred spirits by the likes of Leonard Bernstein (who compared them to Schumann) and the avant-garde composer and diarist Ned Rorem (who threw in Chopin, Monteverdi, and Poulenc).[16] And that conquest had a value far beyond the classical market, because it made all the other listeners feel as if they were joining the cultural elite. The only major audiences the Beatles lost as they became more serious were the little sisters of their first fans, who had loved them as cuddly mop-tops and transferred this affection to the Monkees, and the dancers. (There were also some hard-core rock 'n' rollers who sheared off in favor of the Rolling Stones, but though they grumbled about pretentiousness and slack rhythms, they still bought *Rubber Soul, Revolver,* and *Sgt. Pepper*.) From 1964 through 1970 the Beatles had fourteen number-one albums, and unlike Sinatra's run in the 1950s, those albums were outselling most hit singles. No other group or artist even came close, and not since Whiteman in the 1920s had any band so completely overshadowed an era's popular mainstream.

In the mid-1950s Whiteman had prophesied that rock 'n' roll would go through the same evolution as jazz, saying "they'll get tired of that one- or two-guitar sound, and eventually they'll add fiddles and saxes and brass, like we did when we started the big-band business."[17] In the Beatles' case, the connection was relatively direct: McCartney traced his love of old-fashioned pop melodies to hearing his father play Whiteman's music on the piano, and George Martin, the group's producer and arranger, was an admirer of Gershwin and Ferde Grofé and saw his work with the band as an extension of that tradition.[18] Even the British cachet had been part of Whiteman's story: "I had seen, as everybody must see, the American adoration for the European," he recalled, so he took his orchestra to London in 1923 and began work on the Aeolian Hall concert only after returning with the English nobility's seal of approval, "as if we'd been distinguished foreigners."[19]

There were also striking similarities in the ways the two groups were treated by their eras' respective critics. The reception was not universally laudatory in either case, with plenty of classical gatekeepers moaning about lowered standards and some purist rock 'n' roll fans echoing the complaints of Roger Pryor Dodge that the music they loved was being emasculated by middlebrow pretension. To the English writer Nik Cohn, the evolutions from *Rubber Soul* through *Sgt Pepper* each represented "a big step forward in ingenuity, and...a big step back in guts," and he accused the Beatles of becoming "updated George Gershwins...the posh Sundays called them Art, as Gershwin was once called Art for *Rhapsody in Blue*...but what, by definition, is so great about Art?"[20]

In general, though, there was agreement that for better or worse Whiteman and the Beatles represented the future of their respective styles and a previously unrealized rapprochement between high and low culture. Carl Belz, whose groundbreaking *Story of Rock* opened with the declaration that it would "consider the music *as* art and *in terms* of art,"[21] even provided a parallel to George Seldes's statement contrasting the general superiority of black bands with the specific superiority of Whiteman: "Negro Rhythm and Blues has possessed a consistency which is not present in the white music of the 1960s," Belz wrote in 1969. "And a listener hears a higher percentage of *good* records on the soul stations than on white or integrated programs, although he does not hear anything as artistically advanced as the Beatles."[22]

I want to take a moment to place those statements in the context of their times, because the civil rights movement and rock 'n' roll had dramatically changed the status of black music in white America. So it is a profound irony that the attempt to make highbrow art out of jazz in the 1920s (which put white artists at the forefront of the movement) is generally recalled by historians as an embarrassing wrong turn, whereas the attempt to make highbrow art out of rock 'n' roll in the 1960s (again putting white artists in the forefront of the movement) is generally viewed as a step forward for the genre, which has been led by white artists ever since.

For one thing, the idea of art itself had changed. In the 1920s, jazz was widely compared to Picasso's cubism and the abstractions of Piet Mondrian—that is, popular dance music was being equated with the personal creations of academically trained high modernists. In the 1960s, rock was compared to Roy Lichtenstein's comic book paintings and Andy Warhol's Brillo boxes—that is, "pop art," a name that denied any primacy to individual creation over the mass products of the marketplace and allied the visual arts with what was happening on radios and television screens. And that difference signaled not only shifting fashions but also a shifting balance of power. The combination of technologies of mass reproduction and dissemination—movies, phonographs, radio, television, glossy color printing—with a new degree of economic and educational equality and the intellectual and moral weight of democratic, socialist, and communist ideals had made "popular culture" a potent force in the academic and critical mainstream. In Whiteman's day, almost everyone took it for granted that popular music gained something by being compared to high modern art, but by the 1960s a lot of people were dismissing high art as elitist and irrelevant. As Bob Dylan put it, "Museums are cemeteries. Paintings should be on the walls of restaurants, in dime stores, in gas stations, in men's rooms.... Music is the only thing that's in tune with what's happening.... All this art they've been talking about is nonexistent."[23] Linking pop art to pop music did more for the painters than it did for the musicians, many of whom—Lennon, Pete Townshend, Eric Clapton, Jimmy Page, and Keith Richards among them—had, as it happens, attended art school.

At the other extreme, some critics in the 1920s had hailed jazz as a modern folk music, but in those days that was another way of saying that it was raw material for high art, bearing the same relationship to the *Rhapsody in Blue* that an African mask bore to Picasso's *Demoiselles d'Avignon*. By the mid-1960s, folk music was overtaking classical music as the favored listening for serious young intellectuals, so when rock 'n' roll was described as a folk style (by Belz, among others), that was a claim of roots and authenticity, not an invitation to transform it into something more elevated. As it happened, the Beatles made their New York concert debut at Carnegie Hall, but they emphasized their lack of respect for the venue by opening with "Roll Over, Beethoven." And when they wanted to have their music taken more seriously, they did not attempt to get more bookings in classical concert halls—which, in any case, were by then far too small for them—they just made it more varied and complex, and less dance-oriented.[24] By *Rubber Soul* (their ninth American LP in less than two years[25]) they had added elements of French *chanson* and North Indian sitar, along with a potent dose of American folk and country, and by *Revolver* they were experimenting with tape loops and electronic noise, and McCartney was citing the influence of Karlheinz Stockhausen. (In hindsight, George Harrison would jokingly refer to this as their "'avant garde a clue' music."[26]) With *Sgt. Pepper* they imposed a new aesthetic by refusing to release a single, forcing fans to view the mélange of musical styles from ragtime to raga as a long-form sonic equivalent of the photographic collage on the album's cover.

In terms of their own creations, the Beatles' work was both more daring and more enduring than what Whiteman's crew produced, but that was in part because they had a freedom that would have been unimaginable in earlier eras: The fact that they could retire from performing and make their whole artistic statement on records meant that they could ignore the day-to-day concert and dance business. The later Beatles records were not a take-home equivalent or even a studio-enhanced improvement of live performances. They were, after 1966, the entirety of the group's musical oeuvre: fully conceived, finished objects in the same way that a book or a painting is a fully conceived, finished object. There was a precedent of sorts in previous studio pop productions, but although Brian Wilson and his critical soulmates hailed Phil Spector's "Be My Baby" as a three-minute pop symphony, most fans heard it as a girl-group hit, dancing to it and enjoying it not as a unique work of genius but as part of the commercial collage of Top 40 radio. The later Beatles LPs, by contrast, were treated as musical novels, designed for individual contemplation in their entirety. Although the band continued to release singles that got plenty of radio play, both they and their fans thought of their primary work as a series of albums, and that became the defining form for any band that hoped for its work to be viewed as art rather than disposable commercial pop. It was the age of Marshall McLuhan, and the medium was the message: Musicians who had big ideas made big records.

In retrospect, the critic Robert Hilburn expressed a widespread verdict when he wrote, "Bob Dylan and the Beatles had turned the primitive energy of teen-oriented '50s rock into an art form that could express adult themes and emotions."[27] Looked at another way, the Beatles had joined Dylan in a format that had never been associated with either teen or rock energy. Since the mid-1950s, folk, classical, and jazz musicians had been known for albums rather than singles, and pop performers from Ray Charles to Connie Francis had turned to the LP form when they wanted to record adult material. In the past, though, it had been taken for granted that Charles's and Francis's albums of jazz, country, and Tin Pan Alley standards were aimed at different audiences than the teens who danced to their singles. The Beatles, by contrast, were seen as expanding their genre rather than stepping outside it, and *Sgt. Pepper* as a maturation of their youthful style rather than as an extension of the adult pop they had dabbled in with "A Taste of Honey" and "Till There Was You."

Which is to say that, as usual, the genre labels had more to do with the audience than with the music. Though the Beatles' fan base had changed (screaming teenyboppers ceased to be their core constituency even before the lads grew beards and moustaches) and though they now were hiring symphony musicians as a backing band, the older teens and twenty-somethings who put them at the forefront of a musical movement that included Dylan, the Byrds, the Rolling Stones, the San Francisco psychedelic groups, and soon such phenomenal album-sellers as Simon and Garfunkel and Crosby, Stills, and Nash did not choose to think of themselves or their musical heroes as abandoning youth styles. By the later 1960s, there had clearly been a major change in orientation, and some people were beginning to make a semantic distinction between rock 'n' roll (the earlier, teen-oriented music) and rock (its myriad post-Beatles offshoots). But even the most intellectual rock fans held fast to the notion that the music they now loved was an evolution of the style pioneered by Chuck Berry, Little Richard, and the Coasters rather than an adult style for which they had forsaken the heroes of their adolescence.

It was true that the Beatles and their peers continued to play a lot of music that had links to early rock 'n' roll and, with the exception of a few songs, their work was very different from what was being played and sung by older pop performers. There was a cultural revolution going on, and though in retrospect one can argue that a lot of the changes were more a matter of fashion than of substance, they were grounded in solid and harsh realities. First among these was the Vietnam War, and more particularly the military draft, which threatened a generation of young men with being shipped off to die for a cause that to many of them seemed at best pointless and at worst evil. From early childhood that generation had been threatened with nuclear annihilation, wondering if their world would explode before they had a chance to experience it, and their elders had done little to assuage their fears. So as they reached their twenties, they did not see the obvious paths to security that their parents had followed after World War II. Add to that the contraceptive pill, which meant that sex did not have to lead to babies and thence families. And stir into the mix a new range of drugs, which offered a more interesting escape from those fears than alcohol did, but also could land you in jail. There has been a lot of sneering in later years about '60s-era, antiestablishment hippies settling down to traditional families and careers, but the reality is that during that time a lot of them doubted they would make it to age thirty—and when they did, the world naturally looked different.

Rock also set itself apart from other teen and adult styles by creating new radio, print, and concert scenes. Since the mid-1950s, commercial radio stations had been experimenting with variations of the Top 40 format, in which the same few hits were played over and over, and the payola scandal pushed more broadcasters to take musical choice out of the hands of deejays in favor of restricted committee- and chart-determined playlists. This meant that chart positions ceased to be just measures of popularity and became self-fulfilling prophecies: On Top 40 stations, the top-charting records were pretty much all that were played, day in and day out. (Repetitive as this was, it was a far cry from the genre-specific commercial format of later years, as a typical Top 40 playlist would mingle the Beatles and Herman's Hermits with Motown, Frank and Nancy Sinatra, Herb Alpert, and Dionne Warwick.) By the later 1960s, though, FM stations in many cities were letting young deejays program free-form mixes that included album cuts and leaned heavily to the new rock styles. Meanwhile, a new kind of music magazine was appearing, first *Crawdaddy* in January 1966, then *Rolling Stone* in November 1967 and a host of short- and occasionally longer-lived competitors, which focused on rock not simply as music but as the voice of a generation. And in San Francisco a new kind of concert scene emerged, bringing the bohemian attitude of college-town coffee-houses to huge, free outdoor performances and ballroom gatherings that mixed the music with light shows, hallucinogenic drugs, and a spirit of community that captured the imaginations of young people across the country.

It is easy, and was easy even then, to regard 1967's "summer of love" with cynicism, and all the critiques have elements of truth to them. But so did the romantic myths, and it was natural to counter the nightmare of planetary destruction with the utopian dream of building a new world in the shell of the old. Nor was it all airy dreaming. San Francisco was full of young people who just wanted to "turn on, tune in, and drop out," but there were also plenty of young activists who had traveled to Mississippi to register voters, who would travel to Chicago to protest at the Democratic convention, and who were working with the Black Panthers or the United Farm Workers—and both hippies and activists were growing their hair, smoking dope, and listening to rock bands.

In terms of the broad history of popular music, though, something odd was happening. As rock was vested with more and more importance, both as an art form and as the voice of a young counterculture, its acolytes began to be bothered by the blatantly commercial, dance-hit mentality that had been taken for granted in the music's early days. And, with increasing frequency, that meant that rock was being separated from black music. Or, more accurately, from recent black styles, since blues bands, white and black, were a bigger part of the rock scene than ever before. Indeed, in an odd twist, many writers have described the British Invasion as a discovery of black music, applauding the Beatles, Stones, and Animals for introducing European Americans to African-American masters from Muddy Waters and Howlin' Wolf to Bo Diddley and Chuck Berry. The British stars certainly distinguished themselves from previous rockers by focusing attention on their early idols, and gave a vital boost to some important and deserving artists, but this was part of a larger process in which black music was being recast as the roots of rock 'n' roll rather than as part of its evolving present. Venues like the Fillmore West booked Waters, John Lee Hooker, and B. B. King, along with the racially mixed Butterfield Blues Band and a new generation of white blues-rockers that included Janis Joplin, the Blues Project, and Canned Heat, and at times they added gospel-infused soul singers like Otis Redding and Aretha Franklin to that mix. But it was in much the same spirit that the 1965 Newport Folk Festival—at which Dylan famously went electric—presented Butterfield, Wolf, and Berry alongside acoustic elders like Mississippi John Hurt, Son House, and the Reverend Gary Davis.

Until the mid-1960s, white and black rock 'n' roll styles had evolved more or less in tandem, whether it was Little Richard and Jerry Lee Lewis, the Drifters and the Belmonts, Hank Ballard and Joey Dee, Ray Charles and Bobby Darin, or the Crystals and the Shangri-Las. The black artists may have pioneered more new styles than the white ones, and their share of the rewards was frequently incommensurate with their talents, but they were competing for the same radio and record audiences and appearing in a lot of the same clubs, concert packages, and TV showcases. The pop music world had been becoming less segregated with every passing year, and by 1964 *Billboard* stopped publishing separate pop and R&B charts, apparently deeming the division both politically and musically untenable. The big success stories on the rock 'n' roll scene that year were the British Invasion and Motown, and the Beatles and Berry Gordy both took pains to emphasize that, in Gordy's words, "They're creating the same type of music as we are and we're part of the same stream."[28] As a friend of mine who was then a Midwestern teenager recalls, "we all dreamed of being a Supreme and of dating a Beatle."

That blend of musical and racial integration had defined rock 'n' roll since Alan Freed's time, but the stream divided with the arrival of "folk rock" (or "rock folk," as it was often called at first), which stressed poetic or socially conscious lyrics over dance rhythms, and the sonic explorations of the Beatles, the Byrds, the Beach Boys, and the San Francisco groups. To an audience caught up in these developments, contemporary black artists seemed to be lagging behind, still focusing on dance beats and AM hits. As *Crawdaddy*'s founder, Paul Williams, wrote in a review of a new Temptations LP, "One of the curious things about the year 1966 is that for the first time in the history of America, the best contemporary music is not being made by the American Negro."[29]

It was inescapably true that black performers, by and large, were thinking in different terms from the new rock groups. When Michael Lydon interviewed Smokey Robinson for *Rolling Stone* in 1968, Robinson made no bones about Motown editing his records to fit Top-40 programming strictures. Of one recent hit, "I Second That Emotion," he said:

> It was 3:15 when it was done and Berry—who has an ingenious sense of knowing hit records, it's uncanny—he heard it, he told us, 'It's a great tune, but it's too long, so I want you to cut that other verse down and come right out of the solo and go back into the chorus and on out.' So we did and the record was a smash.... The shorter a record is these days, the more it's gonna be played, you dig? If you have a record that's 2:15 long it's definitely gonna get more play than one that's 3:15, *at first*, which is *very* important.

That logic would have made perfect sense to the Beatles circa 1964, but by 1968 it was not at all the *Rolling Stone* aesthetic, and Lydon responded by suggesting that Robinson "was not aware that for many people in rock and roll, the Top-40 has become an irrelevant concern." Robinson wasn't buying it, though: "Everybody who approaches this, approaches it with the idea of being in the Top Ten," he insisted, "because...let's face it, this is the record *industry*, one of the biggest industries going nowadays."[30]

The idea that music should be treated as an industry was exactly what the new rock fans rejected. Gordy had patterned Motown's production process on the Ford assembly line, and when he wasn't stamping out hits, he was putting his artists through intensive training in dance and deportment and planning the conquest of the Copacabana and Las Vegas. Both his methods and his aspirations exemplified everything that the counterculture despised—but he and his artists were coming from a very different place. They were not convinced by the Beatles' assurances that all they needed was love and everything would be all right if they could free their minds.[31] As a member of the Fifth Dimension, a pop-oriented black group from Los Angeles that ran up a string of hits in the late 1960s, told an interviewer:

> When you start talking about the fact that the black man is still hung up with status symbols, man, don't forget that he's trying to grab on to exactly the things that the white kids are trying to give up. Drop out? Wow, man, what we got to drop out of, anyway? You don't want your fancy house or your good job? Shit, let me have it, man, 'cause I've been trying to get something like that all my miserable life.[32]

Beyond that cultural disconnect, and despite all the changes in the music scene, Robinson was right that top ten hits continued to drive record sales. Even Dylan, the prototypical modern album artist, got very different sales when one of his LPs spawned a hit single. Clive Davis, the head of Columbia Records' pop division during the late 1960s, recalled, "*John Wesley Harding* sold 500,000 albums without a single; but *Nashville Skyline*, with 'Lay Lady Lay's AM-radio help, sold 1.2 million."[33] For Dylan's fans, of course, that was irrelevant. His enduring victory is not that he sold a lot of records but that he forever changed popular songwriting, and everyone from the Beatles and Stones to Marvin Gaye, Stevie Wonder, and the Brill Building pros rethought their styles in response to his work.

But it was no accident that most of the early Dylan hits were for other singers— Peter, Paul, and Mary, the Byrds, and Johnny Cash all charted with his compositions before he did, and they were soon joined by the Turtles and Cher. His nasal voice and aggressively unpolished instrumental backings won him a uniquely devoted following but also turned a lot of listeners off. And that polarization meant not only that his record sales were incommensurate with his influence but that they were even lower than the charts suggest: "His cult besieged record stores when a new album arrived," Davis recalled. "The charts always reflect a concentrated buying spree, so any new Dylan album immediately zoomed to the top. Ray Conniff [an easy-listening arranger], by contrast, might have sold three times as many albums over a longer period of time, but nobody was rushing into the stores to buy him, so his chart action was relatively minimal."[34] A good example of this pattern is Dylan's 1967 *Greatest Hits* package, which charted lower than his previous few records because his fans didn't need it, but was his first million-selling LP because it sold to the larger, less fervent audience (my father, for example) that had become aware that he was important and wanted a representative sample of his work.

As for *Nashville Skyline*, although its hit single undoubtedly helped, it was also a very different sort of album from Dylan's previous work, and its broader acceptance is a reminder that in some ways the world had not changed all that much since the days of Mitch Miller. As at the end of the swing era, the shift away from dance music led to a partial rapprochement between urban pop and country and western. So in 1969 Bobbie Gentry and Jeannie C. Riley had country ballads on top of the pop charts, and Dylan's disc featured Nashville studio backing and a guest appearance and liner notes by Johnny Cash. New Yorkers and San Franciscans associated folk music with leftist politics, but a lot of people between the coasts had welcomed the Weavers, the Kingston Trio, and Peter, Paul, and Mary as wholesome alternatives to jazz or rock 'n' roll, and shifting technologies extended country music's popularity to a broader audience than ever before. In Miller's day, pop singers reliably outsold country artists when they did the same songs, but in 1969, thanks to the success of his weekly TV program and live recordings at Folsom and San Quentin prisons, Cash sold 6.5 million albums, more than any previous solo performer in any genre.[35]

The youth market was huge, and rock was getting most of the headlines, but there were still plenty of older and more conservative listeners, and, as in the past, the biggest-selling artists were those who appealed across the widest range of generational and cultural boundaries. The Rolling Stones were rock's most celebrated live band, and within that world were often placed on a level near or equal to the Beatles, but they didn't sell as well as the mellower folk-rock stars whose songs were played not only on FM rock and Top 40 radio but also on middle-of-the-road (MOR) stations. In a 1972 *Rolling Stone* interview, Paul Simon expressed disappointment that his first solo album had sold only 850,000 units, and when the interviewer pointed out that this was more than any Stones LP except *Sticky Fingers*, Simon's response was "Yeah, but, permit me my arrogance....I always was aware that S&G was a much bigger phenomenon in general, to the general public, than the Rolling Stones."[36] Indeed, with the exception of their acoustic debut, all the Simon and Garfunkel LPs had sold at least two million units, and a couple were already over three million, because they appealed not only to rock fans but also to fans of Cash, Joan Baez, and Barbra Streisand.

Those were incredible numbers, and the rewards that Simon and the Beatles were reaping not only for themselves but also for their record and publishing companies were changing the music business. There had been popular performer-songwriters before, from Duke Ellington and Johnny Mercer to Chuck Berry and Paul Anka, but they had always been a minority, and in any case the money one earned from writing and recording even a million-selling single was peanuts compared with what one got for writing and recording every song on a string of million-selling albums. The combination of prestige and wealth was irresistible, and by the later 1960s it was taken for granted that any serious rock group would create its own material.

What is more, although Lennon and McCartney had started out as fairly traditional songwriters, their later albums were not just written but produced and directed with a degree of effort and thought that had previously been reserved for filmmaking—in George Martin's words, they were "making little movies in sound."[37] After they devoted a fabled 700 hours to recording *Sgt. Pepper* and it was acclaimed a masterpiece, studio experimentation became the order of the day even for a lot of unproven groups, and bands and songwriters came to see themselves less as musicians than as sonic auteurs.[38] Records seemed to emerge from the inspired mind of a single artist or small groups of artists in a communal process, and Judy Collins expressed a widespread belief when she imagined a future in which "we will have pop song cycles like classical *Lieder*, but we will create our own words, music, and orchestrations, because we are a generation of whole people."[39]

Some of the top African-American singers were also writing their own material, and a few were arranging and producing their own records. James Brown had taken full control of his work in the early 1960s, and his *Live at the Apollo* LP, which made it to number two on the *Billboard* album chart in 1963, had proved that his talents were not limited to dance beats and hit singles. But no one was comparing his music—or Robinson's, or Aretha Franklin's—to classical *Lieder*, and white listeners and critics, if they knew him at all, celebrated him as a gritty shouter and phenomenal showman, not as a sonic auteur.

It was not that white rock fans necessarily were unaware of the innovations in recent African-American styles or disrespected the current black stars. But as Robert Christgau noted in his review of the Monterey Pop Festival, by 1967 the relationship was very different from what it had been just three or four years earlier:

> White rock performers seem uncomfortable with contemporary black music. Most of them like the best of it or think they do, but they don't want to imitate it, especially since they know how pallid their imitation is likely to be. So they hone their lyrics and develop their instrumental chops and experiment with their equipment and come to regard artists like Martha & the Vandellas, say, as some wondrous breed of porpoise, very talented, but somehow...different. And their audience concurs.[40]

By that time, there was also a new genre name to express that difference. In January 1965, recognizing that the British Invasion and folk-rock trends had reopened the gap between white and black styles, *Billboard* had reinstituted its R&B chart, but there were obvious problems with maintaining the old rubric of segregation. So by 1967 the magazine was running an annual *World of Soul* section, and in 1969 the black music chart was renamed "Best-Selling Soul Singles." What "soul" meant was a bit vague: The first *World of Soul* was largely devoted to older blues styles, including articles on 78-rpm record collecting, on John Hammond's role as a blues promoter, and on Billie Holiday; and just as with R&B there was always some question of whether it was a musical or simply a racial designation. But at least it acknowledged that black artists were playing a modern style—indeed, the name change was accompanied by the claim that soul was "the most meaningful development in the broad mass music market within the last decade"—while at the same time separating that style from rock.[41]

There were genuine musical differences between the styles favored by white and black groups in the later 1960s, but the problem, as always, was that the categories were neither distinct nor homogeneous. In the continuum of singers, Janis Joplin was a lot closer to Tina Turner and James Brown than she was to Grace Slick or Mick Jagger, so the choice to regard her as a rocker rather than a porpoise was not made on musical grounds. Nor was it true that white players couldn't master the new soul sounds: The records that Otis Redding, Aretha Franklin, and Wilson Pickett cut at Stax and Muscle Shoals were considered even funkier than what was coming out of Motown, and the Stax house band was racially mixed, while the Muscle Shoals musicians were all white. If the spectrum of pop now ranged from James Brown to Simon and Garfunkel rather than from Count Basie to Guy Lombardo, there was still a lot of middle ground, and Booker T and the MGs could potentially have been a unifying a force on the order of the Benny Goodman Quartet—indeed,

Otis Redding and the MGs' Steve Cropper created a perfect fusion of the folk-rock and soul sensibilities with their acoustic-guitar-backed "Dock of the Bay."

But if the victories of the civil rights movement were dismantling de jure segregation, the de facto segregation of American culture was in some ways growing stronger. On the black side, there were radical voices calling for racial separatism and many more promoting self-determination and a fairer share of power—in 1969, only five of the country's 528 soul stations were black-owned, and listeners were bringing pressure on the others to hire not only more black deejays but also more black program directors and executives[42]—and a lot of white people, liberals included, were beginning to realize that the racial divide went much deeper than separate schools and drinking fountains. It was easy for sympathetic Euro-Americans to sing along with "We Shall Overcome," but "Say It Loud, I'm Black and I'm Proud" was another story, even though James Brown's ferociously danceable anthem made *Billboard*'s pop top ten in 1968. As Jonathan Eisen put it, explaining the absence of current black styles from his 1969 anthology, *The Age of Rock*:

> In recent years, young black musicians on the whole have been involved within an entirely different milieu, both social and musical, most of them concentrating on developing greater nationalistic self-consciousness. The electronic music "bag" has been primarily confined to white musicians, with most of the blacks working in the area of jazz and soul ... speaking to different constituencies in different idioms and with different meaning—though with equal infectiousness and intensity.[43]

Some black artists would have echoed Eisen's statement, but it was also a handy way to excuse the fact that rock books, magazines, radio stations, and festivals were including only a token selection of black performers and, however complimentary the language, white formulations of "separate but equal" had never been anything but a trap. Black stars were getting behind the pride movement and singing about "Respect," but as Marvin Gaye bluntly put it, "Everyone wanted to sell [to] whites, 'cause whites got the most money."[44] So, far from isolating themselves in a separate world of soul, most of them were doing their best to maintain the racial overlap that had defined the earlier rock 'n' roll scene, recording songs by the Beatles, the Stones, Simon and Garfunkel, Dylan, the Band, the Doors—even the Archies. Motown hired white guitarists in "the electronic music bag" to give a contemporary rock feel to the Temptations' "Psychedelic Shack," and Atlantic used Eric Clapton and Duane Allman on recordings by Franklin and Pickett. But it was becoming increasingly difficult to overcome the rock-soul division. In 1961, Ike and Tina Turner's "It's Gonna Work Out Fine" had been one of three records by black artists among the five nominees for the first rock & roll Grammy. By 1966, the Grammys had three "contemporary (rock & roll)" performance categories, but there was not one black name among the sixteen nominees, an omission made more galling for the Turners by the fact that Tina had teamed up with Phil Spector that year to make "River Deep—Mountain High." As Ike pointed out:

> [That]'s not a groove record for dancin'... it's the same kind of record "Good Vibrations" was... but right away when they see Tina Turner on the record they name it r&b... and it would have to go number one r&b before the Top 40 station would play it, well man I don't think this is fair... Negroes not going to buy that record... it's strictly... for the white market.[45]

The Turners would eventually become one of the few black acts to break into the rock scene, but only after touring and appearing in a movie with the Rolling Stones and recording covers of the Beatles' "Come Together" and Creedence Clearwater Revival's "Proud Mary."

In hindsight, it is striking to watch *The T.A.M.I. Show*, a concert filmed in Santa Monica in 1964, and see the Beach Boys, Chuck Berry, Lesley Gore, the Supremes, Smokey Robinson and the Miracles, Gerry and the Pacemakers, James Brown, and the Rolling Stones all greeted with equally fervent screams by an overwhelmingly white, female audience, then to watch the effort Otis Redding had to make just three years later to connect with the audience of white hippies in Monterey. By the most generous count, Monterey Pop presented six acts featuring black artists out of a total of thirty-two—and that includes the MGs, the Electric Flag (a white band led by Mike Bloomfield, but with Buddy Miles on drums and vocals), and the Jimi Hendrix Experience, which was arriving from London on Paul McCartney's recommendation, had a white, British rhythm section, and was introduced by the Stones' Brian Jones. Still, that was better than Woodstock two years later, where, out of thirty-three acts, the only featured black performers were Hendrix, Richie Havens, and Sly and the Family Stone. And the decline was more than numeric: In 1964, rock 'n' roll was still a completely biracial genre; in 1967, Monterey booked Redding, the MGs, and Lou Rawls specifically to include a taste of contemporary black music; at Woodstock, Hendrix and Havens were both primarily associated with the white market, while Sly Stone had carved out a unique position as a bridge builder between ghetto funk and the hippie scene, becoming, in the words of *Rolling Stone*'s Jon Landau, "the only major rock figure who has a deep following with both whites and blacks."[46]

Some people in the rock world were clearly troubled by this split. Bill Graham experimented with bills at the Fillmore West in which white stars introduced their black peers, pairing the Al Kooper-Mike Bloomfield Super Session with Sam and Dave, and Janis Joplin with Mavis Staples. Landau and Christgau both pushed their readers to keep on top of what was happening in black music and on AM radio. The Stones frequently toured with black groups, helping both the Turners and Stevie Wonder to cross over to a larger white audience, and they also made some effort to keep up with current dance rhythms, getting their last number-one hit in 1978 with the disco-inflected "Miss You." The Young Rascals (later just the Rascals) took a particularly explicit stand against the racial divide: Three of the band's members had worked in Joey Dee's Starliters, and they carried on Dee's attempt to be part of the R&B scene, evolving along with Brown and the Southern soul artists and becoming one of the few white acts to get regular play on black radio. (The two names mentioned most often by black deejays as examples of their integrated playlists in the later 1960s were the Rascals and, oddly enough, Frank Sinatra.) Though rarely remembered in the same breath with the Beatles and Stones, the Rascals earned seven gold records in 1968 alone—including one for "People Got to Be Free," an ode to racial harmony—and in 1969 they announced that they would no longer appear on programs that were not racially balanced. "We can't control the audience, guaranteeing it will be integrated, and you better believe they're still segregated, if only by psychological forces," said the group's organist and main composer, Felix Cavaliere. "But we can control the show. So from now on . . . all our major concerts will be half black, half white, or we stay home."[47]

It is worth noting that, whereas the Starliters of 1962 had been racially mixed and that fact had excited little comment, the Rascals of 1969, despite their strong antisegregation stance, were not. Rock had become a white genre, and the Rascals' announcement only underlined that change. From now on, when rock bands shared double bills with black artists or invited black musicians to join them as guests, it would be seen as an attempt to cross boundaries or add a touch of blues, soul, or funk, rather than because they were all part of a single musical movement.

The Beatles and their peers had made rock into the most popular concert and album category of their time, and in the process expanded the style beyond anything its previous practitioners had imagined. Indeed, the later 1960s brought a respect for popular music and a popularity for complex artistic experimentation that had not been matched in any previous era—Whiteman's symphonic excursions, famous as they were, were never as broadly influential as his dance music, and jazz attained widespread respectability only after it had ceased to be a mainstream pop style.

In the process, though, they had led their audience off the dance floor, separating rock from its rhythmic and cultural roots, and while the gains may have balanced the losses in both economic and artistic terms, that change split American popular music in two. When similar splits had happened in the past, the demands of satisfying live audiences had always forced the streams back together, but by the end of the 1960s live performances had lost their defining role on the pop music scene. So the Beatles and the movement they led marked the end not only of rock 'n' roll as it had existed up to that time but also of the whole process explored over the course of this book, in which white and black musicians had evolved by adopting and adapting one another's styles, shaping a series of genres—ragtime, jazz, swing, rock 'n' roll—that at their peaks could not be easily categorized by race. The shifts in recording technology, radio, television, race relations, global politics, and an infinity of other factors might have brought a similar result even if the Beatles had never met—as always, we can only know what happened, not what might have happened. But what happened was that they were the catalysts for a divide between rock and soul that, rather than being mended in later years, would only grow wider with the emergence of disco and hip-hop. And that fundamental split would create myriad splinters over the following decades.

When the Beatles appeared on the *Ed Sullivan Show*, it was the last time a live performance changed the course of American music, and when they became purely a recording group, they pointed the way toward a future in which there need be no unifying styles, as bands can play what they like in the privacy of the studio, and we can choose which to listen to in the privacy of our clubs, our homes, or, finally, our heads. Whether that was liberating or limiting is a matter of opinion and perception, but the whole idea of popular music had changed.

EPILOGUE

THE ROCK BLOT AND THE DISCO DIAGRAM

Historians have been making apocalyptic pronouncements about the state of American popular music since before the ragtime era. When I was growing up, it was common to hear that the golden age of pop ended with the Big Band era, or when rock 'n' roll wiped out the "American songbook." So, after devoting much of this book to exploring the continuities between those periods, it would be strange if I ended by nominating my own candidate for a similar apocalypse. The British invasion brought a racial split in American music that has grown wider over the past forty years, and by now we are all aware that the single ubiquitous hit parade is long gone. But the world did not end on the cusp of the 1970s, and the break that came in that era was part of a process that this book has traced over the previous eighty years. If I view this break as particularly significant, that is in part because I am so acutely aware of what has happened since; as I emphasized in my introduction, historians are shaped by our own situations and experiences, and I entered high school in 1973.

At that point the Beatles were still very much a dominant influence on the rock scene: Paul, George, and Ringo all had number one hits that year, Elton John was ascendant, and Pink Floyd, Chicago, and Jethro Tull were expanding the art-rock concept in their various ways. If someone picked up a guitar, they would typically play the introduction to "Blackbird" or "Stairway to Heaven" or something by Crosby, Stills, Nash, and/or Young.

Meanwhile, the records I recall from parties were "TSOP (The Sound of Philadelphia)," "Rock the Boat," "Kung Fu Fighting," "Do It ('Til You're Satisfied)," "The Hustle," "Baby Face," and "That's the Way (I Like It)." That list runs over several years because I think of it as a dance mix and can't remember which records arrived when, nor do I recall at what point we started calling the style "disco." Everybody danced to the disco hits, regardless of race, but we definitely thought of it as a black style—my sister recalls an African-American friend freaking out at the discovery that KC (of Sunshine Band fame) was a white guy.

We were particularly conscious of race at that moment because we were across the river from Boston, and the city was caught up in a ferocious battle over school busing. The atmosphere was tense, and although everybody knew each other, we also knew which bathrooms the white kids hung out in and which were the black kids' territory. The divide was not strictly genetic—there were some black kids who were socially white and some white kids who were socially black—and we all danced to more or less the same records, but we certainly classified musical styles along racial lines, with a few artists like Wonder and KC who overlapped or crossed the boundaries.

I was playing blues guitar by that time and thought of myself as being into black music, and I had chosen that high school as an escape from my white, upper-middle-class neighborhood, so I wanted to feel a kinship with the current black styles. But, try as I might, I found virtually all the disco hits boring and repetitive. For one thing, I had dreams of playing professionally and hated the idea that producers with synthesizers were replacing musicians—if anyone had quizzed me, I would have had to admit that I had no idea how those records were made or how many musicians were actually involved, but the final products sounded utterly mechanical to me. And I was far from alone: Reading back over the pop criticism of that time, it is common to find writers bemoaning the formulaic rhythms of the disco grooves, while at the same time lamenting the blandness and pretentiousness of the rock scene. And in the context of this book, I see those complaints as two sides of the same coin.

In 1962, the British art historian Kenneth Clark gave a talk titled "The Blot and the Diagram," in which he suggested that premodernist painting had functioned both to excite the imagination and to convey specific information, whereas modern painting fulfilled only the former function. Leonardo da Vinci was his example of the ideal old master, drawing inspiration from water stains, colored stones, and burning embers, "because from a confusion of shapes the spirit is quickened to new inventions," but also attaining an unprecedented knowledge of anatomy and geometry, so that his paintings were noted as much for their physical accuracy as for their beauty.[1]

The mainstream of American popular music, at least as I have traced it in this book, was a similar interaction between the desire to provide an emotional or intellectual charge that quickened people's spirits and to provide the best possible accompaniment for dancers. Not all popular music was for dancing, but all of the significant movements were connected to dance styles (the one exception being the studio ballads of the postwar era, whose dominance was the result of a dance slump). Many musicians felt trapped and constrained by the need to satisfy dance crowds, just as many painters undoubtedly found it a burden to have to depict saints and patrons or, later, pretty landscapes. And it was natural for them to envy the evident social status and apparent freedom of classical artists whose audiences sat quietly and paid attention to long, intellectually challenging performances. So there were regular attempts to "elevate" pop styles: Scott Joplin's opera *Treemonisha*, *Rhapsody in Blue*, Ellington's suites—indeed, the whole attempt to reimagine jazz as a classical form—and even, in their way, Sinatra's mood albums.

Until the later 1960s, though, all of these attempts were limited by the fact that pop audiences are overwhelmingly young and their idea of a fun or exciting evening only occasionally involves sitting quietly and listening, even to music they like. So virtually any pop band that worked regularly played a lot of dances, whether the musicians wanted to or not. The bands that stood out combined efficient dance rhythms with some special spark that set them apart, but efficient dance rhythms were a given.

By the late 1960s, that was no longer the case for the top rock bands. As *Billboard* reported in 1968, "Psychedelic dance halls, begun in San Francisco two years ago, and now rolling in other cities, have developed into a new form of concert hall where... young people are not dancing, just digging."[2] Reporters had written the same thing about Benny Goodman's and Count Basie's audiences in the swing era, but the economics of the industry had ensured that the big bands continued to play a lot of dances and disappeared when the dancers stopped coming. In the great scheme of popular music, a similar thing happened to rock: Since the 1960s, there have been relatively few rock bands outside the upper echelons that can support themselves with live performances, and the vast majority of young musicians either "make it" or take up another profession. The equation is simple: People will go to hear dance music as often as they feel like dancing—which in the case of people in their teens and twenties can be pretty much any free evening—but they will only go to hear a concert band when they feel like listening, and no one but a band's most dedicated fans cares to listen to it every week, good as it may be.

If the rock musicians of the 1970s did not feel obliged to please dancers, that was to a great extent because there was no longer much call for dance bands of any kind. We danced to records, and although those records were not made by rock bands, neither were they made by bands that were competing with the rock bands for live gigs. There were some dance bands that toured—Earth, Wind and Fire were famous for their concerts—but that was not the music we typically expected to hear when we went out to see a band, and when it came to making dance records, it was irrelevant whether a disco group even existed outside the studio.

Revisiting Clark's metaphor, rock music was the blot and disco the diagram—the first was no longer expected to fulfill any function beyond exciting, inspiring, or pleasing its listeners; the latter was purely functional. And that held true whether the rock in question was made by Carole King or the Sex Pistols: Both singer-songwriters and punks are, albeit in different ways, making art music. Disco, by contrast, was all about dance rhythms, and though some disco hits were catchier or quirkier than others, if I complained that a particular song was unimaginative or repetitious, most of my friends would just respond with variations of the old *Bandstand* rate-a-record criteria: "It's got a good beat and it's fun to dance to."

Critics, by their nature, want to hear music that is not only functional but interesting—after all, they need to listen to it carefully and find something to say about it. So when straightforward dance music is turned into something more complex and better suited to seated listening, they naturally see this as a step forward. As a result, both *Rhapsody in Blue* and *Sgt. Pepper* were hailed not only for being different from the dance music of their periods but also as signposts to the future. (A London *Times* story about the latter was headlined "The Beatles Revive Hopes of Progress in Pop Music."[3]) Few if any critics in the 1920s imagined that the blues-rooted improvisations of King Oliver's Creole Jazz band would in retrospect sound more modern than Whiteman's orchestral masterpieces. Nor, in the 1960s, did any critics describe James Brown as more advanced than the Beatles. Many celebrated Brown's rootsy power, and some recognized the rhythmic innovations of funk, but when those rhythms were mechanized in the disco era, everyone but the dancers saw it as a dead end. As with previous evolutions of black dance music, it was even described as a regression, more boring and beat-oriented than what had come before it.

I was no more prescient than my rock-loving peers. When Bruce Springsteen, Patti Smith, and the Ramones appeared, I was still into blues and didn't run out to buy their records, but I certainly thought of their music as a breath of fresh air and considered them more interesting than Chic. So it is striking to me, listening to the same music thirty years later, to find that those interesting white artists all sound as if in one or another way they were holding onto the past, while Chic sounds ahead of its time.

That is not an aesthetic judgment. I don't believe that music progresses in aesthetic terms: Every era has good music and bad music and a wealth of disagreement about which is which, and most of my favorite music not only holds onto the past but is from the past. For my own tastes, the split between white and black popular styles in the Beatles era—the increasing divide between rock and soul, listening music and dance music, the blot and the diagram—was bad for both. Revisiting the top rock and R&B hits from the 1960s through the 1970s, I consistently prefer the R&B selection but also hear an overall decline, and I think that decline can be traced to the fact that bands were no longer forced to play each other's styles. As long as every working band had to master the full range of pop styles, any advance forced everyone to adapt and stretch—Fletcher Henderson learned *Rhapsody in Blue*, Guy Lombardo learned some swing rhythms, rockabillies learned "Shout," soul singers learned country and Beatles songs, and everyone played lots of romantic slow dances and a least a few Latin numbers.

As the pop scene became increasingly divided between deejayed dance venues and rock acts that had no need to keep up with the latest rhythmic fashions, there was no reason for anyone to maintain that kind of versatility. Fans continued to dance at rock shows, but the bands did not see their main job as pleasing the dancers, and they certainly were under no pressure to learn the latest disco hits. Meanwhile those hits were increasingly recorded by studio specialists, hired on a track-by-track basis to do whatever each did best. This was arguably liberating, as it allowed everybody to concentrate on the music that most closely suited their tastes or abilities, but in the greater scheme of things the pure rhythm of disco, the pure energy of punk, and the pure self-expression of the singer-songwriters were all less interesting than what might have evolved if musicians had continued to be forced to sacrifice their purity to satisfy audiences that wanted all three.

Indeed, that is one of the reasons that black popular music has consistently tended to be more exciting than white popular music. Black performers have rarely been accorded a level of acclaim and financial security that allowed them to stop worrying about their audience, so they always retained what Clark called "the bracing element of craftsmanship." The Beatles could ignore the rhythmic advances of their time, and if in the process they stopped being part of the teen dance mix, they still sold millions of records to people who regarded them as musical prophets. Black pop performers, by contrast, were expected to keep up with the latest beats. Of course, that was unfair and limited some very talented artists: In the 1970s, even Aretha Franklin was caught in the black-equals-dance-music bind, and though she made the best of a bad situation, I still hold a grudge against the labels that assembled superb '60s-style soul bands for the Blues Brothers and Joe Cocker at a time when Aretha and Wilson Pickett were singing over disco tracks. With a few exceptions—Isaac Hayes, Stevie Wonder, Marvin Gaye, Michael Jackson, Prince, and a handful of others—there was no support for black auteurs to spend hundreds of hours making an album, and even those exceptions were expected to sell a lot more records than Dylan did or the cash flow disappeared.

Nonetheless, unfair as that was, the results speak for themselves. In terms of ongoing development, the segregation of American popular music that began with the British Invasion has hurt white music more than it hurt black. Rock and its white relatives stagnated—not in the sense that no good music was made but in that there have been few major advances in the past thirty-plus years. Meanwhile, the black dance music of the 1970s led into hip-hop and rap, which have inspired and transformed popular styles around the world.

As always, that is a simplification, and if I were carrying this story forward rather than wrapping it up I would be drawing a far more complicated picture. In the process of writing this book, I found that my sense of each period changed in the process of researching and writing about it, and the same would no doubt hold true for the 1970s and beyond.

For example, having experienced the black music of my youth as increasingly dance-focused and studio-created, in retrospect I am struck by the size of that period's soul-funk orchestras. Two decades after the fabled death of the big bands, James Brown continued to lead a horn-heavy orchestra based on the Basie model, most soul stars were using ten- to fifteen-piece groups, and in the 1970s Isaac Hayes and Barry White were touring with several dozen musicians, including full string sections, while Parliament/Funkadelic's ensemble included over sixty dancers, singers, and players. In the long run, the big soul sound probably contributed to the shift away from live music, since very few clubs could afford a large orchestra and the working combos could not recreate that sound any more than they could duplicate the synthesized disco productions. Nevertheless, the survival of big bands on the soul scene deserves a good deal more attention than it has received from pop music historians.

Another thing is that, although I equated disco with black music, the trend found room for everyone from a Donald Duck imitator to the Anglo-Australian Bee Gees and the Village People. (In retrospect, disco has often been equated with gay club culture, but at the time most of us were unaware of those roots, nor did we recognize the Village People as gay.) The third single ever to be certified platinum was Wild Cherry's "Play That Funky Music (White Boy),"[4] and even if most of the disco performers were black, dance floors were more integrated than ever before. A lot of older white fans also continued to support black stars: In June 1969, a writer cruising through Las Vegas noted that Ray Charles, Solomon Burke, Gladys Knight, Aretha Franklin, Little Richard, and Fats Domino were all appearing within a few blocks of each other on the city's entertainment strip, and in 1972 there were two separate weeks when eight of the ten top records on the *Billboard* pop chart were by black singers, with the performers ranging from Michael Jackson and the Staple Singers to Roberta Flack and Sammy Davis Jr.[5]

The 1970s also brought plenty of musical developments that I have not even mentioned: Female singers tended to have a hard time in both rock and dance music, but Carole King and Joni Mitchell blazed trails that have been followed by generations of later singer-songwriters. Country music escaped most of the trends I have discussed in the last few chapters, continuing to please both dancers and listeners, and there are still plenty of country bands earning a living by covering the latest hits for bar crowds. Led Zeppelin and Black Sabbath inspired generations of heavy metal bands, attracted huge concert audiences, and sold millions of eight-track tapes. Salsa burst out of New York with a mix of funk instrumentation, Afro-Caribbean rhythms, hot soloists, and lyrical dexterity that inspired imitators and fusions around the world. And, as always, a lot of people were listening to jazz, classical, blues, polka, and dozens of other styles, barely aware of the music on any pop charts.

In the twenty-first century, nonmainstream styles may account for a larger share of listeners than ever before—it depends on how one defines the mainstream, and on whether one even grants that there still is such a thing. Between downloading, burning, and file sharing, there is no way to form even a rough estimate of how many people are acquiring any particular recording these days, and what gets played on the radio is no indicator in a world where most young people are listening to their own digital playlists.

I do not lament this change, although both as a performer and as a listener I feel threatened by the decline of live music venues. Facing an audience for four or five hours a night, seven nights a week, was tough work, but that was how virtually all my favorite musicians got their education, and it is an education that very few artists will ever have again. But I have to balance that regret with the fact that without the Internet, e-mail lists, and MP3 files it would have been impossible for me even to conceive of writing this book. As always, there have been gains and losses, and if there is one thing to be learned by looking closely at the past, it is that there was no era that did not have its own drawbacks, mediocrities, and disasters. As A. J. Liebling wrote many years ago, "the world isn't going backward, if you can just stay young enough to remember what it was really like when you were really young."[6]

That may not seem like much of a moral, but perhaps it is the most valuable lesson that history can teach us. When I began this book, my nephew Zeke was a twelve-year-old dancing with his friends to Beatles records. Now he is in high school, and he and his classmates are dancing to the current hip-hop hits. I find this reassuring, because it frightened me to think that he felt more comfortable in my past than in his present.

As for me, this journey has forced me to confront some long-standing prejudices and to listen to a lot of artists I would never otherwise have heard, and I have thoroughly enjoyed reliving eighty years of musical history. But now I am ready for the present myself: The time has come to turn off my computer, get up from my desk, and go out and play some music.

NOTES

INTRODUCTION

The epigraph for this chapter is quoted from Charles Rosen, *Critical Entertainments: Music Old and New* (Cambridge, MA: Harvard University Press, 2000), 305.

1 *Atlantic Monthly* (Sept. 1920), quoted in Richard M. Sudhalter, *Lost Chords: White Musicians and Their Contribution to Jazz, 1915–1945* (New York: Oxford University Press, 1999), 19.

2 Bennie Moten's Kansas City Orchestra, "Get Low-Down Blues" (Camden, NJ: Victor Record 21693, 1928).

3 Jim Miller, *The Rolling Stone Illustrated History of Rock 'n' Roll* (New York: Rolling Stone Press; Random House, 1976), 30.

4 Peter Guralnick, *The Sun Sessions*, CD notes, RCA 6414, 1987.

5 Peter Guralnick, *Lost Highway: Journeys and Arrivals of American Musicians* (Boston: Godine, 1979), 135. On other occasions he picked other records for this honor, but as far as I can tell they were always ballads or gospel songs.

6 Thomas A. DeLong, *Pops: Paul Whiteman, King of Jazz* (Piscataway, NJ: New Century, 1983), 307.

7 Ellen Willis, "Records: Rock, Etc.," *New Yorker*, 6 Apr. 1968, 148.

8 Rosen, *Critical Entertainments*, 285.

CHAPTER 1 AMATEURS AND EXECUTANTS

1 John Philip Sousa, "The Menace of Mechanical Music," *Appleton's Magazine* 8 (1906), 278–284 (http://www.explorepahistory.com/odocument.php?docId=418; accessed 15 Dec. 2008).

2 Paul Edmund Bierley, *The Incredible Band of John Philip Sousa* (Urbana: University of Illinois Press, 2006), 78.

3 Charles K. Harris, "After the Ball" (Milwaukee: Charles K. Harris & Co., 1892).

4   Charles K. Harris, *After the Ball: Forty Years of Melody* (New York: Frank-Maurice, 1926), 87.

5   Pete Seeger, *The Goofing-Off Suite* (Folkways LP 2045, 1954); Pete Seeger, *Henscratches and Flyspecks* (New York: Berkley Medallion Books, 1973).

6   Sousa, "Menace of Mechanical Music."

7   Russell Sanjek, *American Popular Music and Its Business* (New York: Oxford University Press, 1988), 2:77.

8   Rosen, *Critical Entertainments*, 217.

9   "Music," *Putnam's Monthly Magazine of American Literature, Science and Art* 1, no. 1 (Jan. 1853):119–120.

10 Sanjek, *American Popular Music*, 2:78.

11 "Bessie Smith & Co. at the Avenue," *Chicago Defender*, sec. 1, 10 May 1924, 6.

12 Margaret McKee and Fred Chisenhall, *Beale Black and Blue: Life and Music on Black America's Main Street* (Baton Rouge: Louisiana State University Press, 1981), 231.

13 Elijah Wald, "John Jackson: Down Home Rappahannock Blues," *Sing Out!* 39, no. 1 (1994): 10–19.

14 Frederika Bremer, *The Homes of the New World: Impressions of America* (New York: Harper & Brothers, 1853), 307–308.

CHAPTER 2 THE RAGTIME LIFE

1   Eileen Southern, *The Music of Black Americans: A History* (New York: Norton, 1971), 68.

2   Gene Jefferson and R. S. Roberts, "I'm Certainly Living a Ragtime Life" (New York: Sol Bloom, 1900).

3   Robert C. Toll, *The Entertainment Machine: American Show Business in the Twentieth Century* (New York: Oxford University Press, 1982), 104.

4   David Ewen, *Music Comes to America* (New York: Thomas Y. Crowell, 1942), 279.

5   Rudi Blesh and Harriet Janis, *They All Played Ragtime* (New York: Alfred A. Knopf, 1950), 223. Even the *Penguin Encyclopedia of Popular Music* (Donald Clarke, ed., London: Penguin Books, 1990), 955, although in general it shares my broader view, argues that "Alexander" "was not ragtime at all."

6   Henry O. Osgood, *So This Is Jazz* (Boston: Little, Brown, 1926), 74.

7   Roger Pryor Dodge, *Hot Jazz and Jazz Dance: Collected Writings, 1929–1964* (New York: Oxford University Press, 1995), 26.

8   David Meltzer, *Writing Jazz* (San Francisco: Mercury House, 1999), 126.

9   Richard Meryman, *Louis Armstrong: A Self-Portrait* (New York: Eakins Press, 1971), 57.

10 The formation of the jazz canon is explored in Scott DeVeaux, "Constructing the Jazz Tradition," in Robert G. O'Meally, ed., *The Jazz Cadence of American Culture* (New York: Columbia University Press, 1998), 483–512.

11 Osgood, *So This Is Jazz*, 69.

12 Sanjek, *American Popular Music*, 2:299.

13 Ibid., 2:296.

14 Kerry Mills, "At a Georgia Campmeeting [*sic*]" (New York: F.A. Mills, 1899).

15 Advertisement, *Indianapolis Freeman*, 14 July 1900.

16 "Intruding at a Cake Walk," *New York Times*, 26 Feb. 1886.

17 "New Cotillion Figure," *Brooklyn Eagle*, 10 Jan. 1901, 15.

18 "A Plantation Cake Walk Makes Much Merriment," *Brooklyn Eagle*, 20 July 1902, 4.

19 Tom Fletcher, *100 Years of the Negro in Show Business* (New York: Da Capo Press, 1984), 19.

20 "Minstrelsy and Cake Walks," *Cleveland Gazette*, 21 Jan. 1899, 2; Dave Riehle, "The Great Cuba Pageant of 1898 and the Struggle for Civil Rights," *Ramsey County History*, Winter 1999 (http://www.laborstandard.org/Vol2No1/Cuba_Pageant.htm; accessed 5 Feb. 2007).

21 Fletcher, *100 Years*, 108.

22 "A Mystery Explained," *New York Times*, 13 Dec. 1874.

23 Mills, "At a Georgia Campmeeting."

24 Lynn Abbott and Doug Seroff, *Ragged but Right: Black Traveling Shows, "Coon Songs," and the Dark Pathway to Blues and Jazz* (Jackson: University Press of Mississippi, 2007), 45, 66.

25 Blesh and Janis, *They All Played Ragtime*, 217.

26 Lawrence Gushee, *Pioneers of Jazz: The Story of the Creole Band* (New York: Oxford University Press, 2005), 100.

27 James Weldon Johnson, Preface to *The Book of American Negro Poetry*, in *Writings* (New York: Library of America, 2004), 713.

28 Ibid., 690.

29 Irving Berlin, "That Society Bear" (New York: Waterson, Berlin and Snyder, 1912).

30 Marshall W. Stearns and Jean Stearns, *Jazz Dance: The Story of American Vernacular Dance* (New York: Macmillan, 1968), 122; "Challenge to a Cake Walk," *New York Times*, 13 Jan. 1898.

31 *Musical Courier*, 1899, quoted in Stearns and Stearns, *Jazz Dance*, 123.

CHAPTER 3 EVERYBODY'S DOIN' IT

1 "Contemporary Dancing Has Evolved the Concave Man," *New York Times Sunday Magazine*, 18 Jan. 1914, 11.4.

2 Edward A. Berlin, *Scott Joplin: Brief Biographical Sketch*, http://www.edwardaberlin.com/work4.htm (accessed 11 Feb. 2007).

3 Irving Berlin, "That International Rag" (New York: Waterson, Berlin & Snyder, 1913).

4 M. F. Ham, *Light on the Dance* (San Antonio, TX: San Antonio Printing Co., 1916), 13, 54.

5 Thomas A. Faulkner, "From the Ballroom to Hell," quoted in Maureen Needham, ed., *I See America Dancing: Selected Readings, 1685–2000* (Urbana: University of Illinois Press, 2002), 117.

6 Maurice Mouvet, *Maurice's Art of Dancing* (New York: Schirmer, 1915), 36; "Dancer from Paris Introduces New Steps to Society," *New York Times Magazine*, 10 Dec. 1911, 10.1.

7 The Seldes and Castle quotations are both from Irene Castle, *Castles in the Air* (Garden City, NY: Doubleday, 1958), 87.

8 Castle, *Castles in the Air*, 88.

9 Mr. and Mrs. Vernon Castle, *Modern Dancing* (New York: World Syndicate, 1914), 177; "Contemporary Dancing," 11.

10 "Contemporary Dancing," 11.

11 Reid Badger, *A Life in Ragtime: A Biography of James Reese Europe* (New York: Oxford University Press, 1995), 143.

12   Ibid., 115. The Castles said they based the fox-trot on a step Europe showed them. A dancer named Harry Fox made a rival claim, as did others, but the Castles were the dance's most influential popularizers.

13   Fletcher, *100 Years*, 191.

14   James Weldon Johnson, "The Poor White Musician," in Johnson, *Writings*, 618.

15   Badger, *Life in Ragtime*, 136.

16   Al Rose, *Eubie Blake* (New York: Schirmer, 1979), 58–59.

17   James Reese Europe, "A Negro Explains Jazz," *Literary Digest*, 26 Apr. 1919, 28–29, reprinted in Eileen Southern, ed., *Readings in Black American Music* (New York: Norton, 1983), 240. *New York Tribune*, 1919, quoted in Gerald Early, *Culture of Bruising: Essays on Prizefighting, Literature, and Modern American Culture* (Hopewell, NJ: Ecco Press, 1994), 190.

18   Charles Dickens, *American Notes* and *The Uncommercial Traveler* (Philadelphia: T. B. Peterson & Bros., n.d., ca. 1850), 118–119; Laurence Bergreen, *As Thousands Cheer: The Life of Irving Berlin* (New York: Viking, 1990), 25. In other versions, Berlin refused the tip.

19   Herbert Asbury, *The Barbary Coast: An Informal History of the San Francisco Underworld* (Garden City, NJ: Garden City, 1933), 292.

20   *San Francisco Examiner*, 29 Nov. 1910, quoted in Tom Stoddard, *Jazz on the Barbary Coast* (Berkeley, CA: Heyday Books, 1998), 38.

21   Stoddard, *Jazz on the Barbary Coast*, includes several chapters devoted to LeProtti's memoirs.

22   Wallace Irwin, *The Love Sonnets of a Hoodlum* (San Francisco: Elder, 1901), verse XIV.

23   "Social Workers See Real 'Turkey Trots,'" *New York Times*, 27 Jan. 1912, 1, 2.

24   *Variety*, 16 Dec. 1925, quoted in William Howland Kenney, *Chicago Jazz: A Cultural History, 1904–1930* (New York: Oxford University Press, 1993), 74.

25   Curt Sachs, *World History of the Dance* (New York: Norton, 1937), 399.

26   Royal L. Melendy, "The Saloon in Chicago," *American Journal of Sociology*, vol. 6, no. 3 (Nov. 1900): 293, 304.

27   Kathy Peiss, *Cheap Amusements: Working Women and Leisure in Turn-of-the-Century New York* (Philadelphia: Temple University Press, 1986), 34.

28   New York Committee of Fourteen, 1912 and 1914, in Danielle Anne Robinson, "Race in Motion: Reconstructing the Practice, Profession, and Politics of Social Dancing, New York City 1900–1930" (PhD diss., University of California Riverside, 2004), 10.

29   Louise de Koven Bowen, *The Public Dance Halls of Chicago* (Chicago: Juvenile Protective Association of Chicago, 1917), 6, 9.

30   Peiss, *Cheap Amusements*, 106.

31   H. W. Lytle and John Dillon, *From Dance Hall to White Slavery: The World's Greatest Tragedy* (N.p.: Charles C. Thompson, 1912).

32   Jane Addams, *The Spirit of Youth and the City Streets* (New York: Macmillan, 1909).

CHAPTER 4   ALEXANDER'S GOT A JAZZ BAND NOW

The epigraph for this chapter is quoted from *Louis Armstrong, in His Own Words* (New York: Oxford University Press, 1999), 218–219.

1   F. T. Vreeland, *New York Sun*, 4 Nov. 1917, quoted in H. O. Brunn, *The Story of the Original Dixieland Jazz Band* (London: Jazz Book Club, 1963), 55.

2   "The Story of J. Russell Robinson," *The Second Line*, vol. 6, no. 9/10 (1955), quoted in Lawrence Gushee, "The Nineteenth-Century Origins of Jazz," *Black Music Research Journal*, vol. 22, Suppl. (2002): 152; Frederic Ramsey Jr. and Charles Edward Smith, *Jazzmen* (New York: Harcourt, Brace, 1939), 51.

3   Tom Stoddard, *Jazz on the Barbary Coast* (Berkeley, CA: Heyday Books, 1998), 77.

4   Willie Smith, *Music on My Mind: The Memoirs of an American Pianist* (Garden City, NY: Doubleday, 1964), 35–36.

5   Ibid., 90. This was late in 1919.

6   Gushee, *Pioneers of Jazz*, 40.

7   Stoddard, *Jazz on the Barbary Coast*, 12.

8   Smith, *Music on My Mind*, 66. James P. Johnson, composer of "The Charleston," likewise traced the song to cotillions at the Jungle Casino, and mentioned schottisches, adding that a typical dance lasted fifteen to thirty minutes (Scott E. Brown, *James P. Johnson: A Case of Mistaken Identity* [Metuchen, NJ: Scarecrow Press and the Institute of Jazz Studies, 1986], 55–56).

9   Sudhalter, *Lost Chords*, 17.

10 Edward B. Marks, *They All Sang: From Tony Pastor to Rudy Vallée* (New York: Viking Press, 1934), 158. Roberts's middle name is sometimes spelled Luckeyeth, and he seems to have used both spellings of the nickname, calling the club he ran in Harlem "Luckey's Rendezvous" but signing his draft card "Charles Lucky Roberts."

11 O. M. Samuels, "New Orleans Makes a Claim," *Variety*, 1 July 1911, in Gushee, "Nineteenth-Century Origins of Jazz," 170.

12 Winthrop Sargeant, *Jazz: Hot and Hybrid* (New York: Dutton, 1946), 227.

13 Abbott and Seroff, *Ragged but Right*, 45–46.

14 Gushee, *Pioneers of Jazz*, 14.

15 Stoddard, *Jazz on the Barbary Coast*, 42.

16 Johnny Danger, *Los Angeles Record*, 3 July 1914, quoted in Gushee, *Pioneers of Jazz*, 86.

17 "Ben's Jazz Curve," *Los Angeles Times*, sec. 3, 2 Apr. 1912, 2.

18 E. T. "Scoop" Gleeson, "Seals Return from the Spa to Tackle the Famous White Sox," *The Bulletin* (San Francisco), 6 Mar. 1913, 16; *San Francisco Examiner*, 12 Sept. 1919, in Bruce Vermazen, "Art Hickman and His Orchestra," http://www.gracyk.com/hickman.shtml (accessed 20 Feb. 2007).

19 Paul Whiteman and Margaret McBride, *Jazz* (New York: J. H. Sears and Company, 1926), 122.

20 Osgood, *So This Is Jazz*, 18.

21 Alan P. Merriam and Fradley H. Garner, "Jazz—the Word," in O'Meally, *Jazz Cadence*, 19; Daniel Cassidy, "Dat Ol' Jazz: How the Irish Invented Jazz," http://www.edu-cyberpg.com/pdf/Jazz.pdf (accessed 20 Feb. 2007).

22 Gordon Seagrove, "Blues Is Jazz and Jazz Is Blues," *Chicago Tribune*, 11 July 1915, E8.

23 Sudhalter, *Lost Chords*, 7.

24 Whiteman and McBride, *Jazz*, 141.

25 Scott Alexander, "The First Jazz Records," http://www.redhotjazz.com/jazz1917.html (accessed 17 Feb. 2007).

26 Tim Gracyk, "'Jass' in 1916–1917 and Tin Pan Alley," http://www.gracyk.com/jasband.shtml (accessed 15 Aug. 2006); Scott Alexander, "The First Jazz Records," http://www.redhotjazz.com/jazz1917.html (accessed 17 Feb. 2007).

27 Tim Gracyk, "Earl Fuller's Famous Jazz Band," http://www.redhotjazz.com/fuller.html (accessed 17 Feb. 2007).

28 *New York Clipper*, 22 Aug. 1917, quoted in Sudhalter, *Lost Chords*, 25.

29 Mark Miller, *Some Hustling This! Taking Jazz to the World, 1914–1929* (Toronto: Mercury Press, 2005), 36.

30 Kenney, *Chicago Jazz*, 18.

31 Robert J. Cole, "Conspiracy of Silence against Jazz," *New York Times Magazine*, 21 Sept. 1919, 84.

CHAPTER 5 CAKE EATERS AND HOOCH DRINKERS

1   George Wald, unpublished memoir transcribed by Elijah Wald, ca. 1990.

2   "Matador Pants Ruined," *Los Angeles Times*, sec. 2, 23 Aug. 1922, 1.

3   Fred W. Edmiston, *The Coon-Sanders Nighthawks: "The Band That Made Radio Famous"* (Jefferson, NC: McFarland, 2003), 29.

4   *The Sidewalks of New York*, 1923, scenario at http://www.geocities.com/emruf1/sidewalks.html (accessed 2 Mar. 2007); "Now Finale-Hopper," *Los Angeles Times*, sec. 1, 4 Mar. 1922, 15.

5   Bertram Reinitz, "New York Faces a Hatless Fad," *New York Times*, 9 Sept. 1928.

6   Kathleen Drowne, *Spirits of Defiance: National Prohibition and Jazz Age Literature, 1920–1933* (Columbus: Ohio State University Press, 2005), 76. The quotation is from William Faulkner's *Sanctuary* (New York: Vintage International, 1993), 29.

7   "He Flapper Rivals Sister," *Los Angeles Times*, sec. 3, 23 Sept. 1923, 13.

8   F. Scott Fitzgerald, "May Day," section 7, in *The Short Stories of F. Scott Fitzgerald* (New York: Charles Scribner's Sons, 1989), 122.

9   Kenney, *Chicago Jazz*, 20.

10 "Vincent Lopez, Inc.," *Time*, 19 Jan. 1925, http://www.time.com/time/magazine/article/0,9171,927648,00.html.

11 Sally Fairfield Burton, "The Folly Test of Fashion," *New York Times*, 25 Mar. 1923.

12 Kathleen Drowne and Patrick Huber, *The 1920s* (Westport, CT: Greenwood Press, 2004), 33.

13 "Bandsman," *New Yorker*, 7 Feb. 1931, 13; Virginia Waring, *Fred Waring and the Pennsylvanians* (Urbana: University of Illinois Press, 1997), 41.

14 Paul Whiteman, "Guarding the Future of Dance Music," *Talking Machine Journal*, Jan. 1925, 69.

15 "Will Beer Be the First Step Back?" *Metronome*, Feb. 1933, 6.

16 Herbert Asbury, *The Great Illusion: An Informal History of Prohibition* (Garden City, NJ: Garden City, 1950), 190–191.

17 Edmiston, *Coon-Sanders Nighthawks*, 38.

18 Guy Lombardo, *Auld Acquaintance* (Garden City, NY: Doubleday, 1975), 180–181.

19 Joe Darensbourg, *The Jazz Odyssey: The Autobiography of Joe Darensbourg* (Baton Rouge: Louisiana State University Press, 1987), 43.

20 Edward Behr, *Prohibition: Thirteen Years That Changed America* (New York: Arcade, 1996), 87. Some (e.g., Charles Fyffe and Robert M. Hardaway, *No Price Too High: Victimless Crimes and the*

Ninth Amendment [Westport, CT: Greenwood, 2003], 66–67) extend this claim to the country as a whole, but whatever the number of speakeasies, most modern scholars believe that per capita alcohol consumption during Prohibition was much lower than in the 'teens.

21 Charles G. Shaw, *Nightlife: Vanity Fair's Intimate Guide to New York after Dark* (New York: John Day, 1931), 129–131.

22 LeRoy E. Bowman and Maria Ward Lambin, "Evidences of Social Relations as Seen in Types of New York City Dance Halls," *Journal of Social Forces*, vol. 3, no. 2, Jan. 1925, 288.

23 Chip Deffaa, *Voices of the Jazz Age: Profiles of Eight Vintage Jazzmen* (Urbana: University of Illinois Press, 1990), 13.

24 Shaw, *Nightlife*, 73, 75.

25 Helen Josephy and Mary Margaret McBride, *New York Is Everybody's Town* (New York: Putnam, 1931), 17.

26 Michael W. Harris, *The Rise of Gospel Blues: The Music of Thomas Andrew Dorsey in the Urban Church* (New York: Oxford University Press, 1992), 44–45.

CHAPTER 6 THE KING OF JAZZ

The epigraph for this chapter is quoted from Nevin Busch, "The Paid Piper," *New Yorker*, 27 Nov. 1926, 26.

1 Doron K. Antrim, ed., *Secrets of Dance Band Success* (N.p.: Famous Stars, 1936), 5.

2 Paul Whiteman and Margaret McBride, *Jazz* (New York: J. H. Sears and Company, 1926), 33; biographical details from Don Rayno, *Paul Whiteman: Pioneer in American Music*, Vol. 1, *1890–1930* (Lanham, MD: Scarecrow Press, 2003).

3 Whiteman and McBride, *Jazz*, 36.

4 Ibid., 39. The precise quotation is, "Up to that time, there had never been a jazz orchestration. I made the first...."

5 Abbe Niles, "Jazz," *Encyclopaedia Britannica*, 14th ed., vol. XII, 983, s.v. "Jazz," quoted in Bruce Vermazen, "Art Hickman and His Orchestra," www.gracyk.com/hickman.shtml. Grofé has been credited with developing Hickman's style, but Vermazen finds no evidence that they worked together.

6 My description of Hickman is principally from Bruce Vermazen, both the article cited above in the preceding note and personal communication. Vermazen writes that, as far as he knows, most of the Hickman orchestra's arrangements were worked out by the musicians as a group, without written charts, though there are rumors of some written arrangements as well.

7 *San Francisco Examiner*, 11 Apr. 1928, 6, quoted in Bruce Vermazen, "Art Hickman," and His Orchestra," http://www.gracyk.com/hickman.shtml (accessed 20 Feb. 2007).

8 *Talking Machine World*, 15 July 1920, 6; *San Francisco Examiner*, 30 Oct. 1920, both quoted in Bruce Vermazen, "Art Hickman and His Orchestra."

9 "A Tribute to Paul Whiteman," *Talking Machine Journal*, Nov. 1920, 66.

10 Whiteman and McBride, *Jazz*, 99–100. According to the *New York Times*, *Jazz* was out by June 1926, and Harry Osgood's *So This Is Jazz* appeared in October.

11 For example, in James Lincoln Collier, *Jazz: The American Theme Song* (New York: Oxford University Press, 1993), 185; Frank Tirro, *Jazz: A History* (New York: Norton, 1993), 3; and

"Jazz Worlds/World Jazz: The Globalisation of an American Classical Music," conference at the University of Newcastle, Newcastle Uupon Tyne, Feb. 2005.

12   Duke Ellington, "A Royal View of Jazz," *Jazz: A Quarterly of American Music*, vol. 2 (Spring 1959): 84. Whiteman is the only white figure he mentions. 1930s quotations from *Evening Graphic*, 18 June 1932, in Stuart Nicholson, *Reminiscing in Tempo: A Portrait of Duke Ellington* (Boston: Northeastern University Press, 1999), 126; *The Brown American*, Dec. 1936, in Early, *Culture of Bruising*, 183.

13   Samuel B. Charters and Leonard Kunstadt, *Jazz: A History of the New York Scene* (Garden City, NY: Doubleday, 1962), 213.

14   These included Mamie Smith, Lucille Hegamin, and the Carver Boys.

15   Whiteman and McBride, *Jazz*, 241–242. Ray Lopez said Mueller could read music before leaving New Orleans, but possibly not to orchestra standards.

16   Hughes Panassié, *The Real Jazz* (New York: Smith & Durrell, 1943), 170.

17   "The Music Mart," *Talking Machine Journal*, Apr. 1923, 46.

18   *Variety*, 29 Dec. 1922, in Rayno, *Paul Whiteman*, 60.

19   Rayno, *Paul Whiteman*, 80.

20   Howard Pollack, *George Gershwin: His Life and Work* (Berkeley: University of California Press, 2006), 270–274.

21   Maurice Peress, *Dvořák to Duke Ellington: A Conductor Explores America's Music and Its African American Roots* (New York: Oxford University Press, 2004), 91; Rayno, *Paul Whiteman*, 82.

22   Peress, *Dvořák to Duke Ellington*, 90.

23   Lopez presented "The Evolution of the Blues" in November 1924, with music by Sir Arthur Sullivan, Fletcher Henderson, W. C. Handy, and Irving Berlin.

24   DeLong, *Pops*, 88.

25   Dodge, *Hot Jazz and Jazz Dance*, 101.

26   Gilbert Seldes, *The Seven Lively Arts* (New York: Harper & Brothers, 1924), 99.

27   "Meet the Beatles' Favorite American Singer: James Brown," *16 Magazine*, Sept. 1964, 58.

28   Early, *Culture of Bruising*, 182.

29   *New Yorker*, 20 Nov. 1926, 17.

30   Sudhalter, *Lost Chords*, 423–424. Sudhalter writes that the Whiteman orchestra "set free at last the part of Bix that was … reaching beyond the rather modest disciplines of hot improvisation into areas which had long fascinated him," countering Benny Green's contention that "today we only tolerate the horrors of Whiteman's recordings at all in the hope that here and there a Bixian fragment will redeem the mess."

31   Rayno, *Paul Whiteman*, 170.

32   Ramsey Jr. and Smith, *Jazzmen*, 224.

CHAPTER 7   THE RECORD, THE SONG, AND THE RADIO

1   Evan Eisenberg, *The Recording Angel: Music, Records and Culture from Aristotle to Zappa* (New Haven, CT: Yale University Press, 2005); Mark Katz, *Capturing Sound: How Technology Has Changed Music* (Berkeley: University of California Press, 2004).

2   "The Music Mart: 2,000,000 Records of 'Whispering' Sold," *Talking Machine Journal*, Apr. 1923, 46.

3   Ibid.

4   Long works of prose fiction had previously appeared in Greek and Latin, but not for a millennium, nor did they bear much resemblance to the flood of novels that followed the successes of Samuel Richardson and Daniel Defoe.

5   Osgood, *So This Is Jazz*, 85.

6   "He Sings for the Phonographs," *Chicago Daily Tribune*, 8 Apr. 1895, 5. The numbers are surely exaggerated, since to make 250,000 records at the stated pace would require recording daily for almost five years.

7   Columbia began marketing two-sided 78- rpm records in 1908, and by the late 'teens they were the industry standard, though Edison continued to make cylinders through the 1920s.

8   Advertisement, *Chicago Defender*, 16 Dec. 1922, 7.

9   There was one earlier blues record with a black singer, a 1917 version of "St. Louis Blues" by Ciro's Club Coon Orchestra, but it was available only in Britain and is of no significance in this discussion.

10 http://history.sandiego.edu/gen/recording/images4/1894list-of-plates2.jpg (accessed 15 Mar. 2007).

11 Phil. A. Ravis, "Cultivate the Collecting Bug," *Talking Machine Journal*, June 1920, 22.

12 Advertisement, *The Chicago Defender*, 12 Dec. 1931, 2.

13 Paul Sann, *The Lawless Decade* (New York: Crown, 1957), 41; Sanjek, *American Popular Music*, 3:87.

14 Charles Merz, *Bigger and Better Murders: The Great American Bandwagon* (London: Victor Gollancz Ltd., 1928), 53–55.

15 Lombardo, *Auld Acquaintance*, 62.

16 Waring, *Fred Waring*, 124.

17 James P. Kraft, *Stage to Studio: Musicians and the Sound Revolution, 1890–1950* (Baltimore: Johns Hopkins University Press, 1996), 73.

18 Bergreen, *As Thousands Cheer*, 328.

CHAPTER 8   SONS OF WHITEMAN

The epigraph for this chapter is quoted from Gunther Schuller, *The Swing Era* (New York: Oxford University Press, 1989), 199.

1   Vincent Lopez, "Fox Trots and Jazz Bands," *Metronome*, Nov. 1924, 62.

2   Artie Shaw, *The Trouble with Cinderella* (New York: Farrar, Straus, and Young, 1952), 124–125.

3   Marvin Freedman, "Here's the Lowdown on Two Kinds of Women," *Down Beat*, 11 Feb. 1941, 9, quoted in Chris Robinson, "Seeing Through a Blindfold: Gender, Race and Jazz in Leonard Feather's Blindfold Tests" (master's thesis, University of Idaho, 2006), 52.

4   http://www.newcolumbiaswing.com/pdfs/ncstunelist.pdf (accessed 13 June 2007). Having seen many such quotations, I Googled "big bands" and "baseball," and this was the first that turned up.

5   "A New Era Dawns," *Metronome*, Mar. 1931, 12.

6   George Simon, "Dance Band Reviews," *Metronome*, Apr. 1935, 21.

7   Whitburn, *Pop Memories, 1890–1954* (Menomonee Falls, WI: Record Research, 1986). Whitburn's chart tabulations before the 1940s are suspect, but other sources suggest that this list is fairly representative.

8   Of Holly Moyer's band at the University of Colorado, pianist Moyer went into advertising, the drummer became a banker, the banjoist a stockbroker, and one sax player a furniture dealer. Sax player Jack Bunch worked as a Hollywood studio player, then a real estate agent. The trombonist was Glenn Miller. George T. Simon, *Glenn Miller and His Orchestra* (New York: Crowell, 1974), 31–32.

9   George Simon, "Dance Band Reviews," *Metronome*, Nov. 1935, 20.

10   Richard O. Boyer, "Me," *New Yorker*, 11 Mar. 1939, 26–27.

11   *New York Telegraph*, 20 Dec. 1930, quoted in Waring, *Fred Waring*, 100.

12   *Metronome*, Aug. 1937, quoted in George Simon, *Simon Says: The Sights and Sounds of the Swing Era 1935–1955* (New York: Galahad Books, 1971), 92.

13   Duke Ellington, "Situation between the Critics and Musicians Is Laughable," *Down Beat*, Apr. 1939, quoted in Mark Tucker, ed., *The Duke Ellington Reader* (New York: Oxford University Press, 1993), 136.

14   Josephy and McBride, *New York*, 16.

15   Edward Kennedy Ellington, *Music Is My Mistress* (New York: Doubleday, 1973), 80.

16   Gunther Schuller, *Early Jazz: Its Roots and Musical Development* (New York: Oxford University Press, 1968), 340.

17   Marshall W. Stearns, *The Story of Jazz* (New York: Oxford University Press, 1957), 183–184.

18   Abel Green, *Variety*, 7 Dec. 1927, quoted in Tucker, *Duke Ellington Reader*, 31–33. For comparison: "Bands in night clubs have to play a pretty stereotyped kind of music for a pretty stereotyped kind of crowd, leaving all the flash and frills to the little lassies" (George Simon, "Dance Band Reviews," *Metronome*, Aug. 1935, 15).

19   *Check and Double Check* (RKO Radio Pictures, 1930). Ellington and the Rhythm Boys recorded "Three Little Words," but in the film the Ellingtonians mime to a studio orchestra.

20   Waring, *Fred Waring*, 109.

21   "First Prom Girl for Annual Ball Still a Mystery," *The Tech*, 20 Feb. 1929, 1; "Orchestra Lead [*sic*] by Leo Reisman Is Prom Feature," *The Tech*, 21 Feb. 1929, 1.

22   Miley's plunger mute provided the "jungle" sound, and he composed the themes of "East St. Louis Toodle-oo" and "Black and Tan Fantasy."

23   *Rhythms* (Vitaphone film short, June 1929). Some experts doubt that Miley appears in this movie, but if it were a white imitator, there is no reason that only those segments would be in silhouette.

24   "Cuban Invasion," *Time*, 23 Feb. 1931, at http://www.time.com/time/magazine/article/ 0,9171,930373,00.html (accessed 15 June 2007).

25   Gill Blue, "Will Spanish Music Be The Next Craze?" *Metronome*, Jan. 1933, 24.

26   Benny Goodman and Irving Kolodin, *The Kingdom of Swing* (New York: Stackpole Sons, 1939), 249.

27   I am indebted to Dan Morgenstern for the Ellington example.

28   Sudhalter, *Lost Chords*, 303–305; Kirk, *Twenty Years on Wheels*, 73–74.

29   Simon, *Simon Says*, 364.

30 "Harry Varley: The Fascinating Career of Rudall Carte's Chief Salesman," http://www
.jazzprofessional.com/profiles/Harry%20Varley.htm (accessed 17 June 2007).

31 *Amsterdam News*, 5 Oct. 1932, 8, in Walter C. Allen, *Hendersonia: The Music of Fletcher
Henderson and His Musicians* (Highland Park, NJ: Walter C. Allen, 1974), 277, reports that
Lombardo's record was broken by a triple bill of the Calloway, Webb, and Henderson bands.

32 The collector was Russell Sanjek. Ronald G. Welburn, "American Jazz Criticism 1914–1940"
(PhD diss., New York University, 1983), 248.

33 Bob Crease and Helen Clarke, "New York Swing Dance Society Remembers," http://www
.savoyballroom.com/exp/notforgotten/nysds.htm (accessed 6 Jan. 2006); George Simon,
Metronome, Feb. 1942, in George T. Simon, *The Big Bands* (New York: Schirmer, 1981), 321.

CHAPTER 9   SWING THAT MUSIC

The epigraph for this chapter is quoted from Gordon Jenkins, "I Give You Ish Jones,"
Metronome, Sept. 1937, 27.

1   Rose C. Feld, "Tinkling Joy Returns to Tin Pan Alley," *New York Times Magazine*, 18 Dec.
1934, 11.

2   Louis Armstrong, *Swing That Music* (New York: Longmans, Green, 1936), 105–106.

3   Eddie Condon, *We Called It Music: A Generation of Jazz* (New York: Da Capo Press, 1992), 192.

4   Shaw, *Trouble with Cinderella*, 183, 204, 199, 259, 228.

5   Morroe Berger, Edward Berger, and James Patrick, *Benny Carter: A Life in American Music*
(Lanham, MD: Scarecrow Press, 2002), 45–46.

6   Buster Bailey, quoted in Nat Shapiro and Nat Hentoff, *Hear Me Talkin' to Ya: The Story of Jazz
as Told by the Men Who Made It* (New York: Dover, 1966), 331–332.

7   Goodman and Kolodin, *Kingdom of Swing*, 112.

8   Schuller, *Swing Era*, 8.

9   Goodman and Kolodin, *Kingdom of Swing*, 135.

10 Ibid., 143.

11 Murray (a.k.a. Murray Kellner) had been a studio regular since the early 1920s.

12 Jeffrey Magee, *Uncrowned King of Swing: Fletcher Henderson and Big Band Jazz* (New York:
Oxford University Press, 2005), 131–135, 207–212.

13 Goodman and Kolodin, *Kingdom of Swing*, 193–196.

14 Ibid., 199. It is often reported that the Palomar audience was ready for Goodman because
Let's Dance was heard three hours earlier in California, and thus Goodman's closing set was
broadcast in prime time there. In fact, the three bands rotated in half-hour segments for five
hours, with the first three hours being broadcast in the east and central zones, the second
three in the mountain zone, and the last three in the west, so everybody heard it at a similar
time.

15 Ibid., 204.

16 Carl Cons, "Society and Musicians Sit Spellbound by Brilliance of Goodman Band," *Down
Beat*, Dec. 1935–Jan. 1936, quoted in Lewis A. Erenberg, *Swingin' the Dream: Big Band Jazz and
the Rebirth of American Culture* (Chicago: University of Chicago Press, 1998), 91.

17 *Metronome*, May 1936, 15; *Metronome*, Aug. 1940, 15. In 1936 Goodman had 3,384 votes to Casa
Loma's 1,981, Dorsey's 666, Lunceford's 608, and Ellington's 307. In 1940 Goodman, Miller,

Tommy Dorsey, Krupa, and Bob Crosby led, with Basie at 9. In 1943 three black bands made the top ten, but with less than a quarter as many voters.

18   Erenberg, *Swingin' the Dream*, 45.

19   "1,500 Storm Theatre to Receive Goodman," *New York Times*, 27 Jan. 1938, 17; Frank S. Nugent, "Mae West in Her Newest Effort at the Paramount," *New York Times*, 27 Jan. 1938, 17; Frank S. Nugent, "Vendetta or a Clarinetist's Revenge," *New York Times*, 30 Jan. 1938, Drama section, 5.

20   Ross Firestone, *Swing, Swing, Swing: The Life and Times of Benny Goodman* (New York: Norton, 1993), 96; Goodman and Kolodin, *Kingdom of Swing*, 143.

21   Whitburn, *Pop Memories*, 640.

22   David W. Stowe, *Swing Changes: Big-Band Jazz in New Deal America* (Cambridge, MA: Harvard University Press, 1994), 231–232.

23   Condon, *We Called It Music*, 270.

24   Kerry Segrave, *Jukeboxes: An American Social History* (Jefferson, NC: McFarland, 2002), 126.

25   In 1939 Victor cited "That Dixieland Band" and "Don't Be That Way" as Goodman's most popular records; "One Record Can Push a Band Into 'Big Money,'" *Down Beat*, 15 Aug. 1939, 4.

26   "Waltz-Me-Willies Weep," *Billboard*, 2 July 1938, 11.

27   Firestone, *Swing, Swing, Swing*, 150.

28   David M. Faulkner and Farnsworth Elliot, "Swing's for Listeners—Not for Dancers!" *Metronome*, October 1939, 19.

29   "Waltz-Me-Willies Weep," *Billboard*, 2 July 1938, 11.

30   "Mid West Ballrooms Ban Jitterbugs," *Metronome*, Dec. 1938, 29; "Ban on Screwy Steps Betters Dansant Biz," *Billboard*, 31 Dec. 1938, 63.

31   Lawrence Welk, *Wunnerful, Wunnerful!* (Englewood Cliffs, NJ: Prentice-Hall, 1971), 218–219.

32   George Frazier, "Stupid Critics Misjudge 3,000 Ickies' Action," *Down Beat*, June 1938, quoted in Erenberg, *Swingin' the Dream*, 58.

33   Kay and Sue Werner, "Rock It for Me." This song tied with "Stompin' at the Savoy" for third place in a 1941 poll of bandleaders for "Best Rhythm Song of All Time," after "I Got Rhythm" and "Honeysuckle Rose"; *Billboard*, 12 Apr. 1941, 17.

34   "Irene Castle Devises New Dancing Steps," *New York Times*, 3 Aug. 1939.

CHAPTER 10   TECHNOLOGY AND ITS DISCONTENTS

The epigraph for this chapter is quoted from "Musicians to End Making of Records," *New York Times*, 9 July 1942, 1, 8.

1   "Kids Cheer Monroe Act; Brown's Too" *Metronome*, July 1941, 18.

2   Stanley Dance, *The World of Swing* (New York: Da Capo Press, 2001), 131.

3   Peter J. Levinson, *Tommy Dorsey: Livin' in a Great Big Way* (New York: Da Capo Press, 2005), 186.

4   Segrave, *Jukeboxes*, 48, 110.

5   Ibid., 37.

6   Ibid., 48.

7   Vern Countryman, "The Organized Musicians: II," *University of Chicago Law Review* 16, no. 2 (Winter 1949), 254.

8   The negative view of the AFM strike, as well as the union's poor record on integration, is
    explored in Donald Clarke, *The Rise and Fall of Popular Music* (New York: St. Martin's Griffin,
    1996), 257–260.

9   Countryman, "The Organized Musicians: II," 239–240, fn.; Erenberg, *Swingin'
    the Dream*, 12.

10 "Saving the Music Publisher," *Metronome*, May 1932, 10.

11 Jack Gould, "Radio Music Dispute Raises Complex Issues," *New York Times*, 9 Feb. 1941; Alva
    Johnston, "Czar of Song," *New Yorker*, 24 Dec. 1932, 19.

12 "Networks Ban All Ad Libbing," *Metronome*, Jan. 1941, 7.

13 Sanjek, *American Popular Music*, 3:181–182.

14 Kraft, *Stage to Studio*, 63.

15 Ibid., 66–67, 126; Sanjek, *American Popular Music*, 3:128, 169.

16 Kraft, *Stage to Studio*, 127.

17 Ibid., 135.

18 Ibid., 146.

19 Countryman, "The Organized Musicians: II," 250–251.

20 William Howland Kenney, *Recorded Music in American Life: The Phonograph and Popular
    Memory, 1890–1945* (New York: Oxford University Press, 1999), 167.

21 Kraft, *Stage to Studio*, 78.

22 Elliott Grennard, "Bands Down to Bedrock," *Billboard*, 2 Jan. 1943, 47.

23 Levinson, *Tommy Dorsey*, 152; Leo Walker, *The Wonderful Era of the Great Dance Bands* (Garden
    City, NY: Doubleday, 1972), 97, 101; Simon, *Big Bands*, 257.

24 Whitburn, *Pop Memories*, 655.

25 This fund has been diminishing in recent years and may soon disappear, but at its peak in the
    early 1980s it annually received over $20 million and sponsored up to 55,000 concerts; Mike
    Boehm, "Hitting a Sound Barrier," *Los Angeles Times*, 14 June 2008, E1, E14.

CHAPTER 11   WALKING FLOORS AND JUMPIN' JIVE

The epigraph for this chapter is quoted from Wade Hall, *Hell-Bent for Music: The Life of Pee Wee
King* (Lexington: University Press of Kentucky, 1996), 2.

1   Bill C. Malone, *Country Music U.S.A.* (Austin: University of Texas Press, 1975), 200; John
    R. Williams, *This Was "Your Hit Parade"* (Rockland, ME: Courier-Gazette, 1973), 54.

2   Jeffrey J. Lange, *Smile When You Call Me a Hillbilly: Country Music's Struggle for Respectability,
    1939–1954* (Athens: University of Georgia Press, 2004), 43; Nat Green, "Fantastic Grosses
    with Folkshows," *Billboard 1944 Music Yearbook* (Cincinnati: Billboard, 1944), 344–345.

3   Joel Whitburn, *The Billboard Book of Top 40 Country Hits* (New York: Billboard Books, 1996),
    512–513.

4   Don Ryan, "Hillbilly Music," *Los Angeles Times*, 3 Mar. 1940, H9. During the mid-1940s the
    Billboard folk chart measured only jukebox play and listed at most eight records a week, so it
    provides only a limited guide to what was selling in this period, but I have no reason to think
    it exaggerates the accordion's prominence.

5   Bill C. Malone, *Singing Cowboys and Musical Mountaineers: Southern Culture and the Roots of
    Country Music* (Athens: University of Georgia Press, 1993).

6   Holly George-Warren, *Public Cowboy No. 1: The Life and Times of Gene Autry* (New York: Oxford University Press, 2007), 37. Autry's given name was Orvon.

7   Jean Ann Boyd, *The Jazz of the Southwest: An Oral History of Western Swing* (Austin: University of Texas Press, 1998), 25.

8   Drew Page, *Drew's Blues: A Sideman's Life with the Big Bands* (Baton Rouge: Louisiana State University Press, 1980), 7.

9   "Coast Orks Go 'Billy," *Billboard*, 29 May 1943, 25.

10   "The Jitterbug's Lexicon," *New York Times Magazine*, 14 Aug. 1938, 101.

11   *Jubilee*, show number 65, broadcast 7 Feb. 1944.

12   Dominic J. Capeci Jr., "Walter F. White and the Savoy Ballroom Controversy of 1943," *Afro-Americans in New York Life and History* 5, no. 2 (31 July 1981).

13   John Chilton, *Let the Good Times Roll: The Story of Louis Jordan and His Music* (Ann Arbor: University of Michigan Press, 1994), 101.

14   "Lunceford Hands Trianon Notice," *Billboard*, 3 July 1943.

15   Paul Denis, "The Negro Makes Advances," *Billboard*, 2 Jan. 1943, 28.

16   James Brown, *Showtime*, Smash MGS 27054, 1964, includes three Jordan covers.

17   Chilton, *Let the Good Times Roll*, 140.

18   Arnold Shaw, *Honkers and Shouters* (New York: Collier Books, 1978), 66.

19   Chilton, *Let the Good Times Roll*, 136.

CHAPTER 12   SELLING THE AMERICAN BALLAD

The epigraph for this chapter is quoted from David Simons, *Studio Stories* (San Francisco: Backbeat Books, 2004), 34.

1   Kenneth T. Jackson, *Crabgrass Frontier: The Suburbanization of the United States* (New York: Oxford University Press, 1985), 241.

2   "Shaky National Conditions Catch Up with Band Biz," *Billboard*, 2 Nov. 1946, 15.

3   "Hats Off (and On) to Sweet," *Metronome*, Apr. 1948, 18.

4   *Metronome*, Feb. 1943, 7.

5   "Phono Music Survey Proves Public Wants Variety Fare," *Billboard*, 28 Dec. 1940, 132.

6   John Lahr, "Sinatra's Song," http://www.johnlahr.com/sinatraprofile.html (accessed 29 July 2007).

7   Donald Clarke, *All or Nothing at All: A Life of Frank Sinatra* (New York: Fromm International, 1997), 67; Will Friedwald, *Sinatra! The Song Is You* (New York: Scribner, 1995) 123. Friedwald gives Goodman's expletive as "hell," but Clarke's version is supported by Firestone.

8   Martha Weinman Lear, "The Bobby Sox Have Wilted, But the Memory Remains Fresh," *New York Times*, sec. AL, 13 Oct. 1974, 1, 12.

9   Diana Gibbings, "Regarding Mr. Haymes," *New York Times*, 12 Aug. 1945.

10   *Command Performance*, program #165, 8 Mar. 1945.

11   "Found: Male with Some Kind Words for Frank Sinatra," *Billboard*, 12 Feb. 1944, 66.

12   " Billboard First Annual Music-Record Poll," *Billboard*, 4 Jan. 1947, 10–16, 54; "Billboard 3d Annual Music-Record Poll," *Billboard*, 1 Jan. 1949, 11, 19; "The Year's Top Male Vocalists on the

Nation's Juke Boxes," *Billboard Juke Box Supplement*, 22 Jan. 1949. Seven hundred is the lowest estimate I find for Sinatra's fan clubs; two thousand is the highest.

13 "Patti Page," *Metronome*, Apr. 1948, 49.

14 Dorothy O'Leary, "Regarding Miss Jo Stafford," *New York Times*, sec. 10, 7 Nov. 1948, 11.

15 *Your Ballad Man* playlists, Library of Congress, American Folklife Center, Alan Lomax Collection, AFC 2004/004.

16 Lomax apparently disliked the orchestral settings and used them only under pressure from CBS, eventually limiting the orchestral portion to six minutes of his half hour show (Matthew Barton, personal communication).

17 "Change That Band Plattertude," *Billboard*, 15 Feb. 1947, 14, 31.

18 Hal Webman, "Gold in Them Hillbills!" *Billboard*, 27 Dec. 1947, 1, 18.

19 Ronnie Pugh, *Ernest Tubb: The Texas Troubador* (Durham, NC: Duke University Press, 1996), 124, 133.

20 "Many Trends Combined to Give Folk Music a Wider Audience," *Billboard*, 27 Feb. 1943, 93–94.

21 Frankie Laine and Joseph F. Laredo, *That Lucky Old Son: The Autobiography of Frankie Laine* (Ventura, CA: Pathfinder Publishing of California, 1993), 95, 98.

22 Colin Escott, *Roadkill on the Three-chord Highway: Art and Trash in American Popular Music* (New York: Routledge, 2002), 64. Jerry Wexler suggested to Page and her producer, Jack Rael, that they cover the Hawkins disc.

23 Friedwald, *Sinatra!* 187–188.

24 Tony Bennett, *The Good Life* (New York: Pocket Books, 1998), 110–111.

25 Rosemary Clooney, *Girl Singer* (New York: Doubleday, 1999), 74.

26 "How the Money Rolls In," *Time*, 20 Aug. 1951, http://www.time.com/time/magazine/article/0,9171,859303,00.html (accessed 24 Jan. 2008).

27 Mitch Miller, "Mitch, The Bearded Hit-Maker Slaps Musical Snobbishness," *Down Beat*, 16 July 1952, 2.

28 Jonny Whiteside, *Cry: The Johnnie Ray Story* (New York: Barricade Books, 1994), 141; Ted Fox, *In the Groove: The People behind the Music* (New York: St. Martin's Press, 1986), 34.

29 "How the Money Rolls In."

30 "Ban on Novachord Spikes Grofé Job," *Billboard*, 8 Apr. 1939, 23. The article adds that "at last year's AFM meeting a resolution against the Hammond electric organ was proposed."

31 Fox, *In the Groove*, 41–42; Eric Olsen, Paul Verna, and Carlo Wolff, *Encyclopedia of Record Producers* (New York: Billboard Books, 1999), 538.

32 Robert Rice, "The Fractured Oboist," *New Yorker*, 6 June 1953, 62.

33 Bennett, *Good Life*, 112, 127.

34 Whiteside, *Cry*, 78.

35 Ibid., 85.

36 Clooney, *Girl Singer*, 61.

37 *Saturday Evening Post*, 26 July 1952, quoted in Whiteside, *Cry*, 133.

38 Whiteside, *Cry*, 102.

39 Friedwald, *Sinatra*, 24–25.

40 Dimitri Tiomkin and Prosper Buranelli, *Please Don't Hate Me* (Garden City, NY: Doubleday, 1959), 146. He wrote that the prairie "aroused a special feeling in me.... A Russian gazes at the Great Plains with a sense of familiarity."

CHAPTER 13   ROCK THE JOINT

The epigraph for this chapter is quoted from Cecil Smith, "Atomic Age Jazz Vies with Original Radio Crooner on TV Tonight," *Los Angeles Times*, 30 June 1954, 22.

1   ABC signed Whiteman as the first nationwide deejay, but Mutual beat them by two weeks with Martin Block; "King of Jazz Jockeys," *Newsweek*, 14 July 1947, 52.

2   Harry Crafton, Don Keane, and Hank (Doc) Bagby, "Rock the Joint," currently published by Andrea Music (SESAC).

3   Clark hosted *The WOLF Buckaroos* in Syracuse and *Cactus Dick and the Santa Fe Riders* in Utica; John A. Jackson, *American Bandstand: Dick Clark and the Making of a Rock 'n' Roll Empire* (New York: Oxford University Press, 1997), 5–6.

4   All quotes from Charlie Gracie are from author's interview, 5 Jan. 2008.

5   John Swenson, *Bill Haley: The Daddy of Rock and Roll* (New York: Stein and Day, 1983), 28. Swenson is my principal source for Haley's biography throughout.

6   Swenson, *Bill Haley*, 37. The R&B bands were Jimmy Preston and his Prestonians and Chris Powell's Five Blue Flames.

7   Bob Rolontz, "Rhythm & Blues," *Billboard 1952 Juke Box Special*, 15 Mar. 1952, 82.

8   Lionel Hampton, "The Public Is Square—But It Rocks," *Metronome*, October 1942, 8.

9   Ralph Cedrone, who played the guitar solo on both "Rock this Joint" and "Rock Around the Clock"—the recordings were made two years apart, but he repeated the same solo on both—was also a swing musician, though without major orchestra credits, and the drummer on Haley's hit version of "Shake, Rattle and Roll" was the black Savoy regular Panama Francis.

10   Shaw, *Honkers and Shouters*, 64.

11   *Camel Rock and Roll Party*, Armed Forces Radio and Television Service broadcast, 1956.

12   Edith Evans Asbury, "Rock 'n' Roll Teen-Agers Tie Up the Times Square Area," *New York Times*, 23 Feb. 1957, 1.

13   *New York Post*, 24 Oct. 1958, quoted in David Ake, *Jazz Culture* (Berkeley: University of California Press, 2002), 54.

14   Arnold Shaw, *The Rockin' '50s* (New York: Hawthorn Books, 1974), 155.

15   The first mention I find of this word, as 'Rockbilly,' is in Phyllis Battelle, "New Music 'Too Bad to Continue Indefinitely,' Says Disc Executive," *Miami Herald*, 20 June 1956, 4-C, who credits it to a Denver deejay, Ray Perkins.

16   Anita Behrman, "What Alan Freed Really Thinks about Rock 'n' roll," *People*, October 1958, 22; Theodore Irwin, "Rock 'n Roll 'n Alan Freed," *Pageant*, July 1957, 62.

17   Charles Gruenberg, "The Rock and Roll Story: Alan Freed," *New York Post*, 5 Oct. 1956, 64. This comment may confuse some modern fans, since Freed played jazz as well as what we now call R&B, but all of that music was listed on the R&B charts.

18   "The Year R.&B. Took Over Pop Field," *Billboard*, 12 Nov. 1955, 126.

19   Mitch Miller, "June, Moon, Swoon, and Ko Ko Mo," *New York Times Magazine*, 24 Apr. 1955, 78.

20   *Alan Freed Presents the Big Beat*, concert program, ca. 1958, 1, http://www.alanfreed.com/archives/Live_Stage_Shows/Programs/1501%20Big%20Beat%20Program%202.pdf (accessed 14 Feb. 2008).

21   Dick Gregory, *From the Back of the Bus* (New York: Avon Books, 1962), 64.

22   Erik Barnouw, *Tube of Plenty: The Evolution of American Television* (New York: Oxford University Press, 1975), 112–113. As of 1952, there were 108 TV stations in the United States,

all network affiliates; by 1954 there were 354, 90 percent of them network affiliates; in 1960 there were 515, 96 percent of them network affiliates. Christopher H. Sterling and Timothy R. Haight, *The Mass Media: Aspen Institute Guide to Communication Industry Trends* (New York: Praeger, 1978), 181.

23 June Bundy, "TV: The New Home for Disk Jockeys," *Billboard Special Disc Jockey Supplement*, 7 Oct. 1950, 70.

24 Joe Smith, *Off the Record: An Oral History of Popular Music* (New York: Warner Books, 1988), 108.

25 The Platters appeared on *The Ed Sullivan Show* of August 12, 1956, http://www.tv.com/the-ed-sullivan-show/a-tribute-to-the-yankees—phil-silvers—teresa-brewer/episode/126009/summary.html?tag=ep_list;title;46; Tommy "Dr. Jive" Smalls hosted his segment on November 20, 1955 (Marv Goldberg, "Lavern Baker," http://home.att.net/~marvy42/Lavern/lavern.html).

26 Daniel Mark Epstein, *Nat King Cole* (New York: Farrar, Straus and Giroux, 1999), 276.

27 The role of television in broadening radio markets is noted in Steve Chapple and Reebee Garofalo, *Rock 'n' Roll Is Here to Pay: The History and Politics of the Music Industry* (Chicago: Nelson-Hall, 1977), 30. As for the effect on musicians: In 1946, 292 radio stations employed 2,433 staff musicians; in 1956, 120 stations employed 1,011; in 1957, 98 stations employed 576. In the same period, the money spent by the stations on musical guests dropped from $8 million in 1946 to $2.6 million in 1955, to $850,000 in 1956, and to $453,000 in 1957. Kraft, *Stage to Studio*, 198–199.

28 Interview with author, 6 Oct. 1997.

29 "Honor Roll of Hits," *Billboard*, 5 Jan. 1952, 14.

30 "'Davy' Is Shooting Down Disk Marks Like Clay Pigeons," *Billboard*, 4 June 1955, 1.

31 "Compulsory Sheet Music in Top Spot," *Billboard*, 29 Oct. 1955, 12.

32 "R&B Tunes' Boom Relegates Pop Field to Cover Activity," *Billboard*, 26 Mar. 1955, 18; "Honor Roll of Hits," *Billboard*, 19 Mar. 1955, 30.

33 Quoted in Smith, *Off the Record*, 137.

34 Marv Goldberg, "Lavern Baker," http://home.att.net/~marvy42/Lavern/lavern.html (accessed 9 Feb. 2008). Goldberg writes that Mercury also used the same musicians, but in personal communication he expressed some doubt about this.

35 "Lavern Baker Seeks Bill to Halt Arrangement 'Thefts,'" *Billboard*, 5 Mar. 1955, 13.

36 "WINS Issues Ban on Copy Records," *Billboard*, 27 Aug. 1955, 21.

37 Gary Kramer, "With More to Spend, Public in '56 Really Turns Fickle," *Billboard*, 22 Dec. 1956, 22.

38 Chuck Berry's "Maybellene" made number five on the sales chart, number thirteen on the jockey chart; Jerry Lee Lewis's "Great Balls of Fire" made number two on sales, number nine on jockey. By contrast, Sinatra's "The Tender Trap" made number seven on jockey and number twenty-four on sales. Pat Boone's and Elvis Presley's singles tended to behave more like Berry's and Lewis's than like Sinatra's, though the gaps were less extreme.

39 "Victor Quits 'Coverage': Pop Policy to Stress Originals & Exclusives," *Billboard*, 2 Apr. 1955, 16.

40 "Boundaries between Music Types Fall; Deejays Spin 'Em All," *Billboard*, 12 Nov. 1955, 34, 36.

41 "Bestselling Jo," *Time*, 20 Oct. 1952, http://www.time.com/time/magazine/article/0,9171,817126,00.html (accessed 20 Jan. 2008).

42　Ruth Cage, "Rhythm & Blue Notes [*sic*]," *Down Beat*, 6 Oct. 1954, 7.

43　Dwight MacDonald, "A Caste, A Culture, A Market—II," *New Yorker*, 29 Nov. 1958, 91, 97.

44　Ibid., 97.

45　Joel Whitburn, *Top R&B Singles, 1942–1995* (Menomonee Falls, WI: Record Research, 1996), 671; "Chart Toppers of 1958," *Billboard*, 15 Dec. 1958, 44.

46　Brian Ward, *Just My Soul Responding: Rhythm and Blues, Black Consciousness, and Race Relations* (Berkeley: University of California Press, 1998), 140; Michael T. Bertrand, *Race, Rock and Elvis* (Urbana: University of Illinois Press, 2000), 200.

47　"C&W Artists Play Hob with R&B Charts," *Billboard*, 6 Jan. 1958, 16, 25. B. B. King had nine top twenty R&B hits from 1955 through 1957, and Ray Charles had eleven, but both dropped off the chart for a year or more before the retabulation in fall 1958.

48　Sam Chase, "Charts Link New Clarity with Depth," *Billboard*, 20 Oct. 1958, 3, 34.

49　"Hot 100 of the Year" and "Hot C&W and R&B Sides of the Year," *Billboard*, 14 Dec. 1959, 78–80. The twelve records by black artists included "16 Candles" by the Crests, a mixed group; the full "Hot 100" included twenty-seven records by black artists; and two records by Latino artists, Santo and Johnny's "Sleepwalk" and Dave "Baby" Cortez's "Happy Organ," were also in the top fifty on both the pop and the R&B lists

50　Poll conducted by Eugene Gilbert's Teen-Age Survey, Inc., reported in "Kids Dig Pop Vocal Most but Don't Always Buy Them," *Billboard*, 15 Dec. 1956, 29, 31. The article gives Teresa Brewer as favorite female vocalist among college boys but does not say which females were favored by high school boys or college girls. The survey also asked what proportion actually bought records by their favorites, and Harry Belafonte came out as the best-selling male in three of the four categories—again, which three are unspecified, but presumably all but the high school boys.

CHAPTER 14　BIG RECORDS FOR ADULTS

The first epigraph for this chapter is quoted from the named Sarah Vaughan hit, words and music by Bob Merrill, Mercury Records 70469, 1955. The second epigraph is quoted from "Wild about Harry," *Time*, 1 July 1957, http://www.time.com/time/magazine/article/0,9171,809616,00.html.

1　All quotes from "Rise of the Music Room," *Time*, 27 May 1957, http://www.time.com/time/magazine/article/0,9171,824885,00.html.

2　Toll, *Entertainment Machine*, 72, Chapple and Garofalo, *Rock 'n' Roll*, 44.

3　Clarke, *All or Nothing at All*, 79, with details added from personal correspondence with Clarke.

4　"Record Album Business on the Upbeat; Decca Most Prolific; Victor Apathetic to Packaging," *Billboard*, 15 Mar. 1941, 13.

5　"More Releases and Records; Albums Cut Juke Supply," *Billboard*, 29 Apr. 1944, 66.

6　"Ten Years of Long-Play Favorites," *Billboard*, 25 May 1959, 13, 45; Joel Whitburn, *Top Pop Albums, 1955–1996* (Menomonee Falls, WI: Record Research, 1996), 1037. I don't count Doris Day's *Love Me or Leave Me* and Elvis Presley's *Blue Hawaii* as soundtracks, because they presumably sold as Day and Elvis discs. Album sales grew dramatically through the 1950s, so although *Music for Lovers* was the best seller for two years, it claimed sales of only a half million copies. Pink Floyd's 1973 *Dark Side of the Moon* eventually beat both Mathis and *My Fair Lady* for longevity honors, but not until the 1980s.

7   "Sober—Within Reason," *Time*, 22 Feb. 1954, http://www.time.com/time/magazine/article/0,9171,860499,00.html.

8   *Ritual of the Savage*, Capitol T288, 1951, liner notes.

9   Keir Keightley, "'Turn It Down!' She Shrieked: Gender, Domestic Space, and High Fidelity, 1948–59," *Popular Music*, 15 May 1996, 152.

10 Ibid., 168.

11 Bob Rolontz, "Wives Sing Stereo Living Room Blues," *Billboard*, 11 May 1959, 1.

12 Shaw, *Rockin' '50s*, 26.

13 "Sinatra's Pioneering Thoughts on LP Pop Tune Production," *Billboard*, 31 Dec. 1949, 13.

14 Bob Rolontz, "Pop, C&W, R&B Indies Lean Three Ways on Price Change," *Billboard*, 8 Jan. 1955, 12.

15 Leslie Gourse, *Sassy: The Life of Sarah Vaughan* (New York: Charles Scribner's Sons, 1993), 60.

16 Ibid., 76.

17 For example, Keir Keightley, "You Keep Coming Back like a Song," *Journal of Popular Music Studies* 13 (2001): 12–13.

18 "The Man on Cloud No. 7," *Time*, 8 Nov. 1954, http://www.time.com/time/magazine/article/0,9171,857657,00.html.

19 Ibid.

20 "Supper Clubs," *New Yorker*, 27 Oct. 1951, 8.

21 George R. White, *Living Legend: Bo Diddley*, quoted in Ned Sublette, "The Kingsmen and the Cha-Cha-Chá," in Eric Weisbard, *Listen Again: A Momentary History of Pop Music* (Durham, NC: Duke University Press, 2008), 83.

22 Elijah Wald, *Josh White: Society Blues* (Amherst: University of Massachusetts Press, 2000), 113.

23 Howard Taubman, "A Folk Singer's Style," *New York Times*, 7 Feb. 1954, X7.

24 "Music: Stadium Record," *New York Times*, 29 June 1956, 17.

25 Phyllis Lee Levin, "Girls Shun 'Teen' Label, Store's Survey Discovers," *New York Times*, 10 May 1957, Family section, 40.

26 Arnold Shaw, *Belafonte: An Unauthorized Biography* (Philadelphia: Chilton, 1960), 236.

27 Emily Coleman, "Organization Man Named Belafonte," *New York Times*, 13 Dec. 1959, 35.

28 Clarke, *All or Nothing at All*, 158; Shaw, *Belafonte*, 303.

29 Coleman, "Organization Man," 42.

30 Two early readers of this manuscript report that they owned four of those five records, proving the power of Top 40 radio to have been even stronger in this period than I had understood.

31 The *Billboard Market Data Report*, 1962, lists consumer sales for 1961 of 173 million LPs and 132 million singles. An additional 50 million singles were sold to juke box companies, but LPs still accounted for 75 percent of overall dollar sales, jukes included.

CHAPTER 15   TEEN IDYLL

The epigraph for this chapter is quoted from Peter Guralnick, *Last Train to Memphis: The Rise of Elvis Presley* (Boston: Little, Brown, 1994), 289.

1   "Kids Dig Pop Vocal Most But Don't Always Buy Them," *Billboard*, 15 Dec. 1956, 29, 31; James S. Coleman, *The Adolescent Society* (New York: Free Press of Glencoe, 1961), 23; "Top Pop Poll," *'Teen Magazine*, May 1958, 16, 17.

2   Letter from Texas Novelty Co., *Billboard*, 4 Mar. 1939, 71.

3   An early if not definitive example would be Cliff Jackson and his Crazy Cats, formed in 1927; a more typical one is "Hep Cat's Ball," recorded by Louis Armstrong in 1940. Etymologists differ as to the word's origin, some scholars tracing it to the Wolof term *hipikat* and others preferring feline sources.

4   Interview with author, June 1996.

5   *Billboard*, 26 Jan. 1957, 60, 64, 70. Carl Perkins also had one trifecta and one country record in the year's top fifty.

6   Paul Ackerman, "What Has Happened to Popular Music," *High Fidelity*, June 1958, 37.

7   Bernie Asbell, "R&R Fading But Imprint Permanent," *Billboard*, 18 May 1959, 4, 21.

8   Coleman, *Adolescent Society*, 23; based on questionnaires from more than 8,000 students at ten high schools in Northern Illinois.

9   David Ritz, *Divided Soul: The Life of Marvin Gaye* (Cambridge, MA: Da Capo Press, 1991), 30. Gaye's first album was of standards, and Berry Gordy wrote that he wanted to be "a crooner like Frank Sinatra" and had to be forced to sing R&B; Berry Gordy, *To Be Loved: The Music, the Memories of Motown* (New York: Warner Books, 1994), 159.

10   Guralnick, *Last Train to Memphis*, 329–330.

11   Thomas Doherty, *Teenagers and Teenpics: The Juvenilization of American Movies in the 1950s* (Philadelphia: Temple University Press, 2002), 168.

12   "1957's Top Popular Albums: Best Sellers in Stores," *Billboard*, 23 Dec. 1957, 23. The Platters' first LP was also listed, but it consisted largely of standards and presumably made the album list because it appealed to the Mathis/Cole audience as well as to the teens who bought their singles.

13   Karen Schoemer, *Great Pretenders: My Strange Love Affair with '50s Pop Music* (New York: Free Press, 2006), 151.

14   Peter J. Levinson, *Trumpet Blues: The Life of Harry James* (New York: Oxford University Press, 1999), 190–191.

15   Roger Pryor Dodge, "Throwback," *The Jazz Review*, May 1959, in Dodge, *Hot Jazz and Jazz Dance*, 275–277; Rudi Blesh, *Shining Trumpets* (New York: Knopf, 1958), 352. Similarly, Hughes Panassié called Ray Charles "the greatest jazz singer since Louis Armstrong . . . [whose success] contributed more than anything else to show the inanity of progressivist theories"; Hughes Panassié, *La Bataille du Jazz* (N.p.: Albin Michel, 1965), 139, my translation.

16   Laine and Laredo, *That Lucky Old Son*, 82.

17   Josh Alan Friedman, "Tell the Truth Until They Bleed," http://www.wfmu.org/LCD/23/docpomus.html (accessed 5 Mar. 2008).

18   "A Very Young Man with a Horn—Frankie Avalon," *Down Beat*, 19 May 1954, 3.

19   Jackson, *American Bandstand*, 62–63.

20   Connie Francis, *Who's Sorry Now?* (New York: St. Martin's Press, 1984), 103.

21   "1956's Top Popular Records: Best Sellers in Stores," *Billboard*, 26 Jan. 1957, 60; "Chart Toppers of 1958: Popular," *Billboard*, 15 Dec. 1958, 44.

22　Schoemer, *Great Pretenders*, 191. Francis was a normal-looking teenager, but in her first movie, *Where the Boys Are*, she is portrayed as so unappealing that she cannot get a date until one of the male characters breaks his glasses. And a nineteen-year-old singer in a group called the Poni Tails said, "I'd go out and buy a boy's record any day before I'd buy a girl's. ... Girls are the ones who buy most of the single records. I think there is probably some kind of a jealousy angle connected with it when they buy a girl's record"; Ren Grevatt, "On the Beat," *Billboard*, 20 Oct. 1958, 7.

23　Bruce Pollock, *When Rock Was Young* (New York: Holt, Rinehart and Winston, 1981), 161.

24　Paul Ackerman and June Bundy, "20-Year Shift in Music Patterns," *Billboard*, 2 Nov. 1959, 1, 6. Numbers are for the first nine months of each year, based on *Your Hit Parade* for 1939 and *Billboard*'s "Honor Roll of Hits" for 1959.

25　"Teen-ager Rocks Teen-agers," *Life*, 1 Dec. 1958, 123.

26　Joel Selvin, *Ricky Nelson: Idol for a Generation* (Chicago: Contemporary Books, 1990), 64.

27　Bob Dylan, *Chronicles, Volume One* (New York: Simon & Schuster, 2004), 14.

28　"My Bucket" was an early jazz standard that had been revived by Hank Williams, but Nelson copied Burgess's version.

29　Selvin, *Ricky Nelson*, 88–89.

30　Ibid., 84.

31　Ibid., 69–70.

32　Preston Love, *A Thousand Honey Creeks Later: My Life in Music from Basie To Motown—and Beyond* (Hanover, NH: Wesleyan University Press, 1997), 154.

33　Dick Clark and Richard Robinson, *Rock, Roll & Remember* (New York: Crowell, 1976), 231.

34　Clark and Robinson, *Rock, Roll & Remember*, 233–234. The bass player, James William Guercio, would go on to manage the band Chicago and to be the main shareholder in the Country Music Television channel.

35　"No Distinct Trend in Pop Wax Shows on Charts," *Billboard*, 26 Jan. 1959, 16.

36　Interview with author, 8 Mar. 2008.

37　Interview with author, June 1998.

38　Gordy, *To Be Loved*, 208.

39　Interview with author, Aug. 1997.

CHAPTER 16　TWISTING GIRLS CHANGE THE WORLD

The epigraph for this chapter is quoted from Eldridge Cleaver, *Soul on Ice* (New York: McGraw-Hill, 1968), 197, 199.

1　*Dance, Teens* (Santa Monica, CA: Griffin, 1958), 7.

2　Jackson, *American Bandstand*, 208–210.

3　Jim Dawson, *The Twist* (Boston: Faber & Faber, 1995), 9–20. The melody of "The Twist" was copied from a 1955 Drifters record, "What'cha Gonna Do?"

4　*Twist*. Dir. Ron Mann, 1992. DVD: Home Vision Entertainment, 2002.

5　Pollock, *When Rock Was Young*, 106.

6　Dawson, *Twist*, 34.

7　Geoffrey Holder, "The Twist? 'It's Not a Dance,'" *New York Times*, 3 Dec. 1961.

8　*Twist*, Mann.

9　　Gerry Goffin and Carole King, "Let's Turkey Trot," Aldon Music, BMI, 1963.

10　"Irene Castle, 71, Prefers a Waltz," *New York Times*, 4 Apr. 1964.

11　"Ballin' the Jack," words by Jim Burris, music by Chris Smith (New York: Jos. W. Stern & Co., ca. 1913).

12　For example, chic Londoners are shown twisting to modern jazz in Joseph Losey's *The Servant*, from 1963.

13　George Carpozi Jr., *Let's Twist* (New York: Pyramid Books, 1962), 14.

14　Smith, *Off the Record*, 268, 282. Paul Simon says that his father led a band at Roseland twice a week for twenty-five years, but I have not been able to confirm this.

15　"Habitues of Meyer Davis Land Dance the Twist," *New York Times*, 19 Oct. 1961.

16　"Chubby Checker Explains His 'Twist', Dance That Is," *Chicago Daily Defender*, 27 Nov. 1961, 16. Checker mentioned recording with Davis, but this is not confirmed.

17　June Bundy, "R.&B. Tunes Make Strong Hot 100 Chart Comeback," *Billboard*, 19 Sept. 1960, 1, 9.

18　"Old R.&B. Hits Pan New Gold in Pop Category," *Billboard*, 11 Jan. 1960, 4, 52. Dion also hit with "In the Still of the Night" in 1960, and in 1961 the Lettermen hit with another song from the Art Laboe set, "The Way You Look Tonight." Some older black fans also bought the oldies packages, but everyone involved seems to agree that white listeners were their principal market.

19　Jerry Wexler, "Mainstream of Jazz Is R and B," *Down Beat*, 15 July 1953, 15.

20　I have come across various uses of "oldies" in the 1940s, and Keir Keightley informs me that it appears in a *Variety* record review from January 13, 1937.

21　John A. Lucchese, *Joey Dee and the Story of the Twist* (New York: McFadden Books, 1962), 71, 145. The Starliters' personnel changed over the years, but their first record had a black lead singer, Rogers Freeman; the group that recorded "Peppermint Twist" included two African Americans, organist Carlton Lattimore and drummer Willie Davis; and a video from 1962 shows three black members, two white and one indistinct; http://www.youtube.com/watch?v=7WIvZu4dPQQ (accessed 10 Sept. 2008).

22　James Brown, *James Brown: The Godfather of Soul* (New York: Macmillan, 1986), 134.

23　Carpozi, *Let's Twist*, 32.

24　Soul and Bonds were produced by Frank Guida, a record dealer in Norfolk, Virginia, who had sung calypso while stationed in the West Indies during World War II; Don Harrison, "Frankie's Got It," *64 Magazine*, Jan.–Feb. 2001, www.virginiamusicflash.com/Frank.html. "Senora" looks like it should be "Señora," but in both Belafonte's and Bonds's songs it is pronounced like "Sonora," and is apparently a woman's name.

25　"35 Negro Millionaires Are Listed by Magazine," *New York Times*, 2 May 1962.

26　Interview with author, 8 Mar. 2008. The Beatles never officially recorded "Shout," but there are at least two surviving versions of them doing the song on radio and television broadcasts.

27　*Hullabaloo Discothèque Dance Book* (New York: Parallax, 1966), 10.

28　Nathan Poirier, "Discotheque," *Saturday Evening Post*, 27 Mar. 1965, 23, quoted in Sharon Leigh Clark, "Rock Dance in the United States, 1960–1970: Its Origins, Forms and Patterns" (Ph.D. diss., New York University, 1973), 74.

29　*Twist*, Mann.

30　Bruce Pollock, *In Their Own Words* (New York: Macmillan, 1975), 7.

31　Lucchese, *Joey Dee*, 19.

32 "St. Joan of the Jukebox," *Time*, 15 Mar. 1963, http://www.time.com/time/magazine/article/0,9171,870193,00.html.

33 This does not include male-female duets, but does include women with male back-up singers.

34 Gordy, *To Be Loved*, 245. He singles out the covers of the Marvelettes' *Please Mr. Postman* and Mary Wells's *Bye Bye Baby* as examples of this.

35 The Crystals' "He Hit Me (and It Felt Like a Kiss)" is still more notorious, but apparently Phil Spector recorded it only to get out of a contract, and virtually no one heard it.

36 Robert Pruter, *Chicago Soul* (Urbana: University of Illinois Press, 1991), 39.

37 Clint Ballard Jr., "You're No Good," VeeJay 566, 1963.

38 John Madara and Dave White, "You Don't Own Me," Mercury 72206, 1963.

39 Gerri Hirshey, *Nowhere to Run: The Story of Soul Music* (London: Southbank, 2006), 178.

40 Alan Betrock, *Girl Groups: The Story of a Sound* (New York: Delilah Communications, 1982), 112.

41 VeeJay intended to release *Introducing the Beatles* in 1963, but due to legal issues it did not appear until January 10, 1964.

42 "Sibyl with Guitar," *Time*, 23 Nov. 1962, http://www.time.com/time/magazine/article/0,9171,829501,00.html.

43 Baez, *And a Voice to Sing With: A Memoir* (New York: Summit Books, 1987), 28–31.

44 "Pete Seeger Talks to Teens," *Seventeen*, Nov. 1963, 148; "Josh White Talks to Teens," *Seventeen*, Apr. 1965; "The Folk Music Club," *Seventeen*, Feb. 1965, 142; "Spotlight: Popular Music: Janis Ian 15 Years Old," *Seventeen*, Jan. 1967, 44–46; 16, May 1966, 2.

45 Carl Belz, *The Story of Rock* (New York: Oxford University Press, 1969), 83–84.

46 "Music Spotlight," *Hit Parader*, Nov. 1965, 40.

47 "The Beat, Beat of Surf Music," *Billboard*, 29 June 1963, 26.

CHAPTER 17 SAY YOU WANT A REVOLUTION...

The first epigraph for this chapter is quoted from "The Messengers," *Time*, 22 Sept. 1967, http://www.time.com/time/magazine/article/0,9171,837319,00.html. The second epigraph is quoted from Fox, *In the Groove*, 66–67.

1 Royal Variety Performance programs, http://www.richardmmills.com (accessed 18 May 2008).

2 Jonathan Colt, "John Lennon Interview," *Rolling Stone*, 23 Nov. 1968, http://www.dmbeatles.com/interviews.php?interview=67 (accessed 21 Mar. 2008).

3 David Sheff, *All We Are Saying: The Last Major Interview with John Lennon and Yoko Ono* (New York: St. Martin's Griffin, 2000), 93.

4 Michael Bryan Kelly, *The Beatle Myth: The British Invasion of American Popular Music, 1956–1969* (Jefferson, NC: McFarland, 1991), 22.

5 Roy Orbison, "Roy Orbison's Own Rock History, Part 2," *Hit Parader*, Jan. 1968, 64.

6 McCandlish Phillips, "Publicitywise," *New York Times*, 17 Feb. 1964, 20.

7 Howard Taubman, "British a Fixture along Broadway," *New York Times*, 14 Feb. 1963, 5.

8 Lester Bangs stressed this point in "The British Invasion" in Miller, *Rolling Stone Illustrated History*, 164.

9   "Discothèque Dancing," *Life*, 22 May 1964, 97–99; "The Sound of the Sixties," *Time*, 21 May 1965, http://www.time.com/time/magazine/article/0,9171,901728,00.html (accessed 6 June 2008).

10   Francis Traun, *Arthur Murray Presents Discothèque Dance Party*, RCA LP-2998, 1964, LP notes.

11   *Hullabaloo Discothèque Dance Book*, 7.

12   The Beatles, *The Beatles Anthology* (San Francisco: Chronicle Books, 2000), 175.

13   Rather than three eight-bar A sections and an eight-bar bridge—the standard Tin Pan Alley form—"Yesterday" has three seven-bar A sections and an eight-bar bridge, for a total of twenty-nine bars.

14   Hank Fox, "An Age-Old Rule Broken as New Tunes Become Instant Standards," *Billboard*, 13 Aug. 1966, 3, 14.

15   The Beatles recorded "A Taste of Honey" in 1963, two years before Alpert did. The song was inspired by a play about British working-class life that had been made into a 1961 movie starring the young Liverpudlian Rita Tushingham (though the song was not included in the film), and first hit in 1962 in an instrumental version by Martin Denny.

16   "The Messengers," *Time*, 22 Sept. 1967, http://www.time.com/time/magazine/article/0,9171,837319,00.html; Ned Rorem, "The Music of the Beatles," *New York Review of Books*, 18 Jan. 1968, http://www.nybooks.com/articles/11829.

17   DeLong, *Pops*, 307.

18   McCartney recalled "lovely childhood memories of ... listening to my dad play ... music from the Paul Whiteman era (Paul Whiteman was one of his favourites)"; Beatles, *Beatles Anthology*, 18. Martin wrote, "The Beatles couldn't have existed without the Gershwins"; Ron Cowen, "George Gershwin: He Got Rhythm," http://www.washingtonpost.com/wp-srv/national/horizon/nov98/gershwin.htm).

19   Whiteman and McBride, *Jazz*, 70, 84.

20   Nik Cohn, *Rock: From the Beginning* (New York: Stein and Day, 1969), 157; Nik Cohn, *Awopbopaloobop Alopbamboom: The Golden Age of Rock* (New York: Grove Press, 1996), 144–145. (The latter is a revision of the former, which had compared the Beatles to Cole Porter rather than to Gershwin.)

21   Belz, *Story of Rock*, ix.

22   Ibid., 188.

23   Nora Ephron and Susan Edmiston, "Bob Dylan Interview," in Jonathan Eisen, ed., *Age of Rock 2* (New York: Vintage Books, 1970), 71.

24   Jonathan Gould, *Can't Buy Me Love: The Beatles, Britain, and America* (New York: Harmony Books, 2007), 6.

25   *Rubber Soul* was released in December 1965. I'm leaving out two documentary LPs and counting VeeJay's *Introducing the Beatles* and Capitol's *The Early Beatles* as one LP, because they have roughly the same songs.

26   Beatles, *Beatles Anthology*, 210.

27   Robert Hilburn, "A Backstage Pass to Intimate Moments in Rock's Odyssey," *Los Angeles Times*, 22 July 2006, 1.

28   Hirshey, *Nowhere to Run*, 185. In Paul McCartney's words, "For us, Motown artists were taking the place of [Little] Richard. We loved the black artists so much; and it was the greatest accolade to have somebody with one of those *real* voices, as we saw it, sing our own songs (we'd certainly been doing theirs)"; Beatles, *Beatles Anthology*, 198.

29 Paul Williams, "Getting' Ready: The Temptations," *Crawdaddy* 5 (Sept. 1966), 29.

30 Michael Lydon, "Smokey Robinson," *Rolling Stone*, 28 Sept. 1968, 21.

31 John Lennon and Paul McCartney, "All You Need Is Love," 1967, and "Revolution," 1968. The latter song was a flashpoint of contention from the moment it appeared. As Ellen Willis wrote, "It takes a lot of chutzpah for a millionaire to assure the rest of us, 'You know it's gonna be alright.' And Lennon's 'Change your head' line is just an up-to-date version of 'Let them eat cake'; anyone in a position to follow such advice doesn't need it." Ellen Willis, "Records: Rock, Etc.: The Big Ones," *New Yorker*, 1 Feb. 1969, 61.

32 J. Marks, *Rock and Other Four-Letter Words* (New York: Bantam Books, 1968), 19. The group member is not specified.

33 Clive Davis, *Clive: Inside the Record Business* (New York: Morrow, 1975), 63.

34 Ibid., 53.

35 Ibid., 134.

36 Ben Fong-Torres, ed., *The Rolling Stone Interviews, Vol. 2* (New York: Warner Paperback Library, 1973), 429.

37 George Martin, *With a Little Help from My Friends: The Making of Sgt. Pepper* (Boston: Little, Brown, 1994), 139.

38 Gould, *Can't Buy Me Love*, 387, reports that in fact the *Sgt. Pepper* sessions took roughly half the reported 700-hour figure, but the legend persists.

39 Marks, *Rock*, 15.

40 Robert Christgau, "Anatomy of a Love Festival," *Esquire*, Jan. 1968, in Robert Christgau, *Any Old Way You Choose It: Rock and Other Pop Music, 1967–1973* (Baltimore: Penguin Books, 1973), 17.

41 "R&B Now Soul," *Billboard*, 23 Aug. 1969, 3; *Billboard World of Soul*, 24 June 1967. "Rock" and "rock 'n' roll" continued to be used interchangeably by many writers, even in rock publications, at least into the early 1970s, and many people still fail to make a distinction between the terms.

42 Thomas Barry, "The Importance of Being Mr. James Brown," *Look*, 18 Feb. 1969, 56.

43 Eisen, *Age of Rock*, xv–vi.

44 Ritz, *Divided Soul*, 73.

45 "Ike and Tina Are Double Dynamite," *Hit Parader*, July 1970, 12–13.

46 Jon Landau, "Rock 1970—It's Too Late to Stop Now," *Rolling Stone*, 2 Dec. 1970, in Charles Nanry, ed., *American Music: From Storyville to Woodstock* (New Brunswick, NJ: Transaction Books, 1972), 250.

47 "The Rascals: Won't Play Unless Bill Is Half Black," *Rolling Stone*, 1 Feb. 1969, 8. The seven gold records included both singles and LPs.

EPILOGUE THE ROCK BLOT AND THE DISCO DIAGRAM

1 Kenneth Clark, *Moments of Vision and Other Essays* (New York: Harper & Row, 1981), 19.

2 Eliot Tiegel, "Dance Loses Footing as Halls Go Concert," *Billboard*, 3 Aug. 1968, 1.

3 William Mann, "The Beatles Revive Hopes of Progress in Pop Music with Their Gay New LP," *The Times*, London, 29 May 1967, http://entertainment.timesonline.co.uk/tol/arts_and_entertainment/music/article1873296.ece.

4   The Recording Industry Association of America introduced the platinum certification (which at that time signified sales of two million units) only in 1976, though prior hits had sold in that range.

5   Arnold Shaw, "The Rhythm & Blues Revival No White Gloved, Black Hits," *Billboard World of Soul*, 16 Aug. 1969, S-3; "Billboard Hot 100," 13 May 1972 and 24 June 1972.

6   A. J. Liebling, *The Sweet Science* (New York: Viking Press, 1956), 306.

BIBLIOGRAPHY

Abbott, Lynn, and Doug Seroff. *Ragged but Right: Black Traveling Shows, "Coon Songs," and the Dark Pathway to Blues and Jazz*. Jackson: University Press of Mississippi, 2007.

Addams, Jane. *The Spirit of Youth and the City Streets*. New York: Macmillan, 1909.

Ake, David. *Jazz Cultures*. Berkeley: University of California Press, 2002.

Allen, Walter C. *Hendersonia: The Music of Fletcher Henderson and His Musicians*. Highland Park, NJ: Walter C. Allen, 1974.

Antrim, Doron K., ed. *Secrets of Dance Band Success*. N.p.: Famous Stars, 1936.

Armstrong, Louis. *Louis Armstrong, in His Own Words*. New York: Oxford University Press, 1999.

——. *Swing That Music*. New York: Longmans, Green, 1936.

Asbury, Herbert. *The Barbary Coast: An Informal History of the San Francisco Underworld*. Garden City, NY: Garden City, 1933.

——. *The Great Illusion: An Informal History of Prohibition*. Garden City, NY: Garden City, 1950.

Badger, Reid. *A Life in Ragtime: A Biography of James Reese Europe*. New York: Oxford University Press, 1995.

Baez, Joan. *And a Voice to Sing With: A Memoir*. New York: Summit Books, 1987.

Barnouw, Erik. *The Golden Web: A History of Broadcasting in the United States*. Vol. 2, *1933 to 1953*. New York: Oxford University Press, 1968.

——. *Tube of Plenty: The Evolution of American Television*. New York: Oxford University Press, 1975.

Beatles, The. *The Beatles Anthology*. San Francisco: Chronicle Books, 2000.

Behr, Edward. *Prohibition: Thirteen Years That Changed America*. New York: Arcade, 1996.

Belz, Carl. *The Story of Rock*. New York: Oxford University Press, 1969.

Bennett, Tony. *The Good Life*. With Will Friedwald. New York: Pocket Books, 1998.

Berger, Morroe, Edward Berger, and James Patrick. *Benny Carter: A Life in American Music*. Lanham, MD: Scarecrow Press, 2002.

Bergreen, Laurence. *As Thousands Cheer: The Life of Irving Berlin*. New York: Viking, 1990.

Bernhardt, Clyde. *I Remember: Eighty Years of Black Entertainment, Big Bands, and the Blues*. Philadelphia: University of Pennsylvania Press, 1986.

Berrett, Joshua. *Louis Armstrong and Paul Whiteman: Two Kings of Jazz*. New Haven, CT: Yale University Press, 2004.

Bertrand, Michael T. *Race, Rock, and Elvis*. Urbana: University of Illinois Press, 2000.

Betrock, Alan. *Girl Groups: The Story of a Sound*. New York: Delilah Communications, 1982.

Bierley, Paul Edmund. *The Incredible Band of John Philip Sousa*. Urbana: University of Illinois Press, 2006.

Blesh, Rudi. *Shining Trumpets*. New York: Knopf, 1958.

Blesh, Rudi, and Harriet Janis. *They All Played Ragtime*. New York: Knopf, 1950.

Bowen, Louise de Koven. *The Public Dance Halls of Chicago*. Chicago: Juvenile Protective Association of Chicago, 1917.

Boyd, Jean Ann. *The Jazz of the Southwest: An Oral History of Western Swing*. Austin: University of Texas Press, 1998.

Braun, D. Duane. *Toward a Theory of Popular Culture: The Sociology and History of American Music and Dance*. Ann Arbor, MI: Ann Arbor Publishers, 1969.

Braun, Michael. *"Love Me Do!": The Beatles' Progress*. London: Penguin Books, 1995.

Brown, James. *James Brown: The Godfather of Soul*. With Bruce Tucker. New York: Macmillan, 1986.

Brown, Scott E. *James P. Johnson: A Case of Mistaken Identity*. Metuchen, NJ: Scarecrow Press and the Institute of Jazz Studies, 1986.

Brunn, H. O. *The Story of the Original Dixieland Jazz Band*. London: Jazz Book Club, 1963.

Bushell, Garvin. *Jazz: From the Beginning*. As told to Mark Tucker. Ann Arbor: University of Michigan Press, 1988.

Carpozi, George, Jr. *Let's Twist*. New York: Pyramid Books, 1962.

Castle, Irene. *Castles in the Air*. Garden City, NY: Doubleday, 1958.

Castle, Mr. and Mrs. Vernon. *Modern Dancing*. New York: World Syndicate, 1914.

Chapple, Steve, and Reebee Garofalo. *Rock 'n' Roll Is Here to Pay: The History and Politics of the Music Industry*. Chicago: Nelson-Hall, 1977.

Charters, Samuel B., and Leonard Kunstadt. *Jazz: A History of the New York Scene*. Garden City, NY: Doubleday, 1962.

Chase, Gilbert. *America's Music: From the Pilgrims to the Present*. Rev. 3rd ed. Urbana: University of Illinois Press, 1987.

Chilton, John. *Let the Good Times Roll: The Story of Louis Jordan and His Music*. Ann Arbor: University of Michigan Press, 1994.

Christgau, Robert. *Any Old Way You Choose It: Rock and Other Pop Music, 1967–1973*. Baltimore: Penguin Books, 1973.

Clark, Dick, and Richard Robinson. *Rock, Roll & Remember*. New York: Crowell, 1976.

Clark, Sharon Leigh. "Rock Dance in the United States, 1960–1970: Its Origins, Forms and Patterns." Ph.D. diss., New York University, 1973.

Clarke, Donald. *All or Nothing at All: A Life of Frank Sinatra*. New York: Fromm International, 1997.

——. *The Rise and Fall of Popular Music*. New York: St. Martin's Griffin, 1996.

Clooney, Rosemary. *Girl Singer*. With Joan Barthel. New York: Doubleday, 1999.

Cohn, Nik. *Awopbopaloobop Alopbamboom: The Golden Age of Rock*. New York: Grove Press, 1996.

——. *Rock: From the Beginning*. New York: Stein and Day, 1969.

Coleman, James S. *The Adolescent Society*. New York: Free Press of Glencoe, 1961.

Collier, James Lincoln. *Jazz: The American Theme Song*. New York: Oxford University Press, 1993.

Condon, Eddie. *We Called It Music: A Generation of Jazz*. With Thomas Sugrue. New York: Da Capo Press, 1992.

Condon, Eddie, and Richard Gehman, eds. *Eddie Condon's Treasury of Jazz*. New York: Dial Press, 1956.

Cuney-Hare, Maud. *Negro Musicians and Their Music*. Washington, DC: Associated Publishers, 1936.

Dachs, David. *Anything Goes: The World of Popular Music*. Indianapolis: Bobbs-Merrill, 1964.

Dance, Stanley. *The World of Swing*. New York: Da Capo Press, 2001.

Darensbourg, Joe. *Jazz Odyssey: The Autobiography of Joe Darensbourg*. As told to Peter Vacher. Baton Rouge: Louisiana State University Press, 1987.

Davis, Clive. *Clive: Inside the Record Business*. With James Willwerth. New York: Morrow, 1975.

Davis, Paul. *Pat Boone: The Authorized Biography*. Grand Rapids, MI: Zondervan, 2001.

Dawson, Jim. *The Twist*. Boston: Faber & Faber, 1995.

Dawson, Jim, and Steve Propes. *What Was the First Rock 'n' Roll Record?* Boston: Faber & Faber, 1992.

Deffaa, Chip. *Voices of the Jazz Age: Profiles of Eight Vintage Jazzmen*. Urbana: University of Illinois Press, 1990.

DeLong, Thomas A. *The Mighty Music Box*. Los Angeles: Amber Crest Books, 1980.

——. *Pops: Paul Whiteman, King of Jazz*. Piscataway, NJ: New Century, 1983.

Dodge, Roger Pryor. *Hot Jazz and Jazz Dance: Collected Writings 1929–1964*. New York: Oxford University Press, 1995.

Doherty, Thomas, *Teenagers and Teenpics: The Juvenilization of American Movies in the 1950s*. Philadelphia: Temple University Press, 2002.

Driggs, Frank, and Chuck Haddix. *Kansas City Jazz: From Ragtime to Bebop—A History*. New York: Oxford University Press, 2005.

Drowne, Kathleen. *Spirits of Defiance: National Prohibition and Jazz Age Literature, 1920–1933*. Columbus: Ohio State University Press, 2005.

Drowne, Kathleen, and Patrick Huber. *The 1920s*. Westport, CT: Greenwood Press, 2004.

Durante, Jimmy, and Jack Kofoed. *Night Clubs*. New York: Knopf, 1931.

Dylan, Bob. *Chronicles*. Vol. 1. New York: Simon & Schuster, 2004.

Early, Gerald. *The Culture of Bruising: Essays on Prizefighting, Literature, and Modern American Culture*. Hopewell, NJ: Ecco Press, 1994.

Edmiston, Fred W. *The Coon-Sanders Nighthawks: "The Band That Made Radio Famous."* Jefferson, NC: McFarland, 2003.

Eisen, Jonathan, ed. *The Age of Rock*. New York: Random House, 1969.

——. *The Age of Rock 2*. New York: Vintage Books, 1970.

Eisenberg, Evan. *The Recording Angel: Music, Records and Culture from Aristotle to Zappa*. New Haven, CT: Yale University Press, 2005.

Ellington, Edward Kennedy. *Music Is My Mistress*. New York: Doubleday, 1973.

Emerson, Ken. *Always Magic in the Air: The Bomp and Brilliance of the Brill Building Era*. New York: Viking, 2005.

Epstein, Daniel Mark. *Nat King Cole*. New York: Farrar, Straus and Giroux, 1999.

Erenberg, Lewis A. *Steppin' Out: New York Nightlife and the Transformation of American Culture, 1890–1930*. Westport, CT: Greenwood Press, 1981.

——. *Swingin' the Dream: Big Band Jazz and the Rebirth of American Culture*. Chicago: University of Chicago Press, 1998.

Escott, Colin. *Roadkill on the Three-chord Highway: Art and Trash in American Popular Music*. New York: Routledge, 2002.

Evanier, David. *Roman Candle: The Life of Bobby Darin*. Emmaus, PA: Rodale, 2004.

Ewen, David. *Music Comes to America*. New York: Crowell, 1942.

Feather, Leonard. *The Jazz Years: Earwitness to an Era*. New York: Da Capo, 1987.

Ferguson, Otis. *In the Spirit of Jazz: The Otis Ferguson Reader*. Edited by Dorothy Chamberlain and Robert Wilson. New York: Da Capo Press, 1997.

Firestone, Ross. *Swing, Swing, Swing: The Life and Times of Benny Goodman*. New York: Norton, 1993.

Fletcher, Tom. *100 Years of the Negro in Show Business*. New York: Da Capo Press, 1984.

Fong-Torres, Ben, ed. *The Rolling Stone Interviews*. Vol. 2. New York: Warner Paperback Library, 1973.

Fox, Ted. *In the Groove: The People behind the Music*. New York: St. Martin's Press, 1986.

Francis, Connie. *Who's Sorry Now?* New York: St. Martin's Press, 1984.

Friedwald, Will. *Jazz Singing*. New York: Da Capo Press, 1996.

——. *Sinatra! The Song Is You*. New York: Scribner, 1995.

Gabbard, Krin, ed. *Jazz among the Discourses*. Durham, NC: Duke University Press, 1995.

Gabree, John. *The World of Rock*. Greenwich, CT: Fawcett, 1968.

Gelatt, Roland. *The Fabulous Phonograph: 1877–1977*. New York: Macmillan, 1977.

Gendron, Bernard. *Between Montmartre and the Mudd Club: Popular Music and the Avant-Garde*. Chicago: University of Chicago Press, 2002.

Gennari, John. *Blowin' Hot and Cool: Jazz and Its Critics*. Chicago: University of Chicago Press, 2006.

——. *The Death of Rhythm and Blues*. New York: Pantheon, 1988.

George, Nelson. *Where Did Our Love Go: The Rise & Fall of the Motown Sound*. New York: St. Martin's Press, 1985.

George-Warren, Holly. *Public Cowboy No. 1: The Life and Times of Gene Autry*. New York: Oxford University Press, 2007.

Giddins, Gary. *Bing Crosby: A Pocketful of Dreams*. Boston: Little, Brown, 2001.

Gillett, Charlie. *The Sound of the City: The Rise of Rock and Roll*. New York: Da Capo Press, 1996.

Giordano, Ralph G. *Social Dancing in America: A History and Reference*. Vols. 1 and 2. Westport, CT: Greenwood Press, 2007.

Goldstein, Richard, ed. *The Poetry of Rock*. New York: Bantam Books, 1969.

Goodman, Benny, and Irving Kolodin. *The Kingdom of Swing*. New York: Stackpole Sons, 1939.

Gordy, Berry. *To Be Loved: The Music, the Memories of Motown*. New York: Warner Books, 1994.

Gould, Jonathan. *Can't Buy Me Love: The Beatles, Britain, and America*. New York: Harmony Books, 2007.

Greig, Charlotte. *Will You Still Love Me Tomorrow: Girl Groups from the 60s On*. London: Virago Press, 1989.

Guralnick, Peter. *Last Train to Memphis: The Rise of Elvis Presley*. Boston: Little, Brown, 1994.

——. *Lost Highway: Journeys and Arrivals of American Musicians*. Boston: Godine, 1979.

Gushee, Lawrence. *Pioneers of Jazz: The Story of the Creole Band*. New York: Oxford University Press, 2005.

Haas, Robert Bartlett, ed. *William Grant Still and the Fusion of Cultures in American Music*, Los Angeles: Black Sparrow Press, 1972.

Halberstam, David. *The Fifties*. New York: Random House, 1993.

Hall, Wade. *Hell-Bent for Music: The Life of Pee Wee King*. Lexington: University Press of Kentucky, 1996.

Harris, Charles K. *After the Ball: Forty Years of Melody*. New York: Frank-Maurice, 1926.

Harris, Michael W. *The Rise of Gospel Blues: The Music of Thomas Andrew Dorsey in the Urban Church*. New York: Oxford University Press, 1992.

Haslam, Gerald W. *Workin' Man Blues: Country Music in California*. Berkeley: University of California Press, 1999.

Hentoff, Nat. *The Jazz Life*. New York: Dial Press, 1961.

Herndon, Booton. *The Sweetest Music This Side of Heaven: The Guy Lombardo Story*. New York: McGraw-Hill, 1964.

Hirshey, Gerri. *Nowhere to Run: The Story of Soul Music*. London: Southbank, 2006.

Hullabaloo Discothèque Dance Book. New York: Parallax, 1966.

Jackson, John A. *American Bandstand: Dick Clark and the Making of a Rock 'n' Roll Empire*. New York: Oxford University Press, 1997.

——. *Big Beat Heat: Alan Freed and the Early Years of Rock & Roll*. New York: Schirmer, 1991.

Jackson, Kenneth T. *Crabgrass Frontier: The Suburbanization of the United States*. New York: Oxford University Press, 1985.

Johnson, James Weldon. *Writings*. New York: Library of America, 2004.

Jones, Dylan, ed. *Meaty Beaty Big and Bouncy: Classic Rock and Pop Writing from Elvis to Oasis*. London: Sceptre, 1997.

Josephy, Helen, and Mary Margaret McBride. *New York Is Everybody's Town*. New York: Putnam, 1931.

Katz, Mark. *Capturing Sound: How Technology Has Changed Music*. Berkeley: University of California Press, 2004.

Kelly, Michael Bryan. *The Beatle Myth: The British Invasion of American Popular Music, 1956–1969*. Jefferson, NC: McFarland, 1991.

Kenney, William Howland. *Chicago Jazz: A Cultural History 1904–1930*. New York: Oxford University Press, 1993.

——. *Recorded Music in American Life: The Phonograph and Popular Memory, 1890–1945*. New York: Oxford University Press, 1999.

Kirk, Andy. *Twenty Years on Wheels*. As told to Amy Lee. Ann Arbor: University of Michigan Press, 1989.

Kraft, James P. *Stage to Studio: Musicians and the Sound Revolution, 1890–1950*. Baltimore: Johns Hopkins University Press, 1996.

La Chapelle, Peter. *Proud to Be an Okie: Cultural Politics, Country Music, and Migration to Southern California*. Berkeley: University of California Press, 2007.

Laine, Frankie, and Joseph F. Laredo. *That Lucky Old Son: The Autobiography of Frankie Laine*. Ventura, CA: Pathfinder Publishing of California, 1993.

Landry, Robert J. *This Fascinating Radio Business*. Indianapolis: Bobbs-Merrill, 1946.

Lange, Jeffrey J. *Smile When You Call Me a Hillbilly: Country Music's Struggle for Respectability, 1939–1954*. Athens: University of Georgia Press, 2004.

Lawrence, Tim. *Love Saves the Day: A History of American Dance Music Culture, 1970–1979*. Durham, NC: Duke University Press, 2003.

Lees, Gene. *Singers and the Song*. New York: Oxford University Press, 1987.

Leiter, Robert D. *The Musicians and Petrillo*. New York: Octagon Books, 1974.

Leonard, Neil. *Jazz and the White Americans: The Acceptance of a New Art Form*. London: Jazz Book Club, 1964.

Levine, Lawrence W. *Highbrow/Lowbrow: The Emergence of Cultural Hierarchy in America*. Cambridge, MA: Harvard University Press, 1988.

Levinson, Peter J. *September in the Rain: The Life of Nelson Riddle*. New York: Billboard Books, 2001.

——. *Tommy Dorsey: Livin' in a Great Big Way*. New York: Da Capo Press, 2005.

——. *Trumpet Blues: The Life of Harry James*. New York: Oxford University Press, 1999.

Lewisohn, Mark. *The Complete Beatles Chronicle*. New York: Harmony Books, 1992.

Lombardo, Guy. *Auld Acquaintance*. With Jack Altshul. Garden City, NY: Doubleday, 1975.

Love, Preston. *A Thousand Honey Creeks Later: My Life in Music from Basie To Motown—and Beyond*. Hanover, NH: Wesleyan University Press, 1997.

Lucchese, John A. *Joey Dee and the Story of the Twist*. New York: McFadden Books, 1962.

Lytle, H. W., and John Dillon, *From Dance Hall to White Slavery: The World's Greatest Tragedy*. N.p.: Charles C. Thompson, 1912.

Magee, Jeffrey. *The Uncrowned King of Swing: Fletcher Henderson and Big Band Jazz*. New York: Oxford University Press, 2005.

Malone, Bill C. *Country Music U.S.A.* Austin: University of Texas Press, 1975.

——. *Singing Cowboys and Musical Mountaineers: Southern Culture and the Roots of Country Music*. Athens: University of Georgia Press, 1993.

Mancini, Henry. *Did They Mention the Music?* With Gene Lees. Chicago: Contemporary Books, 1989.

Marcus, Greil, ed. *Rock and Roll Will Stand*. Boston: Beacon Press, 1969.

Marks, Edward B. *They All Sang: From Tony Pastor to Rudy Vallée*. As told to Abbott J. Liebling. New York: Viking Press, 1934.

Marks, J. *Rock and Other Four-Letter Words*. New York: Bantam Books, 1968.

Martin, George. *All You Need Is Ears*. With Jeremy Hornsby. New York: St. Martin's Press, 1979.

Martin, George. *With a Little Help from My Friends: The Making of Sgt. Pepper*. With William Pearson. Boston: Little, Brown, 1994.

McCarthy, Albert. *The Dance Band Era*. London: Spring Books, 1971.

McKee, Margaret, and Fred Chisenhall. *Beale Black and Blue: Life and Music on Black America's Main Street*. Baton Rouge: Louisiana State University Press, 1981.

Melly, George. *Revolt into Style: The Pop Arts in Britain*. Harmondsworth, England: Penguin Books, 1972.

Meltzer, David, ed. *Writing Jazz*. San Francisco: Mercury House, 1999.

Meryman, Richard. *Louis Armstrong: A Self-Portrait*. New York: Eakins Press, 1971.

Merz, Charles. *Bigger and Better Murders: The Great American Bandwagon*. London: Victor Gollancz Ltd., 1928.

Miller, Jim, ed. *The Rolling Stone Illustrated History of Rock & Roll*. New York: Rolling Stone Press; Random House, 1976.

Miller, Mark. *Some Hustling This! Taking Jazz to the World 1914–1929*. Toronto: Mercury Press, 2005.

Morgan, Al. *The Great Man*. New York: Dutton, 1955.

Mouvet, Maurice. *Maurice's Art of Dancing*. New York: Schirmer, 1915.

Nanry, Charles, ed. *American Music: From Storyville to Woodstock*. New Brunswick, NJ: Transaction Books, 1972.

Needham, Maureen, ed. *I See America Dancing: Selected Readings, 1685–2000*. Urbana: University of Illinois Press, 2002.

Nicholson, Stuart. *Reminiscing in Tempo: A Portrait of Duke Ellington*. Boston: Northeastern University Press, 1999.

Olsen, Eric, Paul Verna, and Carlo Wolff. *The Encyclopedia of Record Producers*. New York: Billboard Books, 1999.

O'Meally, Robert G., ed. *The Jazz Cadence of American Culture*. New York: Columbia University Press, 1998.

Osgood, Henry O. *So This Is Jazz*. Boston: Little, Brown, 1926.

Page, Drew. *Drew's Blues: A Sideman's Life with the Big Bands*. Baton Rouge: Louisiana State University Press, 1980.

Panassié, Hughes. *La Bataille du Jazz*. N.p.: Albin Michel, 1965.

——. *The Real Jazz*. New York: Smith & Durrell, Inc., 1943.

Peiss, Kathy. *Cheap Amusements: Working Women and Leisure in Turn-of-the-Century New York*. Philadelphia: Temple University Press, 1986.

Peress, Maurice. *Dvořák to Duke Ellington: A Conductor Explores America's Music and Its African American Roots*. New York: Oxford University Press, 2004.

Pleasants, Henry. *The Agony of Modern Music*. New York: Simon and Schuster, 1955.

Pollack, Howard. *George Gershwin: His Life and Work*. Berkeley: University of California Press, 2006.

Pollock, Bruce. *In Their Own Words*. New York: Macmillan, 1975.

——. *When Rock Was Young*. New York: Holt, Rinehart and Winston, 1981.

Pruter, Robert. *Chicago Soul*. Urbana: University of Illinois Press, 1991.

Pugh, Ronnie. *Ernest Tubb: The Texas Troubadour*. Durham, NC: Duke University Press, 1996.

Pyron, Darden Asbury. *Liberace: An American Boy*. Chicago: University of Chicago Press, 2000.

Ramsey, Frederic, Jr. and Charles Edward Smith. *Jazzmen*. New York: Harcourt, Brace, 1939.

Rayno, Don. *Paul Whiteman: Pioneer in American Music*. Vol. 1, 1890–1930. Lanham, MD: Scarecrow Press, 2003.

Ritz, David. *Divided Soul: The Life of Marvin Gaye*. Cambridge, MA: Da Capo Press, 1991.

Robinson, Chris. "Seeing Through a Blindfold: Gender, Race and Jazz in Leonard Feather's Blindfold Tests." Master's thesis, University of Idaho, 2006.

Robinson, Danielle Anne. "Race in Motion: Reconstructing the Practice, Profession, and Politics of Social Dancing, New York City 1900–1930." PhD diss., University of California Riverside, 2004.

Rose, Al. *Eubie Blake*. New York: Schirmer, 1979.

Rosen, Charles. *Critical Entertainments: Music Old and New*. Cambridge, MA: Harvard University Press, 2000.

Rust, Brian. *The American Dance Band Discography, 1917–1942*. New Rochelle, NY: Arlington House, 1975.

——. *Jazz Records, 1897–1942*. Chigwell, Essex: Storyville Publications, 1969.

Sachs, Curt. *World History of the Dance*. New York: Norton, 1937.

Sanjek, Russell. *American Popular Music and Its Business*. Vols. 2 and 3. New York: Oxford University Press, 1988.

Sann, Paul. *The Lawless Decade*. New York: Crown, 1957.

Sargeant, Winthrop. *Jazz: Hot and Hybrid*. Rev. ed. New York: Dutton, 1946.

Schoemer, Karen. *Great Pretenders: My Strange Love Affair with '50s Pop Music*. New York: Free Press, 2006.

Schuller, Gunther. *Early Jazz: Its Roots and Musical Development*. New York: Oxford University Press, 1968.

——. *The Swing Era*. New York: Oxford University Press, 1989.

Segrave, Kerry. *Jukeboxes: An American Social History*. Jefferson, NC: McFarland, 2002.

Seldes, Gilbert, *The Seven Lively Arts*. New York: Harper & Brothers, 1924.

Selvin, Joel. *Ricky Nelson: Idol for a Generation*. Chicago: Contemporary Books, 1990.

Shapiro, Nat, and Nat Hentoff, eds. *Hear Me Talkin' to Ya: The Story of Jazz as Told by the Men Who Made It*. New York: Dover, 1966.

Shaw, Arnold. *Belafonte: An Unauthorized Biography*. Philadelphia: Chilton, 1960.

——. *Honkers and Shouters*. New York: Collier Books, 1978.

——. *The Rockin' '50s*. New York: Hawthorn Books, 1974.

Shaw, Artie. *The Trouble with Cinderella*. New York: Farrar, Straus, and Young, 1952.

Shaw, Charles G. *Nightlife: Vanity Fair's Intimate Guide to New York after Dark*. New York: John Day, 1931.

Sheff, David. *All We Are Saying: The Last Major Interview with John Lennon and Yoko Ono*. New York: St. Martin's Griffin, 2000.

Simon, George T. *The Big Bands*. New York: Schirmer, 1981.

——. *Glenn Miller and His Orchestra*. New York: Crowell, 1974.

——. *Simon Says: The Sights and Sounds of the Swing Era, 1935–1955*. New York: Galahad Books, 1971.

Simons, David. *Studio Stories*. San Francisco: Backbeat Books, 2004.

Singer, Arthur J. *Arthur Godfrey: The Adventures of an American Broadcaster*. Jefferson, NC: McFarland, 2000.

Smith, Joe. *Off the Record: An Oral History of Popular Music*. New York: Warner Books, 1988.

Smith, Willie. *Music on My Mind: The Memoirs of an American Pianist*. Garden City, NY: Doubleday, 1964.

Southern, Eileen. *The Music of Black Americans: A History*. New York: Norton, 1971.

——, ed. *Readings in Black American Music*. New York: Norton, 1983.

Spitz, Robert Stephen. *The Making of Superstars: Artists and Executives of the Rock Music Business*. Garden City, NY: Anchor Press, 1978.

Stark, Steven D. *Meet the Beatles: A Cultural History of the Band That Shook Youth, Gender, and the World*. New York: HarperEntertainment, 2005.

Stearns, Marshall W. *The Story of Jazz*. New York: Oxford University Press, 1957.

Stearns, Marshall W., and Jean Stearns. *Jazz Dance: The Story of American Vernacular Dance*. New York: Macmillan, 1968.

Sterling, Christopher H., and Timothy R. Haight. *The Mass Media: Aspen Institute Guide to Communication Industry Trends*. New York: Praeger, 1978.

Stewart, Rex. *Jazz Masters of the Thirties*. New York: Macmillan, 1972.

Stoddard, Tom. *Jazz on the Barbary Coast*. Berkeley, CA: Heyday Books, 1998.

Stowe, David W. *Swing Changes: Big-Band Jazz in New Deal America*. Cambridge, MA: Harvard University Press, 1994.

Sudhalter, Richard M. *Lost Chords: White Musicians and Their Contribution to Jazz, 1915–1945*. New York: Oxford University Press, 1999.

Swenson, John. *Bill Haley: The Daddy of Rock and Roll*. New York: Stein and Day, 1983.

Tiomkin, Dimitri, and Prosper Buranelli. *Please Don't Hate Me*. Garden City, NY: Doubleday, 1959.

Tirro, Frank. *Jazz: A History*. New York: Norton, 1993.

Toll, Robert C. *The Entertainment Machine: American Show Business in the Twentieth Century*. New York: Oxford University Press, 1982.

Tosches, Nick. *Dino: Living High in the Dirty Business of Dreams*. New York: Doubleday, 1992.

Tucker, Mark, ed. *The Duke Ellington Reader*. New York: Oxford University Press, 1993.

Walker, Leo. *The Wonderful Era of the Great Dance Bands*. Garden City, NY: Doubleday, 1972.

Ward, Brian. *Just My Soul Responding: Rhythm and Blues, Black Consciousness, and Race Relations*. Berkeley: University of California Press, 1998.

Walser, Robert, ed. *Keeping Time: Readings in Jazz History*. New York: Oxford University Press, 1999.

Waring, Virginia. *Fred Waring and the Pennsylvanians*. Urbana: University of Illinois Press, 1997.

Welburn, Ronald G. "American Jazz Criticism, 1914–1940." PhD diss., New York University, 1983.

Welk, Lawrence. *Wunnerful, Wunnerful!* With Bernice McGeehan. Englewood Cliffs, NJ: Prentice-Hall, 1971.

Whitburn, Joel. *The Billboard Book of Top 40 Country Hits*. New York: Billboard Books, 1996.

———. *Pop Memories, 1890–1954*. Menomonee Falls, WI: Record Research, 1986.

———. *Top Pop Albums, 1955–1996*. Menomonee Falls, WI: Record Research, 1996.

———. *Top Pop Singles, 1955–1990*. Menomonee Falls, WI: Record Research, 1991.

———. *Top R&B Singles, 1942–1995*. Menomonee Falls, WI: Record Research, 1996.

Whiteman, Paul, and Margaret McBride. *Jazz*. New York: J. H. Sears and Company, 1926.

Whiteside, Jonny. *Cry: The Johnnie Ray Story*. New York: Barricade Books, 1994.

Williams, John R. *This Was "Your Hit Parade."* Rockland, ME: Courier-Gazette, 1973.

INDEX

Motown Records and style, 5, 214, 223, 224, 225, 239, 240, 244

Mound City Blue Blowers, 112

Mouvet, Maurice, 39–40

Moyer, Holly, 264n8

"Mr. Jazz Himself," 58

"Mr. Lee," 223

Mueller, Gus, 75–76, 262n15

"Mule Train," 157–158, 159

Mundy, Jimmy, 116

Murray, Arthur, 48, 219, 232

Murray, Billy, 87

Murray, Kel, 116

Murray the K, 219

Muscle Shoals recording studio, 243

Music, Martinis and Memories (album), 186

Music for Dreaming (album), 186

Music for Lovers Only (album), 186, 189, 272–273n6

"Music Goes Round and Round, The," 122

Music Out of the Moon (album), 187

music teachers, taste influence of, 20

Music to Make You Misty (album), 186

Musical Courier, 26

musical literacy, 19–20, 43, 49–50

"My Bucket," 275n28

"My Bucket's got a Hole in It," 209

My Fair Lady (album), 186

"My Heart Cries for You," 88, 160

"My Hula Hula Love," 206

"My Mariucci Take a Steamboat," 37

"My Old Kentucky Home," 34

"My Pencil Won't Write No More," 92

"My Wife's Gone to the Country—Hurrah!" 37

Nashville Skyline (Dylan album), 241

National Association of Broadcasters, 133

National Association of Performing Artists, 128–129

National Broadcasting Company, 92

"Nellie Gray," 130

Nelson, David, 208, 211

Nelson, Harriet, 208

Nelson, Ozzie, 208–209

Nelson, Ricky, 191, 197, 203, 204, 208–211

New Deal economic programs, 150, 155

New Lost City Ramblers, the, 226

New Orleans, Louisiana, 49, 52, 54–55

"New Orleans Jazz," 58

New Orleans Rhythm Kings, 112

New York, New York

52nd Street district, 121–122

Bowery, 46

Brill Building songwriters, 207, 231

Broadway restaurants, 57–59, 65–66

cakewalk in, 39

dance halls, 44–46, 47, 61–65, 115–116

Europe's orchestra in, 41–43

Five Points neighborhood, 43–44

Greenwich Village, 184, 193

Harlem, 43–44, 51–52, 53, 67–68, 103–105, 217

music rooms and lounges in, 184, 215–216, 217, 222

musical theater in, 33, 40

musicians' diverse activities in, 113

nightclubs, 39–42, 44–45, 51–52, 65–66, 68–69, 119, 163

Prohibition in, 67–70

recorded music in, 126

television shows from, 208

Tin Pan Alley, 26, 29, 34–35, 36–38

New York Is Everybody's Town, 68

New York Journal-American, The, 215–216

New York Theater Roof Garden, 42

New York Times, The, 31, 36, 41, 59, 62, 64, 92–93, 119, 144, 154, 155, 169, 171, 195, 196, 216, 217, 231

New York World's Fair of 1939, 162

New York World's Fair of 1964, 219

New Yorker, The, 64, 81, 102, 163, 193

Newport Folk Festival of 1959, 226

Newport Folk Festival of 1965, 239

Newsweek, 127

Nichols, Red, 112

Nicholson, Jack, 205

nickelodeons, 127

Nick's Bar (New York), 121